AGING, Fourth Edition

Editor
Harold Cox
Indiana State University

Harold Cox, professor of sociology at Indiana State University, has published several articles in the field of gerontology. His paper, "Priority Needs of Rural Elderly," coauthored by Gurmeet Sekhon, was part of the official proceedings of the 1981 White House Conference on Aging in 1981. He is a member of the Gerontological Society and the American Sociological Association—Occupation and Professions Section, and Youth and Aging Section.

Annual Editions

A Library of Information from the Public Press

Cover illustration by Mike Eagle

The Dushkin Publishing Group, Inc.
Sluice Dock, Guilford, Connecticut 06437

The Annual Editions Series

Annual Editions is a series of over thirty-five volumes designed to provide the reader with convenient, low-cost access to a wide range of current, carefully selected articles from some of the most important magazines, newspapers, and journals published today.

Annual Editions are updated on an annual basis through a continuous monitoring of over 200 periodical sources. All Annual Editions have a number of features designed to make them particularly useful, including topic guides, annotated tables of contents, unit overviews, and indexes. For the teacher using Annual Editions in the classroom, an Instructor's Guide with test questions is available for each volume.

PUBLISHED

Africa
Aging
American Government
American History, Pre-Civil War
American History, Post-Civil War
Anthropology
Biology
Business
China
Comparative Politics
Computers in Education
Criminal Justice
Early Childhood Education
Economics
Educating Exceptional Children
Education
Educational Psychology
Environment
Global Issues
Health

Human Development
Human Sexuality
Latin America
Macroeconomics
Marketing
Marriage and Family
Middle East and the Islamic World
Personal Growth and Behavior
Psychology
Social Problems
Social Psychology
Sociology
Soviet Union and Eastern Europe
State and Local Government
Urban Society
Western Civilization,
   Pre-Reformation
Western Civilization,
   Post-Reformation
World Politics

FUTURE VOLUMES

Abnormal Psychology
Death and Dying
Computers in Business
Computers in Society
Congress
Energy
Ethnic Studies
Foreign Policy
Geography
Judiciary
Nutrition

Parenting
Philosophy
Political Science
Presidency
Religion
South Asia
Twentieth Century American
   History
Western Europe
Women's Studies
World History

Library of Congress Cataloging in Publication Data
Main entry under title:
Annual editions: Aging.
   1. Gerontology—Periodicals. 2. Gerontology—United States—Periodicals. 3. Aged—United States—Periodicals. 4. Aging—Periodicals. I. Title: Aging
HQ1060.A57   301.43 5 0973   78-645208
ISBN 0-87967-549-7

Fourth Edition
Manufactured by The Banta Company, Menasha, Wisconsin 54952

Editors/ Advisory Board

EDITOR

Harold Cox
Indiana State University

Members of the Advisory Board are instrumental in the final selection of articles for each edition of Annual Editions. Their review of articles for content, level, currency, and appropriateness provides critical direction to the editor and staff. We think you'll find their careful consideration well reflected in this volume.

ADVISORY BOARD

Virgil E. Christensen
Mankato State University

Jay J. Coakley
University of Colorado,
Colorado Springs

Larry Cobb
Oklahoma City University

Robert A. Famighetti
Kean College of New Jersey

Darlene Howard
Georgetown University

Charles W. Johnson
University of Evansville

Barry Lumsden
North Texas State University

Gamal Zaki
Rhode Island College

STAFF

Rick Connelly, Publisher
Ian A. Nielsen, Program Manager
Celeste Borg, Editor
Addie Kawula, Acquisitions Editor
Brenda S. Filley, Production Manager
Cheryl Kinne, Permissions/Photo Coordinator
Charles Vitelli, Designer
Jean Bailey, Graphics Coordinator
Libra A. Cusack, Typesetting Coordinator
LuAnn Bishop, Editorial Assistant

To The Reader

In publishing ANNUAL EDITIONS we recognize the enormous role played by the magazines, newspapers, and journals of the *public press* in providing current, first-rate educational information in a broad spectrum of interest areas. Within the articles, the best scientists, practitioners, researchers, and commentators draw issues into new perspective as accepted theories and viewpoints are called into account by new events, recent discoveries change old facts, and fresh debate breaks out over important controversies.

Many of the articles resulting from this enormous editorial effort are appropriate for students, researchers, and professionals seeking accurate, current material to help bridge the gap between principles and theories and the real world. These articles, however, become more useful for study when those of lasting value are carefully *collected, organized, indexed,* and *reproduced* in a *low-cost format,* which provides easy and permanent access when the material is needed. That is the role played by *Annual Editions.* Under the direction of each volume's *Editor,* who is an expert in the subject area, and with the guidance of an *Advisory Board,* we seek each year to provide in each *ANNUAL EDITION* a current, well-balanced, carefully selected collection of the best of the public press for your study and enjoyment. We think you'll find this volume useful, and we hope you'll take a moment to let us know what you think.

The decline in the crude birth rate combined with our ever-improving medical technology, which is keeping most people alive and healthy well into their retirement years, has resulted in a shift in the age composition of the American population. Since 1900 we have seen a gradual reduction in the number and percentage of young people in the total population; simultaneously, there has been a gradual increase in the number of older persons.

In 1900 approximately four percent of our total population was sixty-five years-old or older. Currently, approximately twelve percent of our population is in the sixty-five and above age group. Demographic projections indicate that, by the year 2000, the elderly will comprise fifteen percent of the total population. The rapid growth in the number of older persons has made many of the problems of aging quite visible, and they have become widespread topics of concern.

Today almost all middle-aged people expect to live to retirement age and beyond. Those approaching retirement as well as those already retired have generated considerable interest in the quality of life of older persons. Both the middle-aged and the elderly have pushed for solutions to the problems confronting older Americans. Everyone seems to agree that granting the elderly a secure and comfortable status is desirable. Voluntary associations, communities, and state and federal governments have committed themselves to improving the lives of older persons. Many programs for senior citizens, both public and private, have emerged in the last fifteen years.

This change in the age composition of the American population has not gone unnoticed by the media or the academic community. The number of articles appearing in the popular press and professional journals concerning the problems and opportunities of older Americans has increased dramatically over the last several years. While scientists have been concerned with the aging process for some time, in the last two decades there has been an ever-expanding volume of research and writing on this subject. This growing interest has resulted in this fourth edition of *Annual Editions: Aging.*

This volume is somewhat representative of the field of gerontology in that it is interdisciplinary in its approach and includes articles from the biological sciences, medicine, nursing, psychology, sociology, and social work. These articles are taken from the popular press, government publications, and scientific journals. They represent a wide cross-section of authors, perspectives, and issues related to the aging process. They were chosen because they address the most relevant and current problems in the field of aging and present a variety of divergent views on the appropriate solutions to these problems. The topics covered include demographic trends, the aging process, longevity, social attitudes toward old age, problems and potentials of aging, retirement, death, living environments in later life, and social policies, programs, and services for older Americans. A serious attempt was made to organize these articles into a meaningful and useful anthology for both the student and the teacher.

The overriding goal of this edition was to choose articles that are pertinent, well-written, and useful to those concerned with the field of gerontology. We would welcome comments, suggestions, or constructive criticism to help improve future editions of this book. Please fill out the article rating form on the last page of this volume, and let us know your thoughts and opinions. Any anthology can be improved, and this one will continue to be—annually.

Harold Cox

Harold Cox
Editor

Contents

Unit 1

The Phenomenon of Aging

Eight selections examine the impact of aging on the individual, the family, society, and future social programs.

The concepts in italics are developed in the article. For further expansion please refer to the Topic Guide and the Index.

Unit 2

Longevity and Aging

Four selections consider the implications of living longer as well as the physiological and psychological effects of aging.

Unit 3

Societal Attitudes Toward Old Age

Five selections discuss societal attitudes of discrimination toward the elderly, family structures, social programs for the aged, sexuality in the later years, and institutionalization.

Unit 4

Problems and Potentials of Aging

Six selections examine some of the inherent medical and social problems encountered by the aged and review how, with proper supervision, the psychological and physical well-being of the elderly can be affected positively.

The concepts in italics are developed in the article. For further expansion please refer to the Topic Guide and the Index.

Unit 5

Retirement: American Dream or Dilemma

Five selections look at the broad social implications of
the continuing trend toward early retirement and
examine the necessity of reassessing and reshaping
policies to keep valuable elderly employees in the work
force.

The concepts in italics are developed in the article. For further expansion please refer to the Topic Guide and the Index.

Unit 6

The Experience of Dying

Four selections discuss how increased longevity will affect support programs and the family, and consider the effect of death or terminal illness on the family.

The concepts in italics are developed in the article. For further expansion please refer to the Topic Guide and the Index.

Unit 7

Living Environments in Later Life

Four selections examine the problems of maintaining a positive living environment for the increasing number of elderly people.

Unit 8

Social Policies, Programs, and Services for Older Americans

Seven selections consider the necessity of developing effective and positive support programs, policies, and services for older Americans.

The concepts in italics are developed in the article. For further expansion please refer to the Topic Guide and the Index.

The concepts in italics are developed in the article. For further expansion please refer to the Topic Guide and the Index.

Topic Guide

This topic guide suggests how the selections in this book relate to topics of traditional concern to students and professionals involved with gerontology. It is very useful in locating articles which relate to each other for reading and research. The guide is arranged alphabetically according to topic. Articles may, of course, treat topics that do not appear in the topic guide. In turn, entries in the topic guide do not necessarily constitute a comprehensive listing of all the contents of each selection.

TOPIC AREA	TREATED AS AN ISSUE IN:	TOPIC AREA	TREATED AS AN ISSUE IN:
Alcoholism	19. Alcoholism and the Elderly	Family Relations	2. Acting One's Age
Autonomy	39. The Elderly Person		6. Growing Old Absurd
Baby Boom Generation	5. A Generation at Risk		14. Continuity
	8. Entering Middle Age		22. The Black Elderly Today
Benefits of Aging	1. Profile of Tomorrow		29. Coping with the Reality of Terminal Illness in the Family
	7. Creative Aging		34. Positive Consequences of Institutionalization
	8. Entering Middle Age		37. Model Project Reduces Alienation of Aged from Community
Crime	8. The Elderly Person		42. Widower Self-Help Groups
Cross-Cultural Aging	22. The Black Elderly Today	Gerontology	1. Profile of Tomorrow
Day Care	38. Geriatric Day Care		13. Ageism
Death and Dying	29. Coping with the Reality of Terminal Illness in the Family		16. The New Ageism
	30. Choosing the Good Death		31. Death, Dying, and Bereavement in Old Age
	31. Death, Dying, and Bereavement in Old Age	Handicaps	18. Visual Booby Traps
	32. A New Understanding About Death	Health Care/ Health Problems	3. Successful Aging and the Role of the Life Review
Definitions of Aging	1. Profile of Tomorrow		4. America's Neglected Elderly
	2. Acting One's Age		6. Growing Old Absurd
	3. Successful Aging and the Role of the Life Review		10. The Aging Body
Demography	5. A Generation at Risk		11. Surgery and the Elderly
	8. Entering Middle Age		12. Are Companion Animals Good for Your Health?
	21. Growing Old in Rural America		15. Will You Still Love Me?
	35. Innovative Living Arrangements		17. Sex in the Nursing Home?
Discrimination	4. America's Neglected Elderly		20. Hazards of Drug Use Among the Elderly
	13. Ageism		21. Growing Old in Rural America
	16. The New Ageism		23. Therapy After Sixty
	18. Visual Booby Traps		30. Choosing the Good Death
	22. The Black Elderly Today		36. Alternatives to Institutional Care of the Elderly
	37. Model Project Reduces Alienation of Aged from Community	Hospice	31. Death, Dying, and Bereavement in Old Age
	39. The Elderly Person		32. A New Understanding About Death
Drug Problems	19. Alcoholism and the Elderly		38. Geriatric Day Care
	20. Hazards of Drug Use Among the Elderly	Housing	4. America's Neglected Elderly
Economic Status	2. Acting One's Age		35. Innovative Living Arrangements
	21. Growing Old in Rural America		37. Model Project Reduces Alienation of Aged from Community
	22. The Black Elderly Today		38. Geriatric Day Care
Employment	14. Continuity	Institutionalization	4. America's Neglected Elderly
	25. A New Wrinkle in Retirement Policies		12. Are Companion Animals Good for Your Health?
	26. Reconsidering Retirement		17. Sex in the Nursing Home?
	27. New Roles for Older Workers		31. Death, Dying, and Bereavement in Old Age
	28. As Early Retirement Grows in Popularity		33. The Risk of Institutionalization Before Death
	40. Toward an Aging Policy		34. Positive Consequences of Institutionalization
	41. Planning for an Aging Work Force		35. Innovative Living Arrangements
	43. State Units Launch Employment Initiatives		36. Alternatives to Institutional Care of the Elderly
Euthanasia	30. Choosing the Good Death		38. Geriatric Day Care
	32. A New Understanding About Death		

TOPIC AREA	TREATED AS AN ISSUE IN:	TOPIC AREA	TREATED AS AN ISSUE IN:
Life Expectancy/ Longevity	6. Growing Old Absurd 9. Living Longer 10. The Aging Body 27. New Roles for Older Workers 31. Death, Dying, and Bereavement in Old Age 32. A New Understanding About Death 33. The Risk of Institutionalization Before Death		41. Planning for an Aging Work Force 43. State Units Launch Employment Initiatives
		Sexuality	15. Will You Still Love Me? 17. Sex in the Nursing Home?
		Social Policy	37. Model Project Reduces Alienation of Aged from Community 38. Geriatric Day Care 39. The Elderly Person 40. Toward an Aging Policy
Marketing	8. Entering Middle Age		
Minorities	21. Growing Old in Rural America 22. The Black Elderly Today		41. Planning for an Aging Work Force 43. State Units Launch Employment Initiatives
Nursing Homes	12. Are Companion Animals Good for Your Health? 17. Sex in the Nursing Home? 33. The Risk of Institutionalization Before Death 34. Positive Consequences of Institutionalization 35. Innovative Living Arrangements 36. Alternatives to Institutional Care of the Elderly	**Social Security**	26. Reconsidering Retirement 27. New Roles for Older Workers 41. Planning for an Aging Work Force 43. State Units Launch Employment Initiatives
		Social Services	4. America's Neglected Elderly 5. A Generation at Risk 6. Growing Old Absurd 14. Continuity 27. New Roles for Older Workers 33. The Risk of Institutionalization Before Death 34. Positive Consequences of Institutionalization 36. Alternatives to Institutional Care of the Elderly 37. Model Project Reduces Alienation of Aged from Community 38. Geriatric Day Care 40. Toward an Aging Policy 41. Planning for an Aging Work Force 42. Widower Self-Help Groups
Physiology of Aging	7. Creative Aging 9. Living Longer 10. The Aging Body 11. Surgery and the Elderly 15. Will You Still Love Me? 18. Visual Booby Traps 20. Hazards of Drug Use Among the Elderly 23. Therapy After Sixty 25. A New Wrinkle in Retirement Policies 27. New Roles for Older Workers		
Politics	4. America's Neglected Elderly 37. Model Project Reduces Alienation of Aged from Community 39. The Elderly Person 43. State Units Launch Employment Initiatives	**Social Status**	2. Acting One's Age 21. Growing Old in Rural America 22. The Black Elderly Today
		Sociology of Aging	7. Creative Aging 12. Are Companion Animals Good for Your Health? 22. The Black Elderly Today 37. Model Project Reduces Alienation of Aged from Community 42. Widower Self-Help Groups
Poverty	21. Growing Old in Rural America 40. Toward an Aging Policy		
Psychology of Aging	1. Profile of Tomorrow 2. Acting One's Age 7. Creative Aging 9. Living Longer 12. Are Companion Animals Good for Your Health? 23. Therapy After Sixty 24. Symbolic Interaction and Retirement Adjustment 28. As Early Retirement Grows in Popularity 37. Model Project Reduces Alienation of Aged from Community 38. Geriatric Day Care 42. Widower Self-Help Groups	**Stereotypes**	15. Will You Still Love Me? 16. The New Ageism
		Understanding the Aged	1. Profile of Tomorrow 2. Acting One's Age 3. Successful Aging and the Role of the Life Review 7. Creative Aging 14. Continuity 15. Will You Still Love Me? 16. The New Ageism 23. Therapy After Sixty 28. As Early Retirement Grows in Popularity 36. Alternatives to Institutional Care of the Elderly 38. Geriatric Day Care 40. Toward an Aging Policy
Rural Elderly	21. Growing Old in Rural America		
Retirement	5. A Generation at Risk 24. Symbolic Interaction and Retirement Adjustment 25. A New Wrinkle in Retirement Policies 26. Reconsidering Retirement 27. New Roles for Older Workers 28. As Early Retirement Grows in Popularity		

The Phenomenon of Aging

The process of aging is complex and includes biological, psychological, sociological, and behavioral changes.

Biologically, the body gradually loses the ability to renew itself. Various body functions begin to slow down, and the vital senses become less acute. Psychologically, aging persons experience changing sensory processes. Perception, motor skills, problem-solving ability, and drives and emotions are frequently altered. Sociologically, they must cope with the changing roles and definitions of self that society imposes on the individual. Being a grandparent is different than being a parent, for example. The role expectations and the status of grandparents are different from those of parents. The roles of the retired are quite different from those of the employed. Being defined as "old" may be desirable or undesirable, depending on the particular culture and its values. Behaviorally, these individuals may move slower and with less dexterity. Because they are assuming new roles and are viewed differently by significant others, their attitudes about themselves, their emotions, and, ultimately, their behavior can be expected to change.

Those studying the process of aging often use developmental theories of the life cycle—a sequence of predictable phases, which begins with birth and ends with death—to explain individuals' behavior at various stages of their lives. An individual's age, therefore, is important only because it provides clues about his or her behavior at a particular phase of the life cycle: be it childhood, adolescence, adulthood, middle age, or old age.

The articles in this section are written from biological, psychological, and sociological perspectives. The reader's task is to see and understand how many, complex processes interrelate to produce changes in the aging person.

Looking Ahead: Challenge Questions

What accounts for most behavior changes during the aging process: biological, psychological, or sociological factors?

Biological, psychological, sociological, and behavioral researchers usually work independently to explain the aging process. Will anyone ever be able to combine these disparate perspectives into one single theory of aging?

Will we ever be able to slow down the aging process? Would this be desirable?

What is meant by the concept of successful aging?

PROFILE of tomorrow

Caroline Bird

Caroline Bird writes about the economy's impact on the personal lives of Americans. Her books include The Invisible Scar, Born Female *and the current* The Good Years: Your Future in the 21st Century.

For 200 years, Americans have looked forward to the future. In the 1980s, we are afraid of it.

What we've lost is hope of material advancement. It has been a grievous loss, and for young people a cruel betrayal. We told them that with a little bit of luck and a lot of hard work they could expect to enjoy more money and status than their parents or their peers. We led them to expect that people with talent could always make a place to express it. We told them that there was always room at the top.

This was the American Dream. It was a valid promise during the centuries it took to exploit a continent of untapped resources, but it could not last forever. There is room for all talents only when an economy is growing, and no economy, not even ours, can go on growing forever. We have had reprieves—usually by wars—but now that war is unthinkable the slowdown is upon us.

In the 1980s, we are passing through the uncomfortable moment when the car comes to a stop in the garage after a long fast drive in the night and the children waken and fret, the awkward moment of stepping off the escalator. Beginning with 1981, there was little gain in productivity and no gain in real national income—our measure of all payments made to individuals, corrected for inflation. In 1982, the pileup of budget deficits showed how violently the unexpected slowdown had thrown the economy to the ground.

Everyone wanted to go back to the days of pleasant forward motion. But we can't go back, and in our bones we know it. We are going to have to learn to live in a slower-growing economy, and in some ways this is going to be a relief.

A steady-state economy does not encourage postponing satisfactions available today in favor of bigger ones promised in the future. It does not reward pushers, shovers or driven workaholics. People can afford to be cheerful and friendly while in line for a job or bus.

In the 1980s, some Americans are already living by the values that make sense in a slower-growing economy. They are the people past middle age who are going back to the goals and activities that they had to defer when they were building careers and rearing families.

These quiet few are finding work and relationships that are ends instead of means, and lifestyles that are satisfying rather than symbols of success. They are going back to the identity-finding that they laid aside after college, and even to love affairs that may have been impractical in the heat of midlife.

They are our older people and we need to know much more about them.

If you look around you at the people you know who are over 60, you see that they are divided into two nations: the old, who are in need of welfare services, and people who aren't called old because they are doing all right.

The difference between these two nations isn't based on birthdays. "Ugly, decrepit, stupid, forgetful, toothless, sexless, and ready to fall on the conveyor belt of life after 65" is the way (Gray Panther) Lydia Bragger summarized the media depiction of the old for the 1981 White House Conference on Aging. But when I have had occasion to mention that I was born in 1915, people feel obliged to say, "Oh, but I don't think of you as old!" Actually, of course, each of Bragger's adjectives applies to some young people, too.

So we have these two nations: the old and the ageless.

What makes the difference? We need to know, not only because the number of people over 65 is expected to double by 2030, and because you and I are going to live longer than we think, but because the lifestyles of the ageless of today are examplars for everyone destined to live in the steady-state economy of the future.

In 1980, thanks to a Ford Foundation travel and study grant, I was able to talk with scores of the ageless. The trouble was that they were too lucky to be good role models. It's all very well to be George Burns or Margaret Mead or William S. Paley. It's very nice to be able to turn handsprings at 90. But most of us aren't rich, famous, smart, learned, energetic, or vibrantly healthy, and we are frankly sick and tired of hearing about people who are. Like the successful career women I interviewed in 1966, these older men and women kept telling me that their experience wouldn't help me because they were exceptions.

But there is something to learn from exceptions. What precisely is it about money and privilege and power that makes it so much easier for people to be ageless? Take education. How does a college education ward off old age? It did not seem to me to be the schooling itself, but something in their makeup that had attracted them to schooling. Even those who had not been to college were usually articulate, interested in ideas, well informed, and as curious about the world around them as children.

And then it dawned on me. When the ageless were young, you had to be privileged to go to college, to read books and talk ideas, to escape the environment that dulls curiosity—school chairs bolted to the floor, repetitive machine-tending that bolted the worker to the machine. But no more. In the 1980s, many more adults have easy access not only to higher education, but to the sea of information and stimulation that pours into every home. If words and ideas prolong active life, then many more of today's young adults will be ageless.

And the same thing was true of other characteristics of the ageless. Opportunities for sociability, enjoyable work, good health habits, companionable family relationships were once limited to the privileged. But now they are available to more of us—and this trend is continuing.

If this is so, then the ageless are lucky, not so much in enjoying privileges intrinsically limited to a few, but in enjoying them a generation early. They are important because they are bellwethers, living now the way more people of every age are going to live more of their lives in the future: without children, in small or special-purpose quarters, committed to a higher quality of intimate relationships and nonmaterial satisfactions in their work, cultivating habits that make them feel good.

In the 1980s, our slowdown looks like a passage to a present-oriented, adult society, richer, more various, and more humane than the society based on the ethic of success it seems destined to replace. More and more of us believe that work should be a pleasure to the worker, that money is only one of the measures of value, and that the end of love need not be a child. In spite of discouraging headlines, most of us can expect to spend our later years in a world in which the ageless will outnumber the old.

Today's ageless are people who seem to have succeeded in outwitting Mother Nature. They are not slow, timid, or "disengaged" from society. Their lives are not "characterized by a reduction in physical activities and social interaction," as one textbook of psychology describes them. Nor do they suffer from a "reduction in energy" that makes them "willing accomplices in the process of separation from active society."

Consider Armand Hammer, chairman of Occidental Petroleum. During a few months of his 82nd year he bid on Leonardo da Vinci's notebooks at a London auction, swung by the Kremlin to discuss the Afghan uprising with his old friend Brezhnev, clarified the conversation with reporters, and suggested an oil deal with Mexico via an Op Ed article in *The New York Times*.

We expect the old to mumble or fail to finish their sentences, but words are a way of reaching out to other people, and the ageless take pains to write and speak distinctly. Even when they look physically fragile, their speech remains dry, and clear as rarefied mountain air.

We expect the old to mull over the past, but the ageless look to the future, however long or short they can expect it to be. A 94-year-old retired businessman and his wife are crossing orchids that can't be expected to bloom for at least five years. Francetta Barberis, the former head of Webster College, thinks of her life as "a novel that keeps you turning the pages." V. S. Pritchett, the British man of letters, tells about an 84-year-old friend who was so depressed that he wanted to die at once, but not, he said, until he had found out what was going to happen to Poland, and after that, in Iran. It seems unlikely that the world will calm down long enough to let him die.

But the ageless exceptions to the stereotypes surprise us most by their curiosity. Instead of aches and pains, they are full of what they just saw in China. They are as eager as children to try new things. If they are authors, they are learning to write with a computer. If they are swimmers, they are altering the crawl that has served them for half a century to take advantage of the more effective S stroke.

The ageless I talked with didn't see themselves in terms of decline. When I asked them what had changed in their lives after middle

age, they did not regret that their children were grown and gone, nor did they look wistfully back at the years they spent building careers. When asked to describe the course of their lives, they responded with metaphors of continued growth. An educator thought of the course of his life as "a snowball, gathering size and strength." Jacqueline Wexler, the former president of Hunter College, described it as a "spiral that brings you back to the same problems, but you resolve them each time on a higher plane."

Many thought of their lives as a journey rather than an arrival, but all of the modes of travel suggested were self-directed and self-propelled: Nobody felt like a ship being passively tugged through the predictable locks of the Panama Canal. Margaret Hickey, the veteran editor at *Ladies Home Journal*, thinks of her life as "a voyage of discovery through stormy seas." For Pauli Murray, the civil rights activist who was the first black person to earn a doctorate from Yale Law School, it's a "pilgrimage": In her seventies she has just embarked on a new career as an Episcopal priest. Henry Chauncey, the first president of

Educational Testing Service, thinks of his life as "an obstacle race." I think of mine as a climb up a mountain that rewards each step with a longer view.

The ageless have not planned their lives or followed any pattern. They have simply responded imaginatively to the accidental situations they have encountered. They remind us that human beings are not lilies or frogs that are biologically programmed to grow on a predetermined plan that is exactly the same for every individual of the species, but self-directed individuals who deliberately adapt to the particular circumstances that happen to confront them.

We know very little about the potentials of the later years. On most of the standard maps they are *terra incognita* that is either left blank, or decorated with the kind of mythical beasts early mapmakers sketched on parts of the globe about which they had no information. A few of every generation have spied out this unknown land and brought back curious, half-believed travelers' tales. We have to take these tales seriously now that we are all really going there.

According to one report, in later years the world begins to seem as magical as it did in childhood. For essayist Malcolm Cowley, at 80 "you can sit still and look at things." British essayist V. S. Pritchett concurs. At 80 he reported a "new sensation that living people are a wonder" and found himself "looking at places much longer and more intensely." A 75-year-old sociologist friend reports that the world appears to be getting more miraculous. "I used to wonder why so many things went wrong, but now I find myself wondering how it is that they ever go right." On being asked how it felt to be old, Albert Einstein replied that he felt "neither hope nor fear, but interest in observing the universe."

What happens when you stop climbing and the view ahead is a plateau? The answer is, you feel free.

Free from family obligations. "For true happiness, there is nothing like being a childless widow," an old Welsh woman told Anne Morrow Lindbergh. Anne Morrow Lindbergh didn't like the verdict, but she's a wise old woman herself and she didn't deny it.

Free from self-interest. "When you are 65 you have proved yourself already or you have not," semanticist S. I. Hayakawa pointed out, "You are no longer on the make." He was, of course, providing a reason for sending Hayakawa to the United States Senate, to which he was elected after his retirement from the presidency of turbulent San Francisco State College.

Free from worries about what people think. Maggie Kuhn, the founder of the Gray Panthers, became more militant in her old age because she felt free, as she put it, "to raise hell." Old people I interviewed seldom asked that their names be withheld, even when they were candid about their personal lives. When I asked Rosser Reeves if I could use his name, he said, "Hell, yes. There's nothing you can say that could possibly hurt me."

Free to have fun. Agatha Christie, the mystery writer, enjoyed a "second blooming that comes when you finish life of the emotions and of personal relations and suddenly find—at the age of 50, say—that a whole new life has opened before you. Picture exhibitions, concerts, the opera. It's as if a fresh sap of ideas and thoughts were rising in you."

Free to work for the common good. Once you are on the plateau it is easier to see what is happening to the human race as a whole, and there is less to stop you from doing something about it. Eminent people have invested the precious capital of their reputations in high-risk causes. Albert Schweitzer, the doctor who won world fame for his medical missionary work, launched a campaign for global peace after he was 70. He was joined in this effort by Linus Pauling, winner of the Nobel Prize in chemistry, who lost his passport because he insisted on publicizing the danger of testing the atom bomb.

But the most exciting freedom of later years is the freedom to become a unique individual, different from any other on earth. To do this, you have to go back to a forgotten or undeveloped part of yourself. It may be a challenge you dared not take, a truth you could not face, a talent you were never able to use, an opportunity you could not or would not take the first time you encountered it.

Separations are inevitable in later years. Death and divorce are traumas that visibly age the survivors. But however painful, the experience liberates the energy that was bound in the relationship and relieves the inhibitions that made it viable.

The classic example is the flowering of Eleanor Roosevelt after F.D.R. died. When President Truman asked her to represent the U.S. at the United Nations, she thought she wasn't qualified. But when she finally accepted she learned how to use her name and her inside acquaintance with public affairs to advance her own ideals rather than the political interests of her husband.

Doing what you have always wanted to do can release enough energy to overcome physical handicaps. Izzy Stone, the iconoclastic political reporter, wanted to become a professor of philosophy but he didn't do well in school and never finished college. When late in life he suf-

fered a heart attack, he gave up his newsletter and sought revenge on the academics of his youth. He applied his skill at investigative reporting to the 2,500-year-old mystery surrounding the death of Socrates and produced a plausible solution. A painstaking detail man, he learned Greek from scratch to study the record directly.

Some of the ambitions laid aside during middle years are easily achieved. The grandmother of a friend of mine spent all her working life at a sewing machine in New York's garment center. Her children worried about how to keep her occupied when she was retired, but to their surprise, she bought a ticket to Israel with her first Social Security check and has been happy doing volunteer work there ever since. This was what she had secretly wanted to do for decades.

Later years are the only time when you can be sure of who you are. Only then is your track record long enough to reveal a reliable pattern. It takes a lot of living to become a unique individual. Babies look very much alike in the hospital nursery, and the pictures in a high school yearbook resemble each other more than the graduates do at reunions a decade later.

Only in your later years are you free to look at parts of yourself you have had to shove to the back of your mind. The insights that emerge are not always painless. Dr. Robert N. Butler, the psychiatrist now heading the Department of Geriatrics at New York City's Mount Sinai Medical Center, has urged his profession to help older people review their lives. He reports that they experience the kind of identity crisis that we expect of teenagers and emerge with a firmer sense of themselves. He points out that both take to gazing earnestly at themselves in the mirror.

Luckily, the life review that Dr. Butler describes need not generate a dramatic crisis. The ageless come to understand themselves by a phenomenon of later years that is usually a pleasure. After middle age, memories of scenes and feelings

long forgotten well up into consciousness. Insights often accompany these attacks of memory.

An older person can't undo the years that may have been wasted in the past, but experience may have made him or her more resourceful in devising a solution. Jimmy Carter's mother is a good example. One of her early conflicts was that she wanted to support civil rights for blacks at a time when her husband, like many other Southerners, disapproved of the movement. Lillian Carter was 66 when her husband died, but she joined the Peace Corps, survived its rigorous training course, and even learned to type so that she could qualify for it. She said she chose India for her field work because like her native Georgia, it was "a dark country with a warm climate." But it was also on the other side of the world from disapproving friends and family.

So we come back to the initial question: Why are some people ageless while most merely grow old?

Well, for starters, the ageless are a privileged lot. All rich people aren't ageless, and neither are all college professors. Talents wither, and not even all the healthy people become ageless in the questing sense.

Maybe the trouble is with the question. We have been asking why the ageless keep on growing as if they were in possession of some secret that we could bottle and take by the spoonful if only we could wrest it from their grasp. But maybe there isn't a secret. We just think there is because we have been asking the question the wrong way around. Instead of asking why some people keep growing all their lives, we should ask what prevents the rest of us from growing.

Our problem may be that we have been taught to underestimate ourselves, to think of ourselves as animals instead of as human beings. Babies come into the world a bundle of options. Some keep more of these options longer than others, and as we have seen, a few succeed in going back and picking up those that seemed already lost.

ACTING ONE'S AGE: NEW RULES FOR OLD

BERNICE NEUGARTEN INTERVIEWED BY ELIZABETH HALL

Elizabeth Hall has been editor-in-chief of *Human Nature* and managing editor of *Psychology Today*. She has done 14 previous conversations for *Psychology Today*. She is also the author of six books for children, two of which received honorable mention in the National Media Awards of the American Psychological Association (*Why We Do What We Do* and *From Pigeons to People*), and coauthor, with Robert Schell, of the textbook *Developmental Psychology Today* (Random House, 3rd edition). Her current projects include a college textbook in child psychology and another children's novel.

America is growing older. Fifty years ago, only 4 out of every 100 people in the United States were 65 years old or above. Today, 10 of every 100 Americans have passed that traditional marker for old age, and by the year 2020, the number will be 13 in 100. A man of 65 can now expect to live almost to age 79; a woman, to 83. The aging of the populace, the experts predict, will affect every aspect of society—education, medicine, housing, business, leisure. It will also help to determine where tax dollars go and how many of them are needed.

Next year, the Third White House Conference on Aging will gather to examine the status of old people and to recommend legislation. Given the rapidity of the changes that are taking place, the meeting could have a substantial impact. Many credit the 1951 White House Conference on Aging with responsibility for the passage of Medicare four years later.

Bernice Neugarten was recently appointed deputy chairman of the 1981 conference. A professor at the University of Chicago, Neugarten is one of the major authorities in this country on the psychology and sociology of aging. She is also known for her maverick views on some of the issues. Neugarten argues, for example, that the family is not falling apart, that menopause is neither frightening nor terrible, that women welcome the "empty-nest" syndrome rather than fear it, that old age does not mean poverty, isolation, and sickness, and that far from being placid inhabitants of rocking chairs, grandparents can be the shakers and movers of society.

I recently spent two days talking with Neugarten about the social and economic consequences of the age shift and discovered that they are already real forces in American life, not just speculative predictions from academic ivory towers. Quietly and unobtrusively, the graying of America has made us a very different society—one in which people have quite a different perception of what kind of behavior is appropriate at various ages. Here, in condensed form, is what Neugarten told me about the nature of the changes:

Elizabeth Hall: Dr. Neugarten, you've said on several occasions that the United States is becoming an age-irrelevant society. Just what do you mean by that?

Bernice Neugarten: Simply that chronological age is becoming a poorer and poorer predictor of the way people live. An adult's age no longer tells you anything about that person's economic or marital status, style of life, or health. Somewhere after the first 20 years, age falls away as a predictor.

Hall: Does that mean we are becoming a less rigid society?

Neugarten: Yes, I think so. Lives are more fluid. There's no longer a particular year—or even a particular decade—in which one marries or enters the labor market or goes to school or has children. The whole internal clock I used to write about that kept us on time, the clock that tells us whether we're too young or too old to be marrying or going to school or getting a job or retiring, is no longer as powerful or as compelling as it used to be. It no longer surprises us to hear of a 22-year-old mayor or a 29-year-old university president—or a 35-year-old grandmother or a retiree of 50. No one blinks at a 70-year-old college student or at the 55-year-old man who becomes a father for the first time—or who starts a second family. I can remember when the late Justice William Douglas, in old age, married a young wife. The press was shocked and hostile. That hostility would be gone today. People might smirk a little, but the outrage has vanished.

Hall: Of course, we've always been accustomed to wealthy older men marrying young women.

Neugarten: It's going the other way now. I have a collection of newspaper articles on older women who have married younger men. The age difference is not the 30 or 40 years we see when the man is older, but the stories comment on the way public attitudes are shifting.

Hall: Do you think the cult of youth is over in this country?

Neugarten: Not yet, but it's fading. I think that in another decade or two it will be gone. It's inevitable.

Hall: Are we going to stop regarding the old with distaste?

Neugarten: There obviously has been a change. I see it in my college students. Thirty years ago, when I first gave a course in adult development and aging, only a few students found it of interest. Today, courses in aging on state university campuses commonly have 200 or 300 undergraduates.

Hall: How do you explain the shift?

Neugarten: One reason is just the reality of having more old people around. If you walked down a mythical street and met a mythical group of average people, 1 out of every 10 would be over 65. That obviously has to change your attitude in some way. A second reason is the "roots" phenomenon, which began with ethnic consciousness. Lots of young people are interested in their origins, so they turn naturally to their grandparents—and find them a lot more interesting than they had anticipated. When my students study the three-generation family, they have to find one and interview its members. Invariably, the students find the oldest member of the family most interesting. Long lives are interesting.

Hall: What else helps change people's attitudes?

Neugarten: Currently there are a lot of jobs in the field of service to older people. And there's a subtle difference in the way the press deals with old age. I think the interest is both reflected in and stimulated by government programs in the field of aging. The current joke is that aging is "in."

People are finding that getting older isn't all problems and losses; it brings freedoms and gains, too. I've interviewed a great many people who say, "I am much younger than my mother—or my father—was at my age." The kinds of people they expected to be at, say, 50, 60, or 70 aren't what they are. The difference is great, and it will become even greater. The characteristics of people who become old in future decades will be very different from those of people who are old now.

Another thing is that people are vigorous longer than they used to be. People of 60, 70, and even 80 are doing things they would not have done 30 years ago.

Hall: Is it okay to disco at 70?

Neugarten: No one says "act your age" anymore. We've stopped looking with disfavor on older people who act in youthful ways. So that's one factor in the move toward age-irrelevancy. Another is affluence; in an affluent so-

ciety, there are opportunities to move around and start new careers. People are freer to do the things they want to do And higher educational levels are a factor.

Hall: Is age-irrelevancy primarily a middle-class phenomenon, then?

Neugarten: That's probably so, but it's by no means limited to the middle class. Ever since World War I, working-class women have been moving in and out of the labor market. That movement now is characteristic of women and men in the middle class, who also switch careers and go back to school. We no longer believe people must finish their education before they marry. The rhythm of the life cycle has changed in other ways, too. We marry, divorce, remarry. A man can become a father again at the same time he becomes a grandfather. And think of the young women who are rearing children—first in two-parent homes, then in one-parent homes, and then again with two parents.

Hall: Are all the changes you've mentioned due to social factors?

Neugarten: Not at all. Puberty comes earlier and menopause probably comes later. That extends the period of possible childbearing years, although on the latter point we don't have enough good data to be certain. And grandparents are getting younger and living longer.

Hall: How have all those grandparents in their late 30s and mid-40s changed the role of the grandparent?

Neugarten: Some time back, I did a little study and found that the middle-aged grandparent is generally different from the traditional grandparent. Traditional grandparents play what I call a "formal" role. They are always interested in their grandchildren, may give them treats and indulge them, even do a little baby-sitting, but they seldom offer advice on child-rearing. Today's young grandparent is likely to be in the labor market. In fact, grandchildren are more likely to see their grandmothers working than they are their mothers. That means the image has to shift. Employed grandparents tend to become playmates to their grandchildren, not authoritarian figures.

Hall: But public perceptions lag behind. We still think of Miss Lillian as the typical grandparent—I'll bet even 45-year-old grandparents who are at the peak of their careers think that.

Yet she's the *great*-grandparent. Jimmy and Rosalynn Carter are the grandparents.

You mentioned later menopause. What about having children later? There's a trend among highly educated young women to postpone their first child until their early 30s. What will that do to grandparents?

Neugarten: I don't think it will make much difference. Most women have their children early and closer together than was the custom with their grandmothers. So they're through with childbearing much sooner. Having a first baby late will postpone a woman's entry into grandmotherhood for a few years, but I think that will be offset by the fact that older people feel younger today. I don't believe the interaction will change much, nor will the general pattern of early grandparenthood. Don't forget that we also have a very high rate of children born to teenagers.

Hall: The 14- and 15-year-olds who have their own live dolls. Is that happening in all strata of society?

Neugarten: Unfortunately, yes. It used to be much more frequent in the very lowest income groups, but now it's spreading. Someone told me the other day of a midwestern city in which the chic thing to do in one suburban high school was to get pregnant, and that 1 out of 10 girls in that school had already been pregnant. It's a major social problem.

Hall: I've read that a greater proportion of those girls are refusing abortions and that many of them are keeping their babies. Aren't those babies likely to be reared by grandmothers?

Neugarten: If so, it will force a number of young middle-aged women into roles they don't choose. I can't see many middle-class 40-year-olds willingly taking on the rearing of a baby. Remember, a large proportion of them are in the labor market and don't want to return to full time mothering and homemaking.

Hall: You keep saying that "older people feel younger today." Is that another biological factor that adds to age-irrelevancy?

Neugarten: Feeling younger certainly helps make the added years less constricting. But I don't want to give the impression that we've done anything to change the natural life span of human beings. Most biological research-

11

ers believe the human species is programmed to die at about 100. In a few places, researchers are saying the genetically based life span is 120, but that figure is not generally accepted.

None of the reports about extra-long-lived people in South America and the Soviet Union has held up, by the way. In some places, it turned out that in order to avoid military service, young men had taken the names of older brothers who had died. In others, a number of baptismal records had the same name, and so on.

Hall: I heard that the reason there were more old people in some of those societies was that all the young people had left for the city.

Neugarten: Yes, that gives you a population that appears to be heavily old. But investigators found two very curious things. The age distribution was off. In a population with normal distribution, for every 100-year-old, you should have more 90-year-olds; for every 90-year-old, more 80-year-olds, and so on. But in these publicized populations there was a gap. Lots and lots of 100- and 110- and 140-year-olds, but not many in the younger brackets of the aged. That was very peculiar. But what really debunked these long-life societies was that when investigators returned to a village four years later, people they talked to on their first visit claimed to be 10 years older, not 4.

Hall: So yogurt is not going to save us all.

Neugarten: Nor high mountain climates, nor tilling the soil until we're very old. But there's some evidence that environmental purity might help. Pure air and pure water.

Hall: That may not bode well for us. But to get back to the life span, we've pushed the estimate up from 90 to 100 or so by. . .

Neugarten: By public health measures, by nutrition, sanitation, the conquest of disease. All we've been doing is manipulating life *expectancy*. For example, women didn't start to outlive men until 40 or 50 years ago, when childbirth stopped being a big killer. We've been chipping away at those processes that kill by accident, by stress, by disease, but we haven't changed the life span.

Hall: And there is nothing we can do to extend that natural life span, whatever it is?

Neugarten: Some researchers are try-

A WOMAN FOR ALL SEASONS

Unlike many of those who attack established beliefs, Bernice Neugarten can cite chapter and verse in the scientific literature to back up her views. Indeed, she wrote much of that literature. Many of her findings have come from a study of more than 2,000 midwestern adults whose lives she and her associates began following nearly 25 years ago. (See *Psychology Today*, December 1971.)

Neugarten has pioneered in the study of the human life cycle, now a fashionable field in psychology. Some of today's best known life-cycle theorists, including Roger Gould and Daniel J. Levinson, were originally influenced by her work, although their ideas have since diverged from hers. Currently, she is helping to supervise a series of studies of three-generation families to find out how family members perceive one another, what they disagree about, and how they resolve conflict—or, if they are quite old, how they sometimes choose to ignore it. Some interesting findings have already begun to emerge from interviews with 592 family members. It appears, for instance, that the bond between parent and child remains strong throughout adulthood and even into old age, and that conflict may actually help to cement family ties.

Neugarten calls herself "a University of Chicago product all the way." She arrived at the university as a 16-year-old freshman and has never left. When she was a graduate student in educational psychology, she was invited to enter the program on human development as a doctoral student. This interdisciplinary program in sociology, anthropology, psychology, and biology was the first of its kind in the United States, and Neugarten received its first Ph.D. Her interest in the adult years was partly a matter of chance. "When I was ready to teach," she has said, "the only available course was on adulthood and aging." She is now a professor of human development at the university.

An extraordinarily youthful-looking 64, Neugarten is the mother of two: a son, Jerrold, an assistant district attorney for New York County, and a daughter, Dail, assistant dean of the Graduate School of Public Affairs at the University of Colorado in Denver. Neugarten's airy 13th floor apartment in Hyde Park, near Chicago, shows few signs of being inhabited by a psychologist. Except for the large black bust of Lincoln that symbolizes Neugarten's recognition as Illinois' distinguished psychologist for 1979, the house could be that of a patron of the arts, or of a novelist or literary critic. There are classical records and art books, and the other books that line the living room wall are Shakespeare and Proust, not Skinner and Erikson. Neugarten, it turns out, has a bachelor's degree in French and English literature.

Neugarten has been president of the Gerontological Society, has won numerous awards for outstanding research and distinguished teaching, and since 1978 has been a member of the Federal Council on Aging. Her recent appointment as deputy chairman of the 1981 White House Conference on Aging will increase her influence in policymaking. And when the time comes for Neugarten to join the ranks of the young-old, she has a role model close at hand. Her husband, Fritz, started a new business at the age of 65.   —E.H.

ing to manipulate it. Start with the assumption that there are some basic aging processes that are genetically programmed. If we can find the secret of these processes, maybe we can slow them down. Manipulate the genes of the unborn child, perhaps. Or breed

selectively for long-lived people. Or use drugs to change the action of DNA and RNA. Find a way to keep the genes that control the aging process from turning on. Some experiments show that you can extend an animal's life span by, as it were, starving it.

Hall: Wasn't one of the accompaniments of that experiment a very, very late maturation? A 30-year childhood might not be what we're searching for.

Neugarten: That's right. The side effects were by no means good. As more researchers have been drawn into the area of biogerontology, it's become clear that the problems are extremely complex.

Hall: We've been talking about an increasing segment of old people in society even without genetic manipulation. What will that do to our lives? Will there be a smaller proportion of citizens supporting the economy?

Neugarten: Policymakers have been worrying that the ratio of workers to nonworkers will become so tilted as to create a terrible burden for working people. But those projections have another side. If the birthrate stays low, there will be fewer dependent young people, so the dependency ratio of workers to nonworkers may not shift all that much. But in 40 to 50 years, if the birthrate remains low and manpower needs remain constant, we're going to need to draw some of those older people into the labor pool.

Hall: Now that compulsory retirement at 65 has been outlawed, I wonder how many older people actually want to work?

Neugarten: By and large, people retire just as soon as they feel they have enough money to do so. They either choose to get out of the labor market or poor health forces them out. The notion of the faithful worker who gets laid on the shelf is true for only a small proportion of old people; I'd say no more than 8 to 10 percent. Inflation will keep some at work who would prefer to retire, but the quick way to enlarge the manpower pool is to raise the age at which one becomes eligible for public or private pensions. I hope that won't happen. I hope, instead, that we will make a wide range of attractive options available. Perhaps some people will want to shift careers at 55 or so. Or shift from full-time to part-time work.

Hall: Do we have any idea what sorts of people choose to work longer?

Neugarten: The higher the level of occupation and the more absorbing the work, the longer people stay in it. That's because their self-concept gets built into being successful at work, and they find it hard to draw a line between work and play.

Hall: Then blue-collar workers would be less likely to want to keep working. Of course, you can't lay track with a railroad crew at 70.

Neugarten: Much blue-collar work is physically demanding, but large numbers of blue-collar workers find their work monotonous and are happy to move out as soon as they can. People on the higher rungs of the education ladder usually don't retire all at once; many of them don't *ever* retire. Others pace their work differently, take it easy. Or they take on something new. Many business executives become engaged in community affairs in the last years of their employment and find it relatively easy to move into those areas after they retire. In any case, for both demographic and economic reasons, we won't be able to afford much longer the luxury of saying that when you get to a certain age, you retire.

Hall: Airline pilots are fighting retirement regulations now. They say the new big planes are so efficient they almost fly themselves, and that the publicized midair heart attacks all happened to 40-year-old men.

Neugarten: In the case of airline pilots, you don't have to use age as a predictor. Those men are both physically and psychologically examined at regular intervals; both those measures are better predictors than age.

I recently testified as an expert witness in a case to determine whether judges in Illinois should be retired at age 70. My argument was that there was no reason to presume that reaching 70 marked any turning point in capabilities. One big problem is that we don't have any tests that predict how well a judge will perform. You could give a standardized intelligence test to judges, but except for extreme cases of mental deterioration, you wouldn't be able to predict much about their performance from seeing the test results.

Hall: One would think that if there is any profession in which experience and judgment are important, it's that of judge. A judge doesn't have to have the reflexes of an air-traffic controller. Speed or the ability to do 50 push-ups are hardly criteria.

Neugarten: The average 70-year-old often surpasses the young in what we used to call "power" tests.

Hall: That's an intelligence test that gets very difficult but gives you all the time you need to complete it, isn't it?

Neugarten: Yes. You know, we used to think that old people who continued to create in their 80s—people like Grandma Moses, Georgia O'Keeffe, Pablo Casals—were extremely rare. Now it appears that those exceptions aren't so exceptional.

Hall: That reinforces your suggestion that society should draw on their talents. Right now, however, you say that most people retire just as soon as they can afford it. Is supporting old people going to lead to an intergenerational conflict in the short run—before we need older workers in the labor market?

Neugarten: That question needs tempering, I think, by a major factor that is often forgotten. Asked if they would prefer to pay high Social Security taxes or take over the support of aged family members, young people opt for the taxes. They have no intention of assuming financial responsibility for parents and grandparents.

There's something else that needs to be said about the widespread criticism of Social Security. Most objections have not come from the blue-collar worker, but from the industrial firms whose own contribution to Social Security goes up as the worker's contribution rises.

Hall: And who see it strictly as a tax, because they get no return.

Neugarten: Most of what gets into the press comes from management sources, and in the studies we have, the choices are not put squarely. People are asked if they are against paying Social Security taxes, not whether they would rather pay Social Security premiums or become the sole support of their aging mothers and grandmothers.

Hall: That brings the answer out quickly, doesn't it?

Neugarten: Of course. I don't think there's any doubt that support of the aged is going to be increasingly a public function. The United States is now behind other industrial countries when it comes to the proportion of total budget that goes into income maintenance of old people.

Hall: Let's look at the possibility of intergenerational conflict from the other side. Old people are more likely to vote than the young are; are they going to wield political power?

Neugarten: On specific issues, say school taxes or property-tax relief or increases in Social Security payments, older people tend to vote uniformly, but otherwise, people vote less by age than by income level. A politics of age has not yet developed in the United States.

Hall: What about groups that lobby on behalf of old people? The Gray Panthers, the American Association of Retired Persons, the National Council of Senior Citizens?

Neugarten: We don't really know whether these groups are politically powerful. Some have large memberships, but there's no indication that as groups they represent their members' political attitudes. They may be paper tigers. If, however, they become advocates strictly on the basis of age, they may create a backlash that will wipe out gains and cause the needy aged to lose out.

Hall: How large is that group?

Neugarten: Not nearly so large as most people imagine. The number of old people under the poverty line has dropped dramatically in the past 15 years—from nearly 30 percent to about 14 percent. That's true if you look only at cash income. Cash income usually drops about 50 percent when people retire, but most have assets like private savings. And the great majority of all people over 65 own their own homes—mortgage-free. The proportion of needy old people is no higher than the proportion of the needy young. And it's going to change even more. Many of today's needy old people were immigrants without education who spent their lives in unskilled jobs.

Hall: Jobs that weren't covered by pensions.

Neugarten: That's right. And a large proportion of women over 65 spent most of their lives in a society that didn't expect women to support themselves. They've not had long work careers or regular Social Security coverage. When today's young and middle-aged people grow old, old age is going to be even less precarious than it is now. In the United States, income for most people is highest after they no longer need so much money. Most people hit their earning peak in their 50s, and their incomes don't diminish

until retirement. So assets begin to pile up.

Hall: When we talk about the needy aged, then, we're talking about a group that is going to be an increasingly smaller proportion of the old.

Neugarten: I think that's incontrovertible. The case can no longer be made that the aged are the poor of this society.

Hall: We've established that old age doesn't necessarily mean poverty. What about isolation?

Neugarten: The typical 65-year-old is by no means isolated. According to surveys taken in the past four or five years, loneliness among people over 65 is no greater than among people under 65.

Hall: What about physical segregation—whether it's in retirement communities in the Southwest or in nursing homes? Are we pushing old people out of our lives?

Neugarten: You're talking about a tiny, tiny proportion of older people. People tend to grow old in place. Most don't even move from one house to another. And the ones who do move tend to stay in the same community. Don't forget that most people who go into age-segregated communities—whether it's Leisure World or a trailer camp—move from choice. Interaction and sociability in those communities are high, by the way; they are not necessarily bad for the people who move in.

Hall: Is the trend toward such communities likely to increase?

Neugarten: It may, but it needn't. Some people move into age-segregated communities to get services they cannot get at home: transportation, health services, recreational facilities. Right now the suburbs are populated by families with young children. When the adults in those families grow old, we'll have a ring of old people around the cities. If the services they need are available there, most of them will stay where their roots are—with their families and their friends.

Hall: Then you don't believe the family is falling apart?

Neugarten: No. The family is still a strong, supportive institution for older people. We've not become callous.

Hall: We're not casting off the needy old on the mercies of the state?

Neugarten: If anything, the problem may be the other way round. There are

large numbers of families that are going *too* far in caring for older people, stripping themselves of economic, social, and emotional resources to do so. In fact, one recent study showed that parent-caring is becoming a major source of stress in family life. The institutionalization of a family member usually comes only after the family has already done everything they know how to do. Most people in nursing homes—and that's only 4 or 5 percent of people over 65—don't have families. They've never had children, their wives or husbands are dead, and they have no near kin. Many are immigrants. For example, we have a lot of Oriental men who came to this country alone and never married.

Hall: What you've been describing doesn't sound like a nuclear family.

Neugarten: We don't really have a nuclear family in the United States. Only a small percent of our family households are composed of a husband as the sole breadwinner and a wife who stays home with the approximately two children. We have a pattern of extended kinship, and the four-generation family is becoming prevalent. We even have five-generation families. They don't live under the same roof, but they stay closely connected. Not too many years ago, it was uncommon for a child to have four living grandparents; now many children have living great-grandparents. For all practical purposes, the family of the 1980s is a multigenerational family.

Hall: How does the multigenerational family function?

Neugarten: There is an exchange of services up and down the generational tree: housekeeping, advice giving, child care, gifts, help during an illness, or money. Some studies show that more financial aid flows down than up. The interchange is typical and so strong a component of family life that we should underline it. With the multigenerational family, of course, comes a greater concern for older family members, because you have two generations of old people for the middle-aged to worry about. We often talk about women being caught in the middle, between children and aging parents. But that presumes only three generations; they may also be trapped by aging grandparents.

I was at a conference not too long

ago, and to illustrate how widespread the problem was in this country, I reported that while waiting my turn in a beauty shop, I overheard a woman complaining bitterly to the beautician. When I moved into the chair, I asked, "What were all the complaints about?" "Well," said the beautician, "she was complaining about her 85-year-old mother. But who hasn't got an 85-year-old mother?"

And I just had a letter from a colleague from Austria, who said, "Yesterday, in Vienna, I went to have my hair cut, and the man next to me was complaining about his 85-year-old mother."

Hall: So we're talking about a widespread pattern in industrialized countries.

Neugarten: Concern for the present or future care of parents and grandparents is becoming part of the everyday fabric of life. I asked a group of 60 students how many of them had had a family discussion within the past 30 days about present or future problems involving the care of an older relative. More than a casual comment. All but two or three hands went up.

Hall: We've developed the picture of today's old people as vigorous, economically self-sufficient, able to contribute to society, and very much a part of family life. That doesn't sound at all like the American stereotype.

Neugarten: The American stereotype of the aged is based on the *needy* aged; it doesn't resemble the majority of old people, nor are old people a homogeneous group. The stereotype has it that as people age they become more and more like one another. In truth, they become less and less alike. If you look at people's lives, they're like the spreading of a fan. The longer people live, the greater the differences between them. A group of 18-year-olds is more alike than a group of 60-year-olds. To say a man is 60 years old tells you nothing about him except that he has lived for 60 years.

Hall: When we talk about the old, whom are we talking about? Why is 65 considered the beginning of old age?

Neugarten: In the 1930s, 65 was picked arbitrarily as the date of eligibility for Social Security benefits. The choice had nothing to do with the aging process; it could as easily have been 60 or 70. Gradually, it came to be used as the marker for entry into old age.

Hall: When you ask middle-class people where middle age or old age starts, they always place it much later than working-class people do.

Neugarten: Some people over 70 regard themselves as middle-aged. I think that is tied in part to the longer educational period of the middle class. We ought to drop the term "old," because it has such complex connotations. The average person who says "old" generally has in mind a set of physical attributes and behavior that make the bearer different from the rest of society. Now, if those changes occur later, so that they are more frequently found at 75 or 80, you may need another term. I once suggested the terms "young-old" and "old-old," intending to differentiate old people who are vigorous and healthy from old people who are ill.

Hall: If you were 80 and vigorous and healthy, you would be one of the young-old.

Neugarten: That's right, and it's the young-old who are helping to make this an age-irrelevant society.

Hall: We've talked about some of the ways society is changing. Is this large group of vigorous young-old going to have other influences?

Neugarten: They've already affected the leisure market—the travel industry, especially. It's older people who have enough money to go around the world.

Hall: They're no longer sending children through college. But what about education? Will the young-old affect higher education?

Neugarten: Not only the young-old, but the entire trend toward age-irrelevancy among adults will affect education more and more. At the moment, maybe 5 percent of people over 65 are enrolled in formal classes of some sort. About 10 percent of all people enrolled in post-secondary institutions are over 35. I think the whole adult involvement with education is a wave of the future, and it's going to be very powerful, in the sense of changing patterns of life.

Hall: Are most of the adults who are going back to school in the process of changing careers, or are they getting an education just for pleasure?

Neugarten: Both. A large group, disproportionately women, are changing careers or seeking entry into the labor market. The second group, who are going to school to enrich their personal lives, tend to be older. The number is small, but I think it will grow.

Only a part of adult education goes on at formal institutions. There is a wide array of informal classes: occupational education within industry, classes given through libraries, neighborhood centers, museums, television, and other media. Some studies indicate that the majority of adults are engaged in something they call education—a regular, systematic attention given to learning a new skill or a new field of some sort.

Hall: I was talking to a friend about age-irrelevancy the other day. He was somewhat skeptical until I mentioned older adults in the classroom. Then you could see a light go on. He teaches history and said that there was at least one older adult in every one of his classes. Has the appearance of those older adults in the classroom helped change the attitude of the young toward the old?

Neugarten: I think so. The studies I have seen indicate that the effects have been excellent on both young and old. The young learn to enjoy the presence of an older person in class.

Hall: As we have fewer people of college age, enrollment in higher education shrinks. Perhaps the presence of older people on college campuses will help cushion the economic shock for the colleges.

Neugarten: They may help soften the blow, especially people from 30 to 40. Colleges began to reach out to this group about 10 years ago, and the activity has increased. But an adult population requires a wide variety of options—different methods of scheduling, different administration, different counseling, different curricula.

I'm going to make one prediction about education. I think that in the next decade or so, the curricula of all school systems—probably as far down as junior high school—will give more attention to the family cycle, the life cycle, and aging.

Hall: It suddenly struck me that most of what we know about the psychology of the adult comes to us from studies done in universities on college sophomores. What do those studies on 19-year-olds tell us about adult attitudes and behavior?

Neugarten: Perhaps not much. You absolutely cannot generalize from college sophomores to adults. At the moment, the large accumulation of findings about adults *are* skewed, largely because psychologists had a captive audience of potential subjects. But people have begun to realize that, and psychologists and sociologists have been reaching out for populations that are not in school.

Hall: So we may see some great changes in what we think about the way people function. The irrelevancy of age to life in this society must have implications for public policy. You are one of the deputy chairmen of the 1981 White House Conference on Aging. What is the primary message the conference should get from the sort of things we've been talking about?

Neugarten: The primary message is to stop legislating on the basis of age and start providing services only on the basis of need. It's the needs of the old-old that concern us. But if programs meant to assist them are drawn up in terms of age, then society may become so burdened by similar benefits going to the young-old—who don't need them—that adequate programs can't be funded. For example, no more than 15 percent of people over 65 need special health or social services—and they should have them. But, in a time of inflation, a program that offers those services to everyone over 65 is an easy target for budget-trimmers.

Hall: You're suggesting we provide those services for people who need them—no matter what their age.

Neugarten: That's right. Instead of trying to guarantee a minimum income for old people, first guarantee a minimum income for all citizens, then look to see how the Social Security system should be used within that framework. If we don't approach such problems as income maintenance, housing, transportation, health services, social services, and tax benefits in this way, we're going to find ourselves in trouble.

Hall: We might stir up that intergenerational conflict we were talking about earlier, in spite of good intentions. That's the sort of thing you meant when you said age-advocacy groups might create a backlash.

Neugarten: That could happen. And when we treat all old people as if they were old-old, we reinforce the misperception of "the old" as a problem group. The greater the proportion of young-old among the over-65 group, the less likely it is that age-based programs will relieve the pressing needs for which the programs were devised. And that's also why I think we should use incentives to keep old people working longer instead of raising the age of eligibility for Social Security benefits. Some people have tried to help the old by pressing for special benefit programs. I happen to believe that it's far better to integrate old people into society. Let's make this a truly age-irrelevant society and just ignore age differences whenever we can. Let's worry about the poor, the disabled, and the isolated. If we meet their needs, we'll also have met the needs of the old-old.

Successful Aging and the Role of the Life Review

ABSTRACT: The negative view of old age with its outworn stereotypes (particularly "senility") must be changed if the elderly are to have more opportunities for successful aging. It is time for a more balanced attitude. Health in old age involves mental and social as well as physical well-being. There is a distinct difference between the intrinsic features of aging and the reactions of the elderly to their lives. Old age is a period in which unique developmental work can be accomplished. Life review therapy and life-cycle group therapy are effective aids in this direction.

ROBERT N. BUTLER, MD
Washington, DC

Those who think of old people as boobies, crones, witches, old biddies, old fogies, pains-in-the-neck, out-to-pasture, boring, garrulous, unproductive and worthless, have accepted the stereotypes of aging, including the extreme mistake of believing that substantial numbers of old people are in or belong in institutions. On the contrary, most old people need not be and are not in institutions and, given a fighting chance in a society that has devalued them, can maintain a viable place in society. Indeed, at any one moment, 95 per cent of persons over the age of 65 live in the community. In our social policies and in our therapeutic programs we need to bear in mind a basic standard of health, and not have our thinking dominated by stereotypes of frailty, psychopathology, senility, confusion, decline and institutional living.

However, there is no point in developing illusions concerning healthy, successful old age.

Presented at the Symposium on Geriatric Medicine co-sponsored by the American Geriatrics Society and the Franklin Square Hospital, Baltimore, MD, March 2, 1974.

Research Psychiatrist and Gerontologist, Washington School of Psychiatry; Faculty, Howard and George Washington Medical Schools; Consultant, U. S. Senate Special Committee on Aging, National Institute of Mental Health and St. Elizabeth's Hospital, Washington, DC.

Robert N. Butler is currently director of the National Institute on Aging.

Like all periods in life, it has its difficulties. There are problems to be dealt with and needs to be fulfilled. But old age can be an emotionally healthy and satisfying time of life with a minimum of physical and mental impairments. Many older people have adapted well to their old age with little stress and a high level of morale.

The study of "normal" development has seldom gone beyond early adult years, and the greatest emphasis has been on childhood. There are relatively few centers for the study of adult human development. These few centers have studied small population samples, usually of white, affluent, middle-class people, composed about equally of men and women. Such work at the University of Chicago, Duke University, the University of California and for a brief period at the National Institute of Mental Health has helped provide us with some understanding of successful mental health in aging.

In our culture few people think of old age as a time of potential health and growth. This is partly realistic, in view of the lot of so many old people who have been cast aside to become lonely, bitter, poor, and emotionally or physically ill. American society has not been generous or supportive of the "unproductive" — in this case old people who have reached what is arbitrarily defined as the retirement period. But in a larger sense the negative view of old age is a problem of Western civilization. The Western concept of the life cycle is decidedly different from that of the Orient since they derive from two opposing views about what "self" means and what life is all about. Oriental philosophy places the individual self, his life span and his death *within* the process of human experience. Life and death are familiar and equally acceptable parts of what self means. In the West, on the other hand, death is considered outside of the self. To be a self or person one must be alive, in control and aware of what is happening. The greater and more self-centered or narcissistic Western emphasis on individuality and control makes death an outrage, a tremendous affront to man, rather than the logical and necessary process of old life making way for new. The opposite cultural views of East and West evolve to support two very different ways of life, each with its own merits. But the Western predilection for "progress," conquest over nature, and personal self-realization has produced difficult problems for the elderly and for those preparing for old age. This is particularly so when the spirit of a nation and of an historical period has emphasized and expanded the notion of measuring human worth in terms of individual productivity and power. Old people are led to see themselves as failing with age, a phrase that refers as much to self worth as it does to physical strength. Religion has been the traditional solace by promising another world wherein the self again springs to life never to be further threatened by loss of its own integrity. Thus Western man's consummate dream of immortality is fulfilled by religion while integration of the aging experience into his life process remains incomplete. Increasing secularization produces a frightening void which frequently is met by avoiding and denying the thought of one's own decline and death and by forming self-protective prejudices against old people.

In some respects we now deal somewhat more openly with death itself. But aging, that long prelude to death, has become a kind of obscenity, something to avoid.

Medicine and the behavioral sciences have mirrored social attitudes by presenting old age as a grim litany of physical and emotional ills. Decline of the individual has been the key concept, and neglect has been a major treatment technique. Until about 1960 most of the medical, psychologic, psychiatric and social work literature on the aged was based on experience with the sick and the institutionalized even though only 5 per cent of the elderly were confined to institutions. (This 5 per cent, however, is a most significant minority, with major needs. Ultimately, some 20 per cent of older people require institutional care, at least under the current health care system that does not provide comprehensive home care.) The few re-

search studies that have concentrated on the healthy aged give indication of positive potential. Yet the general, almost phobic dislike of the aged remains the norm, with healthy old people being ignored and the chronically ill receiving half-hearted custodial care. Only those elderly who happen to have exotic or "interesting" diseases or emotional problems, or substantial financial resources, ordinarily receive attention for research and treatment by the medical and psychotherapeutic professions.

Health care is approaching a $100 billion annual business, second only to the food industry. The health care industry, however, does not reflect the various human ills in due proportion. Although chronic disease accounts for two-thirds of our nation's health costs, certainly no parallel proportion of our medical school curriculum, medical manpower, intellectual emphasis, research, and health delivery system is devoted to this important group of disorders. With the advent of a national health insurance plan and the ensuing struggle that is now beginning in Congress and in the Administration with respect to the character of that insurance plan, it has to be recognized that not one of the plans under consideration faces realistically the facts of life, of disease and of aging.

HEALTH IN OLD AGE

What is healthy old age? In thinking about health one must remember that science and medicine have historically been more concerned with treating what goes wrong than with clarifying the complex interwoven elements necessary to produce and support health. Typical of this is the treatment of coronary attacks after the fact rather than establishing a preventive program of diet, exercise, protection against stress, and of smoking. Most of the major diseases of the elderly can be cited as examples of this same phenomenon. The tedious and less dramatic process of prevention requires an understanding of what supports or what interferes with healthy development throughout the course of life. We spend only four cents of every health dollar on prevention.

In 1946 the World Health Organization defined health as "a state of complete physical, mental and social well being and not merely the absence of disease or infirmity." This definition represents an ideal with many possible interpretations. But the three components of health — physical, emotional and social — compose the framework in which one can begin to analyze what is going well in addition to what is going wrong. The attempt must be made to locate the conditions which enable humans to thrive and not merely survive.

One cannot look at health simply as statistical or typical. If one were to do so, the dental caries which affects about 90 per cent of the population might be considered healthy. Moreover, health cannot be regarded simply as a state. It is a *process* of continuing change and growth. What may be apparent health at one moment may already contain the beginnings of illness that will develop fully in still another moment.

Old age is a period when there is unique developmental work to be accomplished. Childhood might be broadly defined as a period of gathering and enlarging strength and experience, whereas the major developmental task in old age is to clarify, deepen and find use for what one has already obtained in a lifetime of learning and adapting. The elderly must teach themselves to conserve their strength and resources when necessary and to adjust in the best sense to those changes and losses that occur as part of the aging experience. The ability of the elderly person to adapt and thrive is contingent upon his physical health, personality, earlier life experiences, and on the societal supports he receives, i.e., adequate finances, shelter, medical care, social roles, and recreation. It is imperative that old people continue to develop and change in a flexible manner if health is to be promoted and maintained. Failure of adaptation at any age under any circumstances can result in a physical or emotional illness. Optimal growth and adaptation may occur all along the course of life when the individual's strengths and potentials are recognized, reinforced and encouraged by the environment in which he lives.

THE STEREOTYPE OF OLD AGE

To develop a clear depiction of what old age can be like we must contrast the mythologic with a realistic appraisal of old age. Let me present a sketch which I first gave in 1959 to a group of nursing home owners in the State of Maryland (1). This is the stereotype of old age, and it hasn't changed much in the last fifteen years:

"An older person thinks and moves slowly. He does not think as he used to, nor as creatively. He is bound to himself and to his past and can no longer change or grow. He can neither learn well nor swiftly, and even if he could, he would not wish to. Tied to his personal traditions and growing conservatism, he dislikes innova-

tions and is not disposed to new ideas. Not only can he not move forward, he often moves backwards. He enters a second childhood, caught often in increasing egocentricity and demanding more from his environment than he is willing to give to it. Sometimes he becomes more like himself, a caricature of a lifelong personality. He becomes irritable and cantankerous, yet shallow and enfeebled. He lives in his past. He is behind the times. He is aimless and wandering of mind, reminiscing and garrulous. Indeed, he is a study in decline. He is the picture of mental and physical failure. He has lost and cannot replace friends, spouse, jobs, status, power, influence, income. He is often stricken by diseases which in turn restrict his movement, his enjoyment of food, the pleasures of well being. His sexual interest and activity decline. His body shrinks; so, too, does the flow of blood to his brain. His mind does not utilize oxygen and sugar at the same rate as formerly. Feeble, uninteresting, he awaits his death, a burden to society, to his family, and to himself."

There are certain major associated myths. First, there is the myth of *aging itself*, the idea of chronologic aging, measuring one's age by the number of years one has lived. It is clear that there are great differences in the rates of physiologic, chronologic, psychologic and social aging from person to person and also within each individual.

Second, there is the myth of *unproductivity*. But in the absence of diseases and social adversities, old people tend to remain productive and actively involved in life. There are dazzling examples like the 82-year-old Arturo Rubinstein working his hectic concert schedule, or the 72-year-old Benjamin Dugger discovering the antibiotic aureomycin. Numbers of people become unusually creative for the first time in old age when exceptional and inborn talents may be discovered and expressed. In fact, many old people continue to contribute usefully to their families and community in a variety of ways including active employment.

Third, there is the myth of *disengagement*, related to the previous myth in holding that older people prefer to be disengaged from life and to withdraw into themselves, choosing to live alone or perhaps only with their own peers. Ironically, a few gerontologists hold these views. One study (2) presented the theory that mutual separation between the aged person and society is a natural part of the aging experience. There is no evidence to support this as a generalization. Disengagement is only one of the many patterns of reaction to old age.

Fourth is the myth of *inflexibility*. The ability to change and adapt has little to do with one's age and more to do with one's lifelong character. But even this statement has to be qualified. One is not necessarily destined to one's character in earlier life. The endurance, the strength and the stability in character structure are remarkable and protective. Yet most, if not all, people change and remain open to change throughout the course of life right up to its termination unless they are affected by major destruction of brain tissue or illiteracy or poverty, which are among the common levelers of mankind.

Fifth is the myth of *senility*, the notion that old people are or inevitably become senile (if they live long enough), showing forgetfulness, confusional episodes and reduced attention. This is widely accepted. Senility, in fact, is a layman's term, unfortunately used by doctors to categorize the behavior of the old. Some of what is called senile is the result of brain damage, but anxiety and depression are also frequently lumped in the category of senility even though they are treatable and reversible. Old people, like young people, experience a full range of emotions including anxiety, grief, depression and paranoid states. It is all too easy to blame age and brain damage when accounting for the mental problems and emotional concerns of later life. Benjamin Rush recognized senility as a distinct illness separate from the process of aging (3). Drug tranquilization, much overused in the United States, is a frequently misdiagnosed but potentially reversible cause of so-called senility. Malnutrition or unrecognized physical illnesses such as congestive heart failure and pneumonia may produce "senile behavior" by reducing the supply of blood, oxygen and food to the brain. Alcoholism, often associated with bereavement, is another cause. Late-life alcoholism is a serious and common problem. Irreversible brain damage, however, is no myth. Cerebral arteriosclerosis or hardening of the arteries of the brain and so-called senile brain disease marked by the mysterious dissolution of brain cells, are major and serious disorders that do impair human development in old age.

Sixth is the myth of *serenity*. In contrast to the previous myths which view the elderly in a negative light, this one portrays old age as a kind of adult fairyland. Old age is presented as a time of relative peace and serenity when people can relax and enjoy the fruits of their labors after the storms of life are over. Visions of carefree, cooky-baking grandmothers and rocking-chair grandfathers are cherished by younger generations. In reality, older persons experience more stresses than any other age group, and these stresses often are devastating. The strength of the aged to endure crises is

remarkable, and tranquility is an unlikely and inappropriate response under such circumstances. Depression, anxiety, psychosomatic illnesses, paranoid states, garrulousness and irritability are some of the internal reactions to external stresses. Depressive reactions are particularly widespread in late life. *Twenty-five per cent of all suicides in the United States occur in persons over 65.* Grief is a frequent companion of old age, grief either for one's own losses or for the ultimate loss of oneself. Apathy and emptiness are common sequels to the initial shock and sadness that follow the loss of close friends and relatives. Physical disease and social isolation can follow bereavement. Anxiety is another common feature. There is much to be anxious about, with poverty, loneliness and illness heading the list. Anxiety may manifest itself in many forms — rigid patterns of thinking and behavior, helplessness, manipulativeness, restlessness, suspiciousness, and sometimes paranoia.

No less a thinker than Aristotle failed to distinguish between the intrinsic features of aging and the reactions of the elderly to their lives. He considered cowardice, resentment, vindictiveness and what he called "senile avarice" to be intrinsic to late life. Cicero took a warmer and more positive view towards old age. He understood, for example, "if old men are morose, troubled, fretful and hard to please . . . these are faults of character and not of aging." So he explained in his famous essay "De Senectute."

Ageism. The stereotyping and myths surrounding old age can be partly explained by lack of knowledge and by insufficient daily and/or professional contact with varieties of older people. But there is another powerful factor, i.e., a deep and profound prejudice against the elderly which is found to some degree in all of us. In thinking about how to describe this I coined the word "ageism" in 1968. "Ageism can be seen as a process of systematic stereotyping of and discrimination against people because they are old just as racism and sexism can accomplish this with skin color and gender. Old people are categorized as senile, rigid in thought and manner, old fashioned in morality and skills. Ageism allows the younger generations to see older people as different from themselves. Thus they subtly cease to identify with their elders as human beings" (4, 5).

A BALANCED VIEW OF OLD AGE

It is time for a more balanced view of old

age. Compare what follows with the earlier stereotype:

"Older people are as diverse as people of other periods in life, and their patterns of aging vary according to the range they show from health to sickness, from maturity to immaturity, activity to apathy, useful constructive participation to disinterest, from the prevailing stereotype of aging to rich forms of creativity.

"Ninety-five per cent of older people live in the community and are not institutionalized or in protective settings. Physical illnesses are frequent and often chronic and limiting. Nonetheless over 80 per cent of older people are ambulatory. This period of life is characterized by complex changes that are multiple, occur rapidly, and with profound effects. Some people are overwhelmed. Others can come to accept or substitute for the loss of loved ones, prestige, social status and adverse physiological changes.

"Old age and brain damage alone do not account for the facade and the modes of adaptation of older people. Diseases, life experience, socio-economic and other forces along with the subjective experience of growing old and approaching death — all interweave to contribute to the picture of old age.

"Older people are apt to be reflective rather than impulsive. Having experienced a great deal and having been burned often, they think before acting. Under suitable conditions the present remains very much alive and exciting to them. But they also turn to the review of their past, searching for purpose, reconciliation of relationships, and resolution of conflicts and regrets. They may become self centered or altruistic, angry or contrite, transcendant or depressed. These old people are optimistic and resourceful and yet at the same time can be painfully aware of the brevity of life and its tragedies. Optimism is tempered by a more balanced view of the joys and sadnesses of life. The old continue to learn and change in response to their experience and of human relationships. Their sexual activity may gain in quality (6). They are not often overwhelmed by new ideas for they recognize how few of them there are. Many are employable, productive and creative. Many wish to leave their mark through sponsoring the young as well as through ideas and institutions.

Over the years I have tried to enumerate certain characteristics which help define tendencies to be observed in older people. They are not inevitable nor are they found to the same degree in each person who manifests them. They do show themselves regularly enough to be considered typical of people who have lived a long time and are viewing the world from the special vantage point of old age.

Old age is the only period of life with no future. Therefore a major task in late life is learning not to think in terms of the future. Children are extremely future oriented and look forward to each birthday as a sign of growing up. The middle-aged, as Schopenhauer said, begin to count the number of years they have left before death rather than the number

of years since birth. In old age one's time perspective is shortened even further as the end of life approaches. Some avoid confronting this fact by retreating to the past. Others deny their age and continue to be future oriented. The latter are the people who fail to make wills, leave important relationships unresolved, put off enjoyments, and experience boredom and frustration. A more satisfying resolution is found among those elderly who begin to emphasize the quality of the present and of the time remaining, rather than the quantity. When death becomes imminent, there tends to be a sense of immediacy, of the here and now, of living in the moment.

Only in old age can one experience a personal sense of the entire life cycle. This comes to its fullness with the awareness of death in the forefront. There is the unfolding process of change, the experiencing of a sense of time, the seasoning or sense of life experience with a broadening perspective and the accumulation of factual knowledge of what is to be expected at the different points of the life cycle.

Old age inaugurated the process of the life review, promoted by the realization of approaching dissolution and death. The life review is characterized by a progressive return to consciousness of past experience, in particular the resurgence of unresolved conflicts which can now be surveyed and integrated. The old are not only taking stock of themselves as they review their lives; they are trying to think and feel through what they will do with the time that is left and with whatever material and emotional legacies they may have to give to others. They frequently experience grief. The death of others, often more than their own death, concerns them. Perplexed, frightened at being alone, and increasingly depressed, they at times become wary or cautious to the point of suspicion about the motivations of others. If unresolved conflicts and fears are successfully reintegrated they can give new significance and meaning to an individual's life, in preparing for death and mitigating fears.

AIDS IN SUCCESSFUL AGING

What can we do to help move society to a more balanced view of older people, and how can we help older people to prevent problems in later life and to favor successful aging? How can we treat already troubled older people to help them successfully age? We cannot review all the relevant factors since they vary so greatly and include preventive measures such as a major attack on the known antecedents of arteriosclerosis which would require a change in dietary habits and physical activity. We certainly must face the enormous problem of alcoholism in the United States. Many people with a lifelong excessive alcoholic intake are now surviving into old age, and many older people are taking up alcohol after experiencing grief and loneliness.

There is need for a major reformation of our culture's sensibility toward old people through use of the media, which can aid in transforming our views of what older people are really like and can provide information about how to help older people enhance their sense of themselves. There is also the political approach. Older people are learning to assert themselves for what they need and win self-respect thereby.

Two forms of psychotherapy can be helpful to older people from both the preventive and therapeutic perspectives: 1) life review therapy, and 2) life-cycle group therapy.

Life review therapy includes the taking of an extensive autobiography from the older person and from other family members. Such memoirs can also be preserved by means of tape recordings, of value to children in the family. When the subject is a person of note, the memoirs have considerable historic importance and should be placed in archives for many reasons including furthering our understanding of creativity and improving the image of our elders. The use of the family album, the scrapbook and other memorabilia in the search for genealogies and pilgrimages back to places of emotional import, evoke crucial memories, responses and understanding in aged patients. The summation of one's life work is useful. The consequences of these steps include expiation of guilt, exorcism of problematic childhood identifications, the resolution of intrapsychic conflicts, the reconciliation of family relationships, the transmission of knowledge and values to those who follow, and the renewal of the ideals of citizenship. Such life review therapy can be conducted in a variety of settings ranging from outpatient individual psychotherapy to counseling in senior centers to skilled listening in nursing homes. Even nonprofessionals can function as therapists by becoming trained listeners as older persons recount their lives. Many old people can be helped to conduct their own life reviews. The process need not be expensive.

Reminiscence by the old has all too often been devalued, regarded as a symptom (usually of organic dysfunction), and considered to represent aimless wandering of the mind or living in the past. We recognize the value of reminiscence as seen in the great memoirs composed in old age, which may give fascinating accounts of unusual and gifted people, e.g., Casanova, Benjamin Franklin or Igor Stravinsky. We see the role of the life review in film and fiction. Ingmar Bergman's beautiful 1957 motion picture, "Wild Strawberries," shows an elderly physician whose dreams and visions concerned his past as he changed from remoteness and selfishness to closeness and love. Literature is replete with examples of the life review: Ernest Hemingway's "The Snows of Kilimanjaro," Samuel Beckett's "Krapp's Last Tape" and Leo Tolstoy's "The Death of Ivan Ilych." The National Archives should support a major program to acquire memoirs not only from distinguished contributors to American life but from average citizens who can illuminate the events of history, e.g., the growth of unions. Ethnic groups should help preserve their heritage through life reviews of their elders.

Life-cycle group therapy. Since 1970 Myrna I. Lewis, a social worker colleague, and I have conducted four age-integrated psychotherapy groups with about 8 to 10 members each with one contrasting middle-aged group. We have integrated persons ranging from the age of 15 years to over age 80 in each of the four groups, based on the belief that age segregation as practiced in our society leaves very little opportunity for the rich exchange of feeling, experience and support that is possible between the generations. The groups are oriented towards persons experiencing a crisis in their life ranging from near normal to pathologic reactions to adolescence, education, marriage or single life, divorce, parenthood, work and retirement, widowhood, illness and impending death. Thus such groups are concerned not only with intrinsic psychiatric disorders but with preventive and remedial treatment of people as they pass through the usual vicissitudes of the life cycle. Criteria for membership include absence of active psychosis and presence of life crisis, acute, subacute or chronic. Reactions to life crises follow traditional diagnostic categories including depression, anxiety states, hypochondriasis, alcoholism, and drug misuse. Our groups are balanced for age, sex and personality dynamics. We meet once a week for half an hour. Individual membership in a group averages about two years. New group members are asked to participate for a minimum of three months. This life-cycle crisis approach to group therapy is neither strictly encounter nor strictly psychoanalytic. Rather it can be equally concerned with the interaction among group members as determined by reality and the past histories and problems of each member. The goal is the amelioration of suffering, the overcoming of disability, and the opportunity for new experiences of intimacy and self-fulfillment. Regarding the elderly, some of the phenomena we have observed include pseudosenility (either the type that is psychologically determined by depression and anxiety or the type that is an expression of role-playing), the Peter Pan syndrome or refusal to grow up, leadership preempted by the middle-aged, and neglect or mascoting of the elderly and young. Unique contributions of the elderly include models for growing older, solutions for loss and grief, the creative use of reminiscence, historic empathy, and a sense of the entire life cycle. We believe that both forms of therapy can be very useful in nursing homes, mental hospitals and other institutions. Age integration helps to recapitulate the family, something woefully missing for many older people. The garrulousness of older people reflects a social symptom and an intense desire in the face of death to deal with one's individual life.

These are just two examples of how we can approach older patients, in or out of institutions. Indeed older persons' families, when they exist (one-fourth of older people have no family at all), can themselves participate in therapeutic processes.

COMMENT

When old people look back on their lives, they regret more often what they did not do rather than what they have done. Medicine should regret its failures to act responsibly in the health care (including mental health care) of the elderly. Physicians, psychotherapists and the public should not assume that nothing can be done for old people. No one should count them out.

REFERENCES

1. Butler RN: Re-awakening interests, Nursing Home J of ANHA 10: 8, 1961.
2. Cumming E and Henry WE: Growing Old: The Process of Disengagement. New York, Basic Books, 1961.
3. Hader M and Schulman PM: Benjamin Rush: an early gerontological psychiatrist, Gerontologist 5: 156, 1965.
4. Butler RN: Ageism: another form of bigotry, Gerontologist 9: 243, 1969.
5. Butler RN and Lewis MI: Aging and Mental Health. St. Louis, Mo, CV Mosby Co, 1973.
6. Butler RN and Lewis MI: Sex After Sixty. New York, Harper and Row (in press).

America's Neglected Elderly

Didi Moore

Didi Moore is a New York based freelance writer with a special interest in family issues.

"The crisis with my mother began when she was just 80," said a 49-year-old public-relations woman from the East Coast. "She'd had a couple of falls before, but this time it happened in the middle of the night. She tried to get to the phone, but she fell again. Fortunately, my uncle just happened to come by the next morning.

"The doctor suspected that she'd had several small strokes," said the distraught daughter, who asked not to be identified. "When it was clear that she couldn't go on living alone, we hired round-the-clock nurses at $400 a week. But first one didn't show up; then my mother didn't like another. Each time it was something else.

"So we brought her to our house for a while, but it was extremely hard on me and the rest of the family. We talked about a nursing home. And though she didn't want to go, it became apparent that it was the only way.

"She started in a minimum-care facility. But she became more and more confused, so they decided to switch her to their skilled-care facility—a decision in which I had no choice. Most of the people at the new place are much more demented than she is, and she's very depressed. It's very sad. She keeps asking: 'When can I get out of here and get on with my life?' "

□

The problem of care for the elderly is rapidly becoming a national crisis. Americans over 65 are probably the fastest growing age cohort in the country, according to the United States Bureau of the Census. Between 1900 and 1980, when the population as a whole tripled, their number increased eightfold. The over-75 group—the segment with the most illness—has grown by more than 37 percent in the last decade alone. By 2030, when the baby boomers are well into their "golden years," the over-65 segment is expected to reach 55 million—nearly one-quarter of the population.

The major reasons for this graying of America are recent medical advances that have virtually conquered diseases which, less than three decades ago, were certain to take lives. Elderly patients who, today, suffer strokes, heart attacks and broken bones are likely to live for many years, albeit in an impaired condition. Of the 26 million Americans over the age of 65, nearly 40 percent suffer from some chronic physical or mental handicap. In addition, as a result of major social and economic changes, families, the traditional support system, are now in less of a position than ever before to take on the extended care of their elderly relatives.

Despite the predictability of this shift in health-care requirements, the country's medical and social-service systems are woefully unprepared. The budget submitted to President Reagan last month by Richard S. Schweiker, the former Secretary of Health and Human Services, recommends a $2.6 billion cut in Medicare, the Federal medical-insurance program that covers Americans over 65 and certain younger disabled people. Although this proposal is likely to meet with some resistance on

While medicine has conquered diseases that used to be fatal, the health-care system has not met the changing needs of our increasingly aging population.

Capitol Hill, Medicare—even with the current allocations—does not cover many of the elderly's greatest needs, including long-term care outside the home and nearly all home care and preventive medicine. And some members of the Reagan Administration have talked about turning it into a means-tested program.

Also threatened with a $2.6 billion cut is Medicaid, for which the 12 percent of Medicare beneficiaries below the poverty level are eligible. This state-run, Federally regulated aid program pays not only for nursing-home care, but also for eyeglasses, hearing aids, dentures and drugs—none of which are covered by Medicare.

When Medicare was enacted in 1965, at a cost of $1 billion, it was aimed at preventing a catastrophic illness from financially destroying the elderly patient. It has succeeded at that goal. During the last 18 years, however, while Medicare's price tag has increased to $43.5 billion, the needs of the elderly have changed. More people now die of chronic diseases, but Federal funding is still strongly biased toward care of acute illness. At present, there are some 50 percent more people in nursing homes than there are in community hospitals. And, while there are waiting lists of a year or more at many nursing homes, community hospitals remain 25 percent empty. But in 1981, when $94 billion in Federal funds was spent on community hospitals, only $24 billion was spent on nursing homes.

Doctors themselves contribute to the problem. The Rand Corporation, the California research organization, estimates that by 1990 the country will need 8,000 to 10,000 geriatric physicians to care for the growing elderly population. But, at present, there is no board-certified specialty in geriatrics; of the nearly 400,000 members of the American Medical Association, only 720 identify themselves as having a major practice commitment to geriatrics.

"We are at a critical juncture in the development of our policy toward the elderly," said Representative Claude D. Pepper, the Florida Democrat who is the chairman of the House Rules Committee and of the Subcommittee on Health and Long-Term Care of the Select Committee on Aging. "We must make a national commitment to take bold steps now to develop a compassionate and sensible long-term care policy. If we fail to do this, we will pay for our timidity with billions of inefficiently spent dollars. Much more importantly, we will suffer the consequences which surely would come to a nation that abandoned those who built it with their labors and with their faith."

☐

With miracles of modern medicine alleviating acute illnesses, it is often after the crisis ends—when it is clear the elderly relative will survive—that the nightmare really begins for the family. Children who are suddenly faced with making decisions regarding the well-being of their parents often find the role reversal lonely and

ILLUSTRATIONS BY DAVID JOHNSON

excruciating—riddled with guilt, shame and ambivalence.

"The single greatest fear we have in this country is the fear of growing old, losing our mind and being put away in a nursing home," said Dr. Robert N. Butler, the chairman of the department of geriatrics and adult development at Mt. Sinai Medical School in New York. "It overshoots cancer as a national phobia. And its impact on the family is enormous."

Though his father was 85 and his mother 78, a 45-year-old New York City surgeon, had found little reason to worry about his parents. They had lived "frugally, but comfortably" in Florida for more than 20 years and had been in reasonably good health. But, three years ago, his father suffered a stroke and, in what almost seemed like a cause-effect relationship, his mother began to show signs of serious senility. "His head was fine, and her body was fine. But she'd do things like put the dish towel over the lit burner on the stove, and he couldn't do anything about it," the surgeon said.

"My father—who then suffered a heart attack—made it clear he didn't want to be alone with his wife. We talked about splitting them up—my sister taking my mother and my wife and I, my father—but by that point my sister was so demoralized that she couldn't cope with it. Since my wife and I both work, we knew we couldn't take the two of them."

A nursing home became the inevitable solution, and they chose one in New York. "We had a real advantage because I'm on the staff of a local hospital, but we still had to wait until two people died before they could get beds."

1. THE PHENOMENON OF AGING

Because nursing homes can choose their patients, they tend to give preference to those who demand the least care and attention. Most good nursing homes have waiting lists of a year and more. Yet, because of high interest rates and threatened cutbacks in Medicaid, construction of new homes is virtually at a standstill.

Furthermore, the financial aspects of entering a home can make what is already a difficult decision even more devastating. The cost of nursing homes averages $1,500 to $2,000 a month and some require a large—often illegal—"donation" of about $10,000 up front. Since the Government shares none of these costs, many residents quickly deplete their entire savings to pay for their care. When they are literally impoverished, they become eligible for Medicaid. According to one study, almost two-thirds of the nursing-home patients in Monroe County, N.Y., were forced to convert to Medicaid within a year of entering the home. Even worse, in many states spouses are legally responsible for the costs of caring for their disabled husband or wife. As a result, the noninstitutionalized mate must go on welfare before any money is made available from Medicaid. And the Federal Government is studying the possibility of requiring adult children to provide some financial support for aging parents.

Although there are times when nursing homes are the best alternative—and despite some improvement in the industry since the scandals of the early 1970's—institutionalization is still a nasty word that conjures up images of maltreatment and neglect. Families complain that medical staffs are incompetent and evade questions about patients' treatment and conditions. "And in most nursing homes," explained Mary B. Barrett, 68, a retired college professor from Middletown, N.Y., and a member of the Long-Term Care Committee of the Orange County Subarea Council of the Hudson Valley Health Systems Agency, "it doesn't take long for a patient to be switched from a health-related to a skilled facility because the proprietor gets more money from the Government for the skilled beds."

After helplessly watching the home make this shift, families often find that a parent slips into senility because the only stimulation is the moaning and senseless palaver that goes on in a skilled-care ward. "When you enter a nursing home there's a feeling that this is the end," said Barbara Silverstone, the executive director of the Benjamin Rose Institute, a geriatric residential and research center in Cleveland, Ohio, and the co-author with Helen Kandel Hyman of "You and Your Aging Parent." "You give up your home, your possessions, your autonomy."

Patricia M. Belanger, the director of the New York City Long-Term Care Ombudsprogram, put it more bluntly: "Most people leave nursing homes horizontally."

□

For six years, Margaret Stump, 57, an occupational therapist who heads the Senior Center in Tenafly, N.J., flew to Lima, Ohio, every three months to see her nonagenarian mother before she made the decision to move her to a New Jersey nursing home. "I felt that she'd be better once she got to a home. But I knew she wanted to be in her own house. It was a very difficult decision. I had to wait until I thought she wouldn't know where she was," Mrs. Stump confessed.

Home care is preferred by most elderly people. Seventy percent of them own their own homes and 84 percent of those have no mortgage. But because there is very little Medicare money for home care, assistance can be prohibitively expensive for someone on a fixed income. Visiting nurses, for example, can cost about $40 for a one- to three-hour house call.

With no umbrella organization to coordinate them, even the choice of services can be bewildering. A given community might have one or more—and sometimes none—of the following: home care, visiting nurses, adult day care, respite service for families, a senior center, meals-on-wheels and nursing homes. Because many of these may be demonstration or pilot projects, they may come and go in a few years. "To a certain extent," said Patricia Belanger, "you have to go where the funding is in your community, which is not necessarily where your needs are. You may just need someone to bathe you, but you end up getting a registered nurse."

At present, the Health Care Financing Administration is funding 16 experimental projects across the country to try to fill this gap. These home-care programs offer a range of personal and homemaker services from transportation to the doctor to preparing and feeding meals. In a three-year New York City demonstration project, three-quarters of the clients are impaired enough to be classified eligible for a nursing home. But between the home-care service and family participation, they are able to stay at home. "We think we're intervening with families at a time when they might have given up and institutionalized their elderly relative," says Roberta S. Brill, director of the Home-Care Demonstration and Research Project of the New York City Department for the Aging.

Unfortunately, translating these projects to national policy does not seem likely today. "The Federal Government still has the attitude that Medicare is not for long-term care," says Mrs. Brill.

Another, more widespread program that has helped keep some older people out of institutions is locally run adult day care. At present, there are 800 such centers in every state but Wyoming and New Hampshire, aimed at the functionally impaired senior citizen. "It's a full-day program geared to maintain or improve the person's condition," says Betty Shepherd, coordinator of the National Institute on Adult Daycare. "There is a lot of reinforcement to keep people focused on reality." And there are other programs, as well, such as the family-respite service, which gives a break to families who are caring for elderly relatives by allowing them to go away weekends or take a vacation.

A major problem in arranging funding for programs such as these is that the Government separates payment for what it considers social needs from medical care. For many of the elderly, such distinctions make no sense. For stroke or arthritis patients, for example, it is as important to their well-being to have help dressing and getting around as it is to have someone give them their medications.

☐

Of the available long-term care options, probably the most difficult one is for an adult child to take an aging parent into his or her home. Despite popular rhetoric that says that Americans have abandoned their elderly, every bit of research indicates that families still remain the predominant care givers. Of those with families (25 percent of older people have no close living relatives), 80 percent live with or near them.

But social and economic changes have altered the nature of the American family. Today's elderly raised their families during the Depression, and, for the most part, they had fewer children than their own parents. Furthermore, with the majority of women currently working, the traditional role of daughter or daughter-in-law as care giver has become obsolete. Houses and apartments are often smaller than they used to be, while increased mobility has spread families over thousands of miles. And, because of greater longevity, the "children" of these elderly parents may well be nearing 65. Despite a willingness, older children may be unable to take on the care of an ailing parent.

Depending upon the needs, condition and temperament of the older person, moving in with a grown child is an intrusion that can easily turn a household upside down. "A great deal of the emotional reaction to having an elderly person in your home is engendered by ignorance of how to care for their physical needs. People are afraid because they don't know what to do," said Mary Barrett. "There are classes for the care of the newborn, but there are no classes to teach families how to deal with incontinence or how to feed an elderly person."

More often than not, however, it is the older people who don't want to move in with their children. Paula Brandis, 86, lives in Kittay House, a pleasant-looking senior-citizen residence in the Bronx. While her only daughter lives in Ann Arbor, Mich., Mrs. Brandis has no intention of moving there. "Of course it's nice to be with your children," she said. "But they have to work, and I'd just sit there alone in their big house. My home is here, and my friends are here—it's more important to be near my friends."

When her husband died in her arms two years ago, Elizabeth Bartsch, 83, of Cresskill, N.J., suffered from amnesia. She was greatly distressed, and her 47-year-old son, Alan, concerned about her being alone, brought her to live with him 15 miles away in Woodcliff Lake, N.J. They closed up Mrs. Bartsch's tiny house, and she

said goodbye to her neighbors. But after 14 months, Mrs. Bartsch decided she wanted to go home again.

Children suddenly faced with making decisions about the well-being of their parents often find the role reversal lonely and painful—riddled with guilt, shame and ambivalence.

"She had trouble adjusting to being in our place," said Mr. Bartsch. "She felt she was intruding. She wanted to do things her way, but it wasn't her home. Two women in a house—it's a problem."

Now Mrs. Bartsch has a boarder. Her son stops by about once a day. She's happy to be back in her familiar neighborhood where she can take walks without getting lost. "I've still got a good pair of pins," she said.

☐

No matter what health-care route a family chooses, the effect on everyone's life is inevitably dramatic. Some feel that care for the aging is a woman's issue. The burden, they say, still falls to the daughter or daughter-in-law, who is frequently torn between the demands of her children, job, home and now parents. "In a way, I feel cheated," said the East Coast public relations woman whose mother is in a nursing home. "While the children were growing up, we were limited by having little children. Now that they are grown, we're constricted by having aged parents."

Because their own old age is less imminent, younger children of elderly parents are sometimes emotionally better able to handle the situation. Seymour Israel, a 36-year-old Manhattan lawyer with a 5-month-old baby, found that caring for his seriously senile 75-year-old father was a tender special experience. When his father had surgery last year, Mr. Israel visited the hospital every day to shave and feed him and take him to the bathroom. "Involvement with an aging parent is not something to be afraid of," said Mr. Israel. "It brings you into a very loving situation. For me it's been a real pleasure to be able to do this for him, to give to him what he gave to me."

Despite the best of intentions, few people, if any, are exempt from the sometimes fleeting, sometimes gnawing feelings of guilt. "Even if you've acted as honestly or decently as you can," said the surgeon from New York City, "you feel terrible. You resent them. You end up wishing they were dead, and you feel guilty because you realize that you're not just wishing them out of their misery; you're wishing yourself out of your misery."

For many children, the guilt intensifies as they find themselves feeling angry at their parent's irresponsible behavior. "My mother fires everyone I hire; she denies that she needs me; then, when she gets herself into a spot she can't resolve herself, she calls me to come get her," said one distressed Boston lawyer about his 89-year-old mother. "She doesn't care how it disrupts my life. I'm furious at her for putting me in this position where I constantly feel imposed upon. I feel helpless. And if I confront her with these things, she gets indignant."

The way people behave when they get old is often an exaggeration of characteristics that were present when they were younger. Manipulative parents will frequently be even more manipulative. And their children—deferring to the parent's physical frailty—will feel even more abused. In many cases, these parents are testing their children. They fear they are being discarded; they want proof that they are loved.

Dr. Robert J. Weiss, a psychiatrist and the dean of Columbia University's School of Public Health, likens many elderly parents to adolescents. "They want to be independent, but they are physically unable to act on what they want to do. Like adolescents, many elderly people just aren't able to judge their own limitations," said Dr. Weiss. "They get angry because restrictions are being put on them by, of all people, their children." Indeed, in their desire to remain in control of their lives, many elderly parents misinterpret the willingness of their children to help as an intrusion on their independence.

For the most part, however, the elderly tend to be pragmatic when confronting their increasing frailty. "They worry about how they will live with disease, who will do the shopping and how they will get to the doctor's office," said Dr. Barry Gurland, a psychiatrist and the director of the Center for Geriatrics and Gerontology of the Columbia University Faculty of Medicine and the New York State Office of Mental Health. While some people adapt to the dependent role more readily than others, many elderly people become increasingly anxious about what is happening to them, how painful it will be and how far it will go.

"The loss of peace of mind, along with the comforts of the body give rise to an increased rate of depression," said Dr. Gurland, adding, however, that the elderly are able to adapt to their situation given the time and support of family, physicians and neighbors.

Less resilient, however, is the rest of the family. The effect of caring for an aging relative can be particularly divisive. A crisis with a parent often forces siblings together after many years, triggering old roles. In most cases, one child takes on the bulk of the responsibility for care. Though this inevitably causes resentment, it can be preferable to decision making by a committee of three or four offspring. "There is easily more potential for fireworks between siblings," said Barbara Silverstone, "than there is with a parent-child relationship."

☐

Public policy can do little to ameliorate the emotional impact on children of caring for a disabled, aging parent. But it clearly has a critical role in resolving what is on its way to becoming a national crisis. "The real challenge is to develop a kind of legislation to shift the focus away from acute care to take into account the changing population and its needs," explained Janet S. Sainer, the commissioner of New York City's Department for the Aging.

To a large extent, that means developing a viable and well-funded program to encourage people to stay at home as long as possible. Such a program, say advocates for the elderly, should offer a continuum of services—home health care, adult day care, physical and occupational therapy, respite care and nursing homes—whereby patients could move back and forth as their needs change. "Clearly this is the wave of the future—more appropriate for the vast majority, and more cost-efficient at the same time," said Representative Pepper, who is working to develop a long-term-care financing bill aimed at benefiting the middle-income person as well as the poor.

Essential to the success of such a program is a division of services. With one agency assessing patients' needs—informing them of the options available—and another assuring that care continues to reflect those needs, the elderly would avoid getting caught in a bureaucratic conflict of interest.

Funding, of course, is the major stumbling block in the establishment of a new health policy for the elderly. Private insurance companies have shown little interest in offering coverage for long-term care. They have assumed it won't be cost effective for them since only the elderly would be interested in it. Dr. Robert N. Butler, of Mt. Sinai, who holds one of only three endowed chairs in geriatrics in the country, hopes policy makers will look at more creative sources of financing, such as pension funds or home equity.

There are also those who call for a revamping of the system altogether (though some say that would open it up for destruction). In his book "America's Old Age Crisis," Stephen Crystal theorizes that too much money is spent on the "young old" who are forced to retire at 65, and then are paid Social Security, pensions and Medicare by the Government. As a result, he said, "we don't have money left to take care of those who really need it."

In the end, in order to effect any change, the physicians in this country have to show their support. "The M.D.'s have the most political influence," said Anne R. Somers, a professor at the University of Medicine and Dentistry of New Jersey-Rutgers Medical School. "They set the tone. It's important that the doctors of the future get as excited about Alzheimer's disease or rehabilitating a stroke patient as they get now about a lung transplant." But before that can happen, medical students need more exposure to elderly patients, explained Dr. Butler.

They have to see role models who are excited about the field.

□

By its very nature, there is no ideal way to handle the deterioration of a parent. It is a terribly sad, emotionally draining experience for which there can be no happy ending. Many children find they do their mourning during this time. They grieve the loss of their parent as they want to remember him or her. "Every month, every week, every day, I felt my mother died a little more," said Margaret Stump, whose mother did die shortly before this article was published. When the parent passes away, the child feels the sorrow of the finality. But he or she also feels relief.

Changes in Government policy could go a long way toward making this phase of life more comfortable and secure for the growing number of the chronically ill elderly and their families. More support from the medical and social-service communities would also help both patients and relatives cope with the experience. But in the end it is up to individual families—even before a crisis arises—to deal as openly as possible with their needs, expectations and capabilities.

"There is no one solution that is right," said Barbara Silverstone. "You have to look at what you can and can't do. And whatever solution you choose, it won't be perfect. Most importantly, though, you have to be honest—really lay your cards out on the table. Most feelings of guilt come from promising too much, and not being able to deliver."

A GENERATION AT RISK

When the baby boomers reach Golden Pond

Robert N. Butler

Robert N. Butler is chairman of the Ritter Department of Geriatrics and Adult Development at The Mount Sinai School of Medicine in New York City. He is the former director of the National Institute on Aging and author of the influential book, Why Survive? Being Old in America *(Harper & Row, 1975).*

The time is now to build into our personal and corporate behavior the realities of a long life ending not in the 60s and 70s but in the 80s and 90s. More and more of us are reaching these years. This is where some revolutionary trends of modern life are taking us as predecessors, successors and members of the baby-boom generation.

We are relatively unprepared. Yes, we do worry about pensions and Social Security income and the costs of Medicare. Only beginning to sting are long-term care expenses and associated taxes affecting corporate, government, individual and family budgets. These costs are harbingers of a complex future that we must begin to plan for systematically, starting now.

The 20th century has seen average life expectancy in this country move from under 50 to over 70. Our society has become incredibly efficient at bringing children into maturity. Today's infant has a 50–50 chance of living more than the biblical three score and 10.

Converging with this expansion of average life expectancy is a second great trend: the aging of that enormous cohort of 76.4 million persons born in the 1946–1964 period. This baby-boom cohort will continue to stress our institutions: the schools were among the first to feel their impact, then the job market; next will be pension plans, Social Security, medical and social care, and other institutions concerned with later life.

The baby boomers constitute a generation at risk. The critical years of their retirement will start about 2010. By 2030, there will be over 50 million retirees, twice today's 65-and-over population. Where 1 in 9 Americans are elderly today, the ratio a half century hence may be 1 in 5, assuming that fertility stays at about the replacement level.

If baby boomers have fewer children per family than their predecessors, this expectation will have profound socioeconomic consequences. The ratio of Americans of typical working age to Americans 65-and-over will reach 2 to 1 as baby-boom retirements increase, considerably under today's 3 to 1. However, the total number of dependents—under 18 and over 65—per 100 working-age Americans will actually be fewer in 2030 than in 1970 or 1960. (See table on page 42.) Presumably, workers will spend less on children and will have more for the elderly.

I disagree with warnings that generational conflict will occur when younger workers are forced to support ever growing numbers of elderly. Not only does this line of argument ignore the decline projected in children per household, which will reduce the overall dependency costs of the baby boomers, it overlooks as well the income transfers that go on from elders to the young.

According to A.J. Jaffe in *The New York Statistician* for November–December 1982, the total dependency ratio in today's population is about 1 to 1, and in 2050 "about half of the total population will still be supporting the other half. . . . The change in the dependency burden is the shift from more younger to more older persons." Jaffe believes that the cost of raising and educating the child population about equals total retirement benefits. "It is evading the issue, if not outright misuse of statistics, only to compare the working force and the over 65," he says.

One of the most divisive measures for meeting costs of dependency would be government-enforced "filial responsibility"—that is, requiring children to help support their elderly parents. The Reagan Administration has announced a regulatory change in the Medicaid program to allow states to recover, when possible, nursing-home expenses from the children of poor patients. Experience with such policies has shown that they are administrative nightmares. Even when effective, they may result in family disruption, as resources are withdrawn from support of younger members of a family and given to older members. We have no need for coercive and disruptive measures in a society that can meet old-age needs humanely and efficiently with private or social insurance. Moreover, "filial responsibility" cannot help the 1 in 4 nursing-home patients who have no family.

On a scale no other birth cohort has confronted, the baby boomers will confront a double challenge. First, as they approach and enter retirement, they will have to balance their own needs with those of parents and even grandparents. This is illustrated by the 68-year-old daughter who oversees the care, at home or in an institution, of an 87-year-old mother while dealing with her own need for chronic care and that of her 72-year-old husband on a slender retirement income.

Second, as the baby boomers reach the oldest ages, they will have fewer family members to turn to for the same kind of help they gave in earlier years. Not only are more people living to the ages of highest sickness rates but family structure is changing: fewer children, more divorce, and more social isolation, especially because of widowhood. Given the continued emphasis on mobility and living independently, the elders of tomorrow may have to turn to strangers, particularly paid employees of social-service and health-care organizations.

This double challenge will grow rapidly as the population of the most frail elders increases: now one third of all elders, they will comprise 40 percent in only 10 years. The challenge will spread faster among older women, blacks, and Hispanics, since these groups of elderly are growing faster than the total 65-and-over population. For older women, the challenge will be particularly intense; they outlive men and typically are the mainstays of long-term care within the family.

The age distribution of the U.S. population seems to me to be far less a matter for concern than is the future of the economy. Whatever economic complications the baby boom causes for itself through low fertility could be compensated for by a more productive economy, one that utilizes the able elderly. Excluding them from roles in wealth production would represent an immense failure of heart and imagination. The longevity revolution will test our economy's capacity to use the added labor potential.

To minimize dependency and maximize productivity, our society will have to spur institutional change.

Age discrimination (as I wrote in these pages in November 1980) serves to maximize dependency and minimize productivity among the elderly. In our personal and corporate lives, we must continue to break down barriers of myth and prejudice.

We will need organized approaches through government and the private sector to improve income maintenance and support systems. This means well-directed investment in biomedical, sociobehavioral and productivity-related gerontological research. We must originate, refine, and routinize programs to help preserve (and recover) health and productivity at any phase of the adult life cycle. Surely this is one of the best ways to reduce the dependency costs of the generation at risk.

Extending the Work Span

How shall we finance the added years of life? Assuming a life span of 85 years, we can imagine the working portion as about half, counting 20 years for retirement and 25 for maturation and education. A 40-year work span could easily accommodate two or more careers.

We could add to savings by extending the work span—by delaying retirement, by taking less leisure time during the working years, and banking the income, and by investing more in public and private pension programs. A delayed-retirement strategy implies a full-employment economy. Will our society have jobs for everyone as the baby boomers move toward old age? If we are evolving into a society that needs fewer people in the conventional work force, how will individuals build up reserves for retirement? Will automation drastically alter the education-work-retirement proportions of the life span?

These questions must be answered if we are serious about reducing risks for the baby-boom generation and its children. Likewise, we must ask hard questions about the solidity and efficiency of retirement-income programs, including Social Security, private pensions, and individual retirement accounts. Major evaluations should be made of the use of tax breaks to encourage people to plan for their own retirement. Should the goal be to encourage those who can to save more, allowing income to escape Federal taxation? Or should the goal be to assure an adequate basic income in retirement for all (for example, through higher Social Security benefits based on higher taxes and more income transferring)? Do we need a better balance between these goals than now exists?

Unfortunately, planning for population aging tends to occur in relatively narrow contexts, in response to perceived institutional crises. The recent deliberations of the National Commission on Social Security Reform extended gingerly into some of the issues of health and productivity. But the approach was to shore up the Social Security financing, and this necessarily

1. THE PHENOMENON OF AGING

limited the explorations. Nonetheless, the Commission's recommendations offer an entrée into some of the practical issues of planning for population aging.

The bipartisan panel dealt with short- and long-range problems. A deficit of somewhere between $150 billion and $200 billion in Social Security revenue was projected for the 1983–89 period. The panel recommended that this could be made up by a combination of taxes and benefit cuts. Some of these proposed actions would also reduce deficits expected after 2020, when the baby-boom retirees would reach a peak. However, an unresolved issue was how to meet fully the long-range gap.

Republican appointees on the Commission endorsed a gradual rise in the age of full entitlement, or indexing of that age to improvements in average life expectancy. They argued that postponing the age to 68 would be sufficient to keep the program sound through the mid-21st century.

Democratic appointees called the proposed age change a benefit cut for young workers confronting higher taxes over the proposed longer period until retirement. Such a step was unnecessary now, they argued, since the long-range deficit might well be made up through economic growth or additional tax increases.

The consensus recommendation of the Commission, however, omitted any call for an age change and instead advocated a policy of encouraging retirement at age 66, 67, or 68 by raising benefits by 8 percent for each year of delay. Congress was divided on the issue, and in the end prescribed a gradual rise to age 67 by the early 21st century. This provision is in the law signed by President Reagan.

Neither the Commission nor Congress directly raised the question of whether the United States spends enough on its Social Security program. Other advanced countries—with proportions of elderly the U.S. has yet to experience—seem able to manage a greater investment. Some devote twice the proportion of gross national product to benefits comparable to those offered under our Social Security system.

A major intent of proposals to raise the full benefits age is clear: each year of delay means the individual will put more money into the system and will take less out of it. Attempts to assure the system's soundness are praiseworthy, but we must consider some implications. Will jobs be available? Will they be open to older workers? Will employers or the government be willing to retrain them? Will they be healthy enough and willing to work? Or will they see delayed retirement as an unprofitable trade of healthy years for sick years?

Corporations in various fields have demonstrated ways of keeping older workers on the job, encouraging their re-entry into the work force, and developing part-time arrangements to meet retirees' needs for supplementary cash, as well as their own needs for their skills and for flexible scheduling. *Young Programs for Older Workers*, published by Work in America Institute in 1980, provides case studies of such programs.

Wm. Wrigley Jr. Company has a long-standing practice of phased retirement for employees at age 65: The first year the employee takes a month off without pay, the second year, two months, and the third year, three months. For each year he works from age 65 to 70, the employee adds 8 percent to his base pension; $100 of pension income at age 65 thus becomes $147 at age 70. The term phased retirement, or flexible

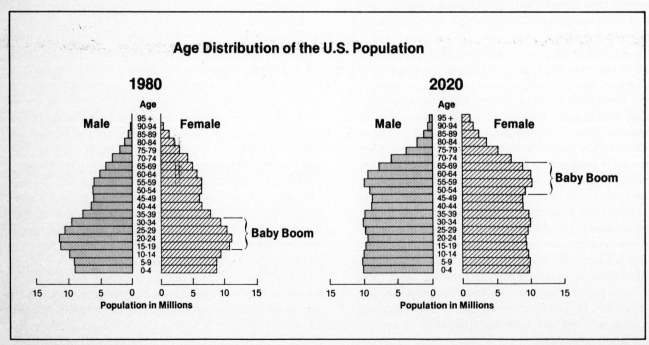

The size of the baby-boom generation in 1980, and the projected size in 2020, compared with the rest of the population. The ratio of working-age Americans to those 65+ will decline to 2:1 as baby-boom retirements increase, considerably under today's 3:1. (Source: The Social Security Administration)

retirement, describes any program that allows the employee to gradually change the proportion of leisure time to work time, whether in the form of shorter days, shorter weeks, or months off.

There are various other arrangements to accommodate older workers. IBM fosters second careers to help individuals adjust to technologic and business changes and, when retirement is imminent, to develop new interests and skills. Tektronix Inc. employs a medical placement specialist to redesign jobs for better efficiency and improved job satisfaction on the part of workers who have physical limitations. A carpenter with a back injury can still saw and use the lathe but can't bend to trim moldings; that part of his job is eliminated, and instead he is given part of another job, say, driving a truck and delivering supplies. The Toro Company has a program that uses part-timers in two ways: some do regular part-time work and others are on call for overload periods.

Surveys show that many retirees want to work, that many workers in their 50s intend to extend their working careers, and that business recognition of older-worker productivity is increasing. Employment agencies for older workers have developed to serve these parties. In Los Angeles, a Second Careers Program—a nonprofit organization administered by the Los Angeles Voluntary Action Center—has been assisting companies since 1975 to begin or enlarge pre-retirement and retirement programs and to identify opportunities for volunteer and paid second-career jobs. Mature Temps, formed by the Colonial Penn Group, provides jobs for people over age 50 through 14 offices around the country.

A lot more has to be done to provide options in employment and retirement for older workers. Robert W. Feagles, senior vice president of The Travelers Insurance Company, which two years ago eliminated mandatory retirement, points out that our society has built a system allowing more people to enjoy retirement but, at the same time, limits choices for older people. "In reality," he says, "most people over 65, whatever they may wish to do, face two stark alternatives: either full-time work or full-time retirement, with few options in between." Most private pension systems define retirement so strictly that even a short interval of paid work threatens loss of benefits. Social Security is a prime example of the earnings test.

We have to differentiate the expectations and conditions of tomorrow's older workers from those of today and yesterday. The fact is that two thirds of Social Security retirements occur before age 65. These individuals have actuarially reduced monthly benefits for the rest of their lives. Some early retirements are for reasons of health. Some of these persons are disabled but do not qualify for disability insurance and, through it, Medicare coverage. The disability definition of Social Security has been criticized as unduly severe: an individual must be unable to perform in any job no matter where it is in the nation; older workers cannot be expected to move thousands of miles just to find a job they are able to do. (The commissioners who proposed a change in the full benefits age also suggested provisions to assist sick early retirees, this group confronts reduced benefits at a time of above-average sickness costs—and no eligibility for Medicare until age 65.)

The One-Hoss-Shay Issue

The Commission also considered the notion that people should be able to have longer work lives because improvements in longevity have been accompanied by improvements in health. In June 1982, as director of the National Institute on Aging, I discussed the point at the panel's request, along with Dr. Jacob Feldman of the National Center for Health Statistics.

The Commission wanted comments on a hypothesis set forth by Dr. James Fries of Stanford University that the natural limit of the human life span is about 85 years. Fries's policy-relevant point is that the period of morbidity in later life is shortening; people are likely to stay healthy longer, deteriorating much like the "one hoss shay" in the poem, almost all at once. If true, the trend might provide support for raising the Social Security full-benefit age beyond 65. In addition, the hypothesis offers the comforting prospect of mod-

Younger and Older Dependents			
Year	Number under 18 per 100 aged 18–64	Number 65+ per 100 aged 18–64	Total
1930	58.9	9.1	68.0
1940	48.9	11.0	59.9
1950	51.0	13.4	64.4
1960	65.1	16.8	81.9
1970	61.4	17.7	79.1
1980	47.2	18.6	65.8
1990	43.5	20.0	63.5
2000	43.2	19.9	63.1
2010	39.2	20.2	59.4
2020	41.2	26.0	67.2
2030	42.0	31.8	73.8
2040	41.2	30.6	71.8
2050	41.7	30.2	71.9

Projections of the numbers of "dependents" in the U.S. population, young and old (derived from U.S. Census figures by Herman B. Brotman, a consulting gerontologist). The table shows that while the proportion of those over 65 will steadily increase, the relative numbers of those under 18 is generally decreasing. Thus, the total "burden" on the working-age population of both young and old would not be unreasonable. In fact, the proportion of dependents may have been higher in 1960 and 1970.

eration in the spiraling costs of Medicare and Medicaid as sickness diminishes in late life.

Trend data from the National Health Interview Survey do not support the Fries hypothesis. Sickness and disability rates by age bracket appear to have held steady over the last decade. Conceivably, this could change. However, applying current rates to the growing elderly population, we project a heavier load of sickness and disability in the 21st century.

Policymakers cannot reasonably ignore this projection, even though some anecdotal evidence suggests that the elders of today are in better health than their forebears. Some surely are. But some reach old age already sick, their lives preserved by medical care. Some live to the oldest ages despite great handicaps. And some maintain good health almost to the very end of life. How this mixed picture relates to ability to work is not precisely clear, since we lack objective criteria for assessing various physical and psychological factors in relation to different kinds of work.

This issue was made most clear to me when the National Institute on Aging, at Congressional behest, reviewed the Federal requirement for mandatory retirement of commercial airline pilots at age 60. Was it medically justified? This was hard to say, since there were no conclusive data on whether pilots were more or less like the general population, in which cardiovascular and other morbidity and mortality rates rise sharply in the 60s. Modern airliners are better staffed and powered than those of 1959 when the rule was imposed. But no one could say definitely that a fine record of passenger safety would be maintained. Undoubtedly, some pilots are mandatorily retired with unnecessary loss of their productivity.

The pilot issue is a special case. But it illustrates the shortcomings of our knowledge of aging and disease processes in relation to practical decisions important in population aging. Based on trends, our best guess is that the proportions of the population with disabilities will stay about the same. For the age bracket 65 to 74, which includes the years relevant to the benefits-age issue, the proportion with a limitation on activity due to a chronic illness or disability is projected to be about the same in 2020 as in 1980: about 35 percent. However, the number will double in that period to 10.7 million, reflecting the baby boom.

The activity limitations—joint stiffness, visual and hearing impairment, cardiovascular problems, and other handicaps—need not be so serious as to prevent employment. Policies could be adopted to promote employment of such people. The working day or week could be adjusted. Work environments and tasks might be modified. For instance, in regard to pilots, a report prepared for the National Institute on Aging notes: "Research on human factor engineering suggests that alterations in cockpit and equipment design can be made that will take into account decrements in performance, so that small changes in physical capability will not significantly affect a pilot's ability to fly safely."

Ways of making such changes for all kinds of jobs are being, and surely will be, researched and tested. The willingness of public and private sectors to pay their fair share for the accommodations would be an important issue. We are already seeing controversy between government and corporate interests over the recent law requiring job-based health insurance to supplant Medicare as the primary coverage for older workers. The companies oppose the law since private insurance costs more for older workers than for younger workers.

But we must also plan for persons with serious functional limitations who require considerable social support, including medical, hospital, nursing home, and at-home services. We must keep in mind that this group constitutes a sizable minority, but a minority nonetheless, of the elderly population. At any one time, only 1 person in 20 of the general elderly population is in a nursing home; the proportion after age 80 is 1 in 5. This is an important point in considering needs for both institutional and community-based services. According to some estimates, a population double the 1.3 million nursing-home residents is in need of long-term care services in the community. If true, the market for major long-term care services is probably about 4 million of the nation's 26 million elderly.

Because mortality and sickness rates accelerate markedly after age 75, the size of this population has implications for the development of health and social services. It is growing fast — over 9 million today, probably 14 million by 2000. The fastest growing segment of the entire U.S. population is the group aged 85 and older. In 1980, there were 2.6 million, or 1.1 percent of the U.S. population at this age. In 2020, there will be 7.6 million, or 2.5 percent.

Between 1980 and 2020, the 75-and-over population with activity limitations due to chronic conditions will increase 2.5 times, to 10.7 million. The number of short-stay hospitalizations will rise to 104.6 million days from 45.8 million. Instead of 1.1 million in nursing homes, there will be 2.7 million. The number of physician visits will double. Personal expenditure for health care will more than double for the aged, while it rises by 50 percent for the entire U.S. population. Nursing-home expenditures will be in the forefront.

The Geriatrics Gap

Geriatric researchers seek ways to prevent a slow decline in various body systems and to help the patient adjust to changed conditions. They also study a variety of special problems of the elderly. The reactions of the older person to drugs, infection, pain, heart attacks, and other conditions may be different from the reactions of younger adults. For example, mental confusion, not chest pain, may be symptomatic of a heart attack in the older person. So-called senility, or senile dementia, may be reversible once the cause of confusion and memory loss is traced to a treatable cause, such as infection, malnutrition, alcoholism, drug abuse, or depression. Geriatric practice must be concerned with educating patients and families on the true nature of illness in old age, lest misconceptions like "it's just old age" delay treatment beyond the time when it can be most effective.

Unfortunately, the field of geriatrics is underdeveloped in this country. Scientific research into the processes of aging did not expand until recently, and some new conclusions are beginning to appear. Several studies have been done that show far less deterioration in information-processing and problem-solving abilities than investigators in the 1930s had thought.

Some of the most significant conclusions from recent gerontologic research are cautionary. First, what sometimes looks like psychological deterioration due to aging may in fact be more the result of a poor socioeconomic background or little education. For example, a 60-year-old born in 1910 may have greater ability than a 60-year-old born in 1880 simply because he has had a better education.

The enactment of Medicare in 1965 was not accompanied by major investments in research, manpower for service and for research, or by the organization and funding of geriatric services. Medicare was, and is, a benefit package based on what young adults need. It emphasizes short-term or acute care.

The Medicare nursing-home benefit, called "extended care" at first, was basically for convalescence after hospitalization. Because costs could not be forecast reliably, Congress omitted long-term care from the Medicare law. Administrative definitions of reimbursable illness costs exclude coverage of what is disparagingly called "custodial services," some of which are essential to the survival or functioning of patients who are not likely to get "better." For want of home care and other mundane assistance, sound geriatric principles cannot be applied, and some patients become expensive institutional cases.

The only large-scale program of long-term care benefits is found in Medicaid, the Federally aided program of state benefits for the poor. Medicaid money accounts for about half the annual $22 billion spent on nursing-home care. (The other half comes directly from patients or families.) The program's growth is threatening many state treasuries. Unless costs can be moderated, taxes will increase and the increases will cut into profits and wages. This is one reason why some forward-looking business groups are examining long-term care issues and their responsibilities for assisting in resolving them.

Private insurance has eschewed coverage of nursing-home and homemaker services. Reimbursement arrangements under conventional health insurance policies are ill suited to geriatric practice. Only grudgingly do they recognize time spent hearing out, examining, and counseling a patient, or the use of experts in medicine, nursing, and social work as a diagnostic and treatment team. The team approach, a cornerstone of geriatrics, disintegrates at the billing office and dies at the bank. A breakthrough in insurance coverage, through private or public approaches, or a combination of them, is sorely needed.

In addition, we will have to somehow meet the demand for more geriatric physicians—a prospect that now seems unlikely since only a small number of the nation's 127 medical schools have professors of geriatrics or required courses in geriatrics.

Organizing for Productive Aging

How may we organize our thinking for action in the interests of today's elderly and the generation at risk? Plans under way at the Mount Sinai Medical Center in New York City may provide one model.

In 1982, the Medical Center established the nation's first medical school department of geriatrics. The Gerald and May Ellen Ritter Foundation funded the department and the Brookdale Foundation supported the chair in geriatrics that I occupy. The department has six faculty members and eight postgraduate fellows. Wholehearted support by the trustees and administration assured substantial room for mandatory instruction in geriatrics in a crowded medical curriculum. A biomedical research program was authorized. Plans for inpatient and outpatient services for geriatric patients and their families were completed. In addition to providing the community with home care and a wellness clinic, the department is creating a geriatric assessment and referral unit to assist physicians, patients, and families in defining and carrying out programs of care. Special clinics will be devoted to patients with senile dementia, menopausal problems, incontinence, and mobility limitations.

Students and medical residents will be exposed to the well and ill elderly in the community at the hospital and at the Jewish Home and Hospital for Aged. The latter, a nationally recognized long-term care institution, will become a teaching nursing home—a counterpart of the teaching hospital.

To conduct policy-related research and analysis and to raise public and professional awareness of population aging, the department is creating an Institute for Studies of Health and Aging. Applying a broad conception of health, the Institute plans to organize these divisions as funds become available:

☐ The Center for Productive Aging, to study and offer consultation services on issues involved in enhancing the contributions of the older population to the economy and to family and civic life. The center will advise on such topics as: personnel policies and programs for long-term health and productivity; objective criteria for personal and corporate decisions on work and retirement, and adaptation of the elderly to work tasks and environments.

☐ The Center for Long-Term Care Systems, to focus particularly on long-term care insurance. The center will provide advice and information to corporations, labor unions, health-care organizations, senior citizen groups, and others concerned about long-term care and geriatrics.

☐ The Leadership Forum on Population Aging, to air the issues of population aging in seminars and other formats of practical use to public and private decision-makers. An Aging Information Service will serve the public and mass media as well as private clients.

☐ The Center for International Aging Studies, to bring policy specialists and social and health-care professionals together to examine population-aging issues of international significance. A program of regular exchange between U.S. and foreign teachers and practitioners is contemplated to accelerate the diffusion of geriatric knowledge and skills.

☐ The National Reference Center on Geriatric Education, to promote the development of geriatric training by collecting and disseminating innovative curricula and teaching materials and by advising schools on how to get started.

With well-conceived policies, later life will be a time of options. Even if impaired in some way, we will have opportunities to be productive; we will maintain our vigor for as long as possible, and we will not easily lose our personal autonomy. Supportive programs will exist, staffed by perceptive and humane practitioners, paid for by some contributory method that protects us against impoverishment and affirms our dignity. We will be proud of these accomplishments and leave them to our children. They will say we knew how to age well.

Growing Old Absurd

Hugh Drummond, M.D.

D O YOU LOOK away when you pass a nursing home? Is there more obligation than affection in your feelings for aged parents? Do you find yourself describing any old man or woman who is not actually obnoxious as "charming" or "cute"? Look a little deeper. Try to understand how you have been taught to despise the elderly—the most unwanted and unneeded of the many unwanted and unneeded in this mad throwaway culture.

Then remember that you, too, will grow old. And by the time those of you who were part of the post-World War II baby boom approach the check-out gate, it is likely that one out of every four Americans will be counted among the elderly.

So this is not about "them," it's about you. I don't want you to become morose and start checking for wrinkles and bathing in vitamin E, but I do think you should begin considering a few aspects of your declining years. As that cigarette ad used to say, "It's not how long you make it, but how you make it long."

It's characteristic of capitalist society not only to grind down the aged as useless nonproducers, but also to refuse to educate the young about how to spend that remaining quarter of their lives when their work-force years are past. The reason for this is obvious. If there were serious attention paid to how one could meaningfully use non-working time, there just might not be a work force—and all the nuclear plants and computers and missiles and Coke machines would crumble to dust.

I am not asking for a major overhaul. A few minor alterations, a couple of shifts in your habits could produce massive effects 20 or 30 years from now, not so much in prolonging your life as in making it worth living.

You see, the issue is not death. It may even be that death is a kind of refuge from a less dramatic but more real source of anxiety: chronic illness. Death is too final, too spiritual, too grand—the stuff of art and philosophy. There is none of that in the chronic health problems that affect 86 percent of the aged. Mahler composed symphonies to death, not to diabetes. There are no odes to cancer. Chronic disease is an unsung presence, which hovers, fluttering, like an uncertain bird of prey.

Moreover, physicians and the rest of the medical establishment know little and care less about chronicity except as something to exploit. It lies in a deep chasm between remote rims of acute illness and nonillness. (There is no health.) It involves constant perturbations of sensation, nagging tugs through the spinal cord into the thalamus; these may not even deserve the word pain, but they are transformed by the imaginations of the cerebral cortex into agony.

There are waves of hope and despair with restless fingers probing for remembered aches. There is fatigue, irritability and an endless preoccupation with numbers on lab reports, the look of urine and how one feels. Mainly there is waiting: in doctors' offices, laboratories, radiology departments, drug stores, for or in hospital beds, and for death itself.

Health becomes less than a memory, more of a mirage, like the voice of a dead lover—thin, unreal, longed for, elusive. Shame and guilt romp like puppies at play: "Why did I?" "Why didn't I?" There is an angry grasping in all directions for foolish, futile rewards: "I'm sick; how in the world can you smile when I'm suffering?"

Bottles of pills stand like grim sentinels—squat, brown, household gods—near beds, in kitchens, in bathrooms. Twenty-five percent of all the medicines in the country goes to the 11 percent of the population over 65. Of that group, a full third take five or more drugs simultaneously. And if you thought that psychoactive drug use was the province of the young, consider that the *average* person over 65 secures three to four prescriptions for Valium, Librium or Darvon each year.

It is not good to be sick and elderly. The medical care in nursing homes is abysmal; one-third of the elderly people who enter such institutions as patients die within the first year. One out of four of the aged makes a trip to the hospital every year; the experience is so stressful that it is thought by some to be more lethal than the illnesses for which they are sent.

The cost of medical care has grown at a faster rate for the aged than for everyone else. It now consumes 30 percent of our whole $200 billion medical bill. Medicare and Medicaid pay for only a quarter of it and were themselves the major initial impetus for the massive leaps in hospital and outpatient costs. It remains a question whether or not there has been a net gain in medical care for the impoverished elderly.

The poorer you are the sicker you are, and the sicker you get the poorer you will become. Nearly 15 percent of the elderly live in "official" poverty; half are getting by on $75 a week. Blacks, especially, are hard hit. Though they pay the same social security taxes as whites, they die more than four years sooner, on the average. Racism always reveals itself in vital statistics.

But, believe it or not, I do not want to depress you. I want to catch your attention so I can convince you to make some microecological changes. While doctors like to make diagnoses of individual diseases, the real business of sickness among the elderly and among the poor (and among everyone else, too) has to do with a synergistic interplay of forces that set up vicious cycles, eddys and currents that even-

1. THE PHENOMENON OF AGING

tually sweep you away in a massive whirlpool.

I'll give you an example. An impoverished person's diet tends to be high in sugar, low in calcium and low in fiber. Poor people also tend to smoke more and lead more stressful lives. Smoking and stress lead to heart disease. Sugar raises the cholesterol level, increases the likelihood of late onset diabetes and causes obesity. Obesity itself increases the likelihood and degree of diabetes. Diabetes causes kidney damage, which raises the blood pressure (which obesity also exacerbates). The hypertension results in worse heart disease and strokes. The reduced calcium intake also increases the severity of heart disease and diminishes bone density (osteoporosis), which increases the likelihood of fractures—resulting in more stress, the danger of blood clots and immobilization, which further thins the bones. Calcium reduction also causes loss of teeth, which results in an

even worse diet with a greater reliance on processed and cooked foods that are low in fiber. The diminished fiber results in a greater likelihood of bowel cancer, prostate disease and constipation—which itself leads to diverticular disease, hemorrhoids and an increased risk of thrombophlebitis (with its attendant consequences of pulmonary embolism, which further damages the heart and lungs). (See the illustration on page 24.)

What modern medicine does is fragment this systemic disaster into modules of diseased organs, each of which is separately and uniquely treated with high technology, high risk and ineffective intervention.

You may decide to live in the hope that an incompetent medical establishment will grope for nuggets of disease amidst this maelstrom and try to cure them by the time you are old. It is like hoping to find someone to tune your engine when a city is being evacuated

during a nuclear power plant accident.

Nor can you really expect to turn off this whirlpool by yourself. That would involve some major changes in the structure of society. What you can do, however, is begin to build a few baffles and place them carefully within your biosphere so that you are not swept away.

One of the most important of these has to do with food. As Ruth Weg points out in her book, *Nutrition and the Later Years,* while poverty, institutionalization, social isolation, diminished taste sensitivity and loss of teeth all play a role in the pathological nutrition of the elderly, food preferences usually tend to be a reflection of a lifetime of eating habits.

The difference between relative health and chronic disease a generation from now is a matter of the smallest shrugging off of a habit or two right now. I really do not want you to be hunkering around health food stores

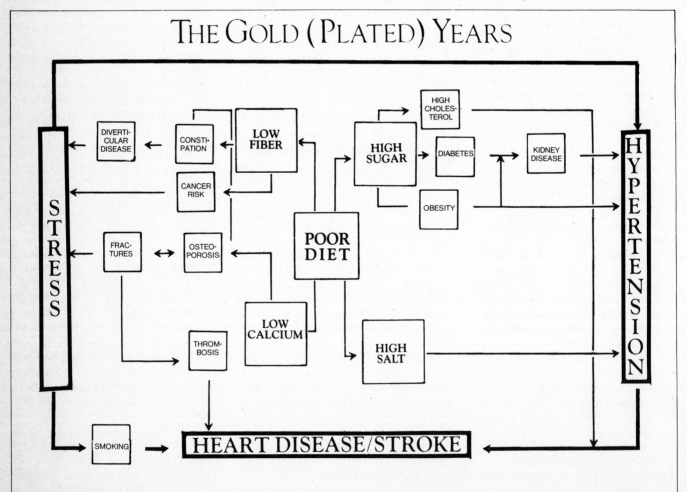

Our culture gives no medals for living to old age. Instead, 86 percent of our elderly are rewarded by being trapped in a maze of health problems. Above, an illustration of how minor conditions and lifelong habits lead to serious illness on any number of paths.

Diagram by Robert Haydock

counting out chromium tablets. A small reduction in the amount of sugar and fat in your diet is not too much to ask in exchange for ten additional years without chronic illness. Three tablespoons of bran a day—you will not choke on it—is enough fiber to prevent a catastrophe in your gut by the year 2000. And while you may insist that you have a hunger for salt, believe me, there is no such thing; each flick of a salt shaker is an unnecessary nudge to your blood pressure. In place of salt, try flavoring your food with lemon juice and as much garlic as your friends can stand. The garlic actually prevents hypertension, and the more natural vitamin C you get the better.

Save on energy: eat vegetables raw instead of cooked, as much as possible. Keep fresh fruit and nuts on the table instead of gooey desserts. That's all.

But the quality of your life in the next century is not just a matter of whole wheat bread alone. One of the major reasons old people become paranoid, depressed and socially isolated is deafness. About 30 percent of people over 65 are hard of hearing. The major source of the problem seems to be the gradual destruction of the receptor cells in the inner ear from too much noise. A 110-decibel dose of the Stones through your headphones may feel like a trip for now, but you will curse Mick Jagger when you can no longer hear the directions to the bathroom.

A decline in your faculties, however, is not inevitable. A switch is not thrown in your nervous system when you reach 65. That age was only an arbitrary invention of the Iron Chancellor, Otto von Bismarck, to define some recalcitrant generals into retirement. How aged you will be, *what* you will be, will be determined by your actions between now and then. If you carry on with our culture's definition of business as usual, you will be a wreck.

I was visiting a patient in a nursing home recently and as I turned to leave I glanced into a room; the sight froze me for a solid minute. It was called the "Recreation Room"; in it sat eight or ten ancient human beings and a huge color TV set tuned loudly to one of those hysterical daytime quiz shows. Not one of those men and women was watching the tube. Nor were any of them asleep. They were, it seemed, imbued with the television, at one with it, their minds so saturated with its flickering images and ghoulish sounds that they no longer needed to focus attention on it. I have observed many visions of hell on earth, but none has seemed more horrible to me than that tableau of old people dimly and dumbly steeped in television. It is worse than hope abandoned; it is hope rendered utterly inconceivable.

Do yourself a favor. Stop watching now. I dropped my set into a Goodwill box after a Clint Eastwood movie. My only regret is that I didn't smash the damn thing.

Instead, spend a half-hour every day with a musical instrument or paint or clay or needlepoint or a journal. In a third of a century you will be an artist, an amateur, a lover of your work. Forget the Grandma Moses success stories. The marketplace is where you are now. Where you want to be is anywhere outside the "rec room" of a nursing home.

Having a "successful" old age is not just a matter of giving up things that are bad for you. The anthropological examples of vigorous longevity in the Soviet Caucasus, in Vilcabamba, Ecuador, and in the principality of Hunza in Pakistan have some things in common. Their people consume frugal diets rich in fruits and vegetables, low in meat and dairy products and totaling about a third of our average calorie intake. But what is also characteristic of them is a high degree of solidarity and physical and social activity. Studies on aging in this country at Duke University conclude that participation in organizations is almost as important a predictor of a happy old age as physical health and economic security.

What this means is that the last quarter of your life should be intensely political—not in the sense of choosing which pack of wolves to vote for, but in the ontological sense, like a bridge between the personal and the public, upon which one's needs and hopes are connected by action.

Everything I have ever told you about the politics of health will be felt by you as a matter of personal experience. It will be *your* scarce dollars counted out for unnecessary and destructive medicines. It will be *your* freedom trivialized in an institution. And it will be *your* cancer providing the capital for the American Hospital Association.

The pharmaceutical industry expects a bonanza in the groans of millions of aged Americans by the end of the century. It is already one of the most profitable industries in the world. Nursing homes (whose parent companies are glamour stocks on Wall Street) will sprout like hamburger stands, and with a little imagination they may become the same places. When you decide that the drug industry should be nationalized and nursing homes effectively regulated, you will be deciding on intensely felt issues and acting on an electorate under your control.

But I do not want you in a nursing home under the best of circumstances. And I do not want you to live alone either. Women will probably continue to outlive men by more than seven years, which means that most couples will not survive together. There is only one solution. You have to plan for a collective lifestyle. Communes and collective houses, which may have been merely hip or cheap in your youth, will be critical in your 70s. The bottom line of all the research is that the only protection against stress is a secure, mutual-support system.

Now there's a pleasant thought for a grim Marxist: that the truest and best expression of communism will be forged by wrinkled hands.

Creative Aging

Charlene Lee Ager, M.A., O.T.R.
Louise Wendt White, M.A., O.T.R.
Wanda L. Mayberry, M.A., O.T.R.
Patricia A. Crist, M.S., O.T.R.
Mary Elizabeth Conrad, M.B.A., O.T.R.

Assistant Professors
Department of Occupational Therapy
Colorado State University
Fort Collins, Colorado

Abstract

The terms 'creative' and 'aging' are antithetical according to dictionary usage—'create' being explicitly described as an active process and 'aging' implicitly defined as a passive reactive one. This paper first briefly explores some divergent attitudes toward aging—negative as well as positive. A neurophysiological framework is then presented to support the belief that aging is an active and creative process. Physical, psychological and sociological aspects are explored in the context of neurophysiological data as it relates to the subject of aging. Finally, three factors which emerge from the discussion as essential to assuring a creative aging process are identified and examined.

In considering the title of this paper, some might question the coupling of the two words 'creative' and 'aging'. Indeed, a dictionary would do little to assuage that thought since 'creative' is defined as "marked by the ability or power to produce or bring about a course of action or behavior . . . and/or the ability to produce through imaginative skill" [1, p. 267], while the definitions given for 'aging' are "to become old . . . to become mellow or mature . . . to acquire a desirable quality by standing undisturbed" [1, p. 22]. (Ostensibly some of the latter phrases are meant to describe wine or cheese, but one cannot help but wonder about this semantic coincidence!) If it is true that dictionary usage reflects the cultural context in which words are given meaning, then it is clear that the term 'aging' has a passive reactive connotation while the term 'creative' envisions an active vital process. Are the terms, then, antithetical?

May describes the creative process as "representing the highest degree of emotional health, as the expression of normal people in the act of actualizing themselves" [2, p. 38] which serves to "interrelate the person and his . . . world." [2, p. 52] Can this phrase be applied to the aging process?

In his summary of attitudes toward aging in this culture, Philibert gives his views on the questions posed above [3]. He states that the aging process is not generally considered to be a creative process, but rather a decline, a deterrent to growth and happiness; the elderly themselves are relegated to minority status, a "target population, to be cared for, controlled, segregated and investigated." [3, p. 385] The 1976 survey conducted for the National Council on Aging [4] concurs with Philibert's views. Time and again, public perceptions of old age and the elderly, while not as devastating as those described above, consistently stereotype and devalue both. Interestingly enough, perceptions of the elderly themselves did not differ significantly from those of the younger population, their own experiences to the contrary: "Putting myths aside, personal testimony shows that the problems of older people . . . are comparable to those of younger people. The message that emerges here, therefore, is that the older public, like the young, have bought the negative images of old age. They apparently assume that life is really tough for most people over sixty-five and that they are merely exceptions to the rule." [4, p. 38] It is unlikely that they would choose the word 'creative' to describe aging.

From a developmental point of view, the term 'creative' can be applied in another context since creativity is, in a sense, basic to the process of adaptation. Neugarten describes the aging process as a "continually changing sense of self and a changing set of adaptations. With the passage of time, life becomes more, not less, complex; it becomes enriched, not impoverished." [5, p. 891] The themes of adulthood do not emerge at a given moment, to be resolved and forgotten. "Identity is made and remade; issues of intimacy and freedom and commitment to significant others, the pressures of time, the reformulation of life goals, stocktaking and reconciliation and acceptance of one's successess and failures— all of these preoccupy the young as well as the old." [5, p. 891] This is a creative process to be sure.

Eastern philosophies of aging also are aligned closely with the creative process proposed in this paper. The emphasis on cultural and spiritual processes, on the continued opportunity for growth in knowledge, experience and wisdom and for self-mastery rather than on the biological processes of deterioration can certainly be viewed as creative [3].

From *International Journal of Aging and Human Development*, Vol. 14, No. 1, 1980-1981. Reprinted with the author's permission.

This paper is offered in support of the proposition that aging can be (and is for many) an active, creative process. Inherent in all the discussion which follows is the assumption that the elderly as a group are not a homogeneous entity, that there is "no such thing as the typical experience of old age, nor the typical older person. At no point in one's life does a person stop being himself and suddenly turn into an 'old person', with all the myths and sterotypes that the term involves. Instead, the social, economic [neurophysiological, physical] and psychological factors that affect individuals when they were younger, often stay with them throughout their lives. Older people share with each other their chronological age, but factors more powerful than age alone determine the conditions of their later years." [4, p. 129]

A neurophysiological foundation which supports the concept of creative aging will be introduced; physical and psychosocial aspects which relate to aging then will be explored in the context of the neurophysiological data. Finally, three factors which emerge from the discussion as essential to assuring a creative aging process will be identified and examined.

Neurophysiological Basis for Creative Aging

The central nervous system (CNS) is immensely complex and many factors influence its function in varying ways. Plasticity, a fundamental property of the CNS, provides one of the most promising foundations for the concept of creative aging.

Bach-y-Rita described plasticity as an adaptive capacity of the CNS, an "... ability to modify its own structural organization and functioning ... an adaptive response to a functional demand." [6, p. 227] Adaptation, the behavioral result of all transactions between a person and his internal and external environments, begins pre-natally and continues throughout life. Sensory information concerning environmental demands is assimilated by the individual. He then "... accommodates to these experiences, and associates, differentiates, and integrates the new experiences with those previously acquired. What continually emerges are newly organized modifications of previous behaviors." [7, p. 2] Behavioral responses are dependent upon movement for expression; that movement, in turn, provides a changing spectrum of sensory experiences—feedback regarding the appropriateness of the responses to changing environmental demands [6, 7]. All development (e.g., motor skills, emotional expression, social skills) depends upon experience with varying environmental demands as well as upon CNS plasticity.

High levels of plasticity in humans are thought to be a reflection of the "dynamic reorganization and adaptation to new circumstances and not to regeneration" of nerve tissue [6, p. 227]. While the actual number of cells (neurons) in the CNS decreases during the lifetime of an individual, they respond to functional demands by sprouting new terminals, thereby increasing the number of synaptic endings at any given neural junction, and/or by changing the size and complexity of the dendritic interconnections. The opposite effect, a decrease in neuronal complexity or number of functional synaptic components, can result from sensory deprivation or injury to brain tissue. The belief that CNS plasticity is associated exclusively with the maturation processes of young developing individuals persists despite evidence to the contrary. "In a recent study of plasticity in the mature and aged human brain, dendritic trees were shown to be more extensive in aged (av. age 79.6) than in adult (av. age 52.1) brains." [6, p. 330]

The concept of engram formation is also pertinent to a discussion of creative aging. This concept incorporates plasticity into its model. An engram is described as a spatio-temporal pattern which is formed within the neural networks of the CNS through repetition; it is basic to the development of skill. The spatial element of engram formation depends upon divergence (one neuron can influence more than one other neuron) and convergence (one neuron can be influenced by more than one other neuron) in the CNS, while the firing of neurons in a sequential pattern contributes the temporal aspect [8]. Sufficient repetition of a sensori-motor event which has meaning to the individual (e.g., riding a tricycle, playing the guitar) promotes the development of an engram for that event.

An engram, once established, enables the individual to perform the event in an automatic or subcognitive manner. In order to change or refine the engram, novelty and purposefulness must exist. Environmental demands (e.g., a new piece of guitar music, increased tempo, riding a bicycle) must be sufficiently different from the usual engram trigger or important enough to the individual to require attention or recognition by the CNS, but not so different that the CNS does not associate the new information with the established engram. Sensory information which does not vary, is too novel for recognition or lacks meaning to the person is not processed by the CNS [9]. Learning and skill increase as the individual elaborates upon his performance, or diminish through disuse. Parts of engrams—or entire patterns of performance—can deteriorate to the point of being unusable.

The necessity for activities or events to be challenging and/or meaningful to the individual provokes discussion, albeit brief, of the reticulolimbic system of the CNS. The reticulolimbic system is "believed to be responsible for emotional tone (behavioral patterns), drives or motivations, short and long term memory storage and retrieval of knowledge or cognition. In other words, it is a vital regulator of the CNS that is necessary for homeostasis as well as for maintaining the functional integrity of the entire nervous system." [9, pp. 70-71] It can be said that nothing that humans sense, do, or think is free from emotion because of the accessibility of the reticulolimbic system to a wide variety of sensory input and its multiple two-way connection with all other CNS systems. All learning (e.g., skill development, emotional expression, acquisition of knowledge) requires that that which is to be learned be important to the person who is to learn [9].

Since plasticity changes and engram development in the CNS depend upon sensory feedback, functional demand, and purposefulness, it follows that humans can influence their own neuronal function in either positive or negative ways. The individual who chooses to perform activities which are meaningful to him and which are rich in a variety of sensori-motor experiences will promote neuronal complexity within his own nervous system. Ultimately his aging process is enriched and expanded because of the existence of an increased number of adaptive responses with which the stresses related to aging can be met. It is reasonable to assume that those individuals who develop and maintain a large variety of engrams throughout life will have the greatest number of alternatives available for choices of action during their later years. The literature suggests that a large number of differing life experiences are more conducive to the development of engrams and flexibility in responses than are many but similar engrams.

Physical Basis for Creative Aging

The obvious physical signs of aging are familiar to everyone—either through personal experience or by observing the aging processes of others. Although some of the superficial signs are similar from one person to another, the aging process increasingly differentiates persons. Engrams developed throughout life—habits and lifestyles—contribute to the uniqueness of each individual. [10]. Some physiologists describe physical aging in terms of the adaptability of the organism to changes in the environment. Early development is characterized by high levels of adaptability, while aging is viewed as a gradual deterioration of adaptability as demonstrated by decreasing ability to respond to stress. While the duration and intensity of physical responses are not equivalent to those seen earlier in life, and the time required to resume homeostasis is longer [11, 12], the ability to adapt to functional demands persists.

Aging occurs differently in different types of cells and tissues. Some cells (i.e., skin, liver, bone marrow) retain the capacity to reproduce themselves throughout the life span although the rate of regeneration decreases significantly with time. Other types of cells, such as those which comprise nerves, muscles and kidneys, lose regenerative capacity even before birth. While these cells are remarkably numerous, cells lost cannot be replaced and ultimately their loss may compromise the function of organs or organ systems [11]. It is agreed generally that the degree of deterioration, in many systems, may not be attributable to the aging process alone, but to other factors such as increasingly sedentary activity performance or changes in diet or living arrangements.

Simple neurological functions, such as reflex activity, which involve few synapses, remain essentially the same throughout life, and, while the speed of nerve conduction slows later in life, the decrease is relatively small [11]. Weg stated that complex coordinated activities or responses to stress show considerably more functional decrement with aging than do less complex ones [12]. Apparently the slowing in nerve function is compounded as more and more processing of information and coordination of responses are required although the formation of activity habit patterns (engrams) tends to promote continuance of ability to perform those patterns. It seems that repeated performance of an activity as age related changes occur enables the individual to adapt his performance to his changing abilities and to continue to perform the activity in a gradually altered but still satisfying fashion.

Several studies have demonstrated that physical exercise acts as a stimulus to the metabolic processes which restore or rebuild body tissue, while lack of physical activity produces deleterious effects. In a longitudinal study with elderly persons [13] the non-exercising population declined in joint mobility, rate of respiration and heart beat, muscle strength, skin condition and nervous and psychological status, while those who performed specified physical activities did not decline and, in many cases, showed improved function.

A number of studies reviewed by Gore indicated that increased physical capacity as a result of exercise markedly improved the quality of life by reversing deleterious non-aging changes and increasing the ability of the individual to adapt to environmental stresses [13]. The necessity for appropriate sensory stimuli to insure adequate physiological function has been stressed in the literature as has the concept that insufficient sensory stimulation ultimately leads to malfunction [9]. A variety of physical activities is seen by many researchers as a logical, natural way to provide sensory stimulation [14] and to promote a physiological, intellectual and emotional function as well. According to Powell, "The unavoidable involvement of the entire brain in physical activity may be an important factor mediating a positive change in mental abilities of the elderly." [15, p. 160] Not only is physical activity a natural way to insure sensory stimulation, but during the performance of activities which are personally meaningful, the type and amount of stimulation, actual exercise, and personal enjoyment can be controlled by the individual. In addition to the obvious possibilities for creative aging, the element of control itself has associated benefits such as increased feelings of psychological well-being.

Psychosocial Basis for Creative Aging

The neurophysiological data emphasizes that CNS

plasticity and flexible engram formation are likely to provide an individual with alternatives for activity performance during later life. There is good reason to believe that multiple and varied early life experiences enhance the personality functions of the maturing individual as well. Adler indicated that heredity endows man with certain abilities while the environment gives him impressions [16]. These abilities and impressions and the manner in which he 'experiences' them comprise his attitude toward life and his relationship to the environment. In his concept of creative self, Adler asserted that man, in essence, creates his own personality by the way he interacts with his environment; the frequency, type and degree of environmental interactions transform the personality into a unified, subjective, personal, dynamic, and unique whole. The creative self, derived through the individual's choices of interactions and activities, gives meaning to life—the individual is master of his own fate.

Jung's theory of personality development also supports the concept of creative aging [17, 18]. Jung sees people as continuing to build on and/or develop new engrams through life. In Jung's view, youth is a time when thoughts, feelings and actions are dependent upon and responsive to external societal pressures. Not until after the age of thirty-five do all aspects of the personality start the process of integration. Middle age extends rather indefinitely. Jung used the term 'old' only for those who lapsed or regressed into 'psychic sleep' (senility?). The later years are seen by Jung as a time of true fruition when the self's internal processes (many of which would not have been allowed into consciousness in younger years) can be contemplated. As men allow themselves to become more 'feminine' (nuturant, subordinate, affiliative) and women allow themselves to become more 'masculine' (dominant, authoritarian, egocentric), members of both sexes more fully experience their humanness and become most whole.

In the sociological context, the mastery of new social roles can be identified as fundamental to creative aging. If one applies the neurophysiological concepts presented, it follows that the more varied the roles one plays in younger years, the greater will be the repertoire of skills acquired, and alternatives available in the later years. Jung would add, parenthetically, that the experimentation with new roles and new activities (expanding one's engram pool), while continuing the old familiar ones, leads a person to become more whole [17, 18]. This is especially true if the new experiences are those which are identified stereotypically with the opposite sex (e.g., women investing themselves in educational and/or political activities and men involving themselves in activities centered in the home such as gardening and nuturing grandchildren).

Many social roles are ascribed to the elderly. The most obvious ones are those which relate to the family (wife, father, grandmother, etc.). 'Retiree' is another role which comes to mind although it is frequently described as a non-role. The role of 'teacher' (in the broadest sense) is also one which is allocated to an elder by virtue of the fact that he becomes a model for younger generations.

Kaplan cites 'leisure' as a social role for the elderly [19]. Increased leisure time, with unlimited flexibility in how that time will be spent, is a reality of older age. Relaxation, self-expression, participation, adventure, learning, and contemplation are all potentially enhancing and rewarding activities, as are service to others, involvement in noncompetitive as well as competitive sports, solitude, companionship, creativity and entertainment [19, p. 224].

McKensie stressed that the criterion for choosing leisure activities in later life should be personal enjoyment [20]. "There is no reason to commit or restrict oneself to those activities that conform to established social expectations concerning old age, such as cooking, gardening, taking walks, or caring for grandchildren." [20, p. 263] The elderly "should not abstain from personally enjoyable activities because society may deem them inappropriate to old age—for example, flying a kite, sun bathing, or frequenting the local discos." [20, p. 262]

The exploratory quality of the use of leisure time is to be emphasized, with enjoyment and personal growth as the goals, rather than perfection of performance or finished products. Just as exploration is important in childhood, so is it important throughout life. Experimentation with the new and unfamiliar expands one's personal and social boundaries and increases CNS complexity and the capacity to adapt.

Conclusion

A neurophysiological framework for creative aging, describing plasticity, engram formation and meaningfulness of activities has been discussed. Attitudes of risk and/or exploration and enjoyment are identified as vital to the expansion of CNS function. Behaviors which the individual incorporates into his CNS as engrams are learned, and the number and variety of engrams which are exercised determines the behavioral options available to that individual. The discussion of physical factors has presented incontrovertible evidence to support the notion that physical fitness, regardless of age, equips an individual to adapt to environmental stresses in more creative ways, thereby enhancing the quality of his life. In considering psychosocial factors, variety, flexibility and personal choice in the process of development to one's full potential surfaced as inherently important. The inevitability of new social roles for the elderly, with the use of leisure time being central to this issue was also raised, and it was emphasized that time commitments should be made to promote enjoyment, health and personal growth.

Three factors emerge from the preceding discussions as essential to assure a creative aging process. The development of an attitude of exploration is the first factor. Neurophysiologically, psychologically, and sociologically this is well-supported. Exploration can promote CNS plasticity and new engram formation; an attitude of exploration can lead to the development of new friends, new interests, and new values, and leads inevitably to personal growth and expansion of life experiences. The earlier such an attitude is adopted, the more diverse the repertoire of behaviors and the more practiced the adaptation processes; opportunities for creative aging seem to be directly related to this process.

The second factor in assuring a creative aging process is exercise—in the broadest sense of the word. The value of physical exercise and fitness is well accepted and cannot be overemphasized; the 'exercise' or practice of the exploratory attitudes described above should not be overlooked; the 'exercise' of choice and responsibility is important as well. The term "creative" strongly implies personal involvement, personal choice and personal action. Creative aging requires that an individual be willing and able to consider available options, to make choices for himself, to follow courses of action, and to assume responsibility for his choices. To be knowledgeable concerning one's options and skillful in making decisions for oneself requires considerable exercise. The earlier in life that this is learned, and the more it is practiced, the more discriminating one becomes in making the right choices for oneself.

The third factor, perhaps less obvious than the others, but equally important to assure creative aging, is planning. Our younger years usually are very carefully planned; education, employment, marriage and/or the start of a family are all scheduled neatly. Planning and organization also mark the middle years which are characterized by further achievements in employment, and landmark accomplishments of children. During the later years, when there is less responsibility for others, when more time is available and when there is greater freedom in how time is spent, planning is especially important. There is no reason why the later years should not be accompanied by realistic personal goals and marked by personal and/or professional accomplishments. The criterion of good planning is that each individual allocates his time and energy according to his own priorities. Such planning can serve only to mark the later years with the same sense of accomplishment that accompanies the earlier years.

The phrase 'creative aging' is far from paradoxial; there is little question that the process of aging is potentially a creative one. The neurophysiological model is compatible with a definition of aging as a developmental process of increasing complexity and enrichment, the adaptation process being identified as the key to a continually changing sense of self.

References

1. *Webster's New Collegiate Dictionary*, G. and C. Merriam Co., Springfield, Massachusetts, 1977.
2. R. May, *The Courage to Create*, W. W. Norton and Co., Inc., New York, 1975.
3. M. Philibert, Philosophical Approach to Gerontology, J. Hendricks and C. D. Hendricks, (eds.), *Dimensions of Aging*, Winthrop Publishers, Inc., Cambridge, Massachusetts, 1979.
4. *The Myth and Reality of Aging in America*, A Study for the National Council on Aging, Louis Harris and Associates, Inc. (second printing), January, 1976.
5. B. Neugarten, Time, Age and the Life Cycle, *American Journal of Psychiatry*, 137:7, July, 1979.
6. P. Bach-y-Rita, Brain Plasticity as a Basis for Therapeutic Procedures, P. Bach-y-Rita, (ed.), *Recovery of Function: Theoretical Considerations for Brain Injury Rehabilitation*, University Park Press, Baltimore, 1980.
7. E. Gilfoyle, A. D. Grady and J. C. Moore, *Children Adapt*, Charles B. Slack, Publisher, Thorofare, New Jersey, 1981.
8. J. Eccles, *The Understanding of the Brain*, McGraw Hill, New York, 1973.
9. J. Moore, Neuroanatomical Considerations Relating to Recovery of Function Following Brain Injury, P. Bach-y-Rita, (ed.), *Recovery of Function: Theoretical Considerations for Brain Injury Rehabilitation*, University Park Press, Baltimore, 1980.
10. R. B. Weg, The Changing Physiology of Aging, *American Journal of Occupational Therapy*, 27:5, pp. 213-217, 1973.
11. J. Hendricks and C. D. Hendricks, *Aging in Mass Society*, Winthrop Publishers, Inc., Cambridge, Massachusetts, 1977.
12. R. B. Weg, Changing Physiology of Aging: Normal and Pathological, D. S. Woodruff and James E. Birren, (eds.), *Aging-Scientific Perspectives and Social Issues*, D. Von Nostrand Co., New York, 1975.
13. I. Y. Gore, Physical Activity and Aging—A Survey of Soviet Literature I. Some of the Underlying Concepts, *Gerontology Clinician*, 14, pp. 65-69, 1972.
14. _____ , Physical Activity and Aging—A Survey of Soviet Literature II. The Effect of Exercise on the Various Systems of the Organism, *Gerontology Clinician*, 14, pp. 70-77, 1972.
15. R. R. Powell, Psychological Effects of Exercise Therapy Upon Institutionalized Geriatric Mental Patients, *Journal of Gerontology*, 29, pp. 157-161, 1974.
16. A. Adler, The Fundamental Views of Individual Psychology, *International Journal Individual Psychology*, 1, 1935.
17. C. G. Jung, The Stages of Life, 1933 (translated by R. F. C. Hull), J. Campbell, (ed.), *The Portable Jung*, Viking Press, New York, 1971.
18. _____ , Conscious, Unconscious and Individuation, *Collected Works*, 9, Part 1, Princeton University Press, Princeton, New Jersey, 1959.
19. M. Kaplan, *Leisure: Lifestyle and Lifespan*, W. B. Saunders, Philadelphia, 1979.
20. S. C. McKensie, *Aging and Old Age*, Scott and Foresman Publishers, Glenview, Illinois, 1980.

Entering Middle-Age

Bryant Robey

The last baby boomer turns 20 this year; teenagers are becoming fewer and harder to find. Not that anybody is looking. By 1990, there will be 18 percent fewer teenagers than there were in 1980. Five million fewer teenagers—you can already hear the national sigh of relief. For the first time in history, the number of people over 65 has now surpassed the number of teenagers.

But such trends may not come as welcome news to companies that have grown accustomed to a diet of teenage fashions, fads, and foods. Businesses thrive on growing markets, so it is no surprise to see many firms retooling to pursue the "mature" market.

Ford Motor Company has even established a Mature Consumer Advisory Board. One such advisor recently observed in the pages of *Ad Forum* that "the percentage of the population age 55 and older is increasing so fast that if we're not aiming our products at them, we'll cut off half the market."

This is the kind of advice that gets auto companies in trouble. For one thing, folks aged 55 do not resemble those aged 85. But even the numbers don't work out right. While nearly half of all Americans are aged 20 to 54; only 21 percent are 55 and older. Nor is the 55-plus set growing as rapidly as is usually credited. And those segments of the older set that are growing the most rapidly are nonetheless much smaller than younger markets.

People aged 85 and over are growing faster than any other age group, thanks to improvements in the treatment of heart disease, and their growth rate shores up the rate for the total 65-and-older population. But the 85-and-up group, we hope, are not avid drivers, so they're not a big market for Detroit. Even after they double between 1980 and 2000, there

The Youth Market

Age Group	Number in 1990 (millions)	Percent Change 1980–1990	Number in 2000 (millions)	Percent Change 1990–2000
10–14	16.8	− 8.0%	19.5	16.4%
15–19	17.0	−19.7	19.0	11.8
20–24	18.6	−14.1	17.1	−7.8

The Middle Market

Age Group	Number in 1990 (millions)	Percent Change 1980–1990	Number in 2000 (millions)	Percent Change 1990–2000
35–39	20.0	41.6%	21.7	8.7%
40–44	17.8	51.8	22.0	23.2
45–49	14.0	26.5	19.8	41.4

The Elderly Market

Age Group	Number in 1990 (millions)	Percent Change 1980–1990	Number in 2000 (millions)	Percent Change 1990–2000
55–59	10.5	−10.1%	13.3	27.1%
60–64	10.6	5.0	10.5	−1.4
65–69	10.0	13.6	9.1	−9.0
70–74	8.0	17.6	8.6	6.6
75–79	6.2	29.3	7.2	16.4
80–84	4.1	36.6	5.0	22.3
85+	3.5	52.2	5.1	48.4

Source: Census Bureau Projections, 1982

will be only five million of them—about one-fourth the number of teenagers aged 15 to 19.

The younger end of Ford's mature market, people aged 55 to 59, will shrink 10 percent between 1980 and 1990. Even after growing 27 percent between 1990 and 2000, the 55-to-59 crowd will be scarcer than the 15-to-19 set.

People aged 60 to 64 will grow even more slowly, as the Depression generation reaches these years. By 2000, there will be scarcely 4 percent more people in their sixties than there were in 1980. At the turn of the century Americans in their sixties will outnumber 15-to-19 year-old teenagers by less than one million. People in their seventies will be growing rapidly, but just 16 million Americans will be in their seventies by the turn of the century.

Perhaps Ford has also formed a "Midlife Consumer Advisory Board" but is hiding its members from public view while it confuses General

Motors and Chrysler with talk about the mature market. The action in the next two decades is going to be among markets of people in their thirties and forties, not in their fifties and sixties.

More than 40 million Americans will turn 30 this decade. People aged 35 to 44 will number almost 44 million by 2000. And the number aged 40 to 44 will grow almost 52 percent during the 1980s alone—second only in growth rate to the small 85-plus group.

As the baby boom grows older, mid-life adults are coming into their own, and marketers should turn their attention to this age group. Already the median age has risen from 30 in the 1980 census to 31 today, and it will keep rising as the boom generation grows older. Ford should put its "mature" market in mothballs for a bit and go after the burgeoning midlifers. But maybe Mercedes, BMW, Volvo, and Toyota already have this market wrapped up.

Longevity and Aging

Although it is true that one ages from the moment of conception to the moment of death, we tend to think of children as "growing and developing" and of adults as "aging." Having accepted this assumption, most biologists concerned with the problems of aging focus their attention on what happens to individuals after they reach maturity. Moreover, much of the biological and medical research dealing with the aging process focuses on the later part of the mature adult's life cycle. A commonly used definition of senescence is "the changes that occur generally in the post-reproductive period and that result in decreased survival capacity on the part of the individual organism" (B.L. Strehler, *Time, Cells, and Aging,* New York: Academic Press, 1977).

As a person ages, physiological changes take place. The skin loses its elasticity, becomes more pigmented, and bruises more easily. Joints stiffen, and the bone structure becomes less firm; muscles lose their strength. The respiratory system becomes less efficient. The individual's metabolism changes, resulting in different dietary demands. Bowel and bladder movements are more difficult to regulate. Visual acuity diminishes; hearing declines; and the entire system is less able to resist environmental stresses and strains.

Increases in life expectancy have resulted largely from decreased mortality rates among younger people, rather than from increased longevity after age sixty-five. In 1900, the average life expectancy at birth was 47.3 years; in 1978, it had gone up to 73.3 years. Thus, in seventy-eight years the average life expectancy increased by approximately twenty-five years. Those who do live to the age of sixty-five do not have an appreciably different life expectancy than their 1900 cohorts. In 1900, sixty-five-year-olds could expect to live an additional 11.9 years. In 1978, persons age sixty-five could expect to live an additional 16.3 years—an increase of only 4.4 years. Although a larger percentage of the population is surviving to age sixty-five today, the chances of being affected by one of the major killers of older persons is still about as great for this generation of sixty-five-year-olds as it was for their grandparents.

We have not appreciably increased life expectancy for persons age sixty-five and older because while medical science has had considerable success in controlling the acute diseases of the young—such as measles, chickenpox, and scarlet fever—they have not been nearly as successful in controlling the chronic conditions of old age—such as heart trouble, cancer, and emphysema. Medical science is now investing considerable effort to bringing the chronic conditions of older people under control. As a result, life expectancy after age sixty-five might be greater for the next generation than it is for this one. An ever-increasing life expectancy will have many implications for American society. This section looks at some of them.

Looking Ahead: Challenge Questions

While medical science has increased life expectancy at birth by controlling the diseases of the young, there has been relatively little success in controlling the diseases of old age and increasing life expectancy after age sixty-five. Can we expect new breakthroughs in medical technology that will increase the life expectancy of sixty-five-year-olds?

While many people expect they will live well into their eighties and nineties, very few imagine living to be 120. Do many Americans really want to live beyond their hundredth birthday?

What changes in business, government, social services, and the economy will be produced by an ever-increasing number of older Americans?

LIVING LONGER

RICHARD CONNIFF

The subject, a healthy white male, is 29 years old, an age he would like to maintain more or less forever. At the moment, he is sitting in front of a computer terminal in a private office in Corona del Mar, California, about an hour south of Los Angeles. He is about to learn electronically, on the basis of key physical indicators, whether he is still in his prime or if his body is already slipping into the long decline to senescence. Forget what the mind feels, or what the calendar and a searching look into a mirror might suggest; this machine aims to tell how much the body has actually aged—and therefore how long the subject is likely to live.

The test takes 45 minutes. It requires no syringes, blood pressure belts or strapped-on electrodes. In fact, the whole experience is less like a medical examination than a stint at a computerized arcade game. Not quite Space Invaders, but then, the subject doesn't want to be Luke Skywalker. He's just a guy who'd like to live to 120, and never feel older than 29.

In all, there are more than a dozen tests. They measure such indicators as the highest pitch the subject can hear (known to decline significantly with age), the ease with which the eye adjusts its focus between near and far objects (lens and supporting structure become less elastic over the years) and the subject's ability to identify incomplete pictures of common objects (perceptual organization begins to fall off at about age 30).

Then comes a brief whirring of electronic thought and, ladies and gentlemen, the computer's analysis: The subject has the hearing of a 21-year-old, skin as sensitive as a child's and, overall, a body that just barely passes for 32. So much for the sweet bird of youth.

But not so fast. It turns out that there may be loopholes in the standard existential contract of birth, aging and death. Even people now approaching middle age can expect a bonus of perhaps several years of extra living, thanks to continuing medical progress against cancer, heart disease, stroke and other killers.

At the same time, gerontologists—specialists in the science of aging—are piecing together the details of diet, exercise, personality and behavior that make it practical to shoot for 80, or even 114—the longest human life span reliably recorded.

Finding the Fountain of Youth

There is hope even for people who fear diet and exercise almost as much as an early death. At the most minute level, scientists are now deciphering the basic biologic mechanisms of aging and of rejuvenation. Gerontologists are so confident about fulfilling the promise of their discoveries that a healthy young man aiming to live 120 years begins to appear reasonable. Writing in The American Journal of Clinical Pathology, one researcher recently predicted: "The discipline of gerontology is now advancing at such a rapid rate, with so much overflow from other fields . . . that I rather confidently expect a significant advance in maximum

life-span potential to be achieved for the human species during what is left of the present century. . . ." One probable means of life extension is already available, in a tentative form, and it suggests that a 16th-century Italian named Luigi Cornaro was far closer than Ponce de Leon to the fountain of youth. More about him later.

The so-called life-extension revolution couldn't come at a stranger time. American society is already on the brink of startling change. It is growing up. Whether longevity improves by only a few more years, as some expect, or by whole decades, mature people will for the first time predominate. Between 1970 and 2025, the median age in the United States will have risen almost 10 years, from 27.9 to 37.6—as substantial an age difference for a nation as for an individual. The number of people 65 and over will double, from 25 million now to 51 million in 2025, and there will be 85 million people over the age of 55. All without major new increases in longevity. In earlier societies, so few people managed to reach old age that they were deemed special, endowed with magical powers to ward off the demons of aging. In the United States over the coming decades, the elderly will be commonplace, and possibly more: a powerful, organized political and economic force.

Elderly Astronauts

What will it mean to live longer in such a society? One public-relations man, a product of the post-World War II baby boom, finds himself caught up in his generation's frantic competition for good homes and the best jobs. He suffers nightmares of an old age in which winning admission to a nursing home will prove harder than getting into Stanford or Yale. Cemeteries will be standing room only. Others worry that an increase in longevity will merely mean an increase in the time they'll spend bedridden, senile, catheterized.

Not so, say the gerontologists. They argue that even if there is no significant medical breakthrough, today's young and middle-aged can still look forward to a more youthful old age than their parents or grandparents. Instead of applying for early admission to the local nursing home, these future elderly may acknowledge their dotage merely by switching from downhill to cross-country skiing, or from running to jogging. Rather than worrying about death or about overcrowding at Heavenly Rest Cemetery, they may instead be considering the personal implications of a study, recently begun by the National Aeronautics and Space Administration, to determine how well 55- to 65-year-

---

LINUS PAULING
Scientist
Born: 1901

"I think people should try to keep healthy. I'm especially interested in vitamin C. I continue to recommend that everyone get a good supply. I take 10 grams a day."

---

old women withstand the stress of spaceflight. K. Warner Schaie, research director of the Andrus Gerontology Center at the University of Southern California, cites three well-known but rarely noted reasons for optimism about future old age:

• **The control of childhood disease.** Aging is cumulative. Instead of simply healing and going away, the minor assaults suffered by the body from disease, abuse and neglect can have "sleeper" effects. Chicken pox in a child, for example, can lead much later in life to the hideous itching affliction known as shingles. But vaccines and other wonders of modern medicine have largely eliminated such time bombs. Says Schaie, who is 53 and has lived through whooping cough, measles and mumps: "Most people who will become old 30 or 40 years from now will not have had childhood diseases. Most people who are now old have had them all. That's an important difference."

• **Better education.** Where a grade-school background was typical for the older generation, more than half of all

Americans now 30 or 40 years old have completed at least high school, and studies show that people with more education live longer. They get better jobs, suffer less economic stress and tend to be more engaged with life and more receptive to new ideas, which may help explain the third factor.

• **The fitness revolution.** "We really have changed our habits with respect to diet and exercise and self-care," says Schaie. Per capita consumption of tobacco has dropped 26 percent over the past 15 years, and the drop is accelerating, promising a decrease in chronic obstructive pulmonary disease and lung cancer. Life-style changes and improved treatment of hypertension have already produced a dramatic national decrease in cerebrovascular disease, one of the major chronic problems of old age.

Gerontologists say that these same future elderly will also benefit from the increasingly accepted idea that aging is partly a matter of choice. Speaking before a recent meeting of the American Academy of Family Physicians, Dr. Alex Comfort, the author and eminent gerontologist, argued that 75 percent of so-called aging results from a kind of self-fulfilling prophecy. "If we insist that there is a group of people who, on a fixed calendar basis, cease to be people and become unintelligent, asexual, unemployable and crazy," said Comfort, "the people so designated will be under pressure to be unintelligent, asexual, unemployable and crazy." Changing the image of the elderly may change the way the elderly behave.

Just as important as the image itself is the way individuals react to it. Performance declines on average with age, but individuals can practice not to be average. A 75-year-old man whose joints should be stiffening into immobility can run the marathon. An 80-year-old woman whose capacity for work is undiminished can model herself after Sir Robert Mayer, who declared at age 100: "Retire? Never! I intend to die in harness." (Now 101, Mayer is still arranging concerts, and recently remarried).

STROM THURMOND
United States Senator
Born: 1902

"I think the advantage of my age is the wisdom and knowledge that comes with experience. For those looking ahead to a long life, I offer this advice: Read the Constitution and demand that public officials, legislators and judges abide by it."

GEORGE GALLUP
Pollster
Born: 1901

"There's no substitute for experience. As I look back on my life, I wonder how I could have been so stupid.

"Intellectual curiosity is important, too. A lot of people die just from boredom. I have a whole program that will keep me going until age 100, at least. Incidentally, some years ago we did a study of people over the age of 95. We interviewed over 450 individuals; 150 of them were older than 100. What we found was that those who live a long time *want* to live a long time. They are full of curiosity, alert and take life as it comes."

This reliance on choice and something more—spunk, exuberance, a positive mental attitude—may sound romantic, and is, admittedly, an exotic notion in some of its permutations. At the State University College in Geneseo, New York, for example, Lawrence Casler, a psychologist, is convinced that aging is entirely psychosomatic. In 1970, to break through "brainwashing" about life span, he gave "an extremely powerful hypnotic suggestion" to 150 young volunteers that they will live at least to 120. "We're planning a big gala champagne party for the year 2070," says Casler. "I'm looking forward to it." He also gave a hypnotic suggestion for long life to residents of a nursing home who were already 80 or older. Casler says that the suggestion appears to have reduced serious illness and added two years to life span in the experimental group.

But even medical specialists in aging take the role of choice seriously. Dr. James F. Fries of the Stanford University Medical Center writes in The New England Journal of Medicine that "personal choice is important—*one can choose not to age rapidly in certain faculties....*" The italics are added, but Fries himself writes that the biologic limits are "surprisingly broad." With training, experimental subjects have repeatedly reversed the pattern of decline in testing for intelligence, social interaction, health after exercise, and memory—even after age 70. Fries, Schaie and every other gerontologist interviewed for this article reached the same conclusion: To stay younger for longer, you must stay physically and mentally active. As Fries put it, "The body, to an increasing degree, is now felt to rust out rather than to wear out." What you don't use, you lose.

2. LONGEVITY AND AGING

The Gray Revolution

A society dominated by old people will inevitably look different. Without a medical breakthrough, even vigorous old people cannot avoid slowing down. Schaie's interpretation is positive: "Young people . . . make many more errors of commission than omission, but the reverse is true for the elderly." Caution. The wisdom of the aged. To accommodate it, traffic lights, elevators, the bus at the corner will also have to slow down and become more patient.

Housing will be redesigned. But that doesn't necessarily mean handrails in the bathroom, wheelchair lifts on the stairway or any of the other depressing impedimenta of old age. "You're thinking of facilities for the ill elderly," says Schaie. Instead, redesign may mean more one-story garden apartments (stairs waste human energy). Homes will be smaller and require less care. House cleaning, home maintenance, dial-a-meal and dial-a-bus services will proliferate. Condominiums for the elderly will be built not near hospitals—an outdated idea, according to Schaie—but near libraries, colleges and shopping and athletic facilities.

The work place will also change, because more old people will stay on the job. As early as 1990, the baby bust of the past two decades will yield a shortage of young workers. Older workers will gain as a result, and there are few things better for an older person's spunk, exuberance or positive mental attitude than a sense of continuing worth in the marketplace and the paycheck that goes with it. The change is already beginning. The personnel department of one high-technology company, unable to find enough job candidates under 30, recently hired Schaie to convince its own top management that gray-haired engineers are just as able to keep the company on the cutting edge of innovation. Schaie says that it will pay to update and retrain older workers, not just for their expertise, but because they are less prone to accidents and absenteeism than their younger counterparts. In the Information Society, automation and robotics will make youth and strength less significant; the premium will be on knowledge and experience.

Indeed, James E. Birren, who runs the Andrus Gerontology Center in Los Angeles, predicts an era of "the experimental aged." A 75-year-old female lawyer came out of the audience once when he was explaining this idea, took his chalk away and told him in detail, with notes, why he was being too restrained. At 62, it seems, Birren still suffered the inhibitions of the conservative young. By contrast, he says, the elderly are past child-rearing and mortgage-paying, and they are also often beyond worrying about what the boss or the family thinks. But they have a much better sense of what they themselves

---

MILLICENT FENWICK
United States Congresswoman
Born: 1910

"Life gets better and better. You know why? You can help someone, and they aren't afraid of you. No one thinks that you're going to seduce them, or breach a promise or be a menace in any way. Here in Washington, your colleagues know that you are not going to interfere with them when they want to run for the Presidency.

"You are free. You aren't a young person, struggling to pay the mortgage and the children's dentist bills, with endless opportunities opening before you. When someone says that youth is the easiest time of life, that person has forgotten the terrible strain of choice."

---

think, and it is often surprising. In a 1971 Gallup poll, for example, substantially more older people thought that the Vietnam War was a mistake than did those in the 21- to 29-year-old group. If they did not do much about it, perhaps it was because they accepted the youth culture's image of old people as doddering and ineffective. But given respect, independence, a steady paycheck, the prospect of continued vigor and the knowledge of their own numbers, the old may replace the young, says Birren, as the experimenters, innovators and all-around hell-raisers of the world.

Which brings us to the question of sex and the elderly. Future elderly will enjoy, and perhaps enforce, a more tolerant public attitude toward their romantic activities. Dr. Leslie Libow, medical director at the Jewish Institute for Geriatric Care in New Hyde Park, New York, blames decreasing sexual interest among older men and women at least partly on the traditional popular expectation that interest ought to decrease. But that expectation shows signs of changing. One company not long ago introduced a line of cosmetics specially designed for older women and met with 400 times the response it had predicted. And a New York-area motel offering X-rated movies recently began advertising a senior-citizens discount. Future elderly will also benefit from subtler changes. Bernice L. Neugarten, a psychologist at the University

---

LATE, GREAT ACHIEVERS

Herein, proof that life begins—or at least continues—after 70.

Konrad Adenauer (1876-1967) 73 when he became the first Chancellor of the Federal Republic of Germany. Resigned 14 years later.
Walter Hoving (b. 1897) Chairman of Tiffany & Company for 25 years; recently left to start his own design-consulting firm at 84.
Pope John XXIII (1881-1963) Chosen Pope at 77; brought the Catholic Church into the 20th century.
Jomo Kenyatta (c. 1894-1978) Elected Kenya's first President at 70. Led the country for 14 years.
Henri Matisse (1869-1954) In his 70's did a series of sprightly paper cutouts that were exhibited at New York's Museum of Modern Art.
Golda Meir (1898-1978) Named Prime Minister of Israel at 71; held the job for five years.
Cathleen Nesbitt (b. 1889) At 92, revived the role she created on Broadway 25 years ago: Professor Higgins's mother in "My Fair Lady."
Pablo Picasso (1881-1973) Complet-

ed his portraits of "Sylvette" at 73, married for the second time at 77, then executed three series of drawings between 85 and 90.
Anna Mary Robertson Moses (1860-1961) Was 76 when she took up painting as a hobby; as Grandma Moses won international fame and staged 15 one-woman shows throughout Europe.
Dr. John Rock (b. 1890) At 70 he introduced the Pill; spent the next 20 years as its champion.
Artur Rubinstein (b. 1887) Was 89 when he gave one of his greatest performances at New York's Carnegie Hall.
Sophocles (c. 496-406 B.C.) Wrote "Electra" and "Oedipus at Colonus" after 70, held office in Athens at 83.
Giuseppe Verdi (1813-1901) Was 74 when "Otello" added to his fame; "Falstaff" followed four years later.
Frank Lloyd Wright (1869-1959) Completed New York's Guggenheim Museum at 89; continued teaching until his death.
Adolph Zukor (1873-1976) At 91, chairman of Paramount Pictures.

of Chicago, suggests that as they put anxiety-producing family and career decisions behind them, men and women are likely to relax more with one another. Sex stereotypes and the arguments they provoke will decline in importance as the years go by. As for male impotence, Libow notes that 20 percent to 40 percent of men continue to have active sex lives well into their 70's even now.

Finally, what about the specter of a long and vigorous life ending wretchedly in a nursing home? The average admission age today is 80, and only 5 percent of the elderly now endure such institutions. Even so, at current rates, the number of nursing-home residents will increase by 57 percent, from 1.3 million now to 2.1 million in 2003. But there are alternatives to terminal "convalescence." Most people now die without what Neugarten calls "a final deterioration that erases individuality." Birren believes that even more people will die "in harness" in the future. Instead of dwindling away, they will remain vigorous longer, then drop away quickly. Temporary "respite care"—an innovation now being imported from Scandinavia—will be available, say, for an octogenarian down with a bad cold. Schaie suggests that old people who are burdened with large homes may also invite friends to come live with them for mutual support. Such communes will give them independence they could never hope for in a nursing home.

Supergenes

So far, all of this assumes that there will be no breakthrough in human longevity, no anti-aging pill or fountain of youth. People will become wrinkled and gray and die at roughly the biblical threescore and ten or fourscore years. But that is no longer a safe assumption.

Dr. Roy Walford is one of the leading gurus of the life-extension move-

ment, and he looks the part. His head is hairless, except for a gray moustache that thickens down past the corners of his mouth. He can seem ferocious on film, but in person he is benign, almost shy. When he tours his complex of laboratories at the School of Medicine of the University of California at Los Angeles, he keeps his elbows close by his sides, and his hands in front of him, tucked like a monk's into the sleeves of his white lab jacket. His colleagues around the country tell you first that he is odd, and second that they respect him more than any other researcher in the field.

Walford believes that he has identified a single supergene that controls much of the aging process. Since 1970, he has been studying a small segment of the sixth chromosome in humans called the major histocompatibility complex. This is the master genetic control center for the body's immune system, and it is a logical suspect in the aging process. The ability to fight off disease peaks in most people during adolescence, and then falls off to as little as 10 percent of its former strength in old age. At the same time, a kind of perversion of the immune system occurs, in which the workhorses of self-defense lose some of their ability to distinguish between friendly and foreign cells. They attack the body's own organs, leading to such characteristic diseases of old age as diabetes and atherosclerosis. The phenomenon is called autoimmunity, and it means that the body is making war on itself.

Walford established the supergene's additional role in aging by comparing 14 strains of mice. The study (conducted by his associate, Kathy Hall) demonstrated significant differences in life span among mice that were genetically identical *except* at key locations in the major histocompatibility complex. Additional study by Walford, Hall and others tied that single genetic variable to two of the most important factors in the aging process as it is now understood. The long-lived mice had improved DNA-repair rates and increased protection against cellular damage from bodily substances known as free radicals. But the most profound idea, first suggested by Richard Cutler of the National Institute for Aging and substantiated by Walford, was simply that genes control longevity. Mice with "good" genes lived longer; the strains with "bad" genes had lives that were nasty, brutish and, above all, short.

Walford points out that there may be other genes controlling longevity. But none has been located so far, and separate studies on the nature of hu-

man evolution suggest that there may be, at most, only a few such supergenes. All of which makes Walford's discovery about the major histocompatability complex more important. What to do about it? Altering the genetic information in the nucleus of every cell of an adult animal is, at least for now, impossible. Instead, scientists are trying to find other supergenes and identify the mechanisms by which they work. If these supergenes have some regulatory mechanism in common, it may then be possible to manipulate the mechanism rather than the gene.

One promising school of thought theorizes that aging results mainly from accumulating errors in the complex, tightly coiled strands of DNA that are each cell's blueprint for accurately reproducing itself. The damage comes from many sources: ultraviolet radiation, viruses, free radicals, toxic chemicals, even the body's own heat. Repair enzymes correct some damage, but some persists. Over the years, tiny breaks and infinitesimal wart-like bulges accumulate, the DNA coils loosen and the cell begins to malfunction.

The theory suggests that those animals most efficient at DNA repair will live longest and age least. And so it happens in nature. The white lip monkey has a low rate of DNA repair, and lives to be only 12 or so years old. Humans have a very high rate of DNA repair, and live longer than any other primate. Differences in the DNA repair rate appear even among members of the same species, along with corresponding differences in longevity. Walford and Hall's long-lived mice displayed a higher rate of DNA repair than their short-lived counterparts. Walford himself has an unusually high rate of DNA repair. This may be why at 56, he still has pink unwrinkled skin, and looks 45.

What if science could boost other people's DNA-repair rates to the same level as Walford's—or perhaps triple them? The theory is that enhanced repair, probably in tandem with other therapies, would delay the accumulation of errors, slow the aging process and extend human life span. It might even be possible to correct old errors, patching breaks that had become a part of the genetic blueprint, excising bulges, retightening the coils of DNA. In a word, rejuvenation.

> ### MOTHER TERESA
> **Missionary**
> Born: 1910
>
> "At the hour of death, when we come face to face with God, we are going to be judged on love—not how much we have done, but how much love we have put into our actions."

Keeping Paramecia Young

Researchers may already have achieved just that in lower animals. Joan Smith-Sonneborn, a professor of zoology and physiology at the University of Wyoming, chose to work with paramecia because the microorganism's single cell in many ways resembles the cells of more complex animals. In an experiment first reported in 1979, she damaged the DNA of paramecia with ultraviolet radiation—the same light waves that cause human skin to tan or burn and, eventually, to age. The damaged animals died sooner than the untreated ones, presumably because they could not repair all the breaks or bumps in their DNA. Damage. Malfunctioning. Old age. Death.

With another group of paramecia, Smith-Sonneborn first induced DNA damage, and immediately stimulated, or "photoreactivated," a repair enzyme known to respond to a particular wavelength of visible light. To her surprise, the photoreactivated paramecia lived not merely as long as untreated counterparts, but substantially longer. They were already at midlife, but somehow achieved a 296 percent increase in their remaining life span, and a 27 percent increase in overall life span. In gerontology, the so-called Hayflick limit represents the maximum life span of each species. It has to do with how many times the animal's cells can divide before they die. There is a Hayflick limit for paramecia and another for humans,

both supposedly inescapable, unmovable. The ultimate deadline. "What we did," says Smith-Sonneborn, "was break through the Hayflick limit for paramecia."

To explain how this happens, Smith-Sonneborn uses the analogy of a sinking ship. When the damage occurs, an S O S goes out. But by the time outside help arrives on the scene, the ship's own crew has plugged the leak and pumped out the bilges. Having no emergency repair to do, the outside help goes to work anyway, overhauling engines and tightening rivets, and may even stay on the scene long afterwards for maintenance. By analogy, the photoreactivated enzymes leave the paramecium more youthful—and youthful for longer—than it was before the damage occurred.

It is, of course, a huge leap from paramecia to human beings. But other scientists have already demonstrated photoreactivation of repair enzymes in human skin. Smith-Sonneborn quickly adds a caveat: No one knows how much ultraviolet damage must be induced in human skin, or with what consequences, before photoreactivation will work as a rejuvenating treatment. So it does not make sense to sit for hours under a light bulb in the hope of unwrinkling or rejuvenating the skin. Then what does any of this matter? The photoreactivation work is important because it demonstrates the possibility of enhancing other DNA-repair mechanisms and other longevity-determining processes elsewhere in the human body. The enhancement may slow aging. And if it is possible to break through the Hayflick limit for paramecia, why not also for people?

> ### MARGARET HICKEY
> **Public affairs editor**
> **Ladies' Home Journal**
> Born: 1902
>
> "With age comes serenity, the feeling of being satisfied with what you have done while still looking forward to what you can do. You begin to like yourself."

The Anti-Aging Diet

Another method of enhancement—the only one that is practical now—takes the life-extension story back to the 16th century and to Luigi Cornaro. Cornaro, a Paduan, led such a profligate youth that by the time he was 40, he found his constitution "utterly ruined

by a disorderly way of life and by frequent overindulgence in sensual pleasures." Told to reform, he entered upon the *vita sobria*, a life of moderation in all things. He restricted himself in particular to just 12 ounces of food daily and lived in robust health until he was 98. Since then, scientists have repeatedly demonstrated that undernutrition—as distinguished from malnutrition—extends the lives of experimental animals. But they mistakenly thought that undernutrition had to start at weaning, when it's riskiest. As Walford puts it, "You can't starve babies and you can't have 10 percent mortality rates in order to have a few people live to be 180." When the underfeeding was delayed until midlife, the experimental animals often died prematurely, Luigi Cornaro to the contrary.

> ### I.F. STONE
> **Author**
> Born: 1907
>
> "There are great joys in one's later years—as many as there are in one's youth. One of them is learning and studying. The things you study have much more significance; you understand them more fully. I'm studying ancient Greek language and civilization. It's difficult work, but very rewarding.
>
> "My advice is to persist. The mind is like a muscle—you must exercise it."

But by refining the technique of previous researchers, Walford and Richard Weindruch, a co-worker, recently achieved a 30 percent increase in maximum life span for test animals whose diet was restricted after they became adults. The crucial refinement seems to have been moderation. Where other experimenters began adult underfeeding abruptly, Walford and Weindruch gradually reduced the intake of their animals, down to about 60 percent of their normal diet. In humans, Walford says, it would work out to a loss of a quarter to a third of body weight over a six-year period—a big loss, but a slow one.

Walford has not yet developed the optimal human diet for longevity through underfeeding, but says he intends to over the next year or so. For himself, he now fasts two days a week and has shed five or six pounds from his already spare frame. But because undernutrition can easily turn to malnutrition, especially outside a doctor's care, he doesn't recommend that people follow his example. In any case, would such a diet be worth the sacrifice? Walford evidently thinks so. One reason is that experimental underfeeding did not merely delay death, it delayed aging. The lack of extra calories forestalled the development, and hence the decay, of the immune system. Autoimmunity, the body's war on itself, actually decreased. And in other underfeeding experiments, the cancer rate dropped markedly.

As for the sacrifice, it may eventually prove unnecessary. At Temple University Medical School in Philadelphia, Arthur Schwartz is working with an adrenal-gland product called dehydroepiandrosterone, or DHEA. His experiments "suggest that DHEA treatment may duplicate the anti-aging and anticancer effects of caloric restriction."

140 and Still Kicking

It is just this piling on of discoveries and developments in all areas of life-extension research that causes Walford, Cutler, Smith-Sonneborn and others to predict a dramatic increase in human longevity. Walford, in fact, believes that it will become possible within this decade to extend maximum human life span to somewhere between 130 or 140 years.

What such a life will be like is anybody's guess. George Bernard Shaw imagined that extraordinarily long-lived people would quickly abandon mating for more mature pursuits, such as higher mathematics. Aldous Huxley wrote of a brave new world in which old men spend their time "safe on the solid ground of daily labor and distraction, scampering from feely to feely, from girl to pneumatic girl."

The possibilities raised by extreme longevity are as numerous as the additional days people will supposedly live. Walford argues that the very vastness of the change is one reason conser-

vative experts on aging prefer to deny the likelihood of significant life extension. "It blows the data base on which they make their projections," he says. A doubling of human life span would, of course, blow anybody's data base. To cite a single example, a young couple starting out with two children, and passing on their belief in zero popula-

---

MICKEY ROONEY
Actor
Born: 1920

'A long time ago I looked around and saw the apathy that the elderly had fallen into. They had nowhere to go, no one to turn to. They were eliminating themselves from the atmosphere of potential. This became a deep concern of mine. So I started a project called Fun Filled Family for people over 45. We have trips, discounts, life insurance policies and gathering places. We have no political or religious ties. We don't use the word age at all, but talk only in terms of experience."

---

tion growth to their offspring, could wind up at the healthy middle age of 90 with 44 direct descendants and descendant-spouses, and at age 150, with six or seven living generations in the family. Alternately, if women were to age much more slowly and reach menopause much later, it might be possible for some future generation to put off parenthood and the whole career-family dilemma until age 50.

Whole new sets of questions arise, and at first they seem to have an absurd Woody Allen quality: If you're going to live to be 150, who's going to pay the rent? But if life extension is as near as

gerontologists suggest, perhaps it is time to begin thinking seriously about seemingly absurd possibilities. Does it make sense, for example, to buy life insurance at 30 if you will be living to 150 and if, barring accidents, medicine makes the time of death ever more predictable? Should you plan now for a second career? (Walford intends to be a researcher in artificial intelligence.) Will longer life encourage a flowering of abilities? Is marriage "till death do us part" practical when there is a good chance that you'll see your 100th anniversary? What if the husband pursues the life-extension therapy and the wife rejects it? What will it mean if marriages and generations become asynchronous? What will happen—in fact, is already happening—to the drilled-in timetables of schooling, mating, childrearing, income-producing, retirement and death?

To many people, the promise and the possibilities suggested by life extension are truly wonderful. "I see humanity as a fragile organism that has been evolving all along into a more complex, autonomous, intelligent species," says F. M. Esfandiary, an author who lectures at the University of California at Los Angeles, "and I believe that in our time this ascent will rapidly accelerate, propelling us into entirely new dimensions. I also believe that our mortality, the very fragility of life, has for eons drastically impaired the quality of life. It is not just the imminence of one's own death that is so cruel, it is the ever-present fear of losing all the people one loves. In the future, people will not be as programmed to finitude and mortality. Instead, they will see a whole avalanche of new options. . . ."

On the other hand, it may be worth remembering that Moses lived to be 120, and still never entered the promised land.

The Aging Body

After twenty, the decades take their toll. You may get wiser, but your memory dims. Your body parts grow, shrink, disappear. It's a process you can only watch with wonder, so you'd do well to know the wonders to watch for.

John Tierney

John Tierney is a staff writer for Science 82 *magazine.*

There are many gruesome things to be said about a man's body as it creeps past the age of thirty. But first a word about the President's hairline:

"It's a hairline you normally see only on a child or a eunuch," says Dr. Norman Orentreich, the inventor of the hair transplant, who has studied men's scalps for three decades and still has a hard time accounting for Ronald Reagan's hairline. Men typically lose hair around the temples. It's an effect of androgen, a hormone produced in the testicles after puberty, and it seems to happen to all men, even those who otherwise keep a thick head of hair all their lives. Yet here is Ronald Reagan with a straight line of hair above his forehead. "He's not wearing a hairpiece," Orentreich says, "and he hasn't been castrated, so I'd have to assume that he happens to have some sort of rare hereditary variation."

This is a comforting fact. Ronald Reagan's scalp is further proof of what gerontologists have come to realize in the past two decades—that the only absolute rule about the aging process is that it eventually stops. The individual variations are enormous at every age and in every part of the body.

THE CATALOG OF DECAY

that follows is merely a list of the average ravages, most of which will hit you sooner or later but some of which you may escape. The victim is a hypothetical American man—one, say, who works in an office, gets a little exercise, has no serious vices, and doesn't dabble in such exotica as macrobiotic diets or megavitamins. At thirty he's not a bad specimen. A little plumper than he used to be, a little slower, a little balder, yet smarter than ever. Still, his body has just passed its peak. It has started dying a little every day, losing about one percent of its functional capacity every year. Cells are disappearing, tissues are stiffening, chemical reactions are slowing down. By seventy his body temperature will be two degrees lower. He will stand an inch or so shorter and have longer ears.

No one understands why. The most appealing theory for why we disintegrate as we get older was offered in an eighteenth-century treatise called *Hermippus Redivivus, Or, The Sage's Triumph over Old Age and the Grave, Wherein, a Method Is Laid Down for Prolonging the Vigour of Man, Including a Commentary upon an Ancient Inscription, in Which This Great Secret Is Revealed, Supported by Numerous Authorities.* A man aged, according to this theory, because he lost vital particles every time he exhaled. The Great Secret— how to find a new source of particles—was revealed by the discovery of a tomb whose occupant had lived to 115. The fellow managed to live so long, according to the tomb's inscription, WITH THE AID OF THE BREATH OF YOUNG WOMEN. Today's physicians advise jogging.

"Exercise will make you feel fitter, but there's no good evidence that it will make you live longer," says Dr. Jordan Tobin of the National Institute on Aging. The same goes for practically every other prescription. Because scientists don't know what causes cells to break down with age, they can't say that anything causes longevity. They can only note that certain types of men age better—those who have long-lived parents, a satisfying job, and plenty of money. Married men tend to outlive bachelors, with one notable exception: if you look at a chart comparing the average life expectancy of men according to their occupations, it turns out that the best job may well be pope (or at least cardinal). Of course, worrying about statistics like these will only hasten the aging process. So your best strategy may simply be to relax, hope that you have the right genes, and accept peacefully the indignities as they occur. You might also consider taking afternoon naps. They don't seem to have hurt Mr. Reagan.

30 In most ways, he is at his peak—the tallest, strongest, maybe the smartest he's ever been. And yet he can see the first lines on his forehead, he can't hear quite as well as he could, his skull's circumference has even started swelling. And his degeneration has just begun.

40 He's an eighth of an inch shorter than he was ten years ago, and each hair follicle has thinned two microns, but not everything's shrinking: his waist and chest are ballooning. All over, he's begun to feel the weight of time's passage: his stamina is greatly diminished.

50 His eyes have begun to fail him, particularly at close range. He notices quirky changes: his speaking voice has risen from a C to an E-flat, his thumbnails are growing more slowly, and his erections have dipped below the horizontal mark. His waist is as big as it will get.

60 By now he has shrunk a full three quarters of an inch, he has trouble telling certain colors apart, trouble distinguishing between tones, trouble making distinctions among the different foods he tastes. His lungs take in just about half what they could thirty years ago.

70 His heart is pumping less blood, his hearing is worse, vision weakening still; yet if he's made it this far, say the statistics, he'll live another eleven years. And if he has the right attitude, he will look back with awe at the wonders that have made him what he has become.

Weight

He loses a bit of his body each day, yet the body just gets bigger. The reason is fat. He's not burning up enough food—both because he's not as active as he used to be and because his basal metabolism (the rate at which the resting body converts food into energy) is slowing down about 3 percent every decade. So while muscle and other tissue is dying, accumulated fat is taking up more of his body. That's the case until middle age, after which his weight levels off and then slowly declines: he starts losing more tissue than he gains in fat.

Age 20: 165 pounds, 15% of it fat
Age 30: 175 pounds
Age 40: 182 pounds
Age 50: 184 pounds
Age 60: 184 pounds
Age 70: 178 pounds, 30% of it fat

Nails

Aged nails grow more slowly, which makes for easy grooming but weathered nails. Measured in millimeters per week, his thumbnail grows:
Age 20: 0.94 millimeters
Age 30: 0.83 millimeters
Age 40: 0.80 millimeters
Age 50: 0.77 millimeters
Age 60: 0.71 millimeters
Age 70: 0.60 millimeters

Stamina

The weakening of our man's heart, lungs, and muscles means that there's less oxygen coming in and that the heart is slower in dispersing it through the bloodstream to the muscles. A healthy seventy-year-old man can still run a marathon if he trains properly, but it will take him at least an hour longer than it did at thirty. The best measure of our man's limits is the work rate, which measures how many pounds he can turn with a weighted crank in a minute and still have his heartbeat return to normal after two minutes of rest:
Age 30: 1,110 pounds
Age 40: 1,020 pounds
Age 50: 950 pounds
Age 60: 870 pounds
Age 70: 800 pounds

Skin

A middle-aged man makes his own wrinkles: the lines on his face are drawn from repeated facial expressions, which is why the surly have more furrows on their brows. But an old man's wrinkling happens automatically—the inside of his skin loses water, and nearby molecules bind to one another, making for a stiffer, less elastic skin structure. Meanwhile, the skin itself thins and spreads out, much like a piece of dough that's been stretched. The result is a baggy suit, with the skin too large for the body. This is especially troublesome in places like the jaw, where the bone is shrinking as the skin is expanding.

Age 30: Lines in forehead are present
Age 40: Lines from other facial expressions show up, especially crow's-feet (from squinting) and arcs linking the nostrils to the sides of the mouth (from smiling)
Age 50: Lines are more pronounced; skin begins to loosen and sag in the middle of the cheek
Age 60: Excess skin and fat deposits etch bags under the eyes
Age 70: Face wrinkles everywhere; skin is rougher and has lost its uniform color—he can see a variety of shades in his face

Eyes

The lens of the eye steadily hardens throughout life and begins to cause problems for a man in his early forties. By then the lens is too big for the eye muscles to focus properly on close objects. Eventually this can cause cataracts, but the odds are that our man will die before that happens. The amount of light reaching the retina steadily declines with age (perhaps because the pupil shrinks), which means that our man will have trouble seeing in the dark; he will need especially bright light to read.

Age 30: 20/20 vision; reads without glasses
Age 50: 20/20 for distance vision, but needs glasses to read; a less elastic eye lens makes him more sensitive to glare; his depth perception is beginning to get worse
Age 60: 20/25 vision; a less elastic, yellower lens filters out some shorter wavelengths of light, making it harder for him to distinguish between blues and greens
Age 70: 20/30 vision; peripheral vision is diminished; night vision is worse, and his eyes take longer to adjust to the dark

Flab

With increased weight comes flab—or, to be precise, an increased subscapular skinfold, which is the best index of flab. This skinfold, measured by pinching the skin beneath the shoulder blade and determining the distance the skin can be stretched, is twelve millimeters wide at age twenty, fourteen millimeters at thirty, and remains about sixteen millimeters after forty. Unfortunately the flab also extends below the shoulder—conspicuously to the waist and chest.

	Waist	Chest
Age 20:	33 inches	36 inches
Age 30:	36 inches	39 inches
Age 40:	39 inches	40 inches
Age 50:	40 inches	41 inches
Age 60:	39 inches	41 inches
Age 70:	39 inches	41 inches

Height

A man is able to withstand gravity only so long. As his muscles weaken, his back slumps. And as the disks between the bones of his spine deteriorate, those bones move closer together. The result: The inexorably shrinking man.

Age 30: 5'10"
Age 40: 5'9⅞"
Age 50: 5'9⅝"
Age 60: 5'9¼"
Age 70: 5'8⅞"

Reflexes

His reflexes slow down, for which his brain is probably more guilty than his nerves. The speed at which signals travel along his nerve fibers declines only 2 percent each decade, which is a relatively minor deterioration compared with other changes in the body. The real slowdown happens because the brain takes longer to process information, make decisions, and dispatch signals. If a man looking at numbers flashing on a screen is told to press a button whenever he sees two consecutive even or odd numbers, this is how long it takes him to react:

Age 30: 0.88 seconds
Age 50: 0.90 seconds
Age 60: 0.92 seconds
Age 70: 0.95 seconds

Teeth

Eating slowly files down a tooth, but not enough to make any significant difference to anyone under the age of two hundred. The problem is keeping the tooth, and it is one problem a man can control. Despite the fact that the amount of enamel on the surface will decrease with age and the layer of dentin underneath will become more translucent, most tooth and gum decay is a result of neglect and disease. The average seventy-year-old man today has lost a third of his teeth; because of fluoridated water and better dental care, his descendants should fare better.

Age 30: 2 teeth missing
Age 50: 7 teeth missing
Age 60: 8 teeth missing
Age 70: 10 teeth missing

Hair

Men actually do get hairier with age, but, alas, not where it does them good. Hair grows in the ears, in the nostrils, and sometimes on the back. Eyebrow hairs tend to get longer and more noticeable. As for the top of the head, there are different hormones at work. Balding usually begins at the temples, producing a widow's peak that recedes with age. Next hit is the monk's spot, that circle on the back of the head—it keeps growing until it meets the receding widow's peak, leaving the top of the head bare. Men bald at different rates, of course, and some never bald at all. Still, if our man is going to bald, he will—no amount of scalp massaging will help. Although there are marked differences among men in the rate at which hair falls out or turns gray, there does seem to be a consistent pattern in the way individual hairs thin. A man's hairs are thickest at about twenty; after that each hair shrinks, and by seventy his hairs are as fine as they were when he was a baby. The diameter of a single hair (measured in microns—millionths of a meter) changes like this:

Age 20: 101 microns   **Age 50:** 94 microns
Age 30: 98 microns   **Age 60:** 86 microns
Age 40: 96 microns   **Age 70:** 80 microns

Muscles and Strength

At thirty, about seventy of his 175 pounds are muscle. Over the next four decades he loses ten pounds of that muscle as cells stop reproducing and die. His shoulders narrow an inch. Connective tissue replaces fiber, causing his muscles to become stiffer and to tense, relax, and heal more slowly. The remaining muscle grows weaker as the fiber becomes frayed, jumbled, and riddled with deposits of waste material. His strength peaks at about thirty and then steadily diminishes. The muscles in his hands perform as follows, as measured by the amount of force that can be exerted by the right (if that's his dominant hand) and left grip:

	RIGHT HAND	LEFT HAND
Age 30:	99 pounds	64 pounds
Age 40:	97 pounds	62 pounds
Age 50:	92 pounds	58 pounds
Age 60:	86 pounds	48 pounds
Age 70:	80 pounds	42 pounds

Head

His features become more distinguished, which is a kind way of saying that they get bigger. Because of the cartilage that begins to accumulate after age thirty, by the time he is seventy his nose has grown a half inch wider and another half inch longer, his earlobes have fattened, and his ears themselves have grown a quarter inch longer. Overall, his head's circumference increases a quarter inch every decade, and not because of his brain, which is shrinking. His head is fatter apparently because, unlike most other bones in the body, the skull seems to thicken with age.

Mouth

He tastes less. When he's thirty, each tiny elevation on his tongue (called a papilla) has 245 taste buds. By the time he's seventy, each has only eighty-eight left. His mouth gets drier as the mucous membrane secretes less. His voice begins to quaver, apparently because he loses some control over his vocal cords. He talks more slowly, and his pitch rises as the cords stiffen and vibrate at a higher frequency: after fifty his speaking voice rises about 25 hertz (cycles per second), from a C to an E-flat (in the octave below middle C).

Now for the Good News...

No wise man ever wished to be younger," said Jonathan Swift, and some gerontologists today might even agree with him. There's no denying that a seventy-year-old body doesn't work as well as it once did, but it's also true that people's fears of aging are greater than they should be. In the course of chronicling decay, researchers have come up with some reassuring findings:

▷ A man becomes less sensitive to pain after the age of sixty. It takes longer for an old man to notice a disturbing stimulus, thus he can endure greater levels of pain without complaining. This is probably due to the degeneration of his nerve fibers and to the decline in the central nervous system's ability to process sensory information.

▷ A man sweats less with age; his sweat glands gradually begin drying up.

▷ Fat isn't as bad as they say—it may even be good for you. Because thin people have always been thought to outlive the obese, doctors have urged patients to conform to a chart of "desirable weights" 15 percent lighter than the men's average. Yet recent studies show that a man ten to twenty pounds above the desirable weight is likely to outlive the virtuous man who follows the chart. "There clearly is something strange going on," says Dr. Reubin Andres of the National Institute on Aging. It could be that the mildly overweight have more reserve capacity to survive illnesses, but no one knows for sure.

▷ Until the age of sixty-five, a smoker is at least twice as likely as a nonsmoker to suffer a heart attack, but after sixty-five, the odds change. The risks are about even for nonsmokers and for men who smoke less than a pack a day. And a man who smokes more than a pack a day is three times *less* likely than a nonsmoker to have a heart attack. This doesn't mean you should take up smoking in your old age, only that a heavy smoker who survives past sixty-five is a hardy fellow.

▷ A nearsighted youth may be able to put away his glasses when he reaches middle age. The thickening of his eyes' lenses cures nearsightedness.

▷ It may be only a small victory in the battle of the sexes, but a man's skin ages about ten years more slowly than a woman's—his skin has more oil, so it's slower to dry out. Shaving also helps: The mild scraping of a razor strips away dead skin and leaves the face smoother. It's not unlike epidermabrasion, a beauty treatment that skin specialists frequently administer to women with more elaborate instruments.

▷ A man's sexual decline isn't usually traumatic. When Clyde Martin, one of the authors of the Kinsey report, asked old men how they'd react to the discovery of a safe drug that could restore their youthful sexual vigor, most said they wouldn't bother taking it. Martin found that men who were most sexually active in their youth showed the least decline in activity during old age; it was the less active men who dropped off most drastically and brought down the average. The conclusion: Old men can continue with sex if they're interested (most men in their seventies can still produce sperm); it's just that most of them aren't. "They bow out gracefully," reported Martin. "They have other interests." Or, as an aged Sophocles said when he was asked about his love life, "Peace, most gladly have I escaped the thing of which you speak; I feel as if I had escaped from a mad and furious master."

▷ If a man reaches seventy, the odds are that he'll live to see eighty. Diseases wreak far more havoc than normal aging; physically, a healthy seventy-year-old has more in common with a healthy thirty-year-old than he does with an ill man of his own age. Seventy is the average life expectancy for a man, but that's only because accidents and disorders kill so many before then. A man who survives until his seventieth birthday, according to actuarial tables, will live eleven more years.

Lungs

As the muscles that operate the lungs weaken and the tissues in the chest cage stiffen, the lungs can't expand the way they used to. A deep breath isn't as deep as it once was. The maximum amount of air he can take into his lungs:

AGE 30: 6.0 quarts
AGE 40: 5.4 quarts
AGE 50: 4.5 quarts
AGE 60: 3.6 quarts
AGE 70: 3.0 quarts

Brain

His brain shrinks as it loses billions of neurons. The cell loss varies in different parts of the brain—the region that controls head posture, for instance, doesn't seem to lose any, while the region that controls sleep stages is hit especially hard (which helps explain why he sleeps about two hours less at night). If IQ tests are any measure, then his intelligence declines. In order to make the average IQ at every age be 100, the test scores are automatically adjusted according to age. If these adjustments weren't made, the average score would be:

AGE 20: 110   **AGE 50:** 100
AGE 30: 111   **AGE 60:** 93
AGE 40: 106   **AGE 70:** 83

This may only mean that old people are out of practice at taking standardized tests; beyond that, a slight loss of memory is probably the most noticeable change after fifty, though even that is more a matter of faulty retrieval than of lost information. If an old man and a young man each try to memorize a list of words and then are given clues to each of the words, the old man recalls them as well as the young man. But without clues, the old man has a harder time remembering what was on the list.

AGE 20: 14 of 24 words recalled
AGE 30: 13 words recalled
AGE 40: 11 words recalled
AGE 50: 10 words recalled
AGE 60: 9 words recalled
AGE 70: 7 words recalled

Can Youth Spring Eternal?

The more realistic question might be "Can aging be slowed?" and, as you would expect, there are two schools of thought about that. Those scientists who believe that an inner clock automatically shuts down each cell at a predetermined time naturally suggest that it's impossible to lengthen the life-span radically. The less deterministically inclined think that a cell dies because of gradual processes that wear it down and that therefore man has the power to somehow slow the decay. They just haven't figured out how.

All of which means that science offers little help for your aging cells at the moment. But whether or not you can ever extend their little cell lives, you can certainly make their stay in your body more comfortable by following these simple health guidelines:

▷ **EXERCISE:** Studies show that regular exercisers outlive their sedentary peers. But it's a chicken-and-egg problem: Are they healthy because they exercise, or do they exercise because they're healthy to begin with? A recent study found that monkeys reduce their risk of heart disease if they work out on a treadmill regularly. This wasn't absolute proof—monkeys aren't men—but it was probably the most compelling evidence yet for the life-lengthening advantages of jogging. And even if exercise doesn't actually prolong life, it produces other rewards—firmer muscles, less fat, stronger lungs, better circulation—worth aspiring to in their own right.

▷ **SUN:** Unless he's a nudist, a man's youngest-looking skin is on his buttocks. That's because exposure to the sun's ultraviolet rays roughly doubles the havoc normal aging wreaks. Protecting your skin from the sun will help keep it from drying and stiffening, and help you avoid brown "age spots" or "liver spots," which can be signs of overexposed skin.

▷ **DIET:** It's probably a good idea to go easy on fats, but nobody really knows what makes the ideal diet. The fact that life expectancy is almost the same in Japan, France, and the United States suggests that vastly different diets can produce similar results. The old rules probably still apply: Keep your food tray balanced, and Eat your vegetables.

▷ **TOBACCO:** It should be avoided, of course. A cigarette smoker's lung capacity is usually equal to that of a nonsmoker ten to fifteen years older.

▷ **ALCOHOL:** Surprisingly, it's probably better to drink a little than not at all. A recent study found mortality 50 percent higher among both teetotalers and heavy drinkers (three to five drinks a day) than among light drinkers (one or two drinks a day). Apparently, moderate amounts of alcohol increase the blood's supply of high-density lipoprotein, which in turn reduces the risk of heart disease.

▷ **VITAMINS:** As you age your stomach takes longer to digest food, but that doesn't really matter. The body can still extract all the nutrients it needs, and a seventy-year-old man who eats a balanced diet shouldn't require any special vitamin supplements. Some gerontologists think we should take extra vitamin E because it stops "free radicals," which the doctors believe cause aging, from forming. But leading gerontologist Dr. Nathan Shock, among others, doesn't think much of this advice: "Taking vitamin E probably won't hurt you," says Shock. "But the main effect is probably just going to be an increase in the profits of the pharmaceutical companies."

For now, there are few other reliable pieces of advice. When asked for any great secrets to be gleaned from all the studies of the aging corpus, Dr. Jordan Tobin of the National Institute on Aging turns his palms heavenward. "I guess the best general rule is to practice moderation in the way you live," he says. "Well, it's probably a good idea not to let yourself get extremely overweight. Don't drink and drive. And wear seat belts."

Bones and Joints

His bones lose calcium. That's bad for the bones and also for the nearby blood vessels, where the lost calcium can accumulate, clogging up the works. His bones become more brittle and slower to heal. Relatively few men suffer rheumatoid arthritis, but after sixty, chances are good that our man will develop a less serious condition called degenerative arthritis. Years of flexing have worn down and loosened cartilage around the joints; the presence of this stray cartilage, coupled with depleted lubricating fluid in the joints, makes for a slower-moving, stiffer man. Movement is further restricted by ligaments that contract and harden with age. The hardened ligaments are more liable to tear.

Sex

By seventy he has found new activities for the nighttime, and he's all but stopped daydreaming about sex. Just why a man's sex drive declines is unclear—lower levels of sex hormones may be a factor, but psychological changes and the general loss of vitality in the body are probably more important. With age, the testes sag and the penis takes longer to become erect, longer to reach orgasm, longer to recover. The orgasm itself is shorter.

ANGLE OF ERECTION
AGE 20: 10% above horizontal
AGE 30: 20% above horizontal
AGE 40: Slightly above horizontal
AGE 50: Slightly below horizontal
AGE 70: 25% below horizontal

FREQUENCY OF AWAKING WITH ERECTION
AGE 20: 6 mornings per month
AGE 30: 7 mornings per month
AGE 50: 5 mornings per month
AGE 70: 2 mornings per month

FREQUENCY OF ORGASMS
AGE 20: 104 per year (49 solo)
AGE 30: 121 per year (10 solo)
AGE 40: 84 per year (8 solo)
AGE 50: 52 per year (2 solo)
AGE 60: 35 per year (4 solo)
AGE 70: 22 per year (8 solo)

Heart

His resting heartbeat stays about the same all his life, but the beats get weaker as his heart muscles deteriorate. As a result, his aged heart pumps less blood with each beat. The decline in blood flow is more marked during exercise, because his pulse can no longer rise as high as it used to.

BLOOD PUMPED BY THE RESTING HEART	MAXIMUM HEARTBEAT DURING EXERCISE
AGE 30: 3.6 quarts per minute	**AGE 30:** 200 beats per minute
AGE 40: 3.4 quarts per minute	**AGE 40:** 182 beats per minute
AGE 50: 3.2 quarts per minute	**AGE 50:** 171 beats per minute
AGE 60: 2.9 quarts per minute	**AGE 60:** 159 beats per minute
AGE 70: 2.6 quarts per minute	**AGE 70:** 150 beats per minute

Heart disease is the most common cause of death in men over forty years old and is responsible for more than half the deaths of men over sixty. As the level of cholesterol in the blood increases with age, the cholesterol accumulates on the artery walls, which are themselves thickening. The net effect is to clog the arteries, increasing the pressure of the blood against the arterial walls, which in turn forces the heart to work harder to pump blood and makes strokes and heart attacks more likely.

AGE 20: 180 milligrams cholesterol; 122/76 blood pressure
AGE 30: 200; 125/76
AGE 40: 220; 129/81
AGE 50: 230; 134/83
AGE 60: 230; 140/83
AGE 70: 225; 148/81

Kidneys

At seventy his kidney can filter waste out of blood only half as fast as it could when he was thirty. He also has to urinate more frequently because his bladder's capacity declines from two cupfuls at age thirty to one cupful at seventy.

Ears

Over the years, things like a good stereo just don't seem as important anymore—a man can't hear the highest notes no matter how well they're reproduced. A child can hear sounds reaching as high as 20,000 hertz, but in early adulthood the range starts decreasing. This seems to be a direct result of a breakdown of cells in the corti, the organ in the inner ear that transforms the vibrations picked up by the outer ear into nerve impulses, as well as of deteriorating nerve fibers. Fortunately, hearing diminishes least in the range of everyday human speech (below 4,000 hertz)—the average old man can hear conversations fairly well. To the young, an old man often seems deafer than he really is simply because he's not paying attention (perhaps with very good reason).

AGE 30: Has trouble hearing above 15,000 hertz (a cricket's chirp)
AGE 50: Can't hear above 12,000 hertz (a "silent" dog whistle)
AGE 60: Can't hear above 10,000 hertz (upper range of a robin's singing); has trouble distinguishing among tones in range he can hear
AGE 70: Misses some words in normal conversation; can't hear above 6,000 hertz (high notes on a pipe organ)

Surgery and the Elderly

Ann Slayton

Mrs. Slayton is a writer with the Public Information Office of the Health Care Financing Administration.

Q: What type of person sees twelve doctors and six nurses a week?
A: The typical American television viewer.

Doctors not only appear frequently on prime time television, but they are characterized as being members of the most successful, humane, and responsive of the professions. "It may well be," conclude researchers at the University of Pennsylvania's Annenberg School of Communications, "that daytime serials are the largest source of medical advice in the United States." They criticize this portrait of doctors—applying the "magic of medicine" to every problem, even ones that have nothing to do with medicine—as "unrealistic" and "idealized."

In real life, doctors know that the practice of medicine is an imprecise art. That is why consultation among physicians is a tradition, almost as old as the practice of medicine itself. The indications for surgery, for instance, are not always precise, and legitimate differences of opinion frequently arise among doctors about what treatment is best.

In recent years, patients have become more insistent about participating in this consultation process, and are less inclined to follow unquestioningly "doctor's orders." In the matter of surgery, more people are taking the initiative to inform themselves about their conditions and seek second opinions when they feel it necessary. Traditionally, consultations have occurred because physicians wanted them; now, second opinions may be sought because patients want them.

The demand among patients to play a more active role in the decision-making process makes some doctors uncomfortable, but most physicians want their patients to understand fully what the problem is and how it should be treated.

 The percentage of patients undergoing multiple surgery during a hospital stay increased from 27.8% in 1970 to 32.6% in 1979. In 1980, 24 million surgical procedures were performed, or 11,000 per

100,000 population. Four of the six most frequent procedures were surgeries on the female reproductive system: hysterectomy, tubal ligation, ovariectomy, and Caesarean section.

Why Have Surgery Rates Climbed?

The escalation of surgical rates over the last decade has multiple causes. The most frequently given reason for the increases is that there are more physicians performing surgery. This is true, but in itself is an insufficient cause. According to a study conducted by the Health Care Financing Administration, increased surgery rates are due to the demand of patients, accessibility of surgical care, and the growth of insurance and other third-party payment sources such as Medicare and Medicaid. There may also be a certain attitude toward surgery as a "once-and-for-all" cure. Certainly, an important factor behind increased rates is the proliferation in the last decade of new diagnostic and surgical procedures, such as the colonoscopy, which permit early surgical intervention for cancer. Improvements in existing technology, for instance the bone cement that is used in hip replacements or the development of the intraocular lens for cataract patients, while contributing to the frequency of certain surgical procedures, make them less risky and more successful in outcome. Finally, major surgical developments, such as the coronary artery bypass for angina pectoris, not only contribute to higher rates of surgery but also are responsible for the escalating overall costs of surgery.

Seeking a second opinion on a recommendation for surgery is especially important for the over-65 population. The elderly have surgery performed and are hospitalized twice as often as the rest of the population. In 1972, the elderly underwent 130.6 operations per 1,000 population. In 1979, that number jumped to 183.4 per 1,000.

Fifteen years ago, one of the most serious problems faced by the elderly was how to pay for increasingly necessary and expensive medical care. Though gaps in its coverage remain, Medicare has largely eliminated this fear, but rising physicians fees and general inflation in the economy have meant that people over 65 are paying for an ever larger share of their medical care in the form of so-called "Medigap" insurance policies that fill in for services not covered by Medicare, and in direct-out-of-pocket costs.

To Have or Not To Have Surgery

Factors determining the need for surgery vary from patient to patient, and according to the condition needing medical attention.

Three procedures—cataract surgery, hernia surgery, and prostatectomy—are among the five most commonly experienced by the over-65 population. Gall bladder removal (cholescystectomy) and arthroplasty/hip replacement are the second and third most frequently performed surgeries among women over 65.

Though surgery can bring about exceptional improvement of a painful condition associated with aging, the risks of surgery increase with age. This is particularly true of major surgery and operations requiring general anesthesia or long hospitalization and recuperation. A general anesthesia, for instance, places an additional strain on the cardio-pulmonary system, which may be weakened in the elderly. Another risk of surgery is a higher frequency of post-surgical infection due to a generally lowered resistance. Depending on individual health status and the procedure done, recuperation periods also may be longer and more difficult than with younger patients.

Every person over age 65 considering surgery should know these general risks. The risks and benefits of individual surgical procedures should be considered carefully.

Cataract Surgery

The leading surgical procedure performed on the over 65 population—cataract surgery—is relatively risk-free. It is usually done with a local anesthetic, and recovery is rapid, but the patient and doctor should agree on the timing of the operation. How much has vision deteriorated from the clouding of the natural lens? Can contact lenses or cataract glasses be worn after surgery? Has the doctor advised not driving at night? To what extent can the condition be ameliorated with glasses? These and other questions are important to the elderly patient who has been advised to have the surgery. Often a second opinion is helpful if the patient is in doubt.

Another decision a person might have to make *before* cataract surgery is whether he or she wants an intraocular lens implant or will be satisfied with wearing contact lenses or cataract glasses. The intraocular lens is a tiny plastic lens that replaces the cataract-clouded natural lens of the eye. It is inserted at the time the diseased lens is removed and, according to the National Eye Institute, offers the best hope for a return to normal vision after surgery. In 1979, 100,000 people or 25 percent of all cataract surgery patients had intraocular lens implants, 90 percent of them between ages 65 and 85.

Ninety-five percent of all routine cataract operations are successful, but it is best, again, for the patient to have a clear understanding of the particular risks and benefits of surgery. Sometimes a doctor will recommend cataract surgery even if the condition is not very advanced and vision is not greatly impaired, if the doctor feels that the cataract condition could lead to some other eye disorder. Usually, however, surgery will be postponed until vision is impaired in both eyes.

In deciding whether to have or postpone the surgery, the patient may want to consult another doctor who can provide more information upon which to base a decision. Some studies have shown, for instance, that aspirin retards the visual deterioration caused by cataracts. One researcher, Dr. Edward Cotelier of Yale University, observed that patients taking large doses of aspirin for arthritic pain have a low incidence of cataracts.

Prostatectomy

Another relatively safe procedure, prostate removal is also performed under a local anesthetic. The prostate, a gland in the male that surrounds the urethra, becomes enlarged with age and sometimes causes painful pressure on the urethra and prevents urine from passing freely. Eventually, the pressure may damage the kidneys.

Removing the prostate is another procedure in which timing is a key consideration. How much discomfort and inconvenience is the person willing to tolerate? Is there any danger of damage to the kidneys? Is another condition likely to be aggravated by the prostate condition? The patient, evaluating such factors with the physician, can come to an informed decision about surgery. Again, should more information be required to make a decision, it is best to get a second opinion.

Cholecystectomy

Removal of the gall bladder, called cholecystectomy, is major surgery, and should not be undertaken lightly by the elderly patient. The gall bladder, part of the digestive system, is a small pouch underneath the liver, in the upper right section of the abdomen. Fatty solids, bile pigment, and lime salts can form stones in the gall bladder or its ducts. Attacks of indigestion or sharp pain in the upper right abdomen are warnings of the presence of gallstones which may or may not be accompanied by infection. Again, whether to have surgery depends on the extent and frequency of infection, and the individual's tolerance of discomfort or pain. Sometimes a change of diet and proper exercise will be sufficient treatment; sometimes surgery is re-

quired. Careful consideration of its risk and benefits, perhaps with the aid of another doctor's opinion, can help ensure the best decision.

As with all forms of major surgery, people considering cholecystectomy, should have a clear understanding from their physicians about the condition as well as the risks of surgery and the nature of the recuperation.

Hernia Repair

Over the last decade, hernia repair has become increasingly safer. Still, the rate of infection is higher for those over 65 than for the younger population, and the rate of recurrence is about 15 percent. In considering surgery, the patient must know what other conditions might be aggravated by the hernia, for example, if it causes an obstruction to the intestine. The patient must decide too, what amount of discomfort he is willing to tolerate.

Arthroplasty and Hip Replacement

The third most frequently performed surgery among women over age 65 is arthroplasty and hip replacement. Hip pain and loss of function come from a variety of disorders, such as arthritis and osteoporosis, and hip replacement is considered a largely successful form of treatment. The patient, with her doctor's advice and, if necessary, a second opinion, must decide if the benefits of surgery outweigh the risks. She should satisfy herself that no other medical treatment is available. The patient should have a clear understanding of any restricted activity following surgery, whether she will limp, need to use a cane, or be limited as to walking distance or the ability to climb stairs. There are many factors involved in arthroplasty, hip repair, and replacement which vary from patient to patient, and postoperative complications are more likely in the elderly. Thus, getting as much information as possible is necessary in making a sound decision.

Being a Good Patient

There are several rules-of-thumb that potential surgical patients can follow to make sure that the surgery they are considering is necessary, safe, and worthwhile in terms of cost.

For people over 65 who are relatively healthy and strive to live independently, being a "good patient" means being adequately informed and taking an active role in deciding about their health care. They will find most doctors want their patients to understand what is happening to them, will encourage questions, and will help the patient find another physician to obtain a second opinion on elective surgery.

A person who is advised to have elective surgery should first ask his or her doctor for a referral to a specialist. If, for some reason, the patient does not want the doctor to know he or she is seeking a second opinion, there are several ways to find a second doctor. The patient can:

• Contact the local medical society or medical schools for the name of a doctor who specializes in the field in which the illness falls,

• Call a toll-free number (800-225-6400 and in Maryland 800-342-6600) to obtain the name of the nearest referral group,

• Call the local Social Security Office,

• Contact his or her private health insurance company to see if it has a second opinion referral service.

Once the patient makes an appointment with the second doctor, he or she should call the doctor who recommended surgery and ask that all pertinent records be forwarded. In doing this, the patient avoids wasting time, money, and possible discomfort by repeating tests that have already been done. Of course, if the patient decides to get a second opinion without the first doctor knowing about it, tests will have to be repeated.

Paying for a second opinion should not be an issue for the elderly. Medicare pays for a second opinion, and in some cases for a third opinion, at the same rate that it pays for other office visits, diagnostic tests, lab procedures, or hospitalization, if required. Since Medicaid payments vary from State to State, the patient should check with the local welfare office to see how much the program will pay.

If the patient decides in favor of surgery, it may be worthwhile to discuss with the doctor the possibility of having surgery on an outpatient basis. Approximately 70 percent of hospitals in metropolitan areas perform outpatient surgery, and there are a growing number of freestanding ambulatory (outpatient) surgical centers. About 100 surgical procedures, including cataract surgery and some hernia repairs and orthopedic procedures, can be done safely without hospital-ization. Not only is outpatient surgery less time consuming, it is also less expensive, and much less stressful for the patient. Medicare now pays 100 percent of the costs of the outpatient facility, though the surgeon's fee is reimbursed at 80 percent unless he agrees to accept assignment from Medicare.

Know the Answers

Before agreeing to any non-emergency surgery, people should know the answers to these questions:

• What does the doctor say is the matter with you?

• What operation does the doctor suggest you have?

• What are the likely benefits to you of the operation?

• What are the risks of the surgery, and how likely are they to occur?

• How long is the recovery period, and what is involved?

• What are the costs of the surgery and recovery period?

• What is likely to happen if you don't have the operation?

• Are there any alternatives to surgery that could be tried first?

Being a "good patient" means being informed about one's medical problems, and being able to get enough information about recommended surgery or alternative medical treatments to make the best decisions. These guides are just as important for the trusted family members and friends whom the elderly depend on for assistance in making health care decisions. The Department of Health and Human Service's Health Care Financing Administration has a booklet that can help patients and their families make good decisions about elective surgery. It can be obtained by mailing a request to:

Surgery
HHS
Washington, D.C. 20201

Are Companion Animals Good for your Health?

A Review of the Evidence

Aaron Honori Katcher, M.D.

Dr. Katcher is Associate Professor of Psychiatry, University of Pennsylvania, Center on the Interaction of Animals and Society.

Does owning a pet improve the physical health of an older person? To describe the state of our knowledge, it is necessary to rephrase the question about the health value of pets as a number of more precise questions.

- Do survey studies in which health is measured at one point in time demonstrate that older people with pets are any healthier than those elderly of similar social characteristics without pets?
- Do longitudinal studies in which an individual's health is measured over a period of time demonstrate that pets improve the health of the elderly when health is defined in terms of either:
  - objective measures like death rate, the incidence of illness, rates of hospitalizations, or different levels of disability, or
  - subjective, less reliable measures of health, such as the subject's estimation of symptoms and morale, or other indicies of health, emotional state, disability, or the quality of life?

- Based on longitudinal or survey studies, what segments of the elderly population stand to gain most from the presence of a pet? Are there any subgroups of the elderly for which a pet may be a detriment rather than an aid?
- Do pets have the capability to alter the emotional state, life style, or physiological state of the elderly in a way that would be expected to result in improved resistance to disease. Are there psychophysiological mechanisms by which pets can alter the "vital balance" so that health is improved?

Pets and the Institutionalized Aged

Before we look at the evidence bearing on these questions, I would like to comment on programs which bring pets to the institutionalized elderly. There is no doubt at all that bringing pets into institutions is a humane and valuable activity that can make dramatic changes in the emotional state of many patients, even those who are severely affected by organic brain disease or lack of social stimulation. The joyous responses of the elderly to even brief contact with pets have been well documented in the accounts of those conducting such programs, the film and still photography provided by Samuel and Elizabeth Corson and

others, and the experimental observations of Robb and Andrysco. The immediate emotional impact is so spectacular that we do not need sophisticated studies to document their presence. Pets are, I hope, a significant wedge in the process of making institutions for the aged more humane and less depriving. I want, however, to address the bulk of my remarks to the questions about the influence of pets on the health of the 95 percent of the aged who live outside of institutions.

Mugford's famous "budgie" experiment (Mugford and M'Comisky 1975) is an example of a longitudinal study in which subjective measures of health and morale were used to describe the outcome of pet placement. In this experiment pensioners were given either a plant or a budgerigar (an Australian parakeet). A balanced design was used so that the two treatment variables (bird or plant) were placed both with people who had, and people who did not have, television sets. Subjects were given a health and morale questionaire at the start of the study and five months later. The number of items on the questionnaire changing in a favorable direction was the outcome measure. Although the numbers used in the study were small (19 subjects were used in the analysis), the authors

"Are Companion Animals Good for Your Health?" Aaron Honori Katcher, M.D., *Aging* Magazine, September/October 1982, pp. 2-7. Reprinted by permission of *Aging* Magazine.

observed a significantly greater level of favorable change in the subjects given the budgerigar. It should be noted, however, that the questionnaire was administered to only 60 percent of the original group. Some subjects died, and others became severely ill or disabled, but the authors do not report how these deaths or illness events were distributed between the treatment groups.

There are no other studies indicating that pets can have a positive influence on health.

There is some consistency in the above findings which suggests hypotheses about the best target populations for pet placement programs.

• We would expect that the influence of the companion animal on health or morale would be greatest when the person is highly attached to the animal. This hypothesis is suggested by the observations of Goldberg and Ory that morale levels among pet owners were higher when the subject was attached to the pet. We could make the same inferences from our observations with hospitalized patients in Baltimore. In our coronary disease study, there were no effects of pet ownership on survival within the population of black patients studied (Friedmann 1979). Moreover the reason for this became clearer when we studied the relationship between hospitalized patients and their companion animals (Friedmann, Katcher et al, 1982), and found that the degree of attachment between black patients and their animals was significantly lower than that of white patients and their pets. In this study we used a 10-question index of attachment which provides a more quantitative measure of the relationship than single questions about the importance of the pet (Katcher, 1981, Katcher, 1982). Again, to be quite clear, I am not suggesting that pet placement programs be restricted to any single group. Instead, I am suggesting that the kind of attachment an individual person develops with a pet has a strong bearing on the effect of that pet on his health or morale. Studies seeking to document the effect of pet ownership should include sufficient numbers of people who develop a close attachment to their pets. Because of the relevance of attachment, I would also suggest that *urban rather than rural populations* might be better study groups, since casual pet ownership is a less common practice in urban areas.

• It is ridiculous to think that animal ownership can reverse the cruel effects of poverty, especially in an aging population. The data from the Goldberg and Ory study are quite explicit. The morale of low-income pet owners was lower than the morale of non-owners, and there was a positive association of morale and attachment only in the higher-income groups. Again, studies of the effect of pet ownership on one's emotional state or health should be careful to include subjects with adequate means. Certainly, a pet, like any other dependent, can become a burden to families or individuals with extremely limited incomes. Programs should consider the cost of maintaining animals. Ownership of a parakeet, to cite an extreme example, is less expensive than a Great Dane, and this may be more desirable for some subjects.

Blood Pressure and Pets

In the long run, it will be necessary to demonstrate that companion animals do indeed influence objective measures of health. It is still useful, however, to study the effect of pets on physiological or psychological parameters of health. For example, it is usually accepted that any factor which results in lower blood pressure might have a favorable influence on health, without demonstrating that it actually influences mortality or morbidity patterns. The practice of meditation,

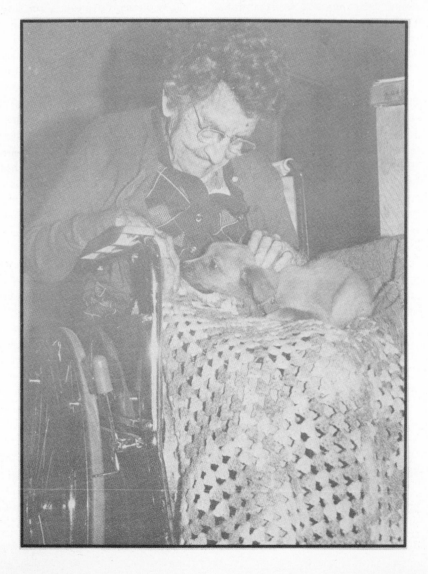

or the "relaxation response" (Benson 1980) is an accepted means of preventing or treating hypertension, yet there are no studies demonstrating that these relaxation procedures extend life. We have studied the influence of animal companions on blood pressure in both healthy and hypertensive adults (Katcher 1981, Katcher, Friedmann and Beck, 1982, Katcher, 1982). These studies provided the following information:

- When people speak to people, blood pressure almost always rises. Sometimes the rises are quite large, bringing the subjects' blood pressure into the hypertensive range. In contrast, when people speak to their pets, blood pressure remains the same and can even fall below the level recorded when the subject is resting quietly.

- When people speak to animals, they touch them as well. Touching is a means of communication that can be highly effective in reducing stress. In previous studies of patients recovering after myocardial infarction in a coronary care unit, the simple act of touching a patient to take his or her pulse was shown to both alter heart rate and change the frequency of abnormal heart beats (Lynch et al 1977).

Pets in the Home

Examination of the first of the questions I raised, "Do health surveys find the health of pet owners to be better than the health of people without pets?" reveals no evidence to support a positive answer. The results of available surveys (Ory and Goldberg, 1981, Lago and Knight, 1981, and Franti et al, 1980) have been equivocal, at best, and indicative of some *negative influence,* at worst.

The best such study was conducted by Ory and Goldberg. They surveyed 1500 older women in a rural Maryland county. They found no overall relationship between pet ownership, health, and morale. However when pet owners were segregated into those who were closely attached to their animal and those who were not, morale was lower in owners who were not attached to their pet. The pet owners who were attached to their pets resembled the

subjects without pets. Hence, subjects who owned a pet but were not attached to them had lower morale scores than people without pets. The relationship between morale, attachment to a pet, and income was then examined. In subjects with relatively high incomes, pet owners who said they were attached to their pets had higher morale scores than those who were not. Among the subjects with lower incomes, there was no relationship between pet attachment and morale. Thus the combination of adequate

> *When people speak to their pets, blood pressure remains the same and can even fall.*

economic means and a close emotional relationship with the animal seems to be a prerequisite for a positive influence of pet ownership on morale.

These findings are partially confirmed by two other studies (Lago and Knight, 1982 and Franti et al, 1980). Lago and Knight analyzed the responses of 137 clients of senior centers and members of senior groups in a rural area of Pennsylvania. These authors found no differences between current pet owners, former owners, and those who had never owned pets on measures of social functioning, health, or morale. The reports correlating health and pet ownership in El Dorado County (Franti et al, 1980) and Yolo County (Franti et al, 1974) provide equivocal results. Some health problems were more frequent in homes without pets and others more frequent in families with pets.

Pets and Our Health

Survey studies are relatively weak lenses for examining the influence of our environment on health. Longitudinal studies examine such effects with more precision. To my knowledge, our study of the influence of social variables on survival after hospitalization for severe coronary artery disease (Friedmann, Katcher, et al 1980) is the

only longitudinal study documenting the influence of pet ownership on an objective measure of health. Parenthetically, I should add that we did not intend to focus on pet ownership when the study was designed; we included a question on pet ownership within a long social inventory. Since such studies are expensive, I hope that the dawning scientific recognition that pets are a significant part of our social environment will result in the addition of simple questions about pet ownership in other studies that examine the impact of social and psychological conditions on health.

The subjects in the reported portion of our study (Friedmann, Katcher et al, 1980) were 93 white patients admitted to a coronary care unit for myocardial infarction or severe angina pectoris. A large number of social and physiological predictors were measured during hospitalization, and the patients were followed for one year. Pet ownership was significantly associated with a lower death rate. The positive effect of pets was not limited to dog owners (dogs being pets which provide a stimulus to exercise). It is extremely important to recognize that there are no data which indicate that dogs or cats influence health or morale more favorably than birds, horses, small mammals, or even fish or lizards.

At this stage in our investigation, we were concerned that pet ownership might reflect better health rather than influence health. To evaluate this question we constructed an index of the severity of the heart disease. A type of statistical analysis called "discriminate function" was used to determine if pet ownership helped in the prediction of survival even when the severity of the disease was taken into account. Pets added significantly to the ability of the "discriminate function" to predict survival, pet ownership accounting for about 3 percent of the variation in death rate. This is a small but significant effect. Considering the number of people who suffer from coronary artery disease, a 3 percent improvement in survival rate could make a significant contribution to a nation's health.

or by mothers with small children. The ability of animals to provide this feeling of intimacy permits another inference. We believe that companion animals can improve health. Human companionship has been shown to have a strong influence on health. People who are single, widowed, or divorced have higher age specific death rates, and higher rates of chronic disease than those who are married (Lynch 1977). Moreover, the loss of a family member can increase death and illness rates in the first few years after the loss.

It is perhaps unnecessary to remind you that large numbers of urban residents consider their cats and dogs as family members. Subjects are quite clear in stating that the pet has the status of a child in the family. Moreover, this statement is supported by other behaviors. Pets are posed in photographs like children, they sleep in the bed or bedroom, providing constant companionship during the entire daily cycle. They are talked to like people, and, in a significant number of instances, act as a kind of "wordless confident." Animals may be the only intimate companion, especially during adolescence, or during late life when people are isolated by the death of relatives and friends.

The Loss of a Pet

At present, we do not have enough information about the health significance of animal companions who are perceived as family members, but we do know that the loss of a loved animal companion can have severe negative influences both upon health and emotional states (Keddie, 1977, Rynearson, 1978, Katcher and Rosenberg, 1979, Quackenbush and Glickman, 1982). Psychotic depression and suicide can follow the death of a pet, as well as the less obvious phenomenon of "giving up" or the "helplessness-hopelessness syndrome" which is frequently a precursor to physical disease. Unfortunately, there are few support mechanisms for those who have lost a pet, and there is a general lack of knowledge among caretakers of the potential importance of such a loss. Indeed, many conceal their grief for fear of frank ridicule. It is obvious that pro-

The pattern of speech used with animals is slower, softer, higher pitched, and strings of words are shorter; this style of speech is associated with lower blood pressure.

The mere presence of a companion animal without any direct contact has been shown to make the experimental environment safer and resulted in lowered recorded blood pressures. Children brought into an experimental setting had lower blood pressures when a dog was present with the experimenter than when the experimenter was alone. Blood pressure was lower in the presence of the dog both when the children were sitting quietly and when they were engaged in the mildly stressful task of reading aloud.

Any phenomenon which attracts our attention away from our private worries and concerns can reduce blood pressure. Techniques of meditation

focus gaze or attention in a formal manner to interrupt thought and reduce stress. We have demonstrated that living objects attract attention and interrupt thought in the same way. Contemplation of a tank of tropical fish can significantly reduce blood pressure in both hypertensive and normal subjects. Reductions are of the same magnitude as those produced by biofeedback and meditation. Fish tanks are not only a visual object that can reduce stress; they also provide an outlet for the important activity of caring for another, and often increase communication with other people.

In addition to these findings, we observed that interaction with animals is characterized by a peculiar comforting combination of touching and talking which defines the feeling of intimacy. The voice tones and facial expressions resemble those used by lovers grams offering pets to people must be cognizant of the effects of the loss of such a pet and be prepared to make the appropriate therapeutic responses.

Many elderly individuals lose pets, not because of the death of the animal but because they are forced out of housing or are not able to enter public housing because of the pet. Having to give up a pet can be a severe source of stress leading to depression, physical illness, or even suicide. The older person who must give up a pet suffers a double loss, he loses the comfort of the pet and is exposed to the severe stress of the depression that follows that loss. There would be a direct therapeutic gain from laws to protect the rights of the elderly to keep the pets they already have.

There have been many epidemiological studies on the influence of social conditions and psychological and emotional states on health. Other than the ones mentioned, none of these investigations have recognized the existence of companion animals (or any other aspect of the non-human living environment). It is possible, however, to infer from this body of work which functions pets perform that might im-

> *A large number of social and physiological predictors were measured during hospitalization, and the patients were followed for one year. Pet ownership was associated with a lower death rate.*

prove the health of their owners (Katcher and Friedmann, 1980). Companionship was one example. In addition to companionship we have listed eight other functions of pets that would be expected to improve health. These are: Something that keeps you active, something to care for, something to touch, something to look at, something that makes you feel safe, a stimulus for exercise, a stimulus for play and laughter, and something that gives constancy to life.

It is not possible to discuss each of these functions in turn, however, one—the ability of pets to give people a feeling of being needed and to stimulate people to care for others—needs special comment. In examining the history of pet ownership in older individuals, we find that many who have loved animals in the past, have given

up caring for pets. Their relatives and friends convinced them to give up their "cares." They have been urged to give up working, give up caring for children, give up caring for houses, and give up civic and social responsibilities. This kind of cultural instruction places older people in a trap. They find that they are progressively worth less and less to others, and are progressively more dependent upon others. The feeling that they have nothing to care for, no one who "needs" them is a common reason for loss of self-esteem and depression in the aged. It is not always possible for older people to acquire relatives, friends, or social organizations that need them. However, companion animals do need their owners, need their care, their attention, and their love. The acts of caring that these animals stimulate may, in the long run, be worth more than an endless series of games and trips that seem to be prescribed for a "carefree" old age.

Conclusions

There is adequate evidence to suggest that companion animals can be a valuable means of improving health and morale in certain populations. While the data indicating a directly measurable health benefit from contact with companion animals are sparse, there is sufficient evidence that pets have important psychological and social functions. These functions have been shown to be important determinants of health or morale in epidemiological studies that investigate only human relationships. We also have direct evidence that pets can reduce stress and lower blood pressure by a variety of mechanisms.

Careful observation of the results of current pet placement projects could provide important data about the relationship between pets and health, *pro-*

vided that those responsible for the programs would collect relatively simple data on health, economic status, and the family status of the pet from the subjects in the programs. In similar fashion, the addition of a simple question about pet ownership to studies investigating the relationship between social factors and disease would greatly increase our knowledge about the true health value of companion animals.

Current data suggest that urban residents of secure means who have had a close relationship with a pet in the past would profit the most from companion animal placement programs.

We urgently require an organized program to protect the rights of the elderly to keep animals they already have. Laws and administrative decisions that deny access to low-cost housing to the elderly with pets pose a direct threat to their health and well-being. We have enough evidence to

suggest that the animal humane and medical communities should press for appropriate legislation to protect the right of the elderly to own pets in any kind of housing.

Because the loss of a companion animal is a direct health threat to the elderly, there is a need to make professionals more cognizant of the role that animals play in the life of some of the elderly and of the danger presented by the loss of an animal. There are almost no social support mechanisms for anyone grieving the loss of a pet. Such grief can be as dangerous to the psychic equilibrium or health of the elderly as the death of a human family member.

Current concepts of appropriate behavior for the elderly encourage them to give up commitments such as the commitment to keep a pet. There is a need to emphasize the value of an alternative way of life; a way of life

characterized by continued engagement in the care of living things. An emphasis on care giving may be one of the most healthy and emotionally sound ways for organizing your life after retirement from a primary career.

It is not necessary to seek positive evidence of a direct improvement in health to justify the continuation of visitation programs with animals for the institutionalized aged. These programs can be justified by their low cost and the large and directly observable positive emotional response of the elderly to contact with animals.

Relationships with companion animals fulfill important psychological and social needs at all stages of the life cycle. Examination of relationships between older people and their companion animals can provide us with important new information about the role of touch, intimacy, and caregiving activities in the aged.

BIBLIOGRAPHY

Franti, C.E., Kraus, J.F., and Borhani, N.O., "Pet Ownership in a Suburban Rural Area of California," *Public Health Repts.*, 89:473, 1974

Franti, C.E., et. al. "Pet Ownership in Rural Northern California (El Dorado County)," *JAVMA* 176:143, 1980

Friedmann, E., et. al. "Animal Companions and One Year Survival of Patients After Discharge From a Coronary Care Unit. *Pub. Health Rep.* 95:307, 1980

Friedmann, E., Katcher, A.H., and Meislich, D., "When Pet Owners Are Hospitalized: Significance of Companion Animals During Hospitalization," in *New Perspectives on Our Life With Companion Animals*, A. Katcher, and A. Beck eds. Univ. of Penna. Press. 1982, (in press)

Katcher, A.H., "Interactions Between People and Their Pets: Form and Function," in *Interrelations Between People and Pets*, Bruce Fogle ed., Charles C. Thomas, Springfield, 1981

Katcher, A.H., et. al. "Talking, Looking, and Blood Pressure: The Physiological Consequences of Interaction With the Living Environment," in *New Perspectives on Our Life*

With Companion Animals, A. Katcher, and A. Beck eds. Univ. of Penna. Press. 1982, (in press)

Katcher, A.H., "Man and the Living Environment: an Excursion Into Cyclical Time," in *New Perspectives on Our Life with Companion Animals*, A. Katcher, and A. Beck eds. Univ. of Penna. Press. 1982, (in press)

Katcher, A.H., and Rosenberg, M., "Euthanasia and the Management of the Client's Grief," *The Compendium on Continuing Education for the Practicing Vet.* 1:887, 1979

Katcher, and Friedmann, E., "Potential Health Value of Pet Ownership," *The Compendium on Continuing Education for the Practicing Vet.* 2:117, 1980

Keddie, K.M.G., "Pathological Mourning After the Death of a Domestic Pet," *Br. J. of Psych.* 131:21, 1977

Lago, D., Knight, B., and Connell, C., "Rural Elderly Relationships with Companion Animals," in *New Perspectives on Our Life with Companion Animals*, A. Katcher, and A. Beck eds. Univ. of Penna. Press. 1982, (in press)

Lynch, J., et. al. "Human Contact and Heart Arrhythmia: the Effects of Human Contact on Cardiac Arrhythmia in Coronary Care

Patients." *J. of Nervous and Mental Dis.* 158-88, 1974

Lynch, J. *The Broken Heart: The Medical Consequences of Loneliness.* Basic Books, New York, 1977

Mugford, R.A., and M'Comisky, J.G., "Some Recent Work on the Psychotherapeutic Value of Cage Birds With Old People," in *Pet Animals and Society,* R.S. Anderson Ed. Bailliere Tindall, London 1975

Ory, M., and Goldberg, E., "Pet Ownership and Life Satisfaction in Elderly Women," in *New Perspectives on Our Life with Companion Animals*, A. Katcher, and A. Beck eds. Univ. of Penna. Press. 1982. (in press)

Quackenbush, J. and Glickman, L., "Social Work Services for Bereaved Pet Owners: a Retrospective Case Analysis" in *New Perspectives on Our Life With Companion Animals*, A. Katcher, and A. Beck eds. Univ. of Penna. Press. 1982. (in press)

Robb, S. "Health Status Correlates of Pet Ownership in a Health-Impaired Population," in *New Perspectives on Our Life With Companion Animals*, A. Katcher, and A. Beck eds. Univ. of Penna. Press. 1982. (in press)

Rynearson, E.K., "Humans and Pets and Attachment," *Br. J. of Psych.* 133:550, 1978

Societal Attitudes Toward Old Age

There is a wide range of beliefs regarding the social position and status of the aged in American society today. Some people believe the best way to understand the problems of the elderly is to regard them as a minority group, faced with difficulties similar to those of other minority groups. Discrimination against older people, like racial discrimination, is based on a bias against physical traits, which can be easily observed. Since the aging process is viewed negatively, it is only natural that the elderly try to appear and act younger. Some individuals spend a tremendous amount of money trying to make themselves look and feel younger.

The theory that old people are a minority group is weak, however, because the exceptions are too numerous. The United States Congress, for example, favors elderly congressmen and senators, and delegates considerable prestige and power to them. Many older Americans are in good health, have comfortable incomes, and are treated with respect by friends and associates.

Perhaps the most realistic way to view the aged is as a status group, like other status groups in society.

Every society has some method of "age grading," by which it groups together individuals of roughly similar age. ("Pre-teens" or "senior citizens" are some of the age grades in our society.) Because it is a labeling process, age grading causes members of the age grade, as well as others, to perceive themselves primarily in terms of the connotation of the label. Unfortunately, the tag "old age" often carries with it a negative connotation in American society.

The readings included in this section illustrate the wide range of attitudes that exist toward older Americans.

Looking Ahead: Challenge Questions

Do most people see older persons as sexually inactive?

Do Americans generally look upon old age as a desirable or undesirable status?

How do the attitudes of children toward older persons differ from those of adults?

How are attitudes toward old age likely to change as older persons become an ever-larger segment of the total population?

Unit 3

AGEISM

The prejudice against
the elderly in this
country runs deep. Yet
scientific evidence
can refute national
fictions, including
the view that
old workers are
like worn-out,
obsolescent
machinery.

Robert N. Butler

Robert N. Butler, M.D., is the Director of the National Institute on Aging. His book Why Survive? Being Old in America *won him a Pulitzer Prize.*

As a society, we pay dearly for our fictions about aging. Since, at birth, everyone in our country stands a better than 50-50 chance of reaching conventional retirement age, our fictions turn out not to involve someone else. They turn out to be self-communications about our worth *in* later life and the worth *of* later life. If we believe in our youth and in our middle age that the older ages are a time of unalloyed depletion and imminent, if not actual, incapacity, then we are painting a dour prospect for our own futures.

Much of it need not come true, unless we insist on making it come true. As I shall show, scientific research offers evidence to refute our fictions, including the view that old workers are in the same class as worn-out, obsolete machinery. The notion that the older worker is necessarily less efficient than the younger worker cannot casually be allowed to pass, unless one already has the attitude that old people don't count. The notion won't pass muster scientifically unless one is talking about feats of strength and endurance, which occupy little of the work force in

our highly mechanized society. It is a most significant aspect of prejudice against the old—ageism.

It is becoming a more and more expensive notion to maintain. The costs of a nonworking elderly population—including many who are able and would like to continue working for the sake of money and emotional satisfaction—are astronomical. Just imagine the value of the population resource our society dismisses because of prejudice or poor planning and lack of imagination in both the public and private sectors. An estimated 2 to 4 million retirees over age 65 show interest in going back to work, full- or part-time, paid or voluntary, according to the National Committee on Careers for Older Americans. (Not included in the estimate are individuals aged 55–65, many of whom retire early in good health when unable to find employment.)

An observation was made not long ago by octogenarian George Burns that people can convince themselves to act according to stereotype—to think of themselves as unproductive, decrepit, and passive. In this instance the comedian wasn't kidding. A lot of people, he said, *practice* getting old. "They start to walk slower and they hold onto things. They start practicing when they're 70, and when they're 75 they're a hit. They've made it. They are now old."

The stereotype is too often fostered by the medical profession, as I, a physician, have observed. Many treatable medical problems in the elderly are assumed to be the inevitable consequences of aging, for which nothing can be done. A prime example is that of the confused older person who is brought into a hospital emergency room in the middle of the night, whose confusion prompts a casual diagnosis of "senility," and returns home in the care of a relative, who is advised to watch the old one carefully. There are scores of treatable causes of confusion. One is infection. The knowing physician will look for it in the confused elderly person. Antibiotics will clear up the infection—and the confusion. In my view, the origin of so-called senility often is not in the elderly patient but in the ageist physician. True organic brain diseases, such as Alzheimer's Disease, indeed exist; they are *not* inevitable results of the aging process, but diseases distinct from normal aging. A tragedy is that these devastating diseases are considered synonymous with old age by many. And also tragic is that, once labeled "senile," a patient can become, irretrievably, by persistent treatment as a sick incompetent, the image of senility.

The power of stereotype to override personal experience was shown in a 1976 survey by Louis Harris Associates for the National Council on the Aging. Survey participants reported favorably their experiences with old people but considered them to be exceptional. In sum, they preferred fiction to fact, at a cost phrased this way by the Harris report:

"If dismissed as a miserable, problem-ridden segment of society, the old will be viewed as merely another of society's problems and not as part of their solution.

"Such perceptions of the elderly can generate only a sense of guilt and pity among the young and not an appreciation for the talents and energies that older people can still contribute. Older people will consistently find themselves excluded from opportunities to pitch in and help. A group for whom there is little social and economic demand will necessarily lose self-esteem."

Among major costs of our fictions is the load placed on our retirement systems and the employers, employees and taxpayers who support them now and in the future. Pressure on people to retire early or at least "on time" and job conditions that make retirement even at a low income preferable to continued work have enlarged the load. Denying people the option to continue working also denies the contributions they could make to their own retirement resources.

At the same time our society has cut people off from major earnings simply because of age, it has extended the vigorous years of life through biomedical and other improvements. The conflict in deliberate and unwitting policy is painfully obvious in current debate over the financing of the Social Security system, a debate that rarely looks beyond the dollar and population statistics to see the new nature of old age in our country.

Gerontology, the study of aging and the aged, has some realities to share about what we are like, individually and as a population, when we become old. One in nine Americans is over age 65. Of the 25 million elderly, about 62 percent are under age 75; many do not resemble in appearance, educational background, and feebleness the elderly of past generations. The "very old" 38 percent of the elderly population cover a large age span, from 75 and up, including 2.3 million persons aged 85 or more. Among these are 12,000 centenarians.

Because women outlive men, the segment aged 75 and over is predominantly female. This group is far more likely to have disabling chronic disease. While relatively few elderly people are in nursing homes (1.1 million), most of their residents (81 percent) are above age 75. The nursing-home population is largely female (74 percent) and widowed or single (83 percent), lacking families to care for them at home.

The key fact is that 20 percent of the elderly population have no chronic condition at all and about 6 percent have at least one such condition—but it does not interfere with mobility and activities of daily living. As modern society has extended life expectancy at birth from the 48 years in 1900 to the 73.3 years in 1978, the additional years have largely been healthy ones. This result would have confounded the expectations of late 19th century Germany, where age 65 was selected as the retirement age under public programs. Why 65? *The belief that few people would survive to collect on contributions.*

At the same time 20th century America produced a large elderly population, its birth rate tended to decline, except for the wave of babies following World War II. When these babies reach age 65 in force, around the year 2020, the projected U.S. population of 290.1 million will have 45.1 million elderly—nearly 16 percent. The 75-plus segment will grow even faster.

These projections assume that the nation's fertility rate (the number of children borne by a woman) will be at a replacement level, one child per parent. Actually, it is now somewhat lower, 1.826. (Because of the large number of young and relatively young resulting from previous high rates, the population continues to grow at a little under one percent a year.) If the fertility rate turns out to be higher, the total U.S. population will be larger in 2020 and the proportion of elders less. If the fertility rate sinks further, more people will be retiring each year than entering the work force to help support them.

Under the fertility and other demographic assumptions already considered, the number of elderly dependents per 100 individuals aged 18 to 64 (as an indicator of the size of the working population) will rise from about 18 today to 29.6 in 2025. At the same time, however, the number of young dependents—persons under age 18—will drop from about 50 to 42. Therefore, the total dependency load will not be considerably larger than it is today. According to Herman Brotman, a consulting gerontologist, the picture indicates "a quite reasonable 'burden' on the (working-age) population under reasonable economic and labor force assumptions." Other commentators are less optimistic.

3. SOCIETAL ATTITUDES TOWARD OLD AGE

Projections are highly perishable products, even when salted with caution. For they obviously cannot take into account the likelihood of biomedical advances that may add years to the average life expectancy. What these advances will be is hard to say, specifically. But if current activity is a gauge, we surely can expect benefits in such areas as cancer and heart-kidney disease research. (As a measure of the effect of advances, total elimination of cardiovascular-renal diseases might add up to 10 years to average life expectancy at age 65; of cancer: 1.2 years.)

Biomedical advances will likely have a variety of effects: (a) to permit persons with extensive disabilities to survive even longer; (b) to prevent disabling conditions from occurring or to delay their occurrence until much later in life than now expected; and (c) to promote wellness and preserve vigor almost to the very end of life.

In the future, families will tend to have three or four generations alive at the same time. If the trend of women to leave home for employment continues, they will not be available, as they were in the past, to assist the disabled elderly. To keep up with inflation, not to speak of raising living standards, many families now and in the future will face hard choices between their elderly and income or the chance for a satisfying career in a work-oriented society. Moreover, the population of elderly persons over age 80—largely women, single and widowed—will continue to grow rapidly. If fertility and longevity projections are accurate, the aged who constituted the post-World War II "baby boom" will find themselves with few adult children to turn to, and these adult children—in or approaching the typically low-income retirement phase of life—probably will be unable to furnish extensive help. Since families today still provide the overwhelming proportion of the assistance many elderly people need to continue living outside of institutions, the future appears to confer a larger role on public and private agencies for financial aid or income maintenance, subsidized housing, and supportive medical and social services.

Beset as contemporary America is with immediate economic problems, it may be easy to push aside projections of things that are likely to haunt us a generation hence. We may well be in a grace period. It takes considerable time to plan and effectuate large societal changes without drastic pain. It is not too early to consider, for example, pressures in the health services area. These will be reflected not only in changing needs for personnel services and facilities to care for the elderly but also in contribution rates for Medicare, taxes for Medicaid, and insurance premiums for expansions to cover chronic physical and mental diseases.

The key population group in this regard is the very old, 75 and up. That population, now 38 percent of the elderly, will rise to 45 percent by the year 2000, or 14.3 million persons. Unless biomedical advances reduce various causes of disability, this population will continue to be a highly disproportionate user of health and social services.

We can choose to let the entire burden of support for the elderly fall all at once on the working populations in 2000, 2020, and after. A commentator on the politics and economics of health care, Anne Somers of New Jersey-Rutgers Medical School, thinks this is a poor option. "We have about 30 years to rethink and reorient our health care delivery and financing systems prior to the catastrophic situation that could confront us by 2020. Perhaps the chief obstacle to that rethinking will be the temporary illusion that it is not really necessary," she says. To ignore the trends may produce a hard conflict between the interests of the elderly and those of society at large.

A reasonable policy would encourage older persons to continue working—or at least not to foreclose the option—for as long as they are willing and able. Last year, average retirement age in 72 large corporations was reported to be 61.8 years, actually lower than in previous years. Officially, at least, the nation raised the retirement age. A 1978 Federal law forbids discrimination, solely on the basis of age, in hiring and firing for most occupations. Mandatory retirement before age 70 is illegal in the vast majority of occupations. Among the few exemptions are those for tenured faculty (until mid-1982) and for high-level executives and policymakers under certain circumstances. Mandatory retirement was entirely eliminated in Federal employment.

The law represents a clear recognition that a person's age is not a relevant qualification for hiring and firing. Dr. Arthur Flemming, a former Secretary of the Department of Health, Education, and Welfare, who has headed the U.S. Administration on Aging and is head of the U.S. Civil Rights Commission, asserts that "mandatory retirement is just a lazy man's device to avoid making a difficult personnel decision."

With the antidiscrimination law on the books, it is more important than ever that employers consider such issues as:

☐ Is there a scientific basis for determining when an individual can no longer handle a job?

☐ Are there elderly individuals who should be encouraged (a) to retire early, (b) to continue working despite handicaps, (c) to transfer to another job that makes use of their capacities, and (d) to be trained for different jobs or retrained for their old jobs?

☐ Are there ways to adapt the job to the worker so that his or her skills, talents, and experience can be utilized and interest in working maintained?

Some of these issues are right at the heart of our stereotypes about the elderly. What gerontology can tell the corporate executive today is fairly straightforward for most occupations:

The biological changes that come with normal aging tend to have little if any practical relevance in most jobs. Disease, of course, is another matter. The ability of human beings to compensate for deteriorations or to adapt to new occupational demands often seems bound only by motivations and expectations.

Much concern about older workers focuses on their cognitive abilities, a concern exemplified in the dreary old saw, "You can't teach an old dog new tricks." What people tend to ignore in that sentence is the "you." Effectiveness is often a matter of the trainer's prowess and expectation.

Does the ability to learn decline with age? Does the capacity to recognize, remember, and solve problems change in important ways as people age? An analysis of scientific findings about cognitive abilities was made recently by Iseli Krauss of the Andrus Gerontology Center at the University of Southern California, Los Angeles. "Though it would be misleading to say that there is *no* decline with age, it appears that significant decline is present in fewer individuals and in fewer abilities than had been thought. Furthermore, those abilities that do decline do so later in life than had been indicated by earlier studies," she observes.

Because of methodological limitations, some studies have fostered biased views of the elderly. In the typical cross-sectional comparison, the performance of elderly persons on an intelligence test is compared with that of young adults. The differences may not really describe aging effects but rather cohort effects. For example, the older individuals probably came from a group born at a stage in our social history when there was much less schooling than now. The older generation may have less facility and familiarity with pen-and-pencil tests. (Consider that the individual marking a 65th birthday now was born in 1915.) What have been called intelligence differences related to aging may be due to personality, or to background or an attitude toward testing that may interfere with performance.

Even where age differences have statistical validity, the results may be of little practical meaning unless test performance can be related to on-the-job performance. An evaluator must be able to identify the aspects of intellectual functioning that make a difference in the real-life situation. Is it a matter of applying skills under great pressure and applying them not simply adequately but with great prudence? Some individuals, as Strauss notes, are superb problem solvers if removed from deadline pressure, while others function best under pressure.

"There are enormous individual differences among the elderly in all areas of intellectual functioning," says Strauss. "Although groups of younger and older adults may differ in level of abilities, there is growing evidence that some older individuals demonstrate abilities at the highest level of the younger groups. It is quite probable that in many instances there are greater differences *within* the older population than between the younger and older populations. This factor has enormous implications for the effective use of older workers."

Are there any instances in which age is a valid indicator of an adult's suitability for a job? The anti-age-discrimination law allows for mandatory retirement of policemen, firemen, certain business executives, and professors. A debate has arisen around the current Federal Aviation Administration requirement that commercial airline pilots retire at age 60. Unable to settle the debate last year, Congress directed the National Institutes of Health to examine data on aging relevant to pilot performance and submit a report. NIH assigned the job to the National Institute on Aging (NIA). The law (PL 96-171) asks for a study to determine, among other things, "whether an age limitation which prohibits all individuals who are older than a particular age from serving as pilots is medically warranted" and the effect of aging on the ability of individuals to perform the duties of pilots with the highest level of safety."

For many years a basic issue in the study of aging has centered on chronological versus functional aging. The concept is that individuals of the same age may have functional mental and physical capacities more like older or younger persons. Surely, employers in an era of anti-age-discrimination law would greatly welcome a scientific criterion for retirement based on physiological capacity. Frankly, I suspect the chances are negligible that scientists could produce a single score or index of physiological age.

In terms of reductions in peak capacity, various organ systems within the body "age" at different rates. The output of the heart at rest declines steadily by about 1 percent per decade in healthy men aged 20 through 90. At any age, however, the range of individual values is large. As shown by the NIA Gerontology Research Center, some 70-year-old individuals have cardiac outputs at about the average of 50-year-old persons. Similarly, there are statistically significant age-related deficiencies, such as declines in blood flow through the kidney, lung capacity, nerve conduction velocity, muscle strength, and auditory and visual acuity. But the trends must be interpreted in the light of variations among individual performances that are quite broad. According to Dr. Nathan Shock, NIA scientist emeritus, there is no evidence that a general factor of "physiological age" exists. Scientists find many physiological ages within an individual, each related to a specific performance.

An attempt to assess physiological age was made recently at the NIA center by Dr. Gary Arthur Borkan and Mr. Arthur Norris, who directs the human performance section. Thanks to more than 850 volunteers who periodically come to the center for examination, a mass of standardized data is available so that these individuals may be compared with their younger selves as well as with one another at the same or different times. (Comparisons of an individual with his or her younger self are the essence of studies called "longitudinal," since they follow the axis of age. By contrast, cross-sectional studies—comparing old and young persons—cut across the age axis.) Borkan and Norris studied results of two dozen tests

What if diseases of late life are eliminated?

Much of what we think of as aging today is actually disease and illness, and not a part of fundamental physical aging. This includes many of the physical, mental and emotional conditions seen in older people. The major diseases of late life may become preventable or at least treatable. The mental depressions of late life and the acute brain syndromes are already treatable and reversible. The removal of pathogenic elements—excessive sun exposure and cigarette smoking (both are causes of skin wrinkles), air pollution and others—may slow down the physical appearances of deterioration. Even genetic traits responsible for such changes as graying and loss of hair may eventually be controllable. What is in the future if acute and chronic disease states are identified and largely eliminated, undesirable genetic traits mainly nullified and pathogenic environmental conditions alleviated? We should see for the first time that flow of human life from birth through death truly called aging. Aging refers to patterns of late-life changes which are eventually seen in all persons but which vary in rate and degree. Although human beings will never be able to live indefinitely, they can live much longer and more comfortably, mostly free from the violent ravages of disease, with perhaps a gradual and fairly predictable decline toward eventual death.

The physical health of the majority of the elderly is already better than is generally believed. Eighty-one percent of those over 65 are fully ambulatory and move about independently. Ninety-five percent live in the community; at any one time only 5 percent are in nursing homes, chronic-disease hospitals and other institutions—a startling fact when one thinks of the popular image of the old "dumped" en masse into institutions by their families because they have become enfeebled.

by Robert N. Butler
from *Why Survive? Being Old in America*,
Reprinted by permission of Harper & Row, Publishers, Inc.
Copyright © 1975 by Robert N. Butler, M.D.

and measurements taken in volunteers at their first visit to the center. The data were grouped in five-year age ranges. Average scores were worked out for each trait by age bracket. Statements could then be made about the extent to which an individual's score resembled the average performance in a trait for his chronological peers or older and younger groups. Taking these rankings for various traits, a biological age profile was constructed. On this basis, a person could be said to be biologically older or younger than his age peers.

As part of the study, physicians who had examined the individuals were asked to appraise whether they looked older or younger than their age. Since some subjects were members of the same families, the profiles could be

assessed for genetic influences. Finally, the first-examination data for volunteers who had died were compared with corresponding data for volunteers still alive. Here are some of the findings:

☐ Individuals who had died were, at first examination, generally biologically older than their age peers.

☐ Physicians' subjective appraisals appeared to agree with Borkan-Norris characterizations of individuals as biologically older or younger.

☐ Individuals in relatively worse physical or mental health, or who were fatter or less active, tended to be biologically older.

☐ To a small extent, life-style variables (e.g., smoking, calisthenics, nutrition) could predict the biological age of individuals.

☐ Since persons biologically younger than their age tended to have biologically young siblings and parents, there may be a genetic component.

My own research convinces me that disease is the pacemaker for incapacity far more than any aging process so far discerned. It may be that subtle bodily changes over long periods of time set the stage for diseases. If so, these changes are, so far, too subtle to be identified as clear heralds or symptoms of disease. A possibility is that a pattern of disease may be the manifestation of aging in one or more body systems or some central mechanism. The clearest support we have for such a speculation comes from the observation that with age the likelihood of fatal disease increases at an accelerating pace.

In 1956, I collaborated in a National Institute of Mental Health study that persuaded me that aging and disease, while interrelated, were not the same. We studied 47 men aged 65 to 91. During a two-week examination period, some 600 characteristics were recorded for each person. Twenty-seven men had no observed evidence of any disease or had only slight evidence of trivial disease, and 20 had only slight evidence of possibly serious disease, evidence so slight as to be undetectable in any but the most sophisticated examination.

These men—vigorous, candid, interesting, and deeply involved in everyday living—were followed for 11 years. In that time, 24 died. We looked back at the records to learn what events and characteristics might have influenced the ability of 23 to survive while 24 died.

The 23 survivors included 17 from the panel of "super healthy" men. This suggested that the little bit of disease found in the other panel indicated greater vulnerability to death.

The chance that half the group would survive for 11 years was considerably less than 50-50 on the basis of average life expectancy for their ages in 1956. The reexamination showed no major reduction in mental performance owing to organic cause. The survivors generally reported some drop in vigor but not enough to discontinue activities at home or in the community. Aware of lessened vigor, they tended to regulate their lives accordingly. The overall picture was one of gradual erosion of physical and mental capacities, especially in the reserves needed for times of heavy stress.

The survivors offered me a glimpse of aging virtually beyond the shadow of disease, a picture hardly like Shakespeare's characterization of old age as "second childishness, and mere oblivion, sans teeth, sans eyes, sans taste, and sans everything."

When disease appeared, deterioration was likely to be systematic. The first signs of such major deterioration appeared in the performance of the chief communicating systems of the body, the cardiovascular and central nervous systems. This raises the speculation that the development of highly refined psychomotor tests, to be given periodically, might provide an estimate of the earliest presence of disease somewhere in the body. With such a tool of preventive medicine to give the alarm, the physician could begin a diagnostic workup to find the specific origins of the functional decline.

Disease-oriented research and aging research have common concerns, but they also differ in the way they look at and approach problems. For example, researchers in the fields of aging and cancer want to know what factors permit the development and spread of tumors. The researcher studying the aging process is primarily concerned with the changes that occur normally with time and set the stage for cancer and other diseases to appear. The National Institute on Aging and the National Cancer Institute have plans for investigators in both fields to confer on common research issues.

Differences between aging and disease-oriented research might best be described simply in this way: The disease-oriented biologist looks for disruptions in normal functioning, such as those caused by an outside chemical or infective agent. The gerontologist looks for changes in the organism that occur normally with time and in its environmental interactions. A product of disease-oriented research may be a vaccine of antibiotic against a specific agent. Aging research would concentrate on ways of preserving the immune system so the old organism is at less risk of succumbing to a wide variety of assaults.

While the main thrust of the National Institutes of Health has been in disease-oriented research, the NIH commitment to the study of aging goes back 40 years to the establishment of a small unit under Dr. Shock. In the early 1960s, Congress created the National Institute of Child Health and Human Development, to which the aging program was attached. In 1974 the National Institute on Aging was created by Congress. The objective: to give prominence and further organization to Federally conducted and supported research in aging. The NIA mandate extends beyond biomedical investigations. It includes study of social and behavioral problems of the elderly. Thus, NIA supports studies in epidemiology (patterns of disease in populations), demography, and research economics (including an attempt to project the macroeconomic consequences of the nation's growing elderly population).

The studies NIA conducts itself or supports at universities, hospitals, and communities provide facts for policymakers, including those in the business world, for physicians, and for individuals to apply in understanding self and society. Besides genetic, cellular, and organ-system investigations, NIA's range of study includes: physical fitness and aging; sleep disturbances in old age; medical and emotional consequences of retirement; methods useful in a flexible retirement system for determining an individual's ability to function; nutritional needs of the aged; organic brain diseases, especially senile dementia; differences in life expectancy between the sexes and among racial and ethnic groups; development of prosthetic devices for persons with sensory and motor impairment; environmental influences on aging; and preventive medicine for older persons.

What is the actual or potential practical value of this research effort? Relevance to criteria for retirement and to medical diagnosis, treatment, and preventive medicine already have been touched on. I expect aging research, in addition, to produce strategies for cost containment and cost effectiveness.

For example, the nation spent about $18 billion last year for nursing-home care. Much of it was financed from Federal-state Medicaid funds, which means taxes paid by individuals and businesses. Individuals who do not meet income-based criteria for eligibility for Medicaid assistance pay out-of-pocket. There is next to no private insurance for long-term care in nursing homes. For some individuals and families, nursing-home expenses are a major cause of indigency. (Medicare, essentially meeting hospital and doctor expenses, does not cover long-term nursing-home care.)

Nursing-home spending by the nation has grown by about 17 or 18 percent annually since 1976, while spending for personal health care in toto has risen between 12 and 14 percent. Mental impairments reputedly are largely responsible for admissions to nursing homes. Senile dementia of the Alzheimer's type is among these impairments. Because the individual is confused or disoriented much of the time, he or she needs constant supervision. Of the 1 million residents of nursing homes, perhaps as many as 500,000 are there because of these impairments. If this estimate is correct, there are billion dollar reasons for focusing research resources on senile dementia of the Alzheimer's type and other causes of mental impairment.

I do not think it is overly optimistic to believe that research will furnish a basis for preventing, ameliorating, and curing some of these cases. Some individuals may be restored to their homes at considerable savings to themselves and to public and private third parties.

Research of potential cost-containment significance is not limited to the biomedical realm. Perhaps 25,000

3. SOCIETAL ATTITUDES TOWARD OLD AGE

Americans die annually following the death of a loved one. The bereavement period is recognized as extremely stressful and may set the stage for disability and dependency as well as for death. NIA is supporting sociobehavioral research on the bereavement period in an effort to find models of successful coping and means of helping people to emerge from bereavement in good health.

One use for research that identifies "successful" aging is that it permits efforts to be focused on the physical, psychological, and social factors that produce it. Gerontology, largely in a descriptive phase of this research, is moving into theory-based investigation.

Considering the potential payoffs, this nation has only lightly invested in aging research. I am told that a criterion of adequate research investment in the industrial sector is 2 to 3 percent of sales. Applying such a criterion to the $35 billion in Federal spending on health benefits in fiscal 1980 for the elderly (construing benefits as "sales"), one would expect an investment of $700 million or more in aging research. The actual fiscal 1980 outlay by the Federal government, the prime funder of aging research, is $57 million. That's 0.16 percent of benefit outlays, hardly a lavish expenditure. This is not to say that the aging research field seeks or could justifiably absorb an enormous increase in funding through public and private sectors. However, when opportunities are recognized, further investment should merit careful consideration.

In addition to possible cost-containment strategies, aging research may produce greater spending obligations—by raising the chances of survival to the oldest ages. With more people living longer and in better health, social policy decisions affecting pensions and other income maintenance programs will be necessary. Will these decisions be made in the context of added years of survival being a "burden" to be paid for grudgingly or a benefit to be paid for willingly? The answer to this question depends on how well our society grasps the new realities of old age and casts off damaging fictions.

The extent to which research and other advances will improve the health status of elderly Americans cannot be stated precisely, but we can have confidence that improvements will occur. Public and private policymakers should begin considering a variety of challenges:

☐ More older workers for whom retirement is not mandated by physical or mental status and for whom it makes no economic sense.

Retirement story

Grace Tully, who was Franklin D. Roosevelt's secretary for 17 years and recently celebrated her 80th birthday, uses a cane to get about. "This isn't arthritis," she explained to *The New York Times*, "this is retirement. Tell people not to retire because you suddenly find yourself not able to walk."

☐ An extension of average life expectancy that will overwhelm income maintenance systems based on obsolete actuarial assumptions.

☐ The lessened ability of families—now extended into three or four generations, with women more likely to be employed outside the home—to provide for very old members.

☐ Restructuring the health establishment to meet the special needs of geriatric patients.

☐ The design or adaptation of communities, houses, shopping centers, roads, and jobs to meet human needs as they change over the entire life course.

☐ Finding ways to employ everyone able and willing to work, including adaptation of jobs to make the most of employee abilities and to maintain interest in working.

☐ Through financial and human capital investment, to create the productivity improvements for supporting good standards of living across the life span.

The elderly are a valuable resource; they are available to contribute to the nation's productivity, out of which retirement needs are supported. At a time of a fertility rate below replacement, a shortage of Depression-born workers, and possibly a lessened ability to maintain the high rate of productivity, it does not make sense to foreclose on the older employee. Nor does it make sense to confer sole responsibility for productivity increases on the 18 to 64 population; rather, the responsibility and the benefits might better be shared across the life span.

Can we cope with the job-creation and job-adaptation issues in the context of changing demography, needs to raise productivity, and pressure to economize on natural resources, and contain inflation? It is and will be extremely important for public and private sectors to share information on successes and failures in dealing with the new demographics. The National Institute on Aging is eager to hear from corporate officials and to make information available from the research it supports.

The time to work on creating choices is now. The growth of the elderly population is more than a problem: it also is a solution, once we remove the blinders of ageism and deal with realities.

Continuity

A Gift From The Older Generation

Carol H. Tice

Carol H. Tice is founder of the T-LC Program in the Ann Arbor schools and president of New Age, Inc., a nonprofit center established to support intergenerational learning in Ann Arbor, Mich.

Today's adult often begins the day to sounds of newscasters reporting variable changes in the weather. These predictions vary—from cloudless skies to forecasts of life-giving rain. The occasional warnings of storms and the possible ensuing destruction remind us of our vulnerability as human beings.

Certainly the weather, with its many moods and changes, holds our attention; its behavior provides, in times of great uncertainty in other parts of our lives, a common base or experience on which we can structure at least some of our immediate plans. The adult knows and understands at a basic level that seasons come and go with reassuring regularity, reminding us of the rhythm and continuity of the life cycle.

While the weather holds meaning for today's children—particularly when a ball game is scheduled—they have lived too few years for the changing seasons to become significant points of reference. Children of earlier, rural America understood the relation of land, water and air in reference to their own survival. They participated in the planting, the caring for and the harvesting of visible and tangible crops that were

Photo: Julie Steedman

Reprinted by permission from *Childhood Today*, September/October 1982, pp. 2-6.

then prepared into meals from recipes handed down through generations and enjoyed at the family table. A sense of the future was transmitted as a child learned to preserve food for the winter months through canning, drying, smoking and pickling. The activity was carried out with brothers and sisters, cousins and aunts, as well as parents. While hands were busy cutting, chopping and grinding, family and community traditions were passed on through the telling of story after story. The heroes and heroines were family members. Sometimes the children themselves were the honored ones.

Celebrations came with regularity and could be counted on as a part of anticipating the year ahead. Family, school, church and community were root systems that substantially nourished growing young lives. Storms of consequence came and went but the roots remained steady through structure and tradition. The seasons continued to foster meaningful activities central to the child's life. Familiarity with the processes of birth, marriage, old age and death contributed toward a child's grasping of his or her place in the world as a youth, a future parent and eventually a grandparent. The life cycle was made visible and explicit.

The social context of children in the United States today is industrialized and characterized by various forms of fragmentation. Higher and higher levels of specialization, occupational mobility and rapid technological change are forces that move us apart rather than bring us together. Feelings of isolation, loneliness and of being disenfranchised are increased. Personal and social alienation often develop.

Family structures are undergoing dramatic changes, too, with large numbers of children living with a single parent while others are adjusting to half-brothers and sisters, stepparents, uncles and aunts in large and newly-merged families.

Age groups have become more and more separated as the number of people over 60 rapidly increases and they seek to live out their retirement years in special buildings or entire communities built exclusively for the old.

The role of education has shifted

Photos: Teaching-Learning Communities

as school buildings near to home are closed and children are transported across town because they are black, white, handicapped or gifted, or because enrollment numbers are down. Instead of continuing as places of nurture, schools often become breeding grounds for vandalism and violence. It has become more and more difficult to focus upon teaching and learning in such settings.

In the midst of dramatic changes that we as adults sometimes find difficulty in comprehending, what kind of guideposts can we provide for our children? Without turning the clock back, what will it take to restore a sense of continuity to them? How can we affirm human values in the midst of the alienation and despair expressed today by so many of our young?

Tapping the vast reservoir of love and wisdom found in our older people could provide that dimension of continuity and a new sense of hope for the children who will one day lead our country.

Increased attention is being given to the potential of bringing old and young together in common activities. The idea, once a natural phenomenon in more rural America, makes sense. A number of programs which have been operating since the early 1970s have brought the groups

together in voluntary teaching/learning and service exchanges. The benefits in growth and feelings of well-being appear to occur at both ends of the age spectrum.

The learning and development of children and youth are nurtured when they receive special attention from loving adults who have the time and patience to listen to and communicate with them. The young gain a vital sense of continuity with traditions of the past, along with guideposts for the future in times of rapid technological and social change. Life-coping skills are mastered in an apprenticeship setting where the personal relationship between, say, an older volunteer in the school and a 5th-grader is as important as the sewing skill being learned. Understanding and respect for the aging process develops through positive, personal association of a child with an oldster, and confidence in the future is encouraged. Both age groups feel less isolated, lonely and disenfranchised. Feelings of usefulness are fostered among the older volunteers when their gifts of shared skills, patience and wisdom are valued. Similar feelings are generated among the young when they reach out to an older person with affection, understanding and encouragement. The physical and mental health of older people often improves as a result of their new contacts and interests.

Within the last decade, increasing efforts have been made toward establishing programs that strengthen communications between senior citizens and the young. The program activities vary, ranging from those in which older adults "coach" parents whose children have been placed in foster care to programs that draw on the arts and humanities as an all-important link in bridging the generation gap. A common thread among programs, regardless of the particular activity being carried out, is often an educational theme of one sort or another.

Such integrating initiatives are being generated by local, state and national agencies that had tradi-

Copyright 1982 U.S. Postal Service

tionally addressed only one segment of the age spectrum. Interest and support in them are growing at a rapid rate. In its *Final Report* to the President, the U.S. National Commission on the International Year of the Child (1980) called for more involvement on the part of older people in the schools. Recognizing the need for continuity in children's lives, the report explains, "Older people, better than anyone else, are able to link children with living history, with diversity in life circumstances and with the roots of cultural heritage."

Another example of this growing interest is seen in the fact that, for the first time, the National Association for the Education of Young Children is planning a day-long intergenerational caucus for its November 1982 meeting.

In 1981, the White House Conference on Aging highlighted the potential of utilizing older people's experience in service of the young for the benefit of both generations. And last May, the Administration on Aging sponsored the first Commis-

sioner's Forum, on the theme of "Aging Together: Intergenerational Relationships," as part of Older Americans Month observances.[1] At the same time, the U.S. Postal Service released a commemorative "Aging Together" stamp that sold out within days of issue.

ACTION's Foster Grandparent Program, which has been pairing older adults with children in institutional settings since 1965, has gained recognition and support from many, including our First Lady, Nancy Reagan. At present, about 18,000 Foster Grandparents are providing companionship and guidance to about 54,300 children in 235 projects in all 50 states and the District of Columbia, Puerto Rico and the Virgin Islands.[2]

Another ACTION program, the Retired Senior Volunteer Program (R.S.V.P.), continues to assist older people in volunteering with the young in a wide variety of settings. Today, 319,000 R.S.V.P. volunteers serve in 728 projects in all the states, the District of Columbia, Puerto Rico, the Virgin Islands and Guam. They serve, on a regular basis, in courts, schools, libraries, day care centers, hospitals and other community service centers.[3]

At the grassroots, thousands of local projects have united old and young in meaningful encounters. At this level, the range of activities is as broad as the country is wide, featuring educational and recreational emphases as well as service dimensions. National clearinghouses are currently making attempts to gather and catalogue programs in the interest of sharing philosophies and strategies.[4]

Many indigenous programs remain local and specific to the group for which they were designed, while others have been adapted on a widespread basis. Tutorial programs in schools where older people become assistants to teachers in defined tasks have been facilitated through the National School Volunteer Program and R.S.V.P. Training materials and assistance are available through these agencies.

In the early 1970s, an innovative intergenerational program, "Teaching-Learning Communities (T-LC)," was begun in the Ann Arbor, Michigan schools. The program is based

on the "common needs" approach: everyone teaches and everyone learns in this "gift exchange" of ideas, skills and interests. The older volunteer who participates in the school programs may select and offer whatever is of the greatest importance to him or her in teaching, sharing and refining a skill or knowledge. Thus a process of continued growth and identity reinforcement is provided for the older person, and a treasure trove of enthusiasm, support and enrichment for the child.

The T-LC program began in one school in Ann Arbor in 1971. The following year the city obtained a small grant from the Michigan Council for the Arts to expand it to three other schools. Two years later Ann Arbor received a $154,000 grant under Title IV-C of the Elementary and Secondary Education Act to develop the project into a demonstration program that could be evaluated and adapted by other communities. The program now operates in all 50 states, in both metropolitan and rural areas.

In Ann Arbor, where eight schools have T-LC programs, the annual cost to the city is $13,165, which pays the salaries of one half-time program coordinator and eight part-time community aides, as well as the cost of supplies. The T-LC program has also served as a resource for possible adaptation in seven other countries, including Australia, Canada, China and Japan.

The Teaching-Learning Communities Program apprentices hundreds of children to volunteer "grandpersons." The elders, coming from their own homes and apartments as well as from nursing and retirement homes, are a multi-ethnic group. Their social, educational and occupational backgrounds vary considerably, and their ages range from 60 to 94. The array of projects undertaken has included fine arts, creative writing and poetry, photography, film making, nutrition and cooking, gardening, and storytelling. Grandpersons come to school once a week and work cooperatively with teachers who wish to welcome a volunteer into their learning environment. Little space is required. The interchange between generations can happen in classrooms, media centers, art rooms and even empty spaces like hallways.

3. SOCIETAL ATTITUDES TOWARD OLD AGE

Creative activity is a clue to the difference between a T-LC project and a tutorial program. For instance, in interviews with potential volunteers, the men and women are asked what they enjoy doing and what their special interests are. In answer to these questions, one women had said she had no special interest. After some more conversation, however, she confided: "Well, I do like to raise moths." "You'll be a smashing success when you share this interest with the children," she was told, and she was.

Another volunteer I knew in Ann Arbor, a woman who had been born in China, showed the children in the school in which she volunteers how to raise silkworms. The children there learned some Chinese along with ancient silkworm culture.

The arts and humanities serve as a foundation upon which other learning disciplines find their place. Thus the dimension of human values is reinforced whatever the activity taking place. The apprentice style of T-LC is informal, allowing for leisurely discussion in which values may be explored and shared along with information and skills. The emphasis is on relationship. Continuity is a natural outcome, linking children to new and beloved older friends, a sense of history about their own community and a dimension of hope in relation to their lives in the future.

Evaluation and research over the past 10 years have indicated that the teaching-learning "gift exchange" approach of the T-LC concept benefits all age groups involved, meeting needs well beyond the given "skill exchange" of a given day's interaction. The children say it best in their own words:

"Seeing you is like seeing the sun get up which is a very beautiful thing to me. Thank you." (Becky)

I LOVE TLC BECAUSE WE DO THINGS WE DON'T JUST TALK ROBERT

". . . .I really like this class, Mrs. Heald. I am proud of the stories I have written here. When I'm in this class is

Photo: Ken Heyman

the only time I can really write well. Thank you for taking the time. . . ."

"I especially like rug-braiding. It's new to me. But I loved doing it because I did it with you." (Phoebe)

"I love the skin on your arm. It looks like the ripples on a stream and it is soft like grandpa's." (A first grader)

"I love T-LC because we do things; we don't just talk." (Robert)

Research relating to the benefits of intergenerational programs for older people has been conducted by the University of Michigan and the Ann Arbor Public Schools.[5]

Margaret Mead, visiting the T-LC project in 1976, referred to it as a process in which children and old people invent the future together.

With the bonds of continuity generated through the teaching-learning concept, informal networks of caring are set in motion. When her grandperson become ill, one 3rd-grader wrote: "I miss you and I feel so worry (sic) about you while you are gone away from everybody. Wish you were here again. Love, Pamela."

Children and grandpersons often stay in contact by phone or mail for several years after the interaction at schools has ended. How important the companionship of older people

can be to some of the children in schools where T-LC volunteers serve was illustrated recently when one 10-year-old boy, who had run away from home, returned. He came back—not to his home—but to his school classroom and his visiting "grandparent."

While the T-LC program began in a local elementary school and was originally designed to meet educational needs of children, the concept has been adapted to other settings, such as libraries, parks, churches, civic theater programs and health care facilities.

In order to provide technical assistance to volunteers and professionals in developing new ways of thinking, planning and working toward intergenerational programs based on the teaching/learning framework, New Age, Inc., a non-profit center for intergenerational education, service and research, was established in Ann Arbor in 1979. Guidelines and other materials based on the T-LC model and other programs adapted from it are available from New Age.[6]

The 3-year-old organization works with Bank Street College of Education in New York City and the Institute of Gerontology, University of Michigan in Ann Arbor, to provide training workshops.[7] It is also developing a film, *All We Can Be*, that will draw on the wisdom of older people to guide young adolescents in planning their future. (As co-producer, with the University of Michigan, of the award-winning 1981 16 mm film, *What We Have*, I learned the value of documenting intergenerational activities and using film as a motivating and teaching resource.)

Also soon to be available to the public is the report on a conference entitled "Linking the Generations for a Caring Society," held two years ago at Wingspread, the Educational Conference Center of the Johnson Foundation.[8] Initiated by New Age, the conference was held in coopera-

tion with the Smithsonian Institution Office of Symposia and Seminars, Michigan State University and others. Additional conferences on related themes are now being planned.

Today's children deserve whatever processes we can set in motion toward affirming values that strengthen families, schools, churches and communities. The arts can provide new images from which to create positive responses to difficult challenges. By bringing old and young together through the arts, perhaps we can all find a touchstone of continuity from which to take hold of life energy and give those images form and function.

---

[1] See "Between Generations," News and Reports Section, CHILDREN TODAY, Jul.-Aug. 1982.

[2] More information on the program may be obtained by writing Foster Grandparents, ACTION, Washington, D.C. 20520.

[3] More information on this program is available from R.S.V.P., ACTION, Washington, D.C. 20520.

[4] For example, information on a variety of programs is available from Intergenerational Clearinghouse, RSVP of Dane County, Inc., 540 W. Olin Ave., Room 137, Madison, WI 53715.

[5] See Tice, Carol, "Creating Caring Communities," *Aging*, May-June 1982.

[6] For information on available materials, write to New Age, Inc., 1212 Roosevelt, Ann Arbor, MI 48104. (A self-addressed, stamped envelope should be enclosed.)

[7] For information on the training workshops, write to New Age, Inc. at the above address.

[8] For the conference report, write to Wingspread, Johnson Foundation, Racine, WI 53401.

Will you still love me?

Morton Puner

Of all the myths about old age, perhaps the cruelest stereotypes concern "dirty old men" and "dried-up old maids." They aren't necessarily so.

This article is adapted from the book To The Good Long Life published by Universe Books. Morton Puner has been a book editor and magazine writer. A member of the Gerontological Society, he now lives and works in St. Tropez, France.

For the old, the sexual revolution came 50 years too late. They can hear and read about it but they cannot touch. For they are burdened with the idea—society's and often their own—that sex isn't for them.

The jokes about the old, usually bad and sometimes terrible, suggest their predicament. A study of "Attitudes Toward Aging as Shown by Humor," by Duke University's Erdman Palmore found that most of the jokes—"especially those dealing with physical ability or appearance, age concealment, old maids and mental abilities"—

reflect a negative view of aging. Some were downright hostile.

His analysis begins with the comment of a 75-year-old acquaintance: "After you reach a certain age, you discover that most jokes about aging aren't funny anymore"—a line which echoes Will Rogers's "Everything is funny as long as it happens to somebody else." Dr. Palmore's collection of jokes about the old, as they appear in *The Gerontologist*, surrounded by interpretation and summary, must be the saddest ever. Among them:

On death—The funeral of a comedian in London was attended by many old-time comedians who had gathered to say a last farewell. During the ceremony, one looked up at his neighbor and asked, " 'Ow old are you, Charlie?" "Ninety," replied the old-timer. " 'Ardly worth going 'ome, eh?"

On declining mental ability—"Four stages of memory loss: (1) forget names; (2) forget faces; (3) forget to zip up fly; (4) forget to zip down fly."

Many of the 264 jokes analyzed by Dr. Palmore are specifically about sexual ability or interest. This is a sampling:

Definition of old age—"The time of life when a man flirts with girls but can't remember why."

Oscar Wilde—"Young men want to be faithful and are not; old men want to be faithless and cannot."

Description of the sexual life cycle of a man—"Triweekly. Try weekly. Try weakly."

"A 90-year-old man married a beautiful 18-year-old girl. He lasted only five days

but it took the undertaker three weeks to get the smile off his face."

Old women are viewed as lonely, frustrated and shriveled:

Definition of an old maid—"A lemon that has never been squeezed."

"An old woman was held up by a robber who proceeded to frisk her for money. After a thorough search all over her body, he gave up. She exclaimed, 'Heavens, young man, don't stop now—I'll write you a check.' "

Dr. Palmore also weighs the significance of the facts that there are no "old bachelor" jokes and that more of the jokes about women are negative (77 percent) than are the jokes about men (51 percent).

Dr. Palmore's materials came from such Middle American standbys as *The Speaker's Treasury of Stories for All Occasions.* There are countless other sources and types of jokes about the old, often more felicitously phrased if more ribald. Frank Harris in *My Life and Loves*, wrote about a witticism of Degas, who lived to 83. Degas heard someone condemning cunnilingus, to which he replied with an old French saying: *"Quelle triste vieillesse vous vous préparez!"* (What a dreary old age you are making for yourself). In his *Rationale of the Dirty Joke*, G. Legman, an authority on erotica, devotes a 40-page chapter to jokes about old age, with section headings such as "Old Wives for New" and "Impotence of Husbands." Among his examples are:

"A young man sees his father coming out of a notorious brothel. 'Father!' he says, shocked. 'Son,' says the father, 'say nothing. I

From *Human Behavior*, June 1974. Originally from *TO THE GOOD LONG LIFE: What We Know About Growing Old*, by Morton Puner, Universe Books, New York, 1974 prefer the simulated enthusiasm of a paid prostitute to the dignified acquiescence of your mother.' "

"An elderly roue at a brothel insists he wants his usual girl, Mamie, who happens to be occupied. The madam vainly offers him various other girls and finally asks: 'Well, what has Mamie got that the other girls don't have' 'Patience,' he replies."

Mr. Legman also includes the French proverb, *Si jeunesse savait; si vieillesse pouvait,"* which has its English equivalent, "If youth only knew; if age only could." Actually, age can. And particularly in marriage or remarriage. All these jokes about the old are gross caricature, cruel and misleading.

There are "two great invalid and destructive myths" about the old, according to sociologist James A. Peterson. One is the idea, held by almost all young and middle-aged persons, that a new marriage for the elderly is foolish and inappropriate. The second myth, "even more devitalizing, is that sexual joy is reserved for those in the first decades of life and that physical intimacy is somehow proscribed" in later years. "These myths are so pervasive and powerful," he says, "that they have caused millions of older persons to live lives of loneliness and frustration." Dr. Peterson cited a number of scientific findings, including those of Dr. William H. Masters and Virginia E. Johnson of the Reproductive Biology Research Foundation and authors of *Human Sexual Response* and *Human Sexual Inadequacy.* There are changes, of course, as there are in any phase of aging, but Masters and Johnson found that there is no age limit to sexual responsiveness and "sexual interaction between older marital partners can be established easily, warmly and with dignity."

Dr. Peterson, an admirer of the Masters-and-Johnson studies, says they assure a man, for example, that he need not ejaculate to have a "rewarding physical closeness" with his wife. "As a male ages, he becomes alarmed when intercourse does not result in ejaculation and he fears that he is becoming impotent," Dr. Peterson says. But if the man understood that intercourse can be rewarding with or without ejaculation, he would soon find out that he can ejaculate periodically and without stress. If he is anxious, he may become impotent and fail in his sexual attempts.

The facts of life for aging women are given in a direct quotation from Masters and Johnson: "There are only two basic needs for regularity of expression in the 70- to 80-year-old woman. These necessities

are a reasonably good state of health and an interested and interesting partner."

The ability to be an interested and interesting partner is often difficult to sustain after four or five years of marriage. To sustain it after 40 or 50 years of the same marriage requires more than simple passion. It also requires more than the repetition of sexual stimuli. Routinized lovemaking is no more exciting than dressing. "As a couple ages, both the man and the woman require new experiences. Habit is the master of the unimaginative. . . ."

"Sexual interaction between older marital partners can be established easily, warmly and with dignity."

In explaining about the increasing joy of sexual play, Dr. Peterson does everything but draw pictures for exciting new approaches to love among the old. As interesting as his statements is the fact that they appear in an article he wrote for *Modern Maturity*, not a scientific journal but a magazine edited with the popular appeal and professionalism of the *Reader's Digest* and published by the American Association of Retired Persons, an organization with about six million members. The magazine is a fine blend of history, current events, criticism, nostalgia, and practical advice for its readers of postretirement age; the fact that its editors approached the subject of sex in old age so directly is an indication of how seriously the problem is felt.

Perhaps no mass-circulation, middle-brow magazine in the world published articles with such candid talk about orgasm, ejaculation and masturbation until 1948, when Dr. Alfred C. Kinsey and his associates at Indiana University issued *Sexual Behavior in the Human Male.* Its publishers felt the need to include a foreword explaining that the book was intended primarily for scientists and other professionals. But mass interest in the subject matter was ready and waiting; Dr. Kinsey and his colleagues handled their studies and publicizing of their findings with such care, skill and taste that their breakthrough into the mass media—and mass idiom—was revolutionary, irreversible and almost painless. The two Kinsey books (the one on women was published in 1953) are now almost unavoidable first citations for new studies of sexual behavior.

Kinsey didn't mean it that way but his studies did little to make the aging feel better. For example, he concluded that— despite all the variables going into sexual behavior—"in the sexual history of the male, there is not a single factor which affects frequency of outlet as much as age." Kinsey was a professor of zoology, not a psychologist or sociologist. Love, life adjustment and the psyche were not his professional fields; "sexual outlet" and its frequency made up his base for measuring sexual behavior. He was looking at the entire *biological* life span of man when he talked of aging:

As far as human sexuality is concerned, aging begins with the onset of adolescence. . . . It seems more correct to think of aging as a process that sets in soon after the initiation of growth. The sexagenarian—or octogenarian—who suddenly becomes interested in the problems of aging is nearly a lifetime beyond the point at which he became involved in that process.

His wisdom was circumscribed only by the limits of his professional interest when he said that "aging studies need to be reoriented around the origins of biologic decline, and that will mean preadolescence or early adolescence in . . . at least in some aspect of human physiology."

Kinsey had a missionary spirit in his fight against the sexual hypocrisy of his time— the difference between what people did and what they talked about or pretended they did. He noted that at least 90 percent of all American males over 17 years old had experience with masturbation and that, "as a question of physical outcome," there was no evidence of harm to it. The harm came, he felt, in telling children or adolescents gruesome tales about the effects of masturbation; it was through his influence that the manual of the Boy Scouts of America finally dropped its unscientific warning about the damage masturbation would do to the mind and body of a scout.

It is true, say, that masturbation persists among men and women into their 60s and beyond; although infrequent, it is sometimes a more important source of outlet than coitus as opportunities shrink, within or without marriage. But to condemn masturbation, or to consider it deviant behavior, is a sanctimony which suits few people. Most authorities go quite the other way. "Masturbation presents no significant problem for the older-age group women," say Masters and Johnson. "When heterosexual contacts are limited or unavailable, the widowed or divorced woman also may revert to the masturbatory practices of her teens and 20s when sexual tensions became intolerable." Dr. Isadore Rubin, a specialist on problems of sex in the aging, notes that "every study of older people has shown that large numbers of them engage in masturbation as an alternative method of gaining release from sexual tension," although they may feel something is wrong in doing so. He quotes, with obvious approval, the advice of marriage counselor Lester W. Dearborn: "It is to be hoped that those interested in the field of geriatrics will take into consideration the sexual needs of the aging and encourage them to accept masturbation as a perfectly valid outlet" when other means are unavailable.

Any study of attitudes or behavior among the old must consider the cultural and social forces which shape, restrain or threaten them. The notion that the old do not really need or cannot partake in sexual activity is a self-fulfilling one; it implies criticism and ridicule and limits the enjoyment of their years.

The old *are* old, born in another time with different ways. Dr. Frederick A. Whiskin, psychiatrist at Cushing Hospital, Framingham, Massachusetts, observed the reading habits of old patients. He found that a number enjoyed rereading best sellers of a 1900 vintage. Biographies of major figures and tales of adventure were popular, too. So were tender love stories, in which all ends well, and religious works.

"Leanings toward genuine intellectual challenge were found to be lacking in our subjects," Dr. Whiskin said. "Wit, humor, drama held little appeal. This lack of interest may be more on the basis of cultural differences than the age factor. Contemporary frankness in discussing sexual matters was generally offensive to the older readers. This could be related in part to their own strict early training, and also a general feeling that older people should not be interested in sex."

Of course, many are—although they are loath to show it. The DeWitt Nursing Home in New York City is a modern home run with considerable imagination and style by Dr. A. Lee Lichtman. Its residents, whose average age is about 83, elect their own local government. A male resident sneaked into a woman resident's room one night and tried to get into bed with her; she did not complain to the doctors but to the residents' government, which took it upon itself to admonish the man. Dr. Lichtman found out about the incident later when another resident confided in him. He was satisfied that it had gone to the local government to handle but was not surprised by the incident. "They keep their sex lives pretty quiet," he said. "But it's definitely there. I get it through the grapevine."

A much longer grapevine has it that there is a senior citizens' community in Florida with its own brothel just outside its confines. The customers are 65 or older, the "girls" from 30 to middle age. The grapevine does not tell what the customers' wives have to say about it.

The feeling that it is repulsive for people over 70 to hold hands, kiss or make love may be about the last barrier of prejudice against the old to fall. Still, that is exactly what the old are doing in greater number, whenever—as in retirement villages—they find the chance and atmosphere that allow it. The fact that the old have strong sexual cravings is hardly a secret to the medical profession.

Perhaps the most illuminating examples of sex as a clinical problem among them come from patient records described by Dr. Freeman. Among them:

A 72-year-old widow had periodic abdominal distress but no organic cause could be found. Finally, alone with the doctor, she started to cry and unburden herself. Her conscience was troubled because she had been dreaming every night that her late husband was returning to her; in the dreams he often made love to her and she found the sexual relation completely satisfying. Now she had a deep sense of guilt, felt that she was cursed and was afraid that her unmarried daughter might learn of her disgrace. The woman was told that her situation was "one of normal possibilities." She rejected this and broke off treatment. However, it was later learned that her abdominal symptoms had disappeared.

A 91-year-old man, highly intelligent and still working daily, was distraught because his wife had denied him a sexual relationship for 50 years. His principles forbade extramarital intercourse and he had relied on masturbation for release. He now masturbated once a month but was depressed each time. He feared and disliked his 89-year-old wife, who was extremely active, still housekeeping, shopping and cooking, and whose virtues were constantly being repeated to him. "This increased not only his distaste but also his self-concern."

A retired fisherman, 71, and his wife, 70, were concerned because they enjoyed a vigorous sex life, with coitus at least once a day. They had fourteen children. Both had the impression that what they were doing was somehow unnatural for older people. The patient record concludes: "A simple expression of reassurance was sufficient to relieve their suspicions of ill health or ill doing."

A man having a general physical review complained that he was upset by his wife's persistent sexual urges. She was a diabetic suffering for atrophic vaginitis and demanded intercourse as the only way of getting rid of her vaginal discomfort. The husband always obliged but said that he was getting "a little tired of it" at his age—84. His wife was 79, and he felt that frequent intercourse was no longer "natural." He asked that his wife be treated vaginally to relieve the problem.

In their report on women, Kinsey and his associates concluded that the decline in intercourse in marriage is the product of the aging process in the male, not in the female. But others believe it is the man's "fear of failure" in sexual activity more than aging itself that accounts for the decline. "There is no way to overemphasize this," say Masters and Johnson.

Once impotent under any circumstances, a man may withdraw from all coital activity rather than have his ego shattered by repeated failure. (Or he may turn to other, young women for reassurance.) But they repeat that sex among married couples—given the right circumstances—can be a joy almost forever. Regular sexual expression, together with physical well-being and a healthy attitude toward the aging process, provides a "sexually stimulative climate within a marriage," they say. And this climate will, in turn, "improve sexual tension and provide a capacity for sexual performance that frequently may extend to and beyond the 80-year level."

This is set against an ideal background. "Fear of failure" on the part of the man has at least its share of counterparts among aging women. After menopause, there are the "mechanical" factors caused by endocrine imbalance. Among them are the thinning of the vaginal walls, reduction in size of the vaginal barrel, shrinking of the major labia. During orgasm, uterine contractions frequently become painful, a condition which, Masters and Johnson say, may be relieved by a balanced combination of estrogen and progesterone. But they note that many facets of the relationship between steroid starvation and female sexual response "remain to be defined" and that, in any event, the psyche—and sexual habits in earlier years—play an equal or greater part than that of an unbalanced endocrine system after menopause.

The menopause itself is not, apparently, the traumatic ordeal many women fear it to be. In a study of attitudes toward the menopause made by Bernice L. Neugarten, Vivian Wood, Ruth J. Kraines and Barbara Loomis, women of varying ages were asked to respond to the statement, "Women generally feel better after the menopause than they have in years." About 68 percent of the women between 45 and 65 years old agreed to the statement; only 26 percent of the women between 21 and 44 had that hope. Another statement put before them was, "Going through menopause really does not change a woman in any important way." Eighty-three percent of the women between 56 and 65, post-menopausal age, agreed, but only 58 percent of the women between 21 and 30 felt the same way. In the same age groups, 21 percent of the older women felt that "a woman is concerned about how her husband will feel toward her after menopause"; more than half—58 percent—of the younger women had that concern. And 21 percent of the women between 56 and 65 agreed that "after menopause, a woman is more interested in sex than she was before." Only 14 percent of the 21 to 30-year-old group felt that to be the case.

Older women seem to feel more confident and freer after the menopause; young women look at it differently, as an ordeal related to aging, something dim and unpleasant. Older women also regard it as unpleasant, but as less important. "It's just the pause that depresses," one said.

This study found that loss of fertility is not an important concern of women, consciously or unconsciously, as they get older. Only four out of 100 women between 45 and 55 said that "not being able to have children" was the worst thing about menopause. (Twenty-six said "not knowing what to expect" was the worst, 19 said "the discomfort and pain" and 18 singled out "it's a sign you're getting old.") This finding disputes the assumption in much psychological literature that "the closing of the gates" is a considerable blow to women. Men—theoretically—never lose the ability to initiate pregnancy. A few years ago, Soviet gerontologists, interviewing men of advanced years, asked at what age they had become impotent. They found that some of the centenarians had not yet reached that stage; indeed, a few had recently become fathers. This bit of knowledge may be comforting but meaningless to most men in more industrial Western society; after middle age their ability or desire to have children has usually long since left them for a dozen other nonbiological reasons.

More recently, Adriaan Werwoerdt, Eric Pfeiffer and Hsioh-Shan Wang of the Duke University Medical Center studied the effects of age, sex and marital status on 254 men and women, 60 to 94 years old, over a three-year period. They found that men were generally more active than women; activity was no great rarity among men surviving into the 80s and 90s. In women, sexual interest was at relatively low ebb during their late 60s and early 70s, probably because of the condition of their husbands, a few years older than they. The Duke University doctors found that there was "a rather sharp drop" in sexual activity among men of the 72-to-74 range. However, there is a greater discrepancy between sexual activity and interest in men than in women at that age and later. They attribute this to psychological stress, as men try to reorient their sexual aims. It may well be that many men in their mid-70s are faced with "the task of finding new outlets for the sexual drive and developing new ways of intimacy," they suggest.

In this study the median age for stopping intercourse was 68 for the men and 60 for women—much earlier for women than the normal difference in age between husband and wife would indicate. Almost all such studies support the idea that women are far more dependent on men than men on women for continuing or stopping and for frequency and type of sexual outlet. Even in reporting their studies, some researchers take time out to comment on the problems of women—and the problems they have

---

The notion that the old do not really need or partake in sexual activity is a self-fulfilling one.

---

with women—in getting direct answers from them. Psychologist Jack Botwinick observes that the problem of determining the effects of age in the female sex drive is more complex than in the male. Dr. Freeman asked a group of older people to give a self-evaluation of their sexual activities throughout their lives and noted, almost parenthetically, how difficult it was for the women to reply. He had sent questionnaires under identical conditions to both men and women, but only one-fourth as many women responded; their answers tended to be informed and indecisive, with "an increased number of free expressions, ranging from indignation to elaboration." Even simple questions would be answered with "I don't know," or "This all depends on my husband."

Women have different attitudes toward sex—and respond differently to questions about sexual behavior—because of their psychologic and sociologic conditioning, Dr. Freeman says. And then, in words that could preface a manifesto for older women's liberation, he says that society "has been less understanding of and less prepared for a continuation of sexual needs and activities in older women—single, married or widowed. Only an occasional woman has the combination of qualities by which to break through this average pattern of her aging, her husband's influence and general customs."

Women have these burdens and more, made worse by the realities of growing old. Among the reasons why it is difficult for older women to marry or remarry is the extreme shortage of older available men. Statistics coming out of the 1970 U.S. Census give an idea of the problem. Overall, there are about 95 males to every 100 females in the United States. But men are usually about two-and-a-half years older than their brides when they marry the first time and they do not live as long. By the time Americans reach the 55-to-64 year age group, there are about 80 men to every 100 women; by 65 to 74, about 72 men to every 100 women; after 75, only 63 men to every 100 women. The ratio of widows to widowers is four to one, with three-quarters of the widows 60 or older. (The situation in Great Britain, with its greater percentage of older people, may be worse. Not only does Britain have many more widows than widowers; it also has an excess of spinsters—14 percent of its women over 65 have never married at all compared to 6 percent in the United States.) There are so many more old women around than old men that, if a man survives his wife, he is apt to step into a bustling marriage market, with himself as a prize. More than two-thirds of men over 65 are married (for the first, second or more times) but only one-third of the women. To borrow again from Dr. Freeman, this time his most poignant line, "Apparently old widowers get married and old widows get lonesome."

It is not the statistics of the situation alone that limit a woman's options. Susan Sontag recently wrote about "the double standard of aging—the social convention that aging enhances a man but progressively destroys a woman." Sontag says that most women of "a certain age" either lie or feel tempted to lie when asked their age. A man doesn't have the same reaction; he knows that he can remain eligible well into old age while even good-looking women become ineligible much younger. Sontag noted that when such men as Pablo Casals, Charles Chaplin, U.S. Supreme Court Justice William O. Douglas or Senator Strom Thurmond take brides many years younger than themselves, it strikes people as remarkable but still plausible. "For the man, a late marriage is always good public relations. It adds to the impression that, despite his advanced age, he is still to be reckoned with."

But an elderly woman who marries a young man is greeted quite differently. It is felt that she has broken a fierce taboo, and she gets no credit for her courage. Rather than being admired for her vitality, she is apt to be condemned as predatory, willful, selfish or exhibitionist. She is also likely to be pitied, since such a marriage is taken as evidence that she is in her dotage. And the younger man who marries her may be thought to be "extremely neurotic, if not mildly contemptible." Sontag says that only three well-known older women who dared such unions—even then only at the

---

If a man survives his wife, he is apt to step into a bustling marriage market, with himself as a prize.

---

end of their lives—come to mind: George Eliot, Colette and Edith Piaf. And all were creative artists or entertainers who had "special license from society to behave scandalously."

There are other obstacles to remarriage which older women have in common with men. One, certainly, is the memory of the first marriage, whether that marriage was good or bad. There is, according to sociologist Peter C. Pineo, a prevalence of "disenchantment" in the later years of marriage, a general drop in marital satisfaction and adjustment. The grounds upon which one decides to marry deteriorate through the years; the "fit" between two individuals, which led them to marry in the first place, reduces with time.

The last years of a marriage may be marked by invalidism or chronic illness; the stresses are great and often haunt the survivor because of compassion for the sufferer, or a feeling of guilt over not having done enough to help, or because of all these together. Whether widow or widower were happy or not in the first marriage, many of them idealize the memory of the dead mate, although the truth may be that, toward the end, the marriage was sustained mainly by memories shared but seen from a different perspective, simple convenience and habit, an easy-to-upset financial structure and a sense that divorce was either impossible, out-of-convention or pointless.

When it comes to marriage, the children of the old don't help much either. Dr. Peterson, in challenging the "almost uni-

versal attitude" of younger persons that a new marriage for those in their later years is "stupid and inappropriate," puts considerable blame on sons and daughters.

The situation forces an increasing number of elderly couples to marry in secret. A 69-year-old widow wrote for advice to syndicated advice-to-the-lovelorn columnist Abigail Van Buren in some desperation: "Is there a state near Iowa where a couple can go to be married in a hurry? We would like to get married as soon as possible as his children want to put him in a rest home."

Ann Landers, Van Buren's sister and a competitive columnist, received a letter from a 59-year-old widow who said she was having a difficult time getting a proposal from an elderly widower because "his children are against it. They do not dislike me but they don't want me to inherit any part of their father's estate. . . . I'd be happy to sign a premarital agreement leaving everything to his children. (I will leave what I have to my daughter.) All I want is his love and companionship."

These two samples of the perils of the old come from the study, *Retirement Marriage,* by Walter C. McKain. McKain and his staff located 100 old couples, all of them previously married and widowed, with a median age of 71 for the women, 76 for the men. The oldest man was 95; he had been 90 when he took a bride of 74. The oldest bride was 78, her husband 76. All the couples had been remarried for five or more years at the time of their interviews.

McKain is a professor of *rural* sociology, which seems to make a difference; his little book describing the study is written in charming, anecdotal, somewhat pastoral style. He says that only a few of the older couples interviewed made even oblique references to their sex life and the interviewers had been instructed not to raise the subject or to appear unduly interested in it. Still, it came up among a few; others got around it indirectly when they discussed the importance of companionship or falling in love. McKain says that older men may use remarriage as proof of their masculinity although having a sexual partner available to them is probably more important than the sex act itself. His conclusion: "The role of sex in the lives of these older people extended far beyond lovemaking and coitus; a woman's gentle touch, the perfume of her hair, a word of endearment—all these and many more reminders that he is married help to satisfy a man's urge for the opposite sex. The same is true for the older wife. One woman had this comment on her remarriage: 'I like the little things; the smell of his pipe, the sound of steps on the back porch,

his shaving mug—even his muddy shoes.' The sex life of older married couples is not confined to the bedroom."

This quaintly romantic attitude seems to blend with an acutely realistic one. Nearly three-fourths of the men and two-thirds of the women mentioned the need for companionship as a major reason for remarriage. "I was lonesome. I hated to be alone. I wanted to share my life with someone who needed me and cared whether I was alive or not," was a characteristic response, age-old and fundamental. Yet they showed much care before deciding on a mate. Some couples mentioned finances as a reason for getting married: a second income, usually from Social Security, would be helpful. "It was either get married or lose my home," one man said bluntly and then, in mitigation, gave other reasons as well. Most couples would have short courtships, small and quiet or secret weddings and forgo honeymoons as being inappropriate to their years. But later they often were eager to spread the news. "We wanted everyone to know so we sent a casserole to the annual church meeting and signed the note 'Mr. and Mrs.,' one couple said. A few spoke of "love at first sight," but were embarrassed to have other old people overhear them.

McKain concludes that the marriages in his sample had the greatest chance of success if both bride and groom knew each other well and shared activities before marriage, if the marriage had approval of friends and relatives, if the couple had enough money and if each partner was well adjusted and satisfied with life generally. There was less chance for success if, imply-

---

"I like the little things; the smell of his pipe, the sound of steps on the back porch, his shaving mug—even his muddy shoes."

---

ing a lack of trust, they kept separate financial accounts and did not pool their resources, or if they continued to live in a house belonging to either mate in a previous marriage. A woman tends to be uncomfortable living in a house, with all its associations, furnished by an earlier wife; a man to feel that home ownership also makes him head of the household.

Whether their widowed parents live with them or apart, many, or most, children hardly ever consider seriously the possibility that a parent will remarry. When the prospect does occur, they suffer surprise, shock and often embarrassment over mother's making a fool of herself or father's turning out to be a dirty old man. About 25 percent of the remarried old couples said that at one point or another they had almost given in to their children's objections or hostility and called off the marriage. (McKain assumes that many more possible remarriages simply don't happen for this reason.) But after five years of remarriage, more than 80 percent of the children were pleased with the outcome; more than half who had opposed it had changed their minds.

One of McKain's chief aims—to determine whether remarriage in old age can, indeed, be successful—was clearly served by the study. He used careful techniques to judge "success." One was an independent evaluation of the marriage by each husband and wife; a negative note from either placed the marriage in the doubtful or unsuccessful category. Another was "internal evidence" based upon a couple's response to a series of questions about their decision-making processes. Finally, each couple was closely observed during the interview, often lasting several hours, for just this purpose: "Outward signs of respect, consideration, affection, pride, together with obvious enjoyment of each other's company were evidence of success, while any serious complaints led to an appraisal of unsatisfactory."

Only six of the 100 marriages appeared to be failures. (In the general United States population, there were 33 divorces for every 100 marriages in 1970.) Twenty others were mainly successful, but "still had problems to overcome." This leaves all the rest, just under three-quarters of the 100 old couples. "Despite the secrecy and shame involved," McKain says, they emerged as "highly successful." And, presumably, bride and groom lived happily ever after.

The New Ageism and the Failure Models: A Polemic

Richard A. Kalish, PhD

Social gerontologists and social geriatricians have made considerable use of the term *ageism* as a counterpart to the more familiar *racism* and *sexism*. The general assumption underlying the application of this term is that ageist individuals and ageist societies or communities or organizations exist.

Ageists, the assumption holds, express overt and covert dislike and discrimination regarding the elderly. This is, they avoid older persons on an individual level, they discriminate against older persons in terms of jobs, other forms of access to financial support, utilization of social institutions, and so forth. Further, the ageist individual derides the elderly through hostile humor, through accusations that the elderly are largely responsible for their own plight, and through complaints that they are consuming more than their share of some particular resource. They may also contend that older people deserve what they get, are in effect a drain on society, are functionally incapable of change or improvement (or, conversely, are capable of change and improvement and should be required to do so with their present resources), and do not contribute adequately to the society from which they are taking resources. Ageism involves stereotyping, prejudice, discrimination, segregation, hostility . . . the list can go on and on.

The New Ageism

I would like to propose that there is another form of ageism, that it is equally pervasive in our society, and that it is found in advocates of the elderly as often — and perhaps more so — than among their antagonists.

This form of ageism, which I will refer to as the New Ageism, although it is certainly not new, has the following characteristics:

(1) It stereotypes "the elderly" in terms of the characteristics of the least capable, least healthy, and least alert of the elderly, although its rhetoric is punctuated by insistence that "all elderly are not alike."

(2) It perceives the older person as, in effect, a relatively helpless and dependent individual who requires the support services of agencies and other organizations.

(3) It encourages the development of services without adequate concern as to whether the outcome of these services contributes to reduction of freedom for the participants to make decisions controlling their own lives.

(4) It produces an unrelenting stream of criticism against society in general and certain individuals in society for their mistreatment of the elderly, emphasizing the unpleasant existence faced by the elderly.

The message of the New Ageism seems to be that "we" understand how badly you are being treated, that "we" have the tools to improve your treatment, and that if you adhere to our program, "we" will make your life considerably better. You are poor, lonely, weak, incompetent, ineffectual, and no longer terribly bright. You are sick, in need of better housing and transportation and nutrition, and we — the nonelderly and those elderly who align themselves with us and work with us — are finally going to turn our attention to you, the deserving elderly, and relieve your suffering from ageism.

The New Ageism obscures individual and group differences within the 23,000,000 or so persons in the country normally defined as elderly. In fact, the definition of "elderly" tends to slip and slide a bit, which permits the New Ageists to seem on more solid ground than they really are. The New Ageists begin by stating that there are 23,000,000 persons over age 65; they often ignore the immense diversity among these persons and they also tend to ignore that most of these persons are intact, functioning effectively on their own, and getting along adequately on what money they have. Then their definition of "the elderly" changes from one based on chronological age to one based on sickness and pover-

California School of Professional Psychology, 1900 Addison St., Berkeley, CA 94704.

ty, but the change is implicit, not explicit, and so the listener is still focused on the 23,000,000 elderly and makes the assumption, without realizing it, that the spotlighted elderly represent the totality of elderly.

The Failure Models

The New Ageism has another message, one which I believe is more subtle and more pervasive than the message described in the previous discussion: the Failure Models. The general message of the Failure Models is that this or that older person has failed or is going to fail. This is accomplished in two related but very different fashions: the Incompetence Model, an approach that constantly reminds older people how incompetent they are; and the Geriactivist Model, an approach that establishes a rigid set of standards for appropriate behavior and faults those who do not adhere to the standards.

The Incompetence Failure Model has been developed in part as a tactic to get funding from governmental and private agencies. In effect, it is the ability to say, "Those persons for whom I am advocate are greater failures than those persons for whom you are advocate. They are such great failures that the only solution to their failure is more money." The obvious difficulty with this model is that as soon as the failures become successes, the incompetents become competent and in need of fewer services, and the advocates will lose their jobs and, more than that, lose their status as serving the "Incompetent Failure of the Year."

This model is best represented by a superficial reading of the distressingly excellent Pulitzer Prize winning book, *Why Survive,* by Robert Butler. I describe this as "best" because it simultaneously is a masterful job of chronicling the ills that have befallen the elderly, basing this chronicle on thorough research and careful documentation, and includes a virtually prototypical example of the Incompetence Failure Model. This book has served effectively to rally the sympathetic and persuade the dubious that the plight of *the* elderly requires remediation. But what accumulative effect does this book, and its kindred media and political writings and speechs, have on older persons? Now that television and columnists have "discovered" the elderly, how has their discovery affected the persons discovered?

I certainly admit that I don't know these answers; indeed I don't think that anyone has a clear idea. There are no research data, and I cannot recall ever having read any analytical article. The very title of Butler's book suggests a possible reaction that an elderly reader or, even more likely, a reader approaching his or her later years, would have: Why Survive? Indeed, what can be gained by living?

One possible effect on older people of the Incompetence Failure Model is that they internal-ize what they read and hear and come to believe it of themselves as individuals. If this is the case, then the work of the advocates of the elderly becomes as damaging to the self-esteem of older persons as is the view of those who damn them with benign neglect or even those who express overt ageism.

A second possibility is that each older individual accepts the information literally, but excludes himself or herself and closer friends. This is the "those-old-people-over-there" position. A third alternative is that the rhetoric and polemic are seen as political in nature and have little or no effect at all. And a fourth is that the elderly individual is strengthened by recognizing the responsibility for his or her plight as emanating from a society that ignores him or her, thus requiring a redoubling of effort which will lead to the assuaging of discomfort.

I suspect that all of these operate, at different times and with different persons, although I believe that the second view prevails. Thus, the elderly person denies that the model applies to him or her, but acknowledges that it is descriptive of "those old folks."

I don't wish to make a scapegoat of *Why Survive?* It served a very important purpose, but unfortunately the valuable discussion of a better life for the elderly in the later part of the book did not receive the attention that the earlier Incompetence Failure Model received. Nor do I wish to present the position that the elderly need all kinds of protection. That notion has been exaggerated: the elderly are much tougher and more resilient than they are given credit for being.

The second message of failure is the Geriactivist Model. I coined this term about ten years ago to describe the older people who are themselves active in the causes of the elderly. They develop a symbiotic relationship with younger advocates, and together they maintain the call for an active and involved old age. The Geriactivist needs the younger associates who have jobs in the community and who can participate in making decisions; the younger advocates — social workers, recreation workers, agency staff, politicians — need the activist older person as both a source of inexpensive support labor and to legitimize the activist position. The activist position is established as the *only* appropriate way for older persons to function. Something is assumed to be wrong with older people who wish to sit around and talk with elderly friends, who wish to stay at home and read, who thoroughly enjoy television, who wish to pray or meditate or jog by themselves, who for whatever reasons prefer their world to be comfortable, comforting and manageable rather than stimulating, challenging, and risky, who prefer their inner worlds to the external world. One geriactivist — my model for this role — went so far as to tell me that any older person who would not participate actively, either socially or politically, was probably lacking in moral integrity or in emotional stability.

Older persons who respond to their inner worlds or who enjoy and desire passive entertainment are seen as challenges to be overcome, rather than as individuals who are adapting to a life-long (or recent) preference that could only be fully realized when retirement and the empty nest made it possible. Thus, once again the sense of failure is communicated. "Those who are not part of the solution are part of the problem; those who do not adhere to my rules of healthy old age are, by definition, failures." Diversity is not recognized, nor are inner life and intrinsic satisfactions seen as a proper definition for a healthy personality.

Overall the Failure Models probably generate anger among the elderly with society and simultaneously with themselves. The implication is that the older person is not only victimized, but also is impotent and powerless to have any significant impact on the society and/or individuals who perpetrate the victimization. The built-in assumption is that change is governed from without, a view guaranteed to intensify the sense of impotence. And since the older person is perceived by others through the lens of this model, the initial response many people have to the older person is that of helpless victim, a view made worse by the assumption that it actually favors the elderly.

The source of the victimization is often stated as being an impersonal bureaucracy and a depersonalizing society, run for the betterment of some vaguely labeled "establishment" or else for some other age or power group. All of this adds up to a perceived conspiracy to deprive the elderly of their entitlements, a situation guaranteed to increase frustration and anger. And made worse by the pity and sympathy that are often the result. Further, to the extent that it is perceived as accurate and authoritative, it will discourage older persons from attempts to gain their rights since this will be seen as a futile action.

Perpetrators or Innocent Bystanders?

Who is really responsible for the Failure Models? Is it the funding agencies that must compete with other funding agencies in their presentation to Congress of the dire need they represent? Perhaps, but only in part, since it is obviously political pressure, as well as extent of need, that produces results.

Are the media responsible? Yes and no. Certainly they exploit the Failure Models, but nonetheless they tend to respond primarily to what they perceive their audience as wanting to view.

Are the members of Congress the true villains? No, since they only respond to some combination of political demand and perceived need.

Is it we gerontologists and geriatricians? Again, yes and no. We are familiar with the successes, and we are familiar with the need to respect diversity, but we are also pressured by the importance of keeping our own programs going, and we can't do this without money and personal support. At the same time, many of us are both active and activists, and our natural inclination is to view these qualities in others in a positive light. Indeed, for some of us, our entire professional value system is predicated on the importance of activity and involvement. What is important to watch here is how we define involvement and that we do not place highly restrictive boundaries on what we consider mentally healthy aging.

So who has perpetrated the Failure Models? All of us, and with many valid reasons, but without adequate thought of consequences. There was a time in history when people who succeeded were considered to be chosen by God, when it was often assumed that those who were healthy or financially successful must be so because of God's will. Now the opposite view seems to prevail, and advocates focus on the weaknesses and victimization of those they represent in order to develop a viable position.

There are no villains, yet we are all responsible.

Some Existing Models and an Alternative

In the 15 or so years that I have been involved in gerontology, I have noted several models in our society that have been used to describe the nature of aging. I'm presenting them here, fully cognizant that they are highly impressionistic and far from being expressed in readily operational terms.

The first model I've termed the Pathology Model. Old age is seen as pathological, a time of sickness and strangeness and falling-apartness. It is also seen as a static period, without much chance for change in a positive direction. It just *is*.

Following that, both in severity and, in my experience, in chronology, is the Decrement Model. This model is based on cross-sectional studies that showed the substantial age-related differences that were initially interpreted as age-related changes. Decrements are not as bad as pathology, but they partake of the same kind of distress.

The third model, initiated when we became aware that longitudinal studies suggested a much smaller decrement than previously assumed, might be termed the Minimal Change Model. Herein older people were presumed to be continuations of what they were as younger people, but with a small degree of decrement. So we talked about biochemical and social and psychological and health impairments that could occur at any age, but occurred more frequently with old age and are sometimes accumulative so that they were, in any event, likely to take a heavier toll in the later years. In these ways, age per se was not the villain, but the age-related changes were.

The fourth model prevails among gerontologists today. It is the Normal Person Model. Older people are simply people, like all other individuals. They are highly diverse. They do resemble each other in some ways, because of when they were socialized to certain values or when they experienced certain events; they share increased likelihood of being grand-parents, being retired, being diabetic, being widowed, but they differ in more ways than they are similar. Their behavior is understandable in terms of the situations they confront, so that any form of conservatism is explained in terms of their social and political values and the economic situation they face; reaction time changes are explained in terms of biochemical changes that the elderly learn to compensate for with considerable success; cognitive changes are likely to arise from isolation as often as from physiological brain change, but in either event, it is a health problem, not an aging problem per se.

I would like to propose a fifth model, perhaps an outgrowth of the Normal Person Model: a Personal Growth model. The later years can be a period of optimum personal growth. Not for everyone: some are not in adequate health, some are too financially restricted, some have been socialized in their early years in ways of thinking and behaving that make later growth impossible. But the later years can be a time for growth. For one thing, many earlier responsibilities are no longer in evidence. Children no longer make significant demands; aged parents are often (but not always) dead; repetitive and unstimulating jobs no longer consume time and energy; stressful competitive needs no longer stir the ego.

Second, older persons no longer need to be constrained by what others think of them. No longer are they likely to be threatened with loss of jobs or the demands of dependent children if they step outside the fences that had previously circled their lives. Of course, they may not be able to do this, or they may not wish to do this, but the option is there.

Third, many elderly have worked through their fears of their own death, and they have therefore learned better than any others how to develop priorities that satisfy them. They have also learned to cope with their own health problems and with losing others. Obviously, death, health, and loss don't cease to be problems, but many older persons have a period of years — sometimes many years — when these are not inhibiting problems.

Fourth, there is tremendous discretionary time. One of the major difficulties of retirement is that of using time for one's own satisfaction. Those who fail to solve this problem probably do not lead enjoyable retirement lives; those who do solve the problem learn how to schedule themselves for optimum pleasure, whether the pleasure comes through physical labor, social relationships, or leisure.

Fifth, there is the motivation caused by knowing the future is finite. For some elderly, this knowledge is so destructive that enjoyment or satisfaction is virtually impossible. Others, however, not only cope more effectively, but respond to the pressure by a highly appropriate use of time. The time boundary justifies their ignoring the minutes of life, if they wish, and to concentrate on what matters to them. This might be gardening or painting or political action or earning money or seeking enlightenment or praying or talking with friends or reminiscing. They do not mark time; they use time for themselves. They learn to enjoy the passing minutes by becoming absorbed in those minutes.

The Personal Growth Model of aging is obviously not one I have created in this paper. The SAGE program, developed by Gay Luce, has been using this model for several years; many senior centers have encouraged personal growth; the rapidly increasing emphasis on facilitating the return of older people to formal and informal educational programs reflects the same intent. Nonetheless, there is too little awareness of the potential for continued growth and personal satisfaction among the elderly and, simultaneously, unduly narrow boundaries as to what constitutes growth and satisfaction.

Some Final Preaching

I am not Pollyanna. Normally I am Cassandra. I do not wish to take a Geriactivist position and place the burden of trying to attain a standard of personal growth on an elderly person who is fighting for life against physical or financial hardship. Rather, I am trying to emphasize the possibility of growth at any time in life and the recognition that the growth that does not occur in the later years is never going to occur.

I am also suggesting that we can develop a Personal Growth model, so that we approach older persons with the expectation that they have the potential for continued growth, that even sickness and financial restriction can be a source of growth, although not desirable, and that our task is to facilitate that growth.

There are programs, many programs, that are doing just that, and there are articles in the media and television programs that show what these programs are doing. Often, of course, the implication of the media is that these older people are unusual and that is why we must put them on display, but the other message can also be heard: you too can be like these people.

3. SOCIETAL ATTITUDES TOWARD OLD AGE

There is also something that each individual can do, rather than feeling helpless to fight the overpowering bureaucracy. We can communicate to older persons that we have faith in their abilities, that we recognize that they are capable of making decisions (even those decisions that we assume, perhaps correctly, will turn out wrong), that we respect their ownership of their own bodies and time and lives. In brief, we can communicate a Success Model instead of the Failure Models.

It is not my point that the elderly in the U.S. and Canada enjoy the best in the best of all possible countries. Many older people are certainly in need of better housing, better transportation systems, better nutrition, more recognition of needs for human relationships and for stimulation and challenge. Nor is this a call for reduced services. Needs and wants will always outrun resources.

The difficulty is that by describing the elderly as helpless individuals, beset by problems, incompetent in finding their own ways, and obligated to meet a set standard of activity, we are expressing the New Ageism. It influences our views of the elderly, their views of themselves, and — I can only assume — the behavior that both the elderly and nonelderly exhibit in regard to aging and older people. If we define older people as victims, we will approach them as victims and expect them to behave as victims. Even by defining something as A Problem, we are initiating a self-fulfilling prophecy.

I would like to see the definition of older people develop so that they are perceived as equally — perhaps more — capable of personal growth and life satisfaction and happiness. This means a Success Model instead of a Failure Model, without blinding us to the very real problems that some older people do face. We can then stop confusing the elderly with the least competent consumers of geriatric services, and begin to work toward the development of a community that recognizes the competent, autonomous, self-esteeming, generative older person as the norm. We can refocus our attention on the later years as opportunities for flexibility, joy, pleasure, growth, and sensuality.

Sex in the Nursing Home? For Lord's Sake, *Why Not?*

Nancy Littell Fox, LPN

The author, who most recently worked as floor supervisor of the St. Catherine Hospital geriatric wing, McCook, Neb., is now a full-time writer and speaker, working from her home in Bend, Ore.

A bosomy blonde with shapely hips sashays down the street, as an 80-year-old man pursues her bouncing figure—with binoculars, from a nursing home window.

"Quick, nurse, a tranquilizer!" the shout goes down the hall.

"Milton again? That dirty old man!" a nursing aide exclaims, convinced that, at his age, her charge should be satisfied to sit snug in a state of sexless senility.

Wait, though. Is this lonely person really a "dirty old man"? It's true that Milton has a reputation for grabbing, pinching, and ogling. But alone and isolated, yet desperate for human contact, he just may be reaching out to others in the only way he can. For, you see, when we stopped Milton's world, he did indeed get off. He's not ill—just mildly impaired. He doesn't belong in an institution, but once committed and often oversedated, he's floundering in unfamiliar space. The farther he strays from the reality he once knew, the more he loses control of his behavior. Perhaps all Milton needs is a touch of genuine affection to keep him from being labeled a dirty old man.

The claim of nursing homes that "Here, all the love needs of the aged are taken care of" is a myth we should destroy. Nurses, more than any other health-care providers, know that sedation is not the answer to this geriatric problem. The desire for personal closeness and physical love isn't dormant in the aged. The need for love holds high priority throughout life, superseded only by the need for the basics of survival—water, food, and shelter. We shouldn't allow nursing home adminis-

trators to provide mere survival while withholding any possibility of fulfilling the emotional needs of residents.

Until retirement, most people are close to spouses, families, or friends of long standing. But in those later years, when many loved ones are lost or far away and the need to belong intensifies, the institutionalized elderly are forced to make a shattering discovery: Not only do these "homes" rarely fulfill their need for love but, as Milton learned, should residents so much as hint that they even *think about* sex, it's a signal to the staff to sedate them—dull their senses.

Why do nursing homes stamp an expiration date on the need for loving relationships? How can the sexual needs of reasonably healthy patients—50% of the nursing home population, according to some estimates—be satisfied in such an environment? These are, perhaps, the most sexually deprived people in our society. In most nursing homes, the taboo on sex is an institutional policy established for no other reason than the convenience of the staff. It's much easier to squelch sexuality, by insisting that the aged should "behave in a proper manner," than to recognize its importance, and allow it to flower.

It's Not 'Dirty' Everywhere

By contrast, people in other nations have a much healthier attitude. In Ecuador, Pakistan, and the Soviet Caucasus, several studies have shown, even centenarians remain sexually active. They've known all along what we're just finding out: Barring serious disorders, the female libido—and the ability to fulfill it—may last a lifetime; and despite a gradual decline, the male, too, can sustain sexual desire and performance well into old age. But in our nursing home system—where the ill and the non-ill, the married and the unmarried, the mentally sound and the senile are thrown together—there's an across-the-board ban on romance.

That's why Carol, a night nurse in one home, could justify shooting down a simple exchange of affection that she witnessed:

Bob, a widower for ten years, and Jean, a long-retired schoolteacher, were watching television one evening, as they frequently did. Gradually, they turned toward each other. So very tenderly, their eyes met. His head tilted toward hers, his hand touched her knee . . . and just then Carol glanced up from her desk and opened fire. "Anna," she commanded an aide, "get those two apart—in separate rooms!"

That's some therapy for dispelling feelings of isolation and worthlessness, isn't it? Whisked apart, stuffed into a convenient asexual vacuum, they each experienced yet another heart-wrenching break, on top of all the other losses in their lives—those countless tearful separations from family, friends, homes, and jobs. And if they did hold any lingering thoughts of tenderness, there'd always be the threat or administration of sedation waiting to counteract them. "Better blah than bliss," these homes seem to say.

Sexuality Isn't Just Sex

Sexuality means more in human relationships than just the performance of physical acts. As sex educator Lester Kirkendall, PhD, explains, there are seven human conditions relevant to human sexuality: "Confidentiality, trust, empathy, mutuality of motivation, affectional expression, emotional investment, and sexual expression." Older couples can share these values and experience these ways of relating to each other in varying degrees. Some institutionalized patients form relationships encompassing all seven conditions. And they have a right to experience these relationships to the degree that naturally develops for them. Others find that, due to sensory impairment, the bridge to a full interpersonal relationship is partly or totally blocked. But even with extreme sensory loss—of sight, hearing, or speech, for example—the sense of touch usually remains. That's why touch is so important to those who have other sensory deficits.

That was Jake's main problem. He had considerable sensory loss, but still yearned to relate to others, to belong, to be close to another human being. One fateful night his needs were misread, and he was sacrificed to policy. Making rounds at 2 AM, the nurse found Jake's bed empty. A frantic search ensued; then an aide cried, from a far corridor, "Here he is, in bed with Bessie!" Both Jake and his friend were fast asleep—until, poking him in his ribs and noisily reprimanding him, the nurse and the aide hustled Jake out of bed and marched him back to his room. "We just can't have Jake jumping in bed with all the women around here," the nurse said as she applied restraints and administered heavy sedation.

From that night on, deeply humiliated, Jake lost interest in life. He started on a steep and rapid descent into oblivion.

Marriage Doesn't Make Any Difference

The policy is the same even for married couples like Ralph and Amy. It was evident to everyone how much this couple missed the intimacy of their married life. So it shouldn't have been a surprise when one day, against regulations, Ralph stealthily made his way to the room of his beloved. Sadly, they couldn't lock the door, because nursing homes invariably make no provision for privacy. Sure enough, enter Gert, an aide, just at the wrong time. Seconds later, exit Gert, blustering with shock and rage. In her rush from the room, Gert ran into a visiting pastor in the hall, and blurted out her problem (and it was, indeed, *her* problem): "The Joneses, Ralph and Amy, do you know what they're doing?"

"Hold on, Gert," the pastor replied. "Just where in the Bible does it say, 'At sixty-seven, thy sex life shall lapse?' And by what right do you censor the private affairs of any couple, of any age? Aren't sexuality and conjugal love gifts from God—a beautiful part of human nature?"

No doubt they are. But in most nursing homes, not only are married couples separated but they are also subjected to the particular watchfulness of the staff. Some homes even impose curfews on late-evening socializing. All this despite the advice of Robert Butler, president of the National Institute on Aging, who says, "It is important for the older person who is interested in retaining sexual capacities to avoid, whenever possible, allowing chronic illness to interfere with sexual functioning. Activity should be resumed at the earliest possible time compatible with successful convalescence." After a long period of abstinence, it becomes less likely that an older person will again take up an active sex life. Residence in a nursing home, it seems, can be as debilitating as chronic illness.

Aside from staff members, those *least* able to cope with our Miltons, Jeans and Bobs, and Jakes and Bessies are the relatives who consigned them to their nursing homes. What happens when two elderly people find each other and decide to tie the knot? Usually, they're met with opposition. Relatives, now in the driver's seat, become vociferous in their objections to a late marriage. "I just can't imagine Grandma getting married to that old man," one cries. "There are too many legal tangles," argues another.

With professional counseling, plus loving support, most tangles could be unraveled. Why *can't* we imagine Grandma in a new love relationship if she needs it and wants it more than anything else in life?

Let's Confront the Issue

There is really no excuse for American nursing homes to be sexless, emotionless mortuaries for the living.

Giving expression to human sexuality, even if it's impaired to some degree, is beneficial in the aging process because it helps to sustain interest in life. As one nursing home resident who had been denied conjugal intimacy with her spouse put it: "We have the right not just to exist, but to live out the rest of our lives to the fullest."

Alex Comfort, the British biologist and gerontologist, warns that the time may come when we will be confronted on this score: "Patients don't forfeit their civil rights by having reached a particular chronological age," he says. "Nursing homes, rehabilitation centers, and even acute-care hospitals will have to change their attitudes about sex among patients. I think it would be possible to sue a nursing home for compromising patients' rights, and I hope somebody does it."

Why Not Act Now?

I don't think nurses have to wait for the courts to decide the needs of our patients. If we are truly patient advocates, all of us—whether in nursing homes or hospitals—should take up the cause of the aged. We must uphold them as individuals of dignity and worth. Let's not just wish them love and fulfillment. Let's begin to change those rules and regulations and policies that *forbid* that love and fulfillment. Let's make sure that the homes to which we send them, or the homes in which we care for them, provide not only the essentials to survive, but also the opportunities to live out the rest of their lives in the joy of human relationships. For who has the right to say that the sunset should be any less beautiful than the sunrise?

Problems and Potentials of Aging

Viewed within the broad perspective of the life cycle, aging might be considered a period of decline, poor health, increasing dependence, social isolation, and—ultimately—death. It often means retirement, decreased income, chronic health problems, the death of a spouse, and a shrinking life space. In contrast, the first fifty years of one's life are periods of growth, development, and ever-increasing life space.

A young child's life usually centers around a house or apartment. As the child grows, he or she begins to move about in a neighborhood. Later, the community and state become a part of one's environment. Finally, the adult is prepared to consider national and international problems—wars, alliances, changing economic cycles, and world problems.

During the later years, however, life space begins to contract. Retirement may remove the individual from involvement in national and international concerns, although he or she may remain actively involved in community affairs. Later, even community involvement may decrease, and the individual may begin to stay fairly close to home and the neighborhood. For some, the final years of life once again may focus on the confines of an apartment or a nursing home.

Many older Americans try to remain the masters of their own destiny for as long as possible. They fear dependence and want to avoid it. Many are successful at maintaining their independence and their right to decide for themselves. Others are not as successful.

The articles in this section are concerned with the problems of older Americans as they attempt to maintain their preferred life styles. We have included articles on visual problems, widowhood, the black elderly, the rural elderly, alcoholism, drug abuse, therapy, and related problems.

Looking Ahead: Challenge Questions

Which aspects of life after sixty-five are desirable and should be looked forward to with some degree of pleasure?

Which aspects of life after sixty-five are undesirable and should be a cause of concern to people of all ages?

The elderly are sometimes considered weak and, therefore, easy targets for criminals and unscrupulous businesspeople. Are the weak always exploited by the unscrupulous in society?

What significant steps might be taken by both business and the local community to assist the elderly in overcoming the problems of aging?

How does drug abuse among young people differ from drug abuse among the elderly?

Visual Booby Traps for Our Aging Population

Jack B. Ralph

Mr. Ralph is an Equal Opportunity Specialist in the Office for Civil Rights, Department of Health and Human Services. He has received an Exceptional Achievement Award for his work in the development and use of design guidelines in the production of information documents for use by the aging, visually limited, and general public.

"If the average person must squint to read these warnings . . . imagine the difficulties of the visually impaired."

Publishers, graphic designers, and editors daily demonstrate their lack of awareness and concern for the special print needs of people with limited vision. Often valuable information and guidance can not be read and understood by those with impaired eyesight because it is published according to ill-considered design and print specifications.

This lack of concern is also obvious in the design and printing of product labels and instruction manuals for appliances and equipment — a situation which increases the danger of accidents in the home.

The group most seriously affected by present design and printing practices are the aged because they have a high incidence of visual problems. With little apparent awareness of the impact of these practices, the publishing and graphics industries are compounding the problems of those suffering loss of visual perception and are contributing to the creation of a special class of handicapped persons.

What good is a written warning if you can't find it, see it, or understand it? The safety of millions of people is jeopardized everyday because they cannot see, read, or understand the cautions on the labels of consumer products. The print on the labels is too small. The color of ink or paper reduces visibility. The vocabulary is too technical,

"Visual Booby Traps for Our Aging Population," Jack B. Ralph, *Aging* Magazine, November/December 1982, pp. 2-6. Reprinted by permission of *Aging* Magazine.

"Reading problems related to abnormal vision occur from childhood to adulthood . . .

. . . But they are frequently compounded in later years by the degenerative visual problems that accompany aging."

specialized, or is not dramatic enough to serve as an adequate warning.

The most visible printing combination is black ink letters on white paper. Any print lighter than black or paper darker than white decreases the contrast. As individuals age, the need for contrast increases because of discoloration in the eye fluids and lens. Such combinations as brown print on tan, or blue ink on pink paper are ill-advised for sight-impaired elderly people. In addition, dark red ink printed on pink paper appears as gray on gray to certain people with degrees of colorblindness.

But contrast is not the only problem. The size of the print is very important. To give the reader a brief initiation into the world of printing, the following common type sizes are presented along with their technical point designations:

This is fourteen (14) point type.
This is eleven (11) point type.
This is twelve (12) point type.
This is eight (8) point type.
This is six (6) point type.

The size of type legally required to warn consumers that a product or medication may be fatal or injurious if improperly used is too small for most people to read easily. In fact, the legally required size print for medication warnings is smaller than the size of print in telephone directories. Help wanted ads generally appear in 6-point type, hampering job hunting efforts by the elderly. Newspapers are often printed in 8- or 9-point type, and many pamphlets and brochures on community services use typewriter type, usually a 10-point size.

The minimum recommended size type for the general population, however, is 11 points. Twelve point size type (about 1/6-inch high) is suggested for the elderly, and 14 points is the minimum approved for the severely visually handicapped.

Unfortunately, the use of these recommended type sizes is often ignored by government agencies, businesses, and manufacturers. For example, room air fresheners are packed in aerosol cans which

must display warnings that puncturing or exposure to 120° heat can cause explosions. This warning on one particular scent of aerosol freshener is displayed in print that is below the 11-point size recommended for the general population. What is worse, however, is that the can has a white background with the hazard warning printed in a chrome reflective paint, offering no visual contrast. Neither the marketing and graphics specialists nor the engineers and technicians of this company seem to have been able to suggest that the design of these labels should effectively warn people with poor eyesight about the explosive hazards of aerosol sprays.

The Number of Visually Handicapped

It is difficult to provide accurate statistics on the number of visually handicapped people in the United States. Reporting of visual impairments is complicated because persons with multiple vision problems can be counted more than once. Consequently, the following category totals should not be added together to make a grand total of people with limited vision. The totals in any one of the categories, however, would seem to justify the need for addressing the problems created by the use of small type size in printed warnings:

- 500,000 persons are seriously visually limited, and need a mechanical apparatus to read even "regular" or 10-point size print.
- 1 million persons are severely visually impaired and cannot read ordinary 8- or 9-point size newsprint with glasses.
- An additional 10.5 million persons cannot read small size 6- to 8-point print and printed materials in certain colors and combinations of ink and paper.
- An estimated 20 million people wear glasses and contact lenses with prescriptions no longer suited to their vision needs.
- It is estimated that another 20 million people have need of some visual correction but do not know it.

Reading problems related to abnormal vision occur from childhood to adulthood, but they are frequently compounded in later years by the degenerative visual problems that accompany aging. The reduction or loss of vision with age, including the decline in near vision, is caused by increased yellowing of the lens with age, retinal disorders, corneal or scleral problems, increasing clouding of the vitreous (eye fluid), and other conditions.

Since it is projected that the proportion of elderly people in the population will rise dramatically over the next several decades, a higher incidence of visual problems should also be anticipated. For a significant number of elderly people who lack adequate financial resources or insurance coverage, these problems are likely to go uncorrected. With eyes unable or ill-equipped to deal with small print, an increasing number of elderly will be excluded from normal visual communication, become more subject to accidents, and be more susceptible to legal entanglements and misunderstandings when signing documents.

While print size will be the largest obstacle for many older people, others will suffer from physiological problems which reduce the amount of light transmitted to the retina, causing an inability to read anything on colored paper. Clouding of the lens (cataracts) also reduces color and contrast recognition. To see color contrast as a cataract-impaired person sees it, put several sheets of amber colored plastic over printed material. The amber may make some colors brighter, but more often reduces perception.

Publishers, advertisers and product manufacturers who do not think about use of color in ink and paper should be made aware that:

- 8.5 million men and 650,000 women in the U.S. are color deficient ("colorblind").
- Thousands of people are color deficient on a temporary basis because of a changing physiological condition.
- Colorblindness often goes undiscovered because the tests to detect this handicap are administered when environmental factors are not correct.

Although this discussion is chiefly concerned with the reading difficulties of the visually impaired, the problems posed by technical vocabulary on instruction and warning labels to people with limited reading and comprehension skills should not be ignored. The extent of reading deficiencies in the general population is reflected in the following statistics:

- The average grade reading level is very low for 14 million citizens who are deaf or hard of hearing.
- About 25 million persons are functionally illiterate (reading at the fifth grade level or less).
- Approximately 37 percent of the adult population, or 45 million persons, read below the eighth grade level.

With so many people unable to read or understand very well, it does not seem satisfactory to allow the listing of the chemical contents and formula of a hazardous product to serve as its only warning. There are many consumers who do not know or understand the ionizing effect of chlorine or the risks of mixing cleaners which, when combined, can release extreme heat and toxic and explosive gases. Not everyone can use the jargon, buzz words, and key terms of chemistry and medicine. The use of words on a label such as caustic soda, lye, corrosive reaction, irritant, hazardous, and volatile make a warning meaningless to many users. Words, such as vertigo, on labels for prescribed or over-the-counter drugs, are also incomprehensible to many people.

Warnings Invisible

For the visually impaired, warnings on prescription drug bottles are printed in such small size type and in such low-contrast ink to paper color combinations that the warnings are effectively invisible to millions of people. In general, the printed cautions about drowsiness sometimes induced by antihistamines and other compounds, the dangers of combining certain medications with alcohol, and the suggested restrictions on driving are visually unacceptable.

Seemingly harmless substances can also present a danger to people with poor eyesight or color blindness. The hazards of using my wife's bath oil beads for "dry skin relief" were dramatically demonstrated to me recently when I slipped getting into a half-full bathtub that contained the miracle beads. While sitting in the tub, recovering from the shoulder strain I sustained in breaking my fall, I examined the clear plastic bottle that contained the solution. The label on the front of the bottle gave the name of the product and its manufacturer in large, beautiful print. On the reverse side of the bottle, through the dark blue solution, I was barely

"Seemingly harmless substances can also present a danger to people with poor eyesight or color blindness"

"What good is a written warning if you can't find it see it, or understand it?"

able to read the caution, printed in 10-point light blue ink, advising me to "guard against slipping in the tub and shower." A cataract sufferer would have had great difficulty reading the light blue printed warning through the dark blue solution. A color deficient person would see very little, indeed.

Try taking a short tour of your own household. Does your oil-based paint and paint thinner carry a clearly visible, large type, properly contrasted, prominently placed warning, stating that proper ventilation should be provided in the room where the do-it-yourselfers are doing it themselves?

Is the "keep away from flame" warning on finger-nail hardener visible enough for women to read to remind them not to smoke while they "do" their nails? Is the warning on the back of a color television set large and visible enough to warn you against taking the back off and exposing yourself to about 25,000 volts of static electricity buildup on the picture tube?

If the average person must squint to read these warnings or hold them up to bright light, imagine the difficulties of the visually impaired.

There is, however, a body of information on printing and graphic design available to publishers and manufacturers which addresses the needs of people suffering from a loss of visual perception and recommends necessary adjustments. These adjustments deal with type size, type style, leading, the color of ink and paper, contrast, paragraphing, hyphenation, margins, capitalization, paper finish, and other specifications.

The author has published guidelines describing these adjustments, and has enlisted the support of experts in vision, aging, and languages to form a non-profit organization, Better Communications, Inc. The purpose of the organization is to research and promote better visual communications for the visually impaired, blind, deaf, and those with poor reading skills.

If minimum guidelines are followed in printing and graphic design, visual communication will be made more accessible to sight-impaired people, young and old, booby traps created by printing design will be eliminated, and printed communication for the general reading public will be greatly improved.

For further information, please contact: Jack B. Ralph, Box 1833, Silver Spring, Md. 20902. Telephone: (202) 245-7196.

Alcoholism and the Elderly

Phyllis K. Snyder and Ann Way, Ph.D.

Ms. Snyder has been Executive Director of Chicago's Alcoholic Treatment Center since 1957 when the facility opened. Dr. Way is a sociologist and demographer. She was formerly Coordinator of Research and Evaluation at the Center.

Alcoholism has been identified as "the most serious of all drug abuse problems" among the aged.[1] The social and emotional costs of alcoholism for the elderly individual and for his family as well as for the community as a whole make it imperative that greater attention be focused on the identification and treatment of the elderly alcoholic.

Drinking Patterns Among the Aged

In considering the patterns of alcohol consumption among the aged, there is evidence that older Americans are less likely to drink than younger Americans. Moreover, if they do drink, they are more likely to be moderate rather than heavy drinkers. In comparing the drinking habits of a national sample, Calahan and his associates found, for instance, that the proportion of abstainers increased with age and that there was a clear decline in the proportion of heavy drinkers after age 65.[2] Some researchers explain these apparent changes in drinking habits with age by contending that alcoholism is a "self-limiting" disease which "burns out" as the alcoholic ages.[3]

The lower proportion of alcohol abuse reported among older Americans is thus considered to be due to the fact that a moderation of even heavy drinking automatically accompanies the aging process. The apparent decline in the proportion of both those who drink and those who drink heavily has been seen as at least partially a result, on the other hand, of the fact that the higher death rates associated with chronic alcohol abuse may insure that the population who survive into their 60's are more moderate in their drinking habits.[4]

Finally, Marden has pointed out that some of the apparent decline in alcohol consumption with age may be due to the disproportionate representation of women in the older age groups.[5] Most studies have found that older women are less likely to drink than older men. Among younger Americans, the gap in drinking habits by age has, however, apparently been narrowing in recent years.[6] If these trends continue, there may be some diminishing in future years of the now-evident sex differentials in alcohol use in the older population.

Despite the fact that drinking appears to decrease with age, there are still a large number of elderly who are problem drinkers. It has been estimated, for example, that there are more than 3 million alcoholics over the age of 60 in the United States.[7] It is important to realize also that many more elderly may misuse alcohol. For instance, the elderly must be particularly aware of the often detrimental effects of combining alcohol with medication they might be taking for various ailments. There is also evidence that alcohol may exacerbate a variety of physical ailments from which the elderly suffer.[8]

Identifying the Elderly Alcoholic

The identification of the elderly alcoholic is one of the major problems in the treatment of alcoholism among the aged. Many senior citizens are retired and living alone, so that problems with alcohol abuse may go undetected by family members or friends who do not interact with them on a regular basis. As is true with female alcoholics, there may also be considerable reluctance on the part of family members to confront the over-60 alcoholic with his illness.

Other factors also contribute to the problem of identifying the geriatric alcoholic. Alcoholism may not be diagnosed by medical personnel who come into contact with older problem drinkers because the symptoms elderly alcoholics present can be attributed to other degenerative diseases common in the aged or because those workers are also reluctant to label an elderly patient as an alcoholic.[9] Furthermore, although denial is a barrier to treatment among all alcoholics, older problem drinkers are even more likely to deny their problems of alcohol abuse because of the social stigma involved in the admission of a drinking problem.

Dobbie cited all of these problems as contributing to the failure to detect alcoholism among the elderly.[10] She suggests, in this regard, that the burden of identifying problem drinkers among the aged must fall heavily upon physicians and social service personnel who treat or provide assistance to the elderly.[11] There is, therefore, an obvious need to educate those individuals to recognize when a patient or client may be an alcoholic or where the misuse of alcohol may be compounding existing physical or emotional illness.

Alcoholism treatment facilities can serve a valuable role in this educational process. For example, Chicago's Alcoholic Treatment Center has cooperated with the Mayor's Office for Senior Citizens in holding training seminars on alcoholism and alcohol abuse for social service personnel working with geriatric clients. Educational programs can also be oriented toward providing senior citizens themselves with information on alcoholism and problem drinking. Warnings concerning the problems that can result from mixing alcohol with prescription and non-prescription drugs should be emphasized in such programs.

Treatment Outlook for the Older Alcoholic

Problems in identifying older alcoholics may not be the only factors which prevent elderly alcoholics from receiving treatment. Dobbie contends that elderly alcohol abusers are actively excluded from the network of existing treatment facilities because their age is regarded as a barrier to successful rehabilitation.[12] There is, however, no evidence to suggest that elderly alcoholics are "untreatable."

Some researchers do consider heavy drinking by older individuals as "more indicative of pathology" than such behavior is among younger persons.[13] On the other hand, there is evidence that older alcoholics actually respond better to treatment than do younger drinkers and that the chances for successful rehabilitation are greater. Rosin and Glatt for instance, argue that geriatric alcoholics do not exhibit the "deep-seated psychological problems" that are characteristic of younger alcoholics.[14]

There may be a pattern of recidivism among elderly alcoholics who do seek and receive treatment. For instance, almost 70 percent of those over 60 who sought admission to Chicago's Alcoholic Treatment Center in a recent 18-month period had participated in another inpatient treatment program prior to their admission to the Center. Around a quarter of the over-60 patients in that same period had, in fact, been treated in the program at Chicago's Alcoholic Treatment Center at least one time previously. The proportion of patients over 60 who had been treated for alcoholism before, either at the Center or in some other inpatient facility, was greater than the proportion for the patient population as a whole during the same period.

The duration of the period of alcohol abuse may have some bearing on treatment success for the elderly alcoholic. Two basic types of geriatric alcoholics have been identified—those who have exhibited a life-long pattern of alcohol dependency and those whose heavy drinking pattern appears to be a reaction to the accumulating stresses of growing old.[15] Cohen observes that where alcohol abuse originates as a coping response to the stresses of aging, there is a good chance for treatment success.[16] He is not optimistic, however, about the recovery possibilities for the geriatric alcoholic whose pattern of alcohol abuse emerged in early adulthood. Zimburg suggests, however, that there is a greater chance for successful rehabilitation even for the latter group of elderly alcohol abusers than there is for younger alcoholics.[17]

Factors in Alcoholism

There is, as has been suggested, an emphasis on stress as a precipitating factor in problem drinking among the aged. Loneliness, for example, is one factor which may contribute to patterns of alcohol abuse. The older person often lives alone, and may be limited in his or her social opportunities for interaction with others. Bereavement over the deaths of family members or friends is another obvious source of stress for older individuals.

Studies have shown that the highest incidence of alcoholism occurs among widowers.[18] The demographic characteristics of patients over 60 who have been admitted to Chicago's Alcoholic Treatment Center tend to confirm social isolation as an acute problem among older alcoholics. Nearly 60 percent of the over-60 admissions to the treatment facility over a recent 18-month period were, for instance, widowed, separated, or divorced, and 15 percent had never married. The majority of these inpatients had been living alone. Cohen has emphasized the need to help the elderly establish new meaningful social relationships as a key variable in the successful treatment of the elderly alcoholic.[19]

Retirement is another factor which may precipitate problem drinking among the over-60 population. The elderly may begin drinking, or increase their level of drinking, to cope with the loss of a sense of self-worth that may accompany retirement. Increased drinking may also be a by-product of the inactivity of retirement as the elderly fill in time with social activities in which drinking is a natural and accepted pattern. Dobbie calls attention to the dangers of social drinking in retirement communities and warns that alcohol abuse is emerging as a major problem in such settings.[20]

In a similar vein, Marden observes that the problem of geriatric alcoholism is likely to be geographically concentrated because the elderly are differentially distributed throughout the country.[21] There is a need, for example, for communities in the Sunbelt to be particularly aware of the possibilities of alcohol abuse among the over-60 population who move South and West after retirement. Within other regions in the United States, there also exist, however, both planned and unplanned residential concentrations of the elderly. These communities and neighborhoods should also be particularly aware of the need to develop programs of education to increase awareness of the dangers of alcohol abuse among the aged and to help in the identification of elderly problem drinkers.

Treatment Alternatives for the Older Drinker

Once he has been identified, there are generally a variety of treatment alternatives available to the elderly problem drinker. Alcoholism treatment programs have, for instance, been established by many private hospitals, and there are also a growing number of publicly supported outpatient and inpatient treatment programs. Each rehabilitation program varies, but group therapy is an important element in many treatment approaches. For example, Chicago's Alcoholic Treatment Center relies on a milieu therapy approach in which group counseling sessions are an integral feature. The sharing of experience among group members as they focus on their problems with alcoholism and the supportive relationships that are developed in the group may be particularly beneficial for the older problem drinker who is, as it has been pointed out, often socially isolated.

It is that social isolation that makes it vital that inpatient rehabilitation programs for the elderly problem drinker be followed by involvement in outpatient treatment programs. Participation in

Alcoholics Anonymous which has a long history of aiding individuals to maintain their sobriety through fellowship with other recovering alcoholics can be very useful too in helping the elderly problem drinker. It is also important that rehabilitation personnel be familiar with programs for senior citizens which can provide them with additional social support.

There are problems in obtaining treatment for the elderly alcoholic. Lack of money may, for example, limit the participation of the older problem drinker in private rehabilitation programs. There are, moreover, few programs specifically designed to serve the elderly alcoholic.[22] More than 20 years' experience at Chicago's Alcoholic Treatment Center suggests there are no major drawbacks in integrating older problem drinkers into a treatment program with young alcoholics.

The treatment of geriatric alcoholics can also be seriously complicated by the fact that they often suffer from a variety of physical ailments which many inpatient alcoholism rehabilitation programs are not equipped to handle. These ailments may also reduce the mobility of an elderly problem drinker and, thus, limit his participation even in outpatient treatment programs. The challenge of aiding older problem drinkers may fall, then, upon the staff of hospitals or nursing homes where the older drinker was admitted primarily for the treatment of other physical problems or on social workers counseling such individuals in other senior citizen assistance programs. It may be possible in such cases to use the services of outreach alcoholism counselors in aiding the elderly alcohol abuser to cope with his problem.[23]

Summary

Although problem drinking has been recognized as a very serious problem among older Americans, there are no ready solutions to the crisis of alcohol abuse among the elderly. The identification of the elderly problem drinker represents the first challenge in efforts to treat the older alcoholic. Programs are needed to educate medical personnel and social workers who work closely with the elderly to recognize when alcohol abuse is a primary or complicating factor in the health or social problems senior citizens experience. Senior citizens themselves can benefit greatly from educational programs that alert them to the dangers of alcohol abuse, and particularly to the problems that arise from mixing alcohol with many medications.

In addition to these educational efforts, there is a vital need to coordinate alcoholic treatment programs with existing geriatric social services.[24]

Those working with senior citizens in a community should be aware of the variety of inpatient, outpatient, and outreach programs where elderly alcoholics can be referred for treatment. In turn, alcoholism treatment workers must learn to utilize the network of senior citizen social services to aid in the post-treatment support of the elderly alcohol abuser. The need for coordination of treatment services with other supportive programs for the aged is particularly acute in neighborhoods, communities, or regions where the over-60 population is concentrated.

Finally, the myth that older alcoholics are untreatable must be dispelled while the unique problems of treating the older problem drinker must be recognized. The problems of aging, particularly the increasing frequency of debilitating illnesses or the possibility of senility, do complicate the treatment outlook for the geriatric alcoholic. The elderly alcohol abuser can, however, be helped, and there is evidence, as has been noted, that he will respond better to treatment than the younger alcoholic. What is clear is that his need for treatment cannot be ignored.

REFERENCES

[1] Sidney Cohen, "Geriatric Drug Abuse", *Vista Hill Foundation Drug Abuse and Alcoholism Newsletter,* March, 1975, p. 4.

[2] Don Calahan and Robin Room, *Problem Drinking among American Men,* Rutgers Center of Alcohol Studies, pp. 73-74.

[3] Leslie R. H. Drew, "Alcoholism as a Self-limiting Disease", *Quarterly Journal of Studies on Alcohol,* December, 1968, pp. 963-968.

[4] Parker G. Marden, "Alcohol Abuse and the Aged", Special Statement Prepared for the Division of Special Treatment and Rehabilitation Programs, National Institute on Alcohol Abuse and Alcoholism, p. 7.

[5] Marden, pp. 7-8.

[6] Jonica D. Homiller, *Women and Alcohol: a Guide for State and Local Decision Makers,* The Council of State Authorities, Alcohol and Drug Problems Association of North America, p. 6.

[7] Janet Ashton Glassock, "Alcoholism on Rise, Long Beach Program Aids Elderly", *Era, New Directions for Aging,* California Department of Aging, September, 1978, p. 4.

[8] Marc A. Schuckit and Paul A. Pastor, "The Elderly as a Unique Population: Alcoholism", *Alcoholism: Clinical and Experimental Research,* January, 1978, p. 31.

[9] Schuckit and Pastor, p. 36.

[10] Judy Dobbie, *Substance Abuse among the Elderly,* Alcoholism and Drug Addiction Research Foundation of Ontario, pp. 6-7.

[11] Dobbie, p. 5.

[12] Dobbie, p. 7.

[13] Grace L. Duckworth and Adylin Rosenblatt, "Helping the Elderly Alcoholic" *Social Casework,* May, 1976, p. 296.

[14] Arnold J. Rosin and M. M. Glatt, "Alcohol Excess in the Elderly", *Quarterly Journal of Studies on Alcohol,* March, 1971, pp. 53-58.

[15] Sheldon Zimberg, "The Elderly Alcoholic", *The Gerontologist,* June, 1974, p. 222.

[16] Cohen, p. 4.

[17] Zimberg, p. 223.

[18] M. B. Bailey, P. W. Haberman, and H. Alksne, "The Epidemiology of Alcoholism in an Urban Residential Area", *Quarterly Journal of Studies on Alcohol,* January, 1965, pp. 19-40, as cited in Zimberg, p. 221.

[19] Cohen, p. 4.

[20] Dobbie, p. 11.

[21] Marden, p. 3.

[22] Dobbie, pp. 7-8.

[23] Duckworth and Rosenblatt, p. 300.

[24] Marden, p. 17.

Hazards of Drug Use Among the Elderly

Lawrence R. Krupka, PhD
Prof. of Natural Science, Kedzie Laboratory, Michigan State Univ., East Lansing, MI 48824.

Arthur M. Vener, PhD
Prof. of Social Science, Michigan State Univ., East Lansing, MI 48824.

The Problem

The elderly (65 and older) comprising 10% of the population consume 22 to 25% of all prescription drugs in the U.S. (Butler, 1975; Rabin, 1972). In the United Kingdom, the elderly representing 12% of the population, consume as much as 30% of the National Health Service funding for drugs (Carlson, 1975).

Multiple pathology, a common phenomenon among the elderly, fosters the practice of polypharmacy in attempts to treat several disorders simultaneously (James, 1976a). The number of drugs prescribed for hospitalized individuals rises with the age of the patient (Hurwitz, 1969). Adverse drug reactions accelerate with increased drug exposure. When six to ten drugs are taken, typically, 7.4% of the recipients have adverse drug reactions (Martin, 1971). Hospital patients who were given one to five drugs had an adverse drug reaction incidence of 18.8%, whereas patients ingesting six or more prescribed drugs, had an incidence of 81.4% (James, 1976a). A reduction in the number of drugs prescribed for older individuals has been recommended to lessen the number of drug interactions (Caird, 1977).

In a study of 138 patients living in an extended care facility, 30 patients had prescriptions for 38 "non-recommended" drugs (Ingman et al., 1975). Furthermore, a study of physicians in Scotland showed that they were generally unaware of the potential interactions involving five groups of drugs—adrenergic neurone blockers, warfarin, antidiabetic agents, monamine oxidase inhibitors and sedatives. Of 185 doctors surveyed only 17% had accurate knowledge of these drug interactions (Petrie et al., 1975).

The problem of multiple drug use among the elderly had serious implications because of pharmacokinetic (differences in absorption, distribution, metabolism and excretion) and pharmacodynamic (alterations of action at receptor sites) considerations (James, 1976b). Attention has been directed to the iatrogenic hazards of drugs to geriatric patients (D'Arcy, 1976). Such potentially harmful, commonly prescribed medicines include antidepressants, antirheumatics, cardiac glycoside, diuretics, barbituates and tranquilizers. Geriatric patients often have decreased renal and liver function resulting in a narrowing of the safety margin between the therapeutic and toxic doses. For example, although phenobarbital is frequently prescribed as a sedative for young people it may be especially hazardous for the older patient. Large doses of the drug can result in stupor and coma. The failure of the liver to metabolize the drug adequately and/or the inability of the kidney to excrete the drug into the urine enhances potential drug toxicity. Furthermore, brain impairment (stroke) in a geriatric patient may result in increased susceptibility to the effect of phenobarbital, wherein a decreased dosage would have the same impact as a larger dose (Felstein, 1969).

In the U.S., only 4 to 5% of the elderly live in institutionalized setting (i.e., nursing facilities). Thus, the overwhelming majority of older people have minimal supervision with respect to their overall exposure to drugs. Several investigators have argued that three drugs seem to be the maximal number for an elderly preson to manage correctly (Lamy & Kitler, 1971). A review of medication errors of patients living at home, has revealed that not less that 25% made errors in the self-administration of their drugs, and in some instances, the figure was as high as 59% (Stewart & Cluff, 1972). In this vein, others have suggested that elderly people who reside in their own households run special drug toxicity risks and need regular reappraisal (Shaw & Opit, 1976).

In a previous study of total drug exposure (prescription, over-the-counter and social—alcohol, caffeine and nicotine) of noninstitutionalized elderly, we found that 67% used at least one prescription drug, 65% took at least one over-the-counter drug and 98% consumed a social drug daily (Vener et al., 1979, in press). In terms of range, 24% ingested zero to two drugs, 55% ingested three to five drugs, and 22% consumed six or more drugs, with one individual consuming 13 different drugs. Of those who used drugs, the average of 2.0 prescription, 1.8 over-the-counter, and 1.8 social drugs amounted to a total of 5.6 drugs per individual with males averaging 7.5 and females 4.7.

Our sample, which ranged from the upper end of the working to the upper end of the middle class, was purposively selected because of their involvement in

This research was supported by the NIH Biomedical Research Support Grant, No. 5 507 RR 07049-11 to Michigan State Univ.

peer interaction networks. When medical attention was needed, they had confidence in both their physicians' diagnoses and the drugs he/she prescribed. As previous research has shown regarding the importance of maintaining interaction with peers (Blau, 1973), our respondents' overall satisfaction with their life condition was relatively high despite their average age of 70 years.

In contrast to this relatively independent (health, financial and social) group of respondents who were ingesting 2.0 prescription per day, we have encountered a number of instances whereby institutionalized elderly were exposed to a larger number of drugs (e.g., up to 18 prescription drugs daily). Some investigators have found that elderly patients in long-term care facilities were taking 3.3 drugs on a daily basis (Kalchthaler et al., 1977) while others found 4.6 (Ingman et al., 1975). In one long-term care institution, 6 of every 10 patients were exposed to major or minor tranquilizers; 3 of 10, sedative-hypnotic agents; and 2 of 10, analgesic agents (Ingman et al., 1975).

In this report, we wish to explore in detail the interactive hazards of the total drug exposure (prescription, over-the-counter and social—alcohol, caffeine and nicotine) of elderly individuals.

Measurement of Drug Interactions

Because of space limitations it would be impossible to analyze extensively the interactions of the drugs of a number of individuals simultaneously. Typically, due to differences in personal habits, health and medical care, individuals ingest a wide array of drugs. Statistical generalizations regarding type, number and frequency

of drug use are more easily arrived at. Therefore, analysis of drug interactions must be examined on an individualized basis. The greater the number of drugs ingested, the greater the opportunity for interactive permutations to develop.

Two case studies have been selected to demonstrate potential drug hazards. One case was selected from our study of 55 noninstitutionalized elderly respondents, while the other was selected from investigations and referrals of individuals residing in long-term care facilities. Neither case is atypical. Both individuals were taking at least 10 drugs, were of approximately similar age, and had several chronic ailments in common.

Case Number 1: Overview

This 79-year-old married male was living in his own residence and consumed 13 different drugs on a daily basis. He had seven chronic illnesses which included allergy and sinus problems, hardening of the arteries, heart trouble, ulcers, arthritis, and two physical impairments—loss of hearing and back trouble.

Despite his chronic illnesses, he had not seen a physician on a regular office visit during the year prior to his being interviewed. However, he was hospitalized on two separate occasions on an emergency basis. In terms of his life condition, he was dissatisfied with cost of medical care, unhappy about his physical health, remorseful about not achieving higher levels of education, and did not like his present family life because his wife had recently been institutionalized and therefore he had to live alone. Also he believed that governmental

Table 1. Daily Drug Exposure of a Noninstitutionalized 79-Year-Old Male.

Drug		Amount	Function
Atromid-S (clofibrate)		1500 mg	Prevent cholesterol build-up
Lanoxin (digoxin)		.25 mg	Regulate heart beat
Aldactazide (hydrochlorothiazide)		25 mg	Diuretic
+ spironolactone)		25 mg	
Motrin (ibuprofen)		1200 mg	Anti-inflammatory
Sorbitrate (isosorbide dinitrate)		20 mg	Treatment of angina pectoris
Pavabid (papaverine hydrogen chloride)		300 mg	Heart muscle relaxant
Ascriptin (aspirin + aluminum hydroxide)		300 mg	Analgesic—gastric distress
Vitamin C		1500 mg	Cold preventive
Vitamin B_1		50 mg	To prevent ear deterioration
Dicalcium phosphate with		100 mg	To provide minerals and Vitamin D
Vitamin D		400 I.U.	
Cefol	Vitamin C	750 mg	
	Niacin	100 mg	
	Vitamin B_1	15mg	
	Vitamin B_2	10 mg	
	Vitamin B_6	5 mg	
	Vitamin B_{12}	6 mg	
	Folic Acid	500 mg	
	Vitamin E	30 I.U.	
Alcohol		2 oz	Enjoyment
Caffeine		1250 mg	Enjoyment

officials had abandoned him along with other older persons.

The repondent's daily drug exposure is listed in Table 1.

Case Number 2: Overview

This 80-year-old female has been living in long-term care facilities since 1971. In 1967 she was widowed and four years later she voluntarily placed herself into a nursing home because of loneliness due to physical isolation. She lived in a rural area and her nearest neighbor resided a mile away. At the time she first entered this facility her physical health was relatively sound and she had no major chronic illnesses. After a year of residence in this original long-term care facility, she became disillusioned with the amount of drugs that she was forced to take and distrustful of the way her pension was being managed. Shortly thereafter she moved to another facility where a number of childhood acquaintances and friends resided. For the first several years she took leadership responsibility in organized social activities. However, within the past several years she has shown a steady decline in both physical and mental health. Presently, she is in a state of extreme lethargy and disorientation and complains of being constipated and frequently is incontinent. She now has four chronic illnesses—hardening of the arteries, high blood pressure, heart trouble and is depressed. She sees a physician once a month who also treats approximately 70 other patients on the day he makes his monthly visit. The 10 drugs that she ingests daily and her weekly injection of vitamin B12 are listed in Table 2.

Drug Interactions

Analysis of the drug interaction of the 79-year-old male exposed to 13 different drugs shows minimal interactive hazards from the prescriptions. He was taking seven prescription drugs daily. His prescriptions indicate that care was taken to avoid potential hazards. For example, the use of Aldactazide as a diuretic was indicated, considering the fact that the respondent was also ingesting digoxin. However, spironolactone, an active ingredient in the drug, has been shown to be a tumorigen in chronic toxicity studies in rats (Physicians' Desk Reference, 1977) and therefore is potentially harmful in itself. The use of Ascriptin (aspirin with aluminum hydroxide) was indicated since the respondent has stomach ulcers and this form of aspirin would be less irritating on the gastric mucosa.

When the respondent's total drug intake is examined, potential interactive hazards become evident. Since the respondent has had severe heart disease (hospitalized twice in the year prior to interview on an emergency basis), his intake of caffeine of approximately 1250 mg per day is more than twice the recommended safe level (Long, 1977). His daily intake of alcohol (minimum of 2 fluid ounces) may interact with the aspirin to exacerbate his ulcers, since alcohol potentiates the effects of salicylates. In addition, his high intake of vitamin C (2250 mg) will interact with the aspirin. Aspirin decreases the effect of vitamin C by increasing its urinary elimination from the body, while vitamin C can increase or potentiate the effect of aspirin by slowing its elimination causing aspirin accumulation and toxicity. The ingestion of vitamin C along with aspirin as well as alcohol with aspirin is not an isolated phenomenon. Twenty percent of elderly respondents in our previous study were taking these drugs simultaneously (Vener et al., 1979, in press). Additionally, Long-term use of aspirin on its own may be hazardous, (e.g., kidney damage [Goldberger & Talmer, 1975]).

Analysis of the drug intake of the 80-year-old institutionalized female indicates that serious health hazards might occur because of her daily prescription regimen. Her lethargic and disoriented state may very

Table 2. Daily Drug Exposure of an Institutionalized 80-Year-Old Female.

Drug	Amount	Function
Atromid-S (clofibrate)	2000 mg	Prevent cholesterol build-up
Lanoxin (digoxin)	.25 mg	Regulate heart beat
Aldoril (methyldopa +	500 mg	Antihypertensive and diuretic
hydrochlorothiazide)	30 mg	
Elavil (amitriptyline hydrochloride)	50 mg	Antidepressant
Thorazine (chloropromazine		
hydrochloride)	75 mg	Strong tranquilizer
Sodium Butisol (sodium butabarbital)	100 mg	Sedative-hypnotic
Donnatal—hyoscyamine sulfate	0.4148 mg	Sedative
atropine sulfate	0.0776 mg	and
hyoscine hydrobromide	0.0260 mg	antispasmodic
phenobarbital	64.8 mg	
Slow-K (potassium chloride)	2400 mg	Potassium depletion
Agoral (phenolphthalein + mineral oil)	1 oz	Relief of constipation
Caffeine	400 mg	Enjoyment
Vitamin B12 (cyanocobalamin) [a]	100 mcg	Treatment for pernicious anemia

[a] once a week

well be symptomatic of behavioral toxicity. Reactions to drugs may be varied and present overlapping symptoms such as insomnia, nightmares, irritability, increased sensitivity to noise, listlessness and restlessness (Davies, 1977). For example, her use of Elavil, a tricyclic antidepressant (amitriptyline) is more likely to cause adverse effects in the elderly. This drug should be avoided if Aldoril (methyldopa and hydrochlorothiazide) is also being taken (Long, 1977). Amitriptyline may cause a dangerous elevation of blood pressure if taken concurrently with methyldopa. Amitriptyline should also be avoided in patients with heart disease, particularly those with disorders of heart rhythm. Amitriptyline taken with a hydrochlorothiazide diuretic may slow its elimination from the body and an overdose could occur. Furthermore, numerous reports have implicated methyldopa as a common cause of depression and other psychiatric disorders such as insomnia and nightmares. Both methyldopa and amitriptyline can cause drowsiness as possible side effects. Amitriptyline may also increase the effects of sedatives, sleep-inducing drugs, tranquilizers and cause oversedation. Since this individual is also taking Thorazine (chloropromazine hydrochloride), a strong tranquilizer as well as several other sedative-hypnotic drugs— sodium butisol (sodium butabarbital), and Donnatal (hyoscyamine sulfate, atropine sulfate, hyoscine hydrobromide, phenobarbital) the present chronic confusional state of this patient may be traceable to these drug interactions and/or side effects. Chloropromazine should be used with caution in the elderly, especially those with impaired heart function. Possible side effects from this drug may include drowsiness, depression, indifference, insomnia and agitation. Chloropromazine may also increase the effects of methyldopa and cause excessive lowering of blood pressure. Lanoxin (digoxin) may cause drowsiness and lethargy as well as confusion and disorientation especially in the elderly. Use of digoxin with hydrochlorothiazide can cause serious digoxin toxicity due to excessive loss of potassium. However, the physician prescribed potassium tablets in order to compensate for this eventuality.

Implications

The elderly male living at home, although having more chronic illnesses than the institutionalized female (three of which were the same), was not taking any tranquilizers, antidepressants or sedative-hypnotics and was able to care for himself and remained active in his network of lifelong friends. The apparent greater use of these drugs in long-term care facilities may be due to the increased pathology of the patients and/or a tendency on the part of physicians working with institutionalized individuals to prescribe more drugs under controlled conditions. In addition, the desire of officials to maintain operational efficiency by controlling the behavior of their patients with disparate needs and dispositions may also be involved.

The use of drug therapy among the elderly should proceed with caution. Multiple pathology of the aging leads to polypharmacy which in turn may lead to a greater number of iatrogenic reactions which frequently are treated with even a greater number of drugs. This cycle can be broken by a greater awareness on the part of health professionals, policy-makers and others who work on behalf of the aging.

Drugs prescribed for the elderly should be as simple as possible and be of relatively short duration (Caird, 1977). A physician explaining why he is prescribing certain drugs to elderly patients or their relatives, in itself, often results in more simple and rational prescribing behavior (Whitehead, 1975). However, in long-term care facilities, as in all total institutions, patients find it difficult to establish and maintain social contacts with individuals from the outside world (Goffman, 1961). Health problems also limit contacts and outsiders as well as loss through death of friends and relatives. Therefore, consideration should be given to the feasibility of utilizing a third party whose prime function would be to act on behalf of the institutionalized elderly patient in lieu of concerned relatives and/or friends. Periodically, this third party would confer with the physician to discuss the patient's medical condition and to explain the rationale for the drugs being prescribed. In order to avoid conflict of interest, the third party should in no way be associated with the long-term care facility in which the elderly patient resides. For example, representatives of state departments of social services or individuals from concerned gerontological organizations could be designated for such a function. Even the best long-term care facilities primarily focus upon the business of medical care, feeding and asepsis (Henry, 1963). Unfortunately, the emotional condition of the patient's mind is often of lesser concern. An additional function of the third party would be to periodically observe and/or confer with the patient to assess his/her overall state of being.

Finally, it is important to note that the two cases analyzed in this report are not bizarre. We have encountered a number of elderly individuals, both institutionalized and noninstitutionalized, who have ingested larger number of drugs. In order to avoid diminishing the importance of the general problem, planners and practitioners should not consider these cases as being exceptional.

References

Blau, Z. S. *Old age in a changing society.* Franklin Watts, New York, 1973.

Butler, R. N. *Why survive? Being old in America.* Harper and Row, New York, 1975.

Caird, F. I. Prescribing for the elderly. *British Journal of Hospital Medicine,* 1977, *17,* 610-613.

Carlson, R. I. *The end of medicine.* Wiley & Sons, New York, 1975.

4. PROBLEMS AND POTENTIALS OF AGING

D'Arcy, P. F. Iatrogenic disease: A hazard of multiple drug therapy. *Royal Society Health Journal*, 1976, *96*, 277-283.

Davies, D. M. *Textbook of adverse drug reactions.* Oxford Univ. Press, Oxford, 1977.

Felstein, I. *Later life: Geriatrics today and tomorrow.* Penguin Books, Baltimore, 1969.

Goffman, E. *Asylums.* Doubleday & Co., Inc. Garden City, 1961.

Goldberger, L. E. & Talmer, L. B. Analgesic abuse syndrome, a frequently overlooked cause of reversible renal failure. *Urology*, 1975, *5*, 728-732.

Henry, J. *Culture against man.* Random House, New York, 1963.

Hurwitz, N. Predisposing factors in adverse reactions to drugs. *British Medical Journal*, 1969, *1*, 536-539.

Ingman, S. R., Lawson, I. R., Pierpaoli, P. G., & Blake, P. A survey of the prescribing and administration of drugs in a long-term care institution for the elderly. *Journal of the American Geriatrics Society,* 1975, *23*, 309-316.

James, I. Prescribing for the elderly: Check the interaction and cut down your calls. *Modern Geriatrics*, 1976, *6*, 7-14. (a)

James, I. Prescribing for the elderly: Why it's best to keep it simple. *Modern Geriatrics*, 1976, *6*, 25-28. (b)

Kalchthaler, D. O., Coccaro, E., & Lichtiger, S. Incidences of polypharmacy in a long-term care facility. *Journal of the American Geriatrics Society*, 1977, *25*, 308-313.

Lamy, P. P., & Kitler, M. E. Drugs and the geriatric patient. *Journal of the American Geriatrics Society,* 1971, *19*, 23-33.

Long, J. W. *The essential guide to prescription drugs.* Harper & Row, New York, 1977.

Martin, E. W. *Hazards of medication.* J. B. Lippincott Co., Philadelphia, 1971.

Petrie, J. C., Durno, D., & Howie, J. G. P., *Clinical effects of interaction between drugs.* J. C. Excerpta Medica, Amsterdam, 1975.

Physician's Desk Reference. 31st Edition, Medical Economics Co., Oradell, NJ, 1977.

Rubin, D. L. Use of medicine: A review of prescribed and non-prescribed medicine use. USPHS, DHEW, Publ. HSM 733012, Reprint Series, 1972.

Shaw, S. M., & Opit, L. J. Need for supervision in the elderly receiving long-term prescribed medication. *British Medical Journal*, 1976, *1*, 505-507.

Stewart, R. B. & Cluff, L. E. A review of medication errors and compliance in ambulant patients. *Clinical Pharmacology and Therapeutics*, 1972, *13*, 463-468.

Vener, A. M., Krupka, L. R., & Climo, J. J. Drug exposure and health characteristics of noninstitutionalized retired individuals. *Journal of the American Geriatrics Society,* 1979. (in press)

Whitehead, A. *World Medicine*, 1975, Sept. 24, 26 (As cited in Atkinson, L., Gibson, I. J. M., & Andrews, J. The difficulties of old people taking drugs, *Age and Aging*, 1977, *6*, 144-150).

Growing Old in Rural America

Anita S. Harbert, Ph.D. and Carroll W. Wilkinson, M.L.S.*

Ms. Wilkinson is an academic librarian and a research assistant with the West Virginia University Gerontology Center. Dr. Harbert is the Director of the West Virginia University Gerontology Center and an associate professor in social work in the School of Social Work at the University.

Scattered across the United States in the mountain hollows of Appalachia, the river valley towns, the wheat farms of the middle and southwest, around the town squares of New England, and in the hills of the Ozarks, are approximately 11 million people aged 60 and over. They are America's rural elderly, a group which includes over one third of the nation's total older population.

Older rural Americans are not evenly distributed throughout the country. They are concentrated in the north central and southern regions of the United States. Most of them live on farms, in small towns with populations of 2,500 or less, or in houses scattered across the open country side.[1] Interestingly, over half of the older people living on farms reside in one of 10 states: Illinois, Indiana, Iowa, Kentucky, Minnesota, Missouri, North Carolina, Ohio, Tennessee, or Texas.

Twenty-one out of the 50 states have at least 40 percent of their older population in rural areas, and in eight states, more than half of the older population is rural.[2] These facts have important policy implications since Federal governmental programs are often set up to serve an urban population.

In the minds of some, the rural elderly are the most disadvantaged of an already disadvantaged minority.[3] There is no question that services are not always made available to those people living in remote areas or to elderly residents who have been too isolated or proud to seek them out.

Robert A. Harootyan of the University of Southern California Andrus Gerontology Center agrees with Louise Gerrard of the West Virginia Commission on Aging. He asserts that, "demographic and socioeconomic data concerning older persons in rural areas suggests that this group of older Americans is especially disadvantaged in various spheres of their lives, particularly health care, economic status, educational attainment, housing and transportation."[4]

According to William Cohen, Senator of Maine, "One out of every ten Americans is over 65, but in rural areas that proportion is one in five. In rural areas, the aged have far fewer public services available to them. The nearest health clinic or doctor may be miles away from an individual's home. In many cases elderly residents in rural areas are poor, and lack everyday conveniences such as telephones and automobiles. Sometimes their lack of mobility in an isolated, rural environment causes serious problems of loneliness. A study done in Maine showed loneliness was one of the four most significant problems faced by the elderly in the state."[5]

Fiscal Neglect

Since the early 1960's and the fiscal crisis of the

cities, rural areas have been subject to benign neglect as far as Federal programs are concerned. The growth of cities called policy makers' attention to high crime rates, urban blight and flight, and pollution. Because of the organized pressures of trade unions and consumer and other special interest groups, much of the focus of social reform during the 60's and 70's has been on urban problems. At the same time, failure to remedy many of the troubles and difficulties, especially the economic ones in the rural areas, led to deterioration of our Nation's small towns and farm communities. This resulted in an extensive out-migration of youth and younger adults to urban areas. Not surprisingly, growth and progress in physical and social development have been slower in rural areas. One writer suggests that rural areas are "out of phase" or behind the present social and physical world.[6]

Special Problems of Rural Areas

Whatever the cause, living in rural areas presents special and unique problems to the elderly of these regions. Perhaps one of the most unique problems is that of sheer distance. The distance "between people, people and towns, and people and services" can create insurmountable problems for rural elderly.[7] Distance complicates meeting basic needs such as food and medical care, it restricts social interaction, and frequently increases living expenses. The rural elderly may have to travel 30, 40, and even 50 miles to obtain necessities; they often live in relative isolation with few neighbors and few social contacts; and frequently, fundamental requirements such as food are more expensive.

Rural areas, in addition, have higher proportions of older residents, which represent another unique aspect of growing old in rural America. The neighbor of an older rural person is very likely to be another older person. In some rural counties the elderly residents may constitute as much as 25 percent of the population. As younger residents are forced to leave their rural homes to find work, they leave behind areas with shrinking tax-bases and a serious shortage of necessary services.[8] Very often in rural states increases in property and sales taxes are becoming a burden to those who can least afford to bear the cost—older rural people.

The rural elderly are more economically oppressed than most older people. Income levels for the rural elderly are relatively lower than those of older people living in non-rural areas. One of the myths about rural life is that it costs less to live in rural areas. Since some people believe that they need less, the lower income levels of the rural elderly are often seen as of no consequence. It is not less expensive to live in rural areas; in some ways it costs more. Transportation costs are higher since one must generally own a car for transportation. Fuel costs for older rural adults, for example, are probably much higher than for non-rural elderly because a higher percentage live in substandard housing which is not properly winterized.[9] The rural elderly frequently neglect such things as health care because they cannot afford it, and the rural elderly generally do with less because they have less.

According to the Bureau of the Census, almost half (49 percent) of the elderly households in rural areas received incomes below $5,000 in 1975 and only 10 percent received $15,000 or more. Their median income was $5,136 or over $1,300 less than for elderly households in metropolitan areas. One-fifth of rural elderly persons were below the poverty level, compared to one-seventh in large cities and one-tenth in suburbs.[10]

Although older rural people are more likely to need to work after retirement, there is a critical shortage of jobs and Federal work programs.

Besides lacking adequate income, the rural elderly often suffer the physical hardships of lack of central heating and adequate plumbing facilities. Sixty percent of substandard housing units in the United States are located in the non-metropolitan areas. Approximately one fourth of these house the rural elderly and nine out of ten older individuals living in these units have incomes below the poverty level.

Rural people 65 and older also have more chronic health conditions and limitations on their activities than non-rural elderly. Disabled rural elderly are doubly disadvantaged by the scarcity of physicians and other health professionals. They lack transportation to medical facilities and many even lack telephones. Access to medical care is very restricted and even further complicated by the low income levels of the rural elderly.

The plight of the rural, minority elderly is even more difficult.[11] Living in neighborhoods and towns surrounded by predominantly white communities subjects them to residues of prejudices and racism, especially in southern states and border areas. The income levels of the Black and native American rural elderly in all sections of the country are substantially below the average. Health, nutrition, and housing are greatly affected by levels of income. The burdens of old age are particularly difficult for the rural minority elderly.

Arnold Auerbach maintains that in addition to their unique economic and social problems, the rural elderly also have attitudinal characteristics that may be seen as problematic. He suggests that, "there is an intensification in the attitudes of the rural aged that emphasizes the insularity, independence, isolation, xenophobia, and individualism that is a reflection of the psychology of rural living."[12] Whatever the reason, the rural elderly are generally apt to know less about available social services, be more indifferent or hostile to government-supported programs, and more difficult to mobilize for participation in social programs.

Very often the attitude of rural people, especially the elderly, is to think in terms of an independent relationship between themselves and government. Most have been very self reliant all their lives. They were their own mechanics, plumbers, carpenters, doctors, grocers—because there were no others.[13] When crisis came, neighbors generally pitched in, frequently without being asked.

Entrenched Traditions

Old age often strips the rural elderly of their resources but not their traditions. These traditions have generated a life style for the rural aged that accepts little of the beliefs prevalent in non-rural areas that government or voluntary agencies have a social responsibility for caring for older people. The rural elderly are more inclined to see those receiving government support of any type as "sponging off public funds."

Among the rural elderly there is basically an indifferent attitude toward government institutions that have neglected them for so long, hostility toward those receiving public aid, and a suspicion of large cities and politicians who have left behind a history of unkept promises. There is also a suspicion of social programs which often infringe on privacy and frequently threaten the very fibers of a long standing way of life.

As one travels the isolated, rutted dirt roads seeking America's rural elderly, one soon becomes aware that frequently the U.S. Postal Service is the only governmental service these people have ever known. With such a sparsity of services, it is not difficult to understand why they do not naturally accept or seek other types of services.

Those developing programs to meet the needs of the urban elderly are conscious of the need to increase their awareness to the new resources available in the community. They often place emphasis on interpretation of services through the media. "Outreach workers and volunteers are dispersed to explain the programs, encourage

participation, and even to cajole the lonely and isolated to participate in group activities or accept the services that have been arranged for them."[14]

These strategies frequently are not effective with rural older people. Many do not own televisions and participation in group activities may involve extensive and expensive travel. Consequently the rural elderly, especially those living in more isolated areas, are unaware of the range of services available to the elderly. In addition, efforts to help the elderly person often are placed on the service—the station wagon or mini-bus, the prescription, the nutrition programs, increased social security benefits—as the measurable end product of a program. But, those who work with older people know that instilling self-respect, dignity, and independence does not happen merely with the proliferation of more and better programs and services.

Especially for the rural elderly, the tangible services and programs must be seen as the means of maintaining their dignity and way of life. According to a White House Conference on Aging report, programs established to meet the needs of the rural elderly living in isolated areas and small towns should be designed to fit their unique way of life. They must deal with them in ways that are not frightening or foreign to them.

This is a challenging task in part due to what Auerbach depicted as the provincialism and isolation of the rural elderly themselves, even more so, however, because of the xenophobia and social narrowness of the general rural atmosphere. In order to overcome these barriers, one must be familiar with some of the idiosyncrasies of rural life. For example, due to the long-standing nature of their problems and generational poverty, those in rural areas may be more resistant to, or suspicious of, change. Rural communities also tend towards greater conformity with conventional norms and remain as the last stronghold for some conventional virtues and prejudices.[15]

Strengths of Rural Life

The strengths which are an inherent part of such conformity must be recognized and valued. One way of dealing with the challenge of creating services for the rural elderly is to build on the strengths and positive aspects of rural life and on the strength and values of the elderly themselves.

Though the temptation is great to portray a bleak picture of the lives of the rural elderly, the circumstances of these people in the United States are not totally grim. There are positive aspects of living in rural areas. According to Melvin A. White of the Rocky Mountain

Gerontology Center, values of the rural aged include independence, self-reliance, ambition, hard work, freedom of choice, a sense of accomplishment, logical "down-to-earthness," political conservatism, integrity and honesty, and a strong sense of responsibility.[16] It is likely that many people would agree that these are highly commendable personal characteristics.

White urges that, in any discussion of the rural aged, we remember certain basic facts about them. He explains that those living on farms and in small towns in the United States are not and never have been homogeneous in nature. White stresses that people living in America's rural areas possess a great cultural diversity which in turn suggests a variety of outlooks on life and a complex mixture of attitudes and personalities.

In West Virginia alone, 21 ethnic groups are heavily represented in the state's population, and the elderly are a significant proportion of each group.

To make matters even more interesting, there is evidence which shows some people leave urban areas to move to rural ones. This creates an even greater variety of backgrounds and outlooks in rural America. Studies completed by the Bureau of the Census since 1970 show that a surprisingly large number of persons migrate to non-metropolitan areas. A substantial percentage of those migrating are retired persons. The elderly in rural areas are increasing in number.[17]

What are the positive aspects of the lives of the rural elderly? Biographical sketches of some older rural Americans are good sources of information for the answers to this question. In reading these sketches, one is forced to see human qualities which are often absent in other lifestyles. Self-reliance of a highly developed and admirable form is evident in many of the rural elderly, as well as general strength and character.

Furthermore rural people, despite their relative isolation, have social systems which support them through life. The family is a significant support system for the rural elderly. In addition there are other informal neighborhood support systems such as churches, friends, and neighbors which are enviable in comparison to the apparent anonymity of some urban centers.[18]

Dora Morris, James Tyree Rexrode, Dr. Margaret Byrnside Ballard, Rosie Lee Shanklin, and Dewey Thompson are, or were, five isolated rural elderly persons. Their average age is 84 and they lived in either Virginia, West Virginia, or Kentucky. Knowing a few facts about their lives helps us understand the isolated rural elderly better than the statistics ever could.

Dora Morris was 88 in 1974 when a front page article about her appeared in the *Washington Post*.[19] She lived alone in her century old mountain home near Lynchburg, Virginia for most of her life without a car, plumbing, power, or much money. Her lifestyle has many elements of the early frontier about it, and she seems quite satisfied. James Tyree Rexrode was an artist who lived in Pendleton County, West Virginia.[20] He amazed his friends by keeping a visual record of happenings in Pendleton County through photographs, cartoons, and paintings for over 50 years. Since he lived in a home one mile north of the tiny town of Sugar Grove, West Virginia, he learned deer hunting, fishing, and searching for gensing early in his life. Mr. Rexrode blended a close relationship to nature with his artistic talents in his rural environment.

Rosie Lee Shanklin, 91 in late 1978, lives on a remote ridge top overlooking the New River in the Cash's Hill section of Summers County, West Virginia. She lives miles from her own mailbox which is located on the nearest paved highway, but that does not present a problem to her. The daughter of a leading local black family and wife of a miner, Mrs. Shanklin is an experienced woman. One of her greatest pleasures is to get out in her garden. Like James Rexrode, Mrs. Shanklin maintains close contact with the out-of-doors and derives a sense of well-being from her isolated environment.[21]

Dewey Thompson of eastern Kentucky, an 80-year-old, mountain chairmaker who does everything by hand including cutting his trees for lumber, demonstrates the maintenance of his trade well into his eighth decade.[22] He too depends heavily on nature for both pleasure and a livelihood.

Finally, Dr. Margaret Byrnside Ballard of Monroe County, West Virginia (who lived from 1900-1976) was a doctor and a local historian who was much loved by her neighbors and friends in Union, West Virginia. She called herself a "simple country woman", and in doing so demonstrated how complex surface simplicity can be. Dr. Ballard helped dispel the myth that all rural elderly persons are poorly educated or unsophisticated.[23]

The lives of the rural elderly are a paradox—they live in severe circumstances yet they have endured eight and in some cases nine decades. That they are alive after what seems so much deprivation is contrary to what common sense would dictate. As we work with and observe the lives of the rural elderly, we can think back on the lives many Americans lived about 150 years ago on the frontier. It was a harsh existence, but the spirit behind it was integral to the American character.[24] This generation of rural elderly is more akin to an earlier time and seems almost anachronistic to us now.

But when this group is gone, what will be left behind? Perhaps while there is still time we need to look closely at the rural elderly and learn from them. According to recent predictions, our future in America will be less abundant and more austere. The rural elderly may offer us models for life which require more self-sufficiency, sacrifice, and independent creativity.

REFERENCES

1 R.C. Atchley, "Introduction to Rural Environments and Aging," in *Rural Environments and Aging,* Gerontological Society, 1975, p. 3.

2 *Ibid.,* p. 3.

3 Dr. Louise Gerrard, "Guest Editorial—The Most Disadvantaged," *Perspectives on Aging,* Jan.-Feb., 1978, p. 2.

4 U.S. Congress. Senate Special Committee on Aging. *The Nation's Rural Elderly,* Part 7, 1977, p. 528. 95th Congress, 1st session, Denver, Colorado, U.S. Government Printing Office, Washington, D.C. 1977.

5 U.S. Congress. House Subcommittee on Health and Long-Term Care, Select Committee on Aging, *Problems of a aine's Rural Elderly,* 1976, p. 67. 94th Congress, 2nd session, Presque Isle, Maine. U.S. Government Printing Office, Washington, D.C., 1976.

6 David L. Adams, "Who Are the Rural Aged?" In Atchley, *op. cit.,* pp. 11-22.

7 1971 White j ouse Conference on Aging, *The Rural and the Poor Elderly,* Washington, D.C., U.S. Government Printing Office, 1972.

8 *Ibid.*

9 We need more research on this problem before proper evidence can be offered.

10 Bureau of the Census, *Current Population Reports,* Series P-60, No. 108, "Household Money Income in 1975, by Housing Tenure and Residence, for the United States, Regions, Divisions, and States (Spring 1976 Survey of Income and Education)," Table 6; and No. 106, "Characteristics of the Population Below the Poverty Level: 1975," Table 9.

11 Arnold J. Auerbach, "The Elderly in Rural and Urban Areas," in Leon Ginsberg, (Ed.), *Social Work in Rural Communities,* New York, CSWE, 1976.

12 *Ibid.*

13 1971 White House Conference on Aging, *op. cit.*

14 Arnold J. Auerbach, *op. cit.*

15 Southern Regional Educational Board Manpower Education and Training Project. "Educational Assumptions for Rural Social Work," in Leon Ginsberg, *op. cit.*

16 U.S. Congress. Senate Special Committee on Aging. *The Nation's Rural Elderly,* Part 7, *op. cit.,* pp. 520-521.

17 U.S. Congress. Senate Special Committee on Aging. *Developments in Aging: 1976,* p. 119. Senate Report No. 95-88, 13171-2, 1977. U.S. Government Printing Office, Washington, D.C., 1977.

18 John Lozier and Ronald Althouse, "Retirement to the Porch in Rural Appalachia," *International Journal of Aging and Human Development,* 6:7-15, 1975.

19 Ken Ringle, "Life on the Mountain," *Washington Post,* 12/15/74, p. 1.

20 Paul Cline, "James Tyree Rexrode 1887-1976: The Man," *Goldenseal,* July-August, 1977.

21 Ken Sullivan, "Out in the Woods and Briers," *Goldenseal,* April-September, 1978.

22 Appalshop, Inc., "Chairmaker," a 16mm film, 1976.

23 George Parkinson, "Dr. Margaret Byrnside Ballard: 1900-1976," *Goldenseal.*

24 Carroll W. Wilkinson, *Comprehensive Annotated Bibliography on the Rural Aged, 1975-1978.* West Virginia University Gerontology Center, Morgantown, West Virginia, 1978.

The black elderly today

Suzanne Murphy

Both are black. Both are 73. Both look young for their age. There, the similarities end.

Retired for nearly a decade, Thurman C. Fletcher and his wife live comfortably on his social worker's pension. He calls himself a professional volunteer and student of gerontology, and is active in a dozen community organizations, including the Los Angeles City Area Agency on Aging.

Harriet Judy, on the other hand, lives in a different world. Self-supporting since age 12, when she was forced to quit school, she has worked as a mother's helper, domestic and caterer. She gets some Social Security, but continues to work in spite of her age. She has no plans to quit; she can't afford to.

Such are the differences among today's American black elderly. Yet this group of two million—the fastest-growing elderly population in the country—has more similarities than differences.

As heirs to centuries of racial prejudice, they share a common legacy of inferior education and limited job opportunities. It's a legacy that has kept them apart from the mainstream of American life and taken its toll in financial, psychological and human terms.

But differences are increasing. Dr. Barbara Solomon of the University of Southern California's Andrus School of Gerontology explains:

"You can't just speak of the black elderly because there is a class of variables that is important to recognize. You look at middle-class elderly teachers who now, after retirement, have incomes that make it possible for them to travel and still participate at a relatively high level in professional organizations.

"These people have a different lifestyle from, say, domestic workers who have never really been able to retire because they've never had the kind of pension plans that would permit it. Retirement isn't a concept that has any meaning to them."

Most observers agree that the social and economic status of the black elderly is significantly better than it was a decade ago. But much remains to be done in the areas of income, housing, health care and transportation if they are to achieve a standard of living comparable to their white counterparts.

Besides that, some social scientists believe that elderly black Americans may be facing an even greater challenge with the slow dissolution of their extended-family system. Blacks are known for their strong ties among generations, which have helped them survive the harsh realities of discrimination.

In households that frequently saw as many as four generations living under one roof, elders held positions of stature and dignity, providing material and spiritual support. As keepers of family history and tradition, they brought cohesiveness to the family, and transmitted values to successive generations.

Such is the view of Dr. William E. Huling, an associate professor at California State University, Northridge, and an authority on the black aged. Now, says Huling, all the breakthroughs in civil rights legislation and desegregation practices over the last 25 years ironically may spell trouble. The result could be the breakdown of special roles once reserved for elderly blacks as more blacks move into the American mainstream, adopting lifestyles comparable to whites and leaving traditional ways behind.

Hazel Lewis, director of the Watts Labor Community Action Center of South-Central Los Angeles, says, "The challenge now is to maintain the dignity and status of our black elderly and foster a new independence in them, new ways of coping with the changing order." The center typifies today's thrust by blacks to deal with change. Established in 1975, it is frequented by low-income persons 65 through 97. Most live on fixed incomes and, when possible, supplement them with part-time work or family aid. The majority live alone near one or more family members.

Lewis says, "If the kids do move to the suburbs, Momma is usually going to stay here where she feels most comfortable, where she has her church, her friends, her social units. She doesn't want to be a burden on anybody.

"She can make it on her own and have her own life as a full functioning person and still see and communicate with the family. I think that's the attitude of the black elderly in coping with the changing order of things."

The center provides a convenient setting for older persons to meet, socialize and give one another support, all in a familiar cultural context. "These people are all in the same boat," explains Lewis. "They have a lot to give one another and to do together. We let them know that there are valuable outlets for their energies—through continuing education programs, recreation projects, and volunteer work."

The center provides meals and a variety of services, including free transportation to and from the center, shopping trips, recreational activities, legal assistance, health services and adult education classes.

"If help is needed in just about any area, we'll either provide it or refer the individual to an agency that can," says Lewis.

But the center's impact on making blacks more assertive may turn out to be its most important contribution.

"We have helped them to develop a more assertive posture toward the system, to become more vocal, says Lewis. "Poverty is the number-one problem for our black seniors, yet many of them were unaware of the benefits available to them under programs like Supplementary Security Income.

"Others were reluctant to apply on their own behalf out of distrust, or because they simply didn't know how to go about dealing with all the red tape. But we've told them, 'Hey, this isn't 1902 or 1920, you don't have to roll over and play dead.'

"It's made a difference. Our seniors have become more aware that they have clout, that they can make their feelings known if they go through the proper channels."

To underscore this approach, the center's management meets regularly with a senior advisory council to confer on policymaking decisions and to deal with suggestions and complaints.

These are all steps in the right direction, says Solomon. "In general, you find the black elderly having a much more positive experience now than they had earlier. It's not to say that they are totally satisfied, but many have told me that they are participating as never before. There are opportunities through a number of older American programs for them to become involved in decisionmaking and other things they never dreamed could happen when they were in the rural South 50 years ago."

Organizations such as the National Center on Black Aged are trying to improve the status of elderly blacks. A "Living Legacy" award program has been established to honor black elderly leaders. Seventeen have been cited so far in such fields as science, art, politics, religion and education. They, in turn, each choose an outstanding young or middle-aged person in the same field and pass on to that younger person their experiences in the form of an oral history.

"The idea," says the center's executive director, Dr. Delores Davis, "is to promote intergenerational relationships; our black elders are passing on the legacy." Last year's choices were honored by President Carter in a special White House ceremony.

On the agenda for 1981, the National Center on Black Aged is planning a salute to aging that will focus on black entertainers—Ella Fitzgerald, Count Basie and Lena Horne, for example—and highlight their contributions to American life.

Many gerontologists foresee increasing involvement by black elderly in the decisionmaking processes that will affect their lives. And for people like Harriet Judy, they predict that retirement will become a reality.

Says Davis, "I certainly think retirement is going to become a concept that will have more significance for blacks than in the past. Given that, there is going to be more concern about how those later years can be spent so that there will be a sense of being worthwhile and productive."

The trends, says Davis, are already toward an increased awareness on the part of blacks about aging and the needs of the elderly.

She says, "We're receiving calls from all levels of the community. National organizations are responding more and more, asking for information on Federal programs and how they can develop housing, social service programs, and nutrition projects. Educational institutions want us to help design programs, seminars and workshops on black aging for their conferences; even private citizens are showing an increased awareness of their own aging, and a growing consciousness of the need for improved programs and services.

"That's good news."

Therapy after Sixty

THE GRAYING OF AMERICA IS COMPELLING THERAPISTS AND PATIENTS TO ACCEPT EACH OTHER.

MARILYN NISSENSON

Marilyn Nissenson is a freelance writer living in New York.

I walked in the door with a box of the sugared almonds she always loved. She put them on the cupboard without a thank-you and said, 'It's a burden for you, coming every week. I can't cook your favorite chicken. We can't go for a walk. I'm too old; there's no reason why I'm still here,' " says a New York attorney, describing his 81-year-old mother, whom we shall call Ann.

"She had been a woman who drove to the store every day, cooked, played cards with her friends, checked in on the neighbors and fussed over my father like the baby he was," he continues. But after her husband's death and an operation she underwent to remove a brain tumor "she couldn't be alone, couldn't get around without her walker, had to depend for every meal on the lady my brother and I hired to take care of her."

The attorney and his brother found a local therapist, whom they introduced to their mother as a person who could help her. After 16 months of once-a-week sessions with the therapist in her own living room, Ann regained a measure of optimism. "Well, I only have a few more years to live. I should enjoy them." She decided to move into a suitable nursing home so that she could enjoy a wider range of social contacts.

At least 25 million Americans—nearly 12 percent of the population—are now 65 or older, and the average 65-year-old can expect to live another 15 or 20 years. Many will face a new set of realities: dealing with less physical energy, greater risk of illness, failing memory, the diminished ability to think quickly and the impact of serious illnesses and deaths of friends and loved ones.

Perhaps 15 or 20 percent of this population will find that for the first time in their lives, they can't cope. Some of them will stop eating. Or they'll misuse the drugs they take for whatever physical condition ails them. Along with their children, they will worry that such ailments signal the onset of senility.

Although they account for 25 percent of what the nation spends on health care and are twice as likely as someone younger to be hospitalized for mental disorder, the aged are still underrepresented in the total population of those receiving psychological aid. Less than 3 percent of the clients treated by clinics or private therapists are older than 65, and as recently as 1981, nearly 70 percent of the clinical psychologists in this country reported that they were not treating any older patients.

Partly, this is the result of attitudes held by practitioners themselves. Many community mental-health workers, psychiatric social workers, clinical psychologists and psychiatrists appear reluctant to take on aging patients, feeling that it is more important to help young people than to assuage the fears of those for whom time is running out. It is not a particularly new prejudice. Freud, for example, wrote that it was inappropriate to try to treat older patients, whom he defined as people beyond 50. In an early version of his developmental stages of human life, Erik Erikson suggested that the appropriate task of old age was to confront despair and preserve a sense of self, no matter how diminished, in the face of death.

Nor is the attitude unrelated to the feelings that older patients sometimes provoke in therapists in the course of treatment. Some therapists find themselves enacting the role of the child, with the patient becoming the parent. Dealing honestly with older people's frailty is also difficult because it forces therapists to face their own mortality. As one psychologist put it, "Many young people come to me with character disorders, or sexual dysfunction, drugs and drinking and so on. Those are problems I'm not personally threatened by. But when I see someone who's 68, depressed, with a crippling case of arthritis, an ill wife and two daughters half a continent away, I can't help thinking 'Is that going to be me, and what will I do if it is?'"

But attitudes are changing. For one thing therapists, like everyone else, react to the marketplace, and America's population is turning gray. The babyboom generation will reach old age in 2010 or so. Robert Butler, former head of the National Institute on Aging and currently at Mt. Sinai School of Medicine in New York, predicts that, given the treatment and cure of cancer and heart disease, "The 21st century will be the first century of old age."

In the early 1960s, Butler published a series of influential papers arguing against the conventional view that the propensity of older people to dwell in the past was regressive, pathological and of little interest to anyone but themselves. Butler declared, on the contrary, that this process of life review was a healthy, normal impulse. Stimulated by approaching death, the older person relives the past in an effort to master the present and maintain a sense of self.

Butler's arguments have encouraged many therapists to take older people more seriously. And in the wake of his theory, many senior-citizen centers have organized reminiscence programs in which the natural process of life review is enhanced and rewarded rather than ignored. Older people are interviewed, sometimes on videotape, or encouraged to write autobiographies. Such projects give older people the satisfaction of being taken seriously, bring them in contact with younger people and provide the

SOME THERAPISTS FIND THEMSELVES ENACTING THE ROLE OF A CHILD, WITH THE PATIENT BECOMING THE PARENT.

community with rich oral history archives.

Older patients seem to entertain fewer illusions about themselves. They are less reticent, less self-deceptive. Stanley Cath, a psychoanalyst from Boston has found that old people present the initial defense: "I'm not worth the trouble, my life is almost over." But once reassured that this is not so, they quickly begin to engage in productive therapy. By reviewing the events of their lives, they can resolve old conflicts and gain a coherent view of themselves. Often a life-review monologue is unconsciously addressed to one person—a parent, a former admirer or spouse, a sibling, a child—to whom the hidden message is "you see, my life has had meaning after all."

Although counseling services are becoming increasingly available to older patients, those who could benefit from them often don't seek help because of what they perceive as the stigma attached. They grew up at a time when psychology was not part of everyday life and to admit the need for psychological help was exceedingly difficult. Some people are also uncertain where or whom to turn to.

Fortunately, a variety of support groups has recently sprung up. Some stress practical skills for coping with medical and social authorities, or communicating with family members. Others offer help to people with a common problem: recent retirement. Still others address themselves to patients with specific physical disorders, teaching them techniques to reduce the anxiety that often accompanies and intensifies their symptoms.

Group participation of any kind tends to be immensely reassuring. It

provides a new social network for people who are otherwise isolated and lonely. They feel the satisfaction of helping others as well as being helped themselves, and they are relieved to learn that they are not alone in anguish or unique in suffering.

Group therapy helped Grace Harper, a 73-year-old New Jersey housewife, who three years ago lost her mother, husband and granddaughter within four months. "I would burst out crying in the supermarket, so I cut down eating. I stopped going to church. I dropped my bridge group. Some days I wore my nightgown till noon. I'm in perfectly good health, but every time I got a little dizzy, I imagined a brain tumor was coming on. I prayed to God to take me too.

"When my sister-in-law told me about this therapist who saw groups of older patients, I thought, 'I could use some help like that, but I can't talk about private matters to perfect strangers.' Yet after I went for a few weeks, I was telling these people things I had hardly even been able to admit to myself. It's much easier if you see other people like yourself who can admit in front of others that they are at the end of their rope."

But it's not always that easy. Some therapists have only limited success with older patients in group treatment. Many older people who can barely bring themselves to discuss personal matters in a private session withdraw completely. Others feel it's too depressing to hear about how other people face bereavement—there's enough grief in their own lives. Still others believe that age-segregation in therapy is just another wall separating older people from the rest of the community.

Group counseling for the elderly is often oriented more toward social work rather than therapy, and it is not always adequate in chronic situations. For example, finding new friends and learning how to cope with practical crises will generally not help elderly people who suffer from oppressive feelings of unworthiness or severe depression. Some problems will benefit more significantly by different therapeutic techniques.

"There's always a debate about what kind of help is best," says Margaret Gatz, a clinical psychologist at the University of Southern California

GROUP PARTICIPATION OF ANY KIND PROVIDES A NEW SOCIAL NETWORK FOR PEOPLE WHO ARE OTHERWISE ISOLATED AND LONELY.

in Los Angeles. "I know a 70-year-old woman who'd begun to stay home all day and stare at the wall. In six weeks of behavior-modification training, she learned to reward herself for social encounters and to stop things that set her back. And I know a 70-year-old who's fascinated and energized by classical analysis. Probably it's a question of finding the right fit. There's some form of help that should work for almost every older person."

Some older people fall into a trap which Martin Seligman, a psychologist at the University of Pennsylvania calls "learned helplessness." Hospitalized patients particularly, but all old people to some degree, have a diminished ability to control the environment. If younger people don't like a job, they can leave. If they don't like school, they can quit. If a romance isn't flourishing, they can end it and seek another partner. Old people have fewer choices, and a sense of restricted control over one area of life can lead to the erroneous belief that all self-assertion is futile.

Ann's sons had expected her therapy to release her pent-up feelings toward her husband and to give her a chance to vent her rage at her recent physical decline. Instead, she spoke for the first time about events in her childhood: the terrors of her trip to America at the age of 5, and the helplessness and guilt she and her mother shared when her father, who stayed behind in Vienna to clear up family business, got stranded at the outbreak of World War I and died before he could join them in Trenton.

After working through this trauma in her therapy, Ann never mentioned it again, but the ice was broken. In several sessions, which her sons were invited to attend, she was willing to listen to their description of their childhoods and answer some questions that none of them had been able to discuss before.

In addition to psychological factors confronting the elderly, therapists must often pay a great deal of attention to their physical condition, including the possible effects of medication and, just as important, eating habits. Dietary irregularities can result in symptoms that mimic serious physical and neurological disorders.

Therapeutic sessions for the elderly are often scheduled differently than for younger patients. Some patients are only able to tolerate a 20- or 30-minute appointment. Sometimes they need help arranging transportation. A few therapists now make house calls, as well as other adjustments. James Haycox, a psychiatrist at the Burke Rehabilitation Center in White Plains, New York, finds his role expanded: "If the patient is hard of hearing, I raise my voice. If he has trouble reading the phone book, I look up the number of the drugstore or the senior-citizen group and even make the call. I do a lot of touching. I do a lot of social work. I do a lot of things a good friend should do."

Not the least of the adjustments that therapists are making relates to the gender gap in older populations, a gap brought about by the difference in longevity between men and women. The average life expectancy for women is 8 years more than it is for men. Demographic realities make it clear that men must face their own earlier demise, while women at this age level will have to deal with the loneliness of widowhood. Since women older than 65 are the fastest-growing segment of

WHERE TO GET HELP

What should you do if you believe that you or your aging parent needs psychological care? First, professional diagnosis is essential. This may involve separate appraisals by an internist, a neurologist and a psychologist.

Short-term memory loss does not necessarily mean serious problems or future deterioration. A skilled diagnostician can distinguish between the events in normal aging and symptoms of depression, delirium—which is brief disorientation or panic—and dementia, the overall term for chronic, progressive brain impairment.

A geriatric center is the best bet for a good cross-disciplinary diagnosis, and such centers are affiliated with many major universities. A sampling of some around the country includes the Andrus Gerontology Center at the University of Southern California in Los Angeles, the geriatric department at Boston University Medical School, or the Geriatric Study and Treatment Program at New York University Medical Center.

Community Mental Health Centers (CMHC's), found in most large towns and cities, are another alternative. Unfortunately, not all CMHC's are responsive to older patients. The Civil Rights Commission stated in a 1982 report that the professionals employed by CMHC centers are likely to be prejudiced against the elderly.

For those who have no university geriatric centers or CMHC's in their areas, some private clinics also provide diagnostic and referral services. In addition, Area Agencies on Aging—social-service organizations located throughout the country—will refer old people to clinics or individuals that offer psychological help.

Financing can be a problem. The limit to Medicare coverage is approximately $300 for outpatient psychological care. And nursing homes are often reluctant to provide inpatient care; if they have more than 50 percent psychiatric patients, Medicare excludes them from all coverage. Many clinics, on the other hand, base their fees on the patients' ability to pay.

—*M.N.*

our population, it is unlikely that most of them will find a new partner. Their psychological vulnerability is also increased by the fact that the years of caring for children and grandchildren have ended, making them candidates for the empty-nest syndrome.

Yet, at least in some cultures, this post-reproductive and post-marital phase does not automatically lead to an ineffectual existence. As David Gutmann, a psychologist at Northwestern University, reports, women in many cultures "become domineering, independent and unsentimental in late middle life." Indeed, even in our own culture, a resurgence of sexuality marks older women. For example, some of the patients of Stanley Cath reveal that he is the subject of explicitly erotic dreams. "On the one hand," he points out, "that's transference; on

the other, it's reflective of the fact that I may be the only man in their lives."

Martin Berezin, a Boston psychoanalyst, reports that many of his widowed patients find release in increased masturbation and need help resolving guilt about it.

In recent years, Erickson has somewhat revised his views of the last stage of life, pointing out that there is a lengthening, productive period when we are "elderly," before the final stage when we are old (see "A Conversation with Erik Erikson," *Psychology Today*, June 1983). He has recently pointed out that we used to think that sex either didn't or shouldn't exist in old age. Now we realize that since it is no longer procreative, it should and does exist for its own sake. He postulates the last sexual stage of development as one of "generalized sensuality."

The recovery of emotional resilience is often the most that can be hoped for from therapy. There is, after all, a limited possibility for life change; practical aspects of coping can be learned, but an ailing or dead spouse, one's own signs of physical limitations and the finiteness of the future cannot be analyzed away.

Old age will always be a time of increased frailty, intermittent grief and reduced options. However, many people face these obstacles with the same wisdom and flexibility that has marked their earlier years. As more therapists turn their attention to the elderly, we can hope that they will be able to transmit to their patients a sense of what successful aging is all about—a renewed zest for life and acceptance of its end.

Retirement: American Dream or Dilemma?

Since 1900 the number of persons in America aged sixty-five and over has been increasing steadily, but a decreasing proportion of that age group remains in the workforce. Epstein and Murray (1967) observed that in 1950, twenty-six percent of all men over sixty-five were employed, but only fifteen percent were employed in 1962. The long-range trend indicates fewer and fewer persons are being employed beyond the age of sixty-five. Some people choose to retire at age sixty-five or earlier; for others retirement is mandatory. A recent change in the law, however, allows individuals to work to age seventy before retiring.

Strieb and Schneider (1971) observed that for retirement to become an institutionalized social pattern in any society, certain conditions must be present: A large group of people must live long enough to retire; the economy must be productive enough to support people who are not in the workforce; and there must be pensions or insurance programs to support these people during their retirement.

Retirement is a rite of passage. People can consider it as either the culmination of the American Dream or as a serious problem. Those who have ample incomes, interesting things to do, and friends to associate with often find the freedom of time and choice that retire-ment offers very rewarding. For others, however, retirement brings problems and personal losses. Often, these individuals find their incomes decreased, and they miss the status, privilege, and power associated with holding a position in the occupational hierarchy. They may feel socially isolated if they don't find new activities to replace their previous work-related ones. Additionally, they must sometimes cope with the burden of the death of a spouse and/or their own failing health. The articles in this section provide a better understanding of why many older Americans feel ambivalent as they approach the retirement years.

Looking Ahead: Challenge Questions

If given the choice of retiring or continuing to work, some people would choose to continue working. How would you explain the desire not to retire?

Why do you believe many older persons decide to retire early? What factors are crucial to this decision?

In your opinion, what are the major advantages of retirement for the individual?

What are the major disadvantages that accompany retirement?

From an economic point of view, should people be encouraged to retire earlier or later?

Symbolic Interaction and Retirement Adjustment: An Empirical Assessment

Harold Cox and Albert Bhak
Indiana State University

Abstract

Using a variety of indicators of retirement adjustment most studies have focused on two variables as the critical ones: the kind of work the individual was involved in prior to retirement with its concomitant style of life or the individual's preretirement attitudes. Focusing on the latter variable and using a symbolic interaction perspective, it was hypothesized that the individual's significant others are crucial to both the development of his pre-retirement attitudes and his post-retirement adjustment. The data upheld both the predicted relationships, and further suggest that the social world of older people is comprised of both primary groups and proximate others. The Lowenthal and Haven concept of confidants as a major factor in the adjustment of older people, though valuable, too narrowly defines their social world. The broader concept of significant others comprised of both confidants and proximate others seems more realistic.

Economic and demographic trends in American society have resulted in an ever increasing number of retirees. Demographically both the number and proportion of people arriving at age sixty-five have increased. In 1900, three million Americans were sixty-five or older and they comprised approximately 2.5 per cent of the population. In 1970, twenty million Americans were over the age of sixty-five comprising approximately 10 per cent of the population. While the number and proportion of the population over sixty-five years of age has been increasing, the proportion of those who remain in the work force has decreased. Epstein and Murray observed that 26 per cent of all men over sixty-five were employed in 1950 while only 15 per cent of that group were employed in 1962 [1].

Past studies have indicated the multiplicity of problems that the individual is confronted with at the time of retirement among which are: the lowering of income, the loss of status, the loss of the privilege and power that were associated with one's position in the occupational hierarchy. These changes necessitate a major reorganization of life's activities since the nine to five work day is now meaningless, a redefinition of self independent of the identity that was formed in response to the demands of major occupational roles. A considerable degree of social isolation will be felt if new activities are not found to replace previous work related ones, and if new meaning and value for one's life are not discovered.[1] Inevitably, the major reorganization of one's life that must take place at retirement is beset with numerous adjustment problems. The major concern here is to identify the critical factors associated with a successful retirement adjustment.

Retirement Adjustment

Using a variety of indicators of retirement adjustment most studies focus on one of two variables as critical: the kind of work the individual was involved in and his style of life prior to retirement or the individual's pre-retirement attitude.

Viewing the former variable as the critical one, Simpson [3] speaks of the disjunctive effects of retirement and asserts that work is one of the most important avenues for integrating the individual into the social system for it provides identity, style of life and social participation patterns.[2] Beginning with the assumption that work places the individual and his family in the hierarchy of the social structure it is argued that retirement undercuts the individual's major social support. It is not retirement, per se, which is responsible for the individual's lack of anchorage and adjustment in retirement, but rather it is work histories which do not allow for the development of other social ties.

Orientation toward work was found to be the main influence shaping pre-retirement attitudes and consequently post-retirement adjustment among upper white collar workers, and income deprivation was the main influence on retirement adjustment for the semi-skilled workers. None of the explanations accounted for much variability within the middle stratum.

Streib and Schneider focus on the attitudinal orientation of willingness or reluctance to retire as the critical factor in retirement adjustment [2]. Their findings indicate that persons who are favorably disposed

126

From *International Journal of Aging and Human Development*, Vol. 9, No. 3, 1979. Reprinted with the author's permission.

toward retirement are much more likely to retire than those who are reluctant and are simultaneously more likely to make a favorable adjustment. This was true whether they voluntarily chose to retire or they were administratively retired.

While viewing retirement as a major role disjuncture due to the loss of the work, Streib and Schneider were led to some conclusions that differed with previous research [2]. Viewing role sets and role changes as dynamic processes they found that the loss of the work role does not inevitably lead to either adjustment problems or disengagement. Many retirees, after losing the work role, expanded activity in other ongoing roles (i.e., wife, grandfather, friend, volunteer, etc.). Their findings suggest that many retirees successfully cope with role realignment precipitated by retirement.

While utilizing a role approach to study the problems of retirement adjustment Streib and Schneider suggest that an alternate approach would be to view the problem in terms of reference groups which are significant for work and retirement, namely, families, friends, cliques at work, etc. [2]. The latter perspective is the one taken here and it is our contention that the "significant others" who comprise the individual's reference groups are critical in the development of both the individual's pre-retirement orientation and his degree of social integration and adjustment in retirement.

Significant Others

In discussing the concept of "significant others" Stryker states that [5]:

> This concept represents the recognition that, in a fragmented and differentiated world, not all persons with whom one interacts have identical or even compatible perspectives and that, therefore, in order for action to proceed the individual must give greater weight or priority to the perspectives of certain others. To speak then of significant others is to say that given others occupy high rank in importance for a given individual.

While not referring specifically to the concept of significant others, numerous studies have noted the relationship between the maintaining of close friendship ties and a successful adjustment to old age. Erickson postulates that the capacity for intimacy is one of the major developmental tasks of life [6]. Blau's study of the structural constraints on friendship of the aged documents the importance of the prevailing age-sex, marital status, patterns in the establishment of friendships [7]. In his study of friendship in an aging population, Arth is concerned with the importance of close friends in the social world of the elderly but does not define closeness [8]. Rosow's study of friendship patterns in varying age density conditions attributes the importance of close friends to the successful adjustment of older Americans [9].

Lowenthal and Haven were the first to carefully consider the quality of the social relationships of older people [10]. Using the concept of "confidant" they observed that the healthiest and happiest of older people often seem to be those who were involved in one or more close personal friendships. They concluded that the maintenance of a stable intimate relationship is more closely associated with good mental health and high morale than is high social interaction, role status or stability of interaction and role.

The composition of an individual's social world can be seen in terms of spheres of social involvement. The primary group of husband, wife, children and a few very close friends would be in the first circle. The second would hold a wider range of associates, including well known friends in the individual's work, environment, social clubs, fraternal and religious organizations. We chose to call this second circle the individual's "proximate others." The third circle contains a much larger group of casual acquaintances usually considered by sociologists as secondary group associations.

The contention here is that the individual's primary groups and proximate others also comprise his major reference groups and significant others. Though the concept of "confidants" is critical, it too narrowly defines the social world of older people and implies a greater disengagement than actually occurs. While retirement removes the individual from many secondary group associations, the loss is mitigated by active involvement with both primary groups and proximate others. Most people at age sixty-five can look forward to fifteen more years in reasonably good health. To view their life in later years as determined entirely by the immediate family or one or two very close friends seems to place too great a limitation on the social worlds of older people.

Hypotheses

An individual's reference groups will, in part, determine both his pre-retirement orientation as well as his post-retirement adjustment. Based on the past research dealing with the friendship patterns and life adjustment of older people the following hypotheses were derived:

1. that a positive view of retirement by the individual's significant others will lead to his holding favorable attitudes toward retirement, and
2. that a positive view of retirement by the individual's significant others will be a major factor contributing to his successful retirement adjustment.

Methodology

The state of Indiana is divided into fifteen regions for the purpose of implementing federal and state programs for older people. The participants (103 elderly) in this study were from region seven of West Central

5. RETIREMENT

Indiana. Region seven, at the time the data was gathered, had three nutrition centers where elderly people met daily to purchase meals, at a nominal cost, and one "senior citizen" center which conducted a number of recreational and social activities. On a designated day a team of interviewers visited these locations and interviewed everyone who was in attendance on that particular day. Only one person refused to be interviewed.

The interview schedule contained questions regarding the individual's pre-retirement attitudes, his significant others' view of retirement, his post-retirement adjustment, his feelings of usefulness after retiring and his own evaluation of his current state of health. Most of the response choices given to participants were Likert-type ranging from strongly agree to strongly disagree and were scored from 1 to 5. A few of the response choices were yes, undecided, and no, and were scored from 1 to 3. The wording of the questions was such that a similar opinion on a number of questions would be forced alternately into agree and disagree choices.

Findings

The first hypothesis stated that a positive view of retirement by the individual's significant others would lead to his holding favorable attitudes toward retirement. In order to test the first hypothesis a correlation coefficient was computed between the individual's significant others' view of retirement and his attitudes toward retirement. As Table 1 indicates this correlation was .53 which proved to be significant beyond the .001 level of probability.

The second hypothesis predicted that the significant others' favorable view of retirement would lead to a successful retirement adjustment on the part of the individual. In order to test the second hypothesis a correlation coefficient was computed between the significant others' view of retirement and the individual's post-retirement adjustment. As Table 1 indicates this yielded a correlation of .55 which proved to be significant beyond the .001 level.

In order to further specify the nature of the relationship one additional correlation and two partial correlations were computed. The first of these was the correlation between the individual's pre-retirement attitudes and retirement adjustment which yielded a correlation of .33 and proved to be significant beyond the .002 level (see Table 1). On the basis of the zero order correlations the individual's significant others are more highly correlated with the individual's post-retirement adjustment than are his pre-retirement attitudes. The partialling out of the relationship proved invaluable in determining the relative strengths of these two variables.[3] The partial correlation between attitude toward retirement and retirement adjustment, while controlling for significant others, was .05 which proved not to be significant (Table 1). The partial correlation between significant others and retirement adjustment, while controlling for attitude toward retirement, was .47 which proved to be significant beyond the .001 level (Table 1).

These results seem to indicate that significant others are the single most critical determinant of retirement adjustment. In the zero-order correlations significant

Table 1. Correlations Between Pre-Retirement Attitudes, Significant Others and Retirement Adjustment

	Correlation coefficient	Degrees of freedom	Probability
Correlation Between the Individual's Attitude Toward Retirement and Significant Others View of Retirement	.53	80	.001
Correlation Between Significant Others and Retirement Adjustment	.55	80	.001
Correlation Between Pre-Retirement Attitudes and Retirement Adjustment	.33	80	.002
Partial Correlation Between Attitude Toward Retirement and Retirement Adjustment While Controlling for Significant Others	.05	79	.31
Partial Correlation Between Significant Others and Retirement Adjustment While Controlling for Attitude Toward Retirement	.47	79	.001

others prove to be more powerfully correlated with retirement adjustment. In the partial correlation between significant others and retirement adjustment, while controlling for attitude toward retirement, the strength of the correlation drops only slightly from the original one (from .55 to .47) and remains significant beyond the .001 level.

Attitude toward retirement, on the other hand, was significantly correlated with retirement adjustment in the zero-order correlation but dropped from a correlation of .33 to .05 in the partial which did not prove to be significant. Remembering that partial correlation removes the effect of the control variable in order to determine what is left of the original relationship, it is apparent that when significant others is pulled out of the relationship between attitude toward retirement and retirement adjustment there is very little left of the original relationship.[4]

Table 2. Multiple Correlation for the Effects of: Attitude Toward Retirement and Significant Others on Retirement Adjustment

Correlation coefficient .56

Analysis of Variance for the Regression

	D.F.	Sum of squares	Mean square	F	Sig.
Regression	2	47.14	23.57	17.61	.0001
	79	105.72	1.33		

A multiple correlation coefficient was computed to determine the combined effects of attitude toward retirement, and significant others on retirement adjustment (see Table 2). This correlation was .56 and proved to be significant beyond .001. Once again, this gives credence to the fact that significant others appears to be the critical variable since the combined effect of attitude toward retirement and significant others is almost identical to the zero-order correlation between significant others and retirement adjustment (.55 and .56). Thus, the combined effect of these two variables produce a correlation that is no stronger than the one produced by significant others alone.

Discussion

Utilizing a symbolic interaction perspective and hypothesizing that the individual's significant others are crucial to both the development of his pre-retirement attitudes and his post-retirement adjustment proved most fruitful as the findings upheld both of the predicted relationships. The concept of significant others seems to suggest some new direction and assumptions with regard to research related to the adjustment patterns of older people. First, it suggests that the social world of the elderly is comprised of both primary groups and proximate others. Second, while other studies have focused on the disjunctive aspects of retirement this study suggests that we focus on the factors which ease the transition to the retired status.

Assuming that significant others assist the individual in shaping his attitudes toward retirement and that anticipatory socialization takes place at each stage of life, there seems little doubt that older people who have already negotiated numerous other changes in status throughout life, begin far in advance to plan for their retirement and that the transition is not necessarily a painful one. Using the concept of reference groups comprised of significant others as an approach to viewing adjustment problems of older people would seem to offer the possibility of further elaborating past findings as well as possibly offering a new direction for future research.

Notes

[1]For a more complete discussion of this point see ref. [2, 3].

[2]Ida Harper Simpson edited a book of readings *Social Aspects of Aging* [3]. Within this book Chapter 2 "Work and Retirement" was written by Ida Harper Simpson, Kurt W. Back, and John McKinney.

[3]For a complete discussion of elaboration techniques of the effect of controlling for additional variables see ref. [11].

[4]The N in the Tables was somewhat lower than the original sample size due to the fact that a person who did not answer every single question in the scales used had to be eliminated from the entire analysis.

References

1. L.A. Epstein and J.H. Murray, The Aged Population of the United States, *Research Report No. 19,* Office of Research and Statistics, Social Security Administration, U.S. Department of Health, Education and Welfare, The Government Printing Office, Washington, D.C., 1967.

2. G.F. Streibe and C.J. Schneider, *Retirement in American Society,* Cornell University Press, Ithica and London, 1971.

3. I.H. Simpson, *Social Aspects of Aging,* Duke University Press, Durham, North Carolina, 1966.

4. I.H. Simpson, K.W. Back, and J. McKinney, Work and Retirement, *Social Aspects of Aging,* Duke University Press, Durham, North Carolina, pp. 45-55, 1966.

5. S. Strykker, Symbolic Interaction as an Approach to Family Research, *Marriage and Family Living, 21,* pp. 111-119, 1959.

6. E.H. Erickson, Identity and the Life Cycle, *Psychological Issues,* International University Press, New York, monograph, 1959.

7. Z.S. Blau, Structural Constraints on Friendship in Old Age, *American Sociological Review, 26,* pp. 429-440, 1961.

8. M. Arth, American Culture and the Phenomenon of Friendship in the Aged, *Social and Psychological Aspects of Aging,* C. Tibbitts and W. Donahue, (eds.), Columbia University Press, New York, pp. 529-534, 1962.

9. I. Rosow, *Social Integration of the Aged,* The Free Press, New York, 1967.

10. M.F. Lowenthal and C. Haven, Interaction and Adoption: Intimacy as a Critical Variable, *American Sociological Review, 33,* pp. 20-30, 1968.

11. Lazarsfeld and Rosenberg, *The Language of Social Research,* The Free Press, New York, pp. 115-125.

A NEW WRINKLE IN RETIREMENT POLICIES

Encouraging employees to stay on the payroll beyond the age of retirement makes good business sense.

Ellen Wojahn

Two days a week, Virginia Coulter rides a commuter train to Warren Publishing Corp., near Boston's old garment-and-leather district, where she types, handles paperwork, and generally functions as an office manager. She also pitches in on the production of the company's weekly newspaper, *Banker & Tradesman*, which caters to financial and real estate interests in Massachusetts. That often means spending hours on her feet, pasting up columns on a tall easel—a tiring task by any standard. But Coulter is used to it. At age 79, she has been on the job for 62 years, longer than anyone else currently employed at Warren. Her routine, she says, is too ingrained in her life to give up—and the same is true of many of her co-workers.

"Just look around this room," she says, gesturing at the typing pool behind her. "Most of these girls are almost my age, and a lot of them work more hours than I do. That one there is in her seventies, and she works at least three days a week. And that one over there—look how fast she types! She even takes work home." But the real workaholic, Coulter says, is her sister—Winifred Church. "She's been running the mail room, five days a week, for 40 years. Did she tell you she's 82?"

Anyone who asks Winifred Church to reveal her age gets a forthright answer—but not without a short speech on her definition of the word "old." Age, Church explains, is only a number, and is no indication of a person's ability to be gainfully employed. She continues working full-time—and braving Boston's commuter-clogged Southeast Expressway twice daily in her new K-car—because, she says, "people do what they want to do, as long as they can do it." Sure, there may be a few older people who are no longer mentally or physically capable of holding a job, but "I've also known some people who were pretty decrepit at the age of 30," she points out.

Eight of Warren's 35 employees are eligible for social security, but they are allowed—or rather, encouraged—to stay on the payroll as long as they like. It is company policy, says president Tim War-

Winifred Church (left) and Virginia Coulter, age 82 and 79, respectively, are two workers who believe strongly that age is no indication of a person's ability to be gainfully employed.

ren Sr. "Why should we tell anyone that they have to stop working at any given age when we can provide a flexible environment that supports them?"

Warren lets his would-be retirees determine how many hours they want to work and, within reason, what duties they would like to retain. He pays them $7 to $9 an hour—at least as much, he says, as what he would have to pay younger workers. There are no exclusions from or restrictions on their participation in company benefits programs; even profit sharing is available to them. The only difference among the older set is that the company prorates its benefits in accordance with the number of days per week the employee works. A two-day-a-week employee, for example, gets 4 of the company's 10 paid holidays, two-fifths of the normal company contribution to a health plan, and a like proportion of the annual profit-sharing sum.

Warren likes to call this his "compassionate retirement program," one in which people are not forced by so-called social engineers to give up work that has,

over long careers, become an integral part of their identity. But, lest his policy be construed as charity, Warren quickly interjects that his $1.5-million company benefits from the program just as much as its post-retirement-age participants do.

"We get tremendous value out of our older workers," Warren says. Because many of the company's jobs are clerical, and work loads fluctuate with publishing schedules, he finds it more cost effective to use part-time employees—and older people, he says, are usually more interested in such positions than younger, more career-oriented workers. In addition, Warren says his older employees can usually teach their younger co-workers a thing or two about what the phrase "work ethic" means.

"When you bring young people in and put them in an environment in which they observe older people working right up to the last minute, paying attention to what they're doing—it's like parenting," Warren says. "This sense of responsibility, these diligent work habits, all of this is very definitely transmitted by older people to younger people. And we like it, because it makes our company a microcosm of the world—young and old, working together."

Warren tends to downplay the novelty of his policies, saying there was never any calculated decision made to create and perpetuate this mix of young and old; it was merely something that evolved over the company's 111-year history. "It's who we are, what we do," says Warren, shrugging. And, he adds, it probably isn't all that unusual.

Flexible-retirement policies enable older employees to remain productive members of the work force.

"But it is!" says Malcolm Morrison, director of the U.S. Department of Labor's National Studies on Mandatory Retirement. "All of the studies I've seen indicate that the companies with flexible-retirement options—those that allow people to work beyond retirement—probably number less than several hundred. A lot of companies won't even examine the issue, won't even cost it out." Why not? "There are negative attitudes and beliefs about the productivity of older workers, and although there are studies that should refute these ideas, many companies aren't swayed." Such studies, Morrison says, show that older people are indeed productive workers, with lower absenteeism, greater job stability, and a more positive attitude than younger employees (age 18 to 35). Retaining older employees, he concludes, is more often a bargain than a burden.

The trend throughout the 1960s and '70s toward early retirement has also played a role in discouraging experimentation with flexible-retirement options, Morrison says. "Companies have not been convinced that people want to keep working. They have seen people leave

rapidly at age 55 or 62, and requests for anything but early or traditional retirement arrangements have been few, so nobody bothers to bend their personnel policies."

But Morrison and consultant Frank Bowe, a visiting professor at the University of Arkansas who specializes in issues involving older and disabled workers, believe that there is considerable, pent-up demand for post-retirement-age, part-time work, and that it will increase.

"Perhaps 75% to 80% of those considering retirement would keep working, if they could only get their job descriptions modified to allow for more safety, diminished physical demands, and, in many cases, fewer hours," Bowe says. What older workers want, he says, is nothing more than what disabled workers are now guaranteed by federal law—"reasonable accommodation." And, although now—with high unemployment levels, particularly among young workers—it may seem less than necessary for companies to make such concessions to older workers, Bowe is convinced that doing so is the best course for both business and society at large.

"We're talking about the fastest-growing segment of our population here. Which is better? Letting these people retire, and spending half of the nation's taxable payroll to support them? Or giving them something productive to do, so that we can quit paying people not to work?"

Government statistics indicate that those who reach the age of 65 today can expect to live to age 81, which means there is nearly a generation of people eligible for retirement. Yet, of the estimated 26 million Americans over the age of 65, only 4 million will hold a job during any given year. At the same time, the number of teenagers entering the labor force is shrinking dramatically. As of last July, the United States had more residents over the age of 65 than teenagers.

"Gradually, certainly by the turn of the century, business will be watching a lot of workers go out the window," Morrison says. "Companies who don't plan for this exodus are going to face labor shortages. Policies will have to change.

Early retirement will have to go." As the labor situation becomes more of a seller's market, he predicts, business will need to offer flexible working conditions to attract and hold retirement-age workers.

As of last July, the U.S. had more residents over the age of 65 than it had teenagers.

To begin assessing the potential impact of these changes, Morrison says, companies should carefully analyze the occupational categories, skills, and age of their work force, with an eye toward how those findings jibe with two more sets of figures: the company's projected labor needs for the next 10 to 15 years, and the expected supply of such workers. Much of this examination relies on guesswork, Morrison concedes, "but you should come away with a sense of whether your retirement policies will be appropriate a decade from now." If the determination is that they won't be, "develop some alternatives, and give them a fair trial."

Bowe and Warren, meanwhile, offer a few tips for how to ensure the success of an experimental flexible-retirement program:

☐ Check job descriptions for duties that may exclude older workers, and eliminate them, or train supervisors to find ways to work around them.

☐ Carefully match employees to jobs, paying strict attention to each worker's strengths and capabilities, then encourage employees to know and enforce their own limitations.

☐ Don't assume that older workers can't learn new skills, or won't welcome feedback and coaching.

☐ Above all, walk a prudent line between being flexible and giving older workers special treatment.

Virginia Coulter's advice? "Just learn to accept older people. We're not so different, you know, once you get used to looking at the wrinkles all day."

Reconsidering Retirement
Understanding Emerging Trends

Bernard I. Forman

Bernard I. Forman is a part-time Mandatory Retirement representative of the National Senior Citizens' Law Center in Washington, D.C. He has a doctorate in education from Rutgers University and is professor emeritus of art at Mankato State University, Mankato, Minnesota.

Dealing with the social and financial problems of older people entails much more than just piecemeal modifications of retirement policies in the United States.

There is a need to change popular attitudes toward work and toward the concept of retirement itself. Yet, sensitivity to emerging social trends and understanding of forces underlying these trends are often conspicuous by their absence.

While the effects of the changing demography on political and socioeconomic realities are widely discussed, practical measures to moderate their impact are mainly temporizing evasions and circumventions. It is seldom disputed, for example, that wholesale reform of the American pension system is sorely needed to make it more equitable and comprehensive. Yet, very little actual improvement has emerged so far from the efforts of several congressional committees and presidential commissions specifically assigned to address the problem.

It is generally acknowledged by most students of American government that the necessary changes will not take place without some form of government intervention. It should be equally evident that

UNITED NATIONS

United Nations interpreter works in a booth overlooking a meeting room at U.N. headquarters. Mandatory retirement often forces highly skilled, experienced workers off the market. A recent congressional report suggests that the wasted know-how of older workers could be the key to increasing American productivity.

 From *The Futurist*, June 1984, pp. 43-47. Published by The World Future Society, 4316 St. Elmo Avenue, Washington, D.C. 20014.

"The American public no longer accepts without question the thesis that retirement is an unadulterated blessing that provides a cure-all for our social and economic ills."

no combination of makeshift, patchwork reforms can succeed in resolving the intricate, interlocking problems that arise from retirement. The economic advisability of continuing to encourage early retirement is especially doubtful. However, there is little agreement among advocates for the aging and pension-fund experts as to the best way to treat retirement.

Balancing Benefits and Consequences

One valid concern is the balancing of short-term benefits of certain common employment practices—like that of mandatory retirement—against their long-term consequences. How wise is it, for example, to focus our current efforts on assuring full employment for young workers when dropping birthrates may bring an acute labor shortage in the not-so-distant future? Who will fill the vacant slots if qualified, experienced older workers are prevented from doing so or are encouraged to withdraw from the labor market? Social considerations aside, can commerce and industry afford to ignore the obvious need to retain the older worker who is willing and able to continue working? Can older workers continue their jobs without jeopardizing the opportunities for younger replacements?

During the Carter administration, Congress tried to find answers to such thorny questions, with mixed results. One report suggested that the know-how of older workers, now being wasted, was the key to increased American productivity. Other studies supported these assertions.

The American public no longer accepts without question the thesis that retirement is an unadulterated blessing that provides a cure-all for our social and economic ills. Nevertheless, Labor Department figures show that American work-

ers continue to opt for early retirement in increasing numbers. The paradox is hard to explain, except in terms of the customary time lag between the availability of information and its digestion by the general public.

International Retirement Policies

In Europe, this trend has been even more pronounced. Max Horlick

---

Workers are opting for early retirement in increasing numbers. But this trend could have several serious long-term consequences—including an acute labor shortage in the not-too-distant future.

---

of the U.S. Social Security Administration describes the anomaly as follows: "Long-range planners discuss the need to extend the working career in order to defer payment of benefits and gain a longer period of contributions. The trend, however, tends to be toward earlier and earlier retirement."

Despite warnings that lowering the retirement age would create additional problems as the aging community grew, social and political pressures caused the warnings to be ignored. European planners seem to be fully aware of the contradictions, but are even more wary of the growing political influence of the elderly.

A substantial number of European countries, including both capitalist and Communist-bloc nations, have experimented with a variety of financial inducements designed to reduce or control unemployment by fostering the retirement of older workers. West

Germany lowered the retirement age from 65 to 63 in 1968, with allowances for part-time employment under certain conditions. Denmark has permitted early retirements for reason of failing health since 1965, as has Norway for "premature aging." Both Norway and Sweden lowered the permissible age for retirement from 70 to 67 in 1974, and then to 65 in 1976.

In these countries, social planners have responded to the perceived needs of their older citizens in a manner that they consider the most humane and equitable. They have reacted to popular criticism of the policy of forced retirement with carefully crafted programs allowing for partial retirement, partial pensions, and other innovative options. They have, in short, tried to provide flexible choices. Yet some form of withdrawal from employment seems to be regarded as an absolute prerequisite for eligibility for government benefits.

Social and economic problems related to aging have become even more troublesome in Great Britain than they are in the United States. The long-held postulate that help for the old and underprivileged is a basic responsibility of government has come under serious challenge. For the first time in decades, it is being argued that even such a previously sacrosanct assumption has practical limitations. The result is that in Britain, as in the United States, the poor, the elderly, and the disadvantaged are the ones most profoundly affected by the reduction of public benefits and subsidies.

It is incontestable that maintaining even minimal standards of living among the world's vast numbers of unemployed is becoming an overwhelming problem. Even in Sweden, a country long associated with progressive social-welfare policies, the electorate seems to be having second thoughts about the feasibility of unlimited public support of social programs. To more and more people it is becoming manifest that if increasing masses of pensioners must be supported by decreasing numbers of the still-employed, the burden will eventually become unbearable.

5. RETIREMENT

The major political and economic systems of the Western world have responded to the current labor glut with what amounts to the same old failed remedies. They have tended to revert back to the solutions of the Great Depression, when it was believed that promoting earlier retirement of older workers would magically solve all problems of mass unemployment. They seem to have forgotten that the relief was only temporary and purchased at great cost.

France, under President Francois Mitterand's socialist government, has once again taken to trying to encourage earlier retirement in an attempt to "distribute" the country's jobs and stem the rising tide of unemployment. Much the same policy is being followed in Great Britain, Belgium, West Germany, the Netherlands, and Italy. Even among Communist-bloc nations— in Yugoslavia, Bulgaria, Czechoslovakia, Hungary, and the Soviet Union—the same tendency is manifesting itself.

In the Orient, we have a somewhat different picture, colored largely by massive overpopulation. Japan, for all its industrial and technological wizardry, is deeply troubled by the clash between the old tradition of reverence for the aged and the new demands of a modern technocracy. Lines have become sharply drawn between the mass of younger workers and a deeply entrenched gerontocracy. Still other cultural factors affect conditions in China, India, and other Asiatic societies. Even with cheap and abundant labor, none of them has completely escaped the socio-economic consequences of a worldwide increase in the number of older survivors.

Future Implications

The inclination to ignore the implications for the future of an aging work force is not necessarily shared by all government agencies. Serious efforts have been made by several governments to encourage later retirement in order to ease the strain on pension and retirement systems. In the Soviet Union, for example, some key officials have argued against removing experienced older workers from the labor

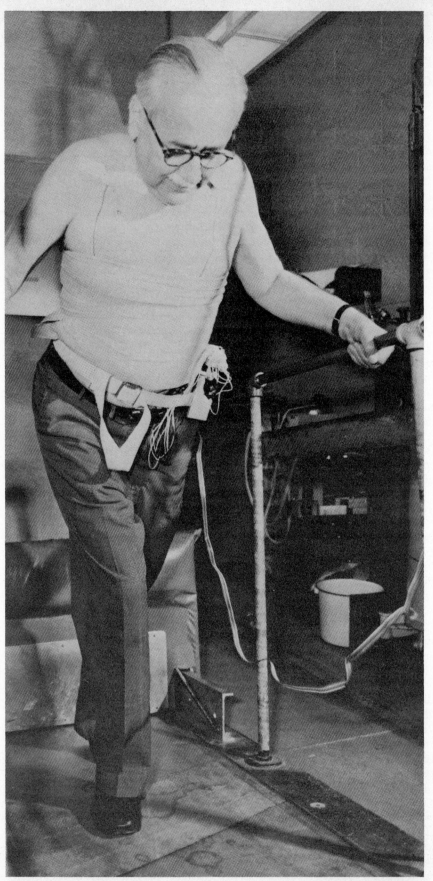

U.S. NATIONAL INSTITUTES OF HEALTH

Elderly man undergoes an exercise test at the National Institutes of Health. Surveys have shown that declining health is no longer a major factor in early-retirement decisions; in fact, a majority of retirees would like to return to work.

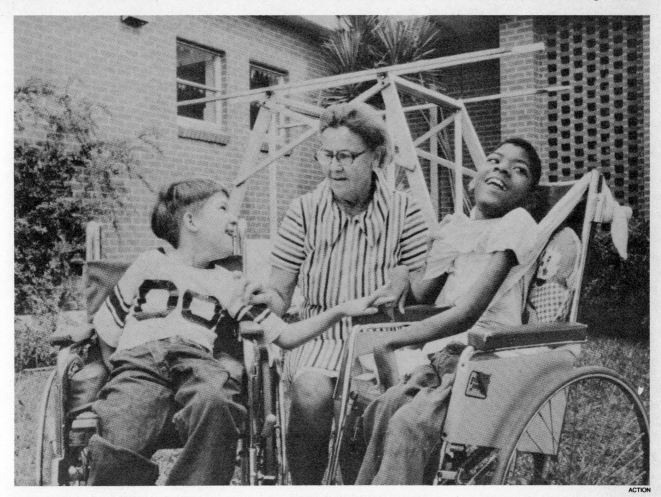

ACTION

Retired woman cares for two handicapped children as part of a "foster grandparent" program in Mississippi. Increasingly, it is seen as good social and economic sense to better utilize the skills and abilities of older Americans, says author Bernard Forman.

force prematurely on the grounds that such actions are wasteful, uneconomic, and ultimately counterproductive.

The United States seems to be trapped between two equally important concerns. On the one hand, the public is becoming increasingly conscious of the aging of the population and the illogic and injustice of current retirement policies. On the other hand, there are worries about the possible effects that changing present retirement policies may have on the employment prospects of younger workers. The concerns may be equally important, but they cannot be treated with a single "generic" remedy, appropriate for all economic ailments.

A 1979 Department of Labor-sponsored study contended that most early-retirement decisions were motivated by declining health rather than by an actual desire to withdraw from work. It saw those decisions as only minimally affected by the mandatory-retirement policies of employers. A Harris survey of the same year, however, disputed that conclusion. It showed that a majority of retirees regretted being induced to leave their jobs and would like to return to work, if that were possible. Harold Sheppard, President Carter's counselor on aging, stated that there were signs the trend toward early retirement was undergoing a definite reversal.

Several recent studies by Jerome Rosow and others at the Work in America Institute make detailed recommendations for alternatives to current retirement policies. One outlines some of the available new options for an "extended working life." Another describes some of the model retirement programs already in operation.

The Changing Public Opinion Of Retirement

There are signs of awakening public awareness of the wastefulness of premature retirement, along with a willingness to rethink and redefine the concept of retirement itself. Innovative pilot programs sponsored by both public and private agencies, aimed at providing meaningful employment for workers at or near retirement age, have emerged. Among notable examples are:

● The personnel policy of Baltimore's WMAR-TV, which deliberately attempts to match older employees with appropriate new jobs.

● The Travelers Insurance Company's ambitious retraining program for older employees, and its allied "Corporation for Older Americans."

● The "Retirement Planning for the 80s" project of the National Council on Aging.

5. RETIREMENT

"The real question is not whether but how to assure all retirees of a comfortable old age without compelling them to retire either too early or too late."

A wide variety of alternatives to total retirement are already available. Among current variations of flexible or partial retirement are combinations of delayed or postponed retirement, in-company part-time work, or temporary assignments. There are also opportunities presented for phased-in or "tapered" withdrawal from full employment and a variety of novel shared-job arrangements.

Some firms offer continued accrual of pension benefits and others are pro-rated, proportionately reduced, offset, or postponed until full retirement occurs. In a few exceptional cases, in-service retraining programs that make possible the "redeployment" of older workers are available. Some companies have even tried copying the Danish experiment of voluntary demotion, which they have found preferable to involuntary retirement. However, it remains inescapable that the continuation of benefits in any situation is still contingent upon the good will and generosity of the employer, in the absence of federal mandates or regulation.

Even if this promising new trend develops into a full-scale readjustment of American employment patterns, some crucial questions remain to be answered. Among them are the feasibility (from the actuarial point of view) of continuing accrual of pension benefits after "retirement" and the political risks of raising the age of eligibility for Social Security.

Dissatisfaction with current retirement policies was seen in Congress with the passage of the Age Discrimination in Employment Amendments of 1978. The drive to eliminate mandatory retirement altogether has most recently been reactivated by Congressman Claude Pepper and others. President Reagan's own personal opposition to mandatory retirement has reinforced the movement,

which is strongly supported by public opinion. Still, most labor unions continue to be ambivalent, mainly because their leadership views the issue as a useful weapon in labor-management negotiations. Academe remains, for its own special reasons, equally resistant to change, while other special-interest groups also persist in favoring traditional retirement policies.

In the business community, the picture continues to be mixed. However, there is evidence of a rising tide of opposition to present retirement practices, along with a belated recognition of their adverse social and economic consequences. More and more businessmen are beginning to see that the mushrooming army of unemployed and unproductive retirees is placing an intolerable strain on younger workers, on Social Security, on the American pension system, and on the economy as a whole. Changing demography, occupational shifts, labor-force composition, pension systems, and the whole gamut of employment issues play an interactive role in affecting the health or sickness of the national economy.

Changes Needed in Retirement Policies

Few Americans seriously question the right of every employee to some kind of livable income (whatever it may be called) after many years of service to an employer. Whether it is received in the form of an earned pension or as a Social Security payment, it is the deserved reward for services rendered. The real question is not whether but how to assure all retirees of a comfortable old age without compelling them to retire either too early or too late.

Should the income derived from a public or private pension be adequate to enable the retired worker to retain his or her pre-

retirement style of living? Since no one has yet come up with a satisfactory estimate of what an adequate or decent standard of retirement living is (or should be), that must remain a moot question.

Nevertheless, there can be little doubt that some combination of private and public income maintenance is necessary to shield the average retired employee from inflation and impoverishment. For that reason, substantial improvements in the administration and distribution of both public and private pension funds are desirable. Yet it is equally important to be sure that the required reforms are not used merely as a pretext by the employer to spur accelerated retirement and circumvent the desire of capable older employees for continued employment on a full- or part-time basis. Some authorities, in fact, maintain that making pension plans more generous for a larger number of workers is tantamount to offering irresistible financial incentives for early retirement.

From a broader perspective, it seems to make good social and economic sense to do whatever we possibly can to utilize the wasted know-how of older workers much more effectively than is being done now. Creating a new, unproductive leisure class of parasitic elders is hardly an acceptable cure for intractable societal ills anywhere in the world. Nor is there any law that decrees we must follow blindly in the footsteps of other nations that have been mistaken in the past and may be repeating the same mistakes today. We are not obliged to use foreign social security programs as absolute models, especially if we are convinced that they are wrong.

American policy-makers are now recognizing that retirement has many faces, not all of them attractive. Some have even begun to reconsider the very idea of retirement. The realization may finally have begun to sink in that a great number of older people are going to have a lot of time ahead of them to weigh the advantages and disadvantages of having nothing really meaningful to do.

New Roles for Older Workers

Jarold Kieffer, Ph.D.

Dr. Jarold Kieffer is a policy and management consultant living in Fairfax, Virginia, who has had a long career in government and education. He was the Deputy Commissioner of Social Security at the close of the Ford Administration, then served as director of the National Committee on Careers for Older Americans, and later as staff director of the 1981 White House Conference on Aging.

This article is based upon the theme of his book Gaining the Dividends of Longer Life: New Roles for Older Workers, *published in December, 1983 by Westview Press.*

In 1983, through amendments to the Social Security Act, Congress and the President signalled that future older workers will be expected to work longer to qualify for full Social Security benefits. In the year 2000, a slow process of increasing the retirement age from 65 to 67 will begin. Also, those contemplating early retirement under Social Security in the future can expect sharper decreases in their starting benefits. These moves to require or induce people to work longer were considered necessary because most workers over age 62 have been retiring as soon as they could qualify for Social Security benefits, and many have been retiring even earlier under private or public pension systems.

The early retirement phenomenon has been accompanied by the phenomenon of longer life expectancy. From 1960 to 1983, the average life expectancy of men, once they reached

"New Roles for Old Workers," Jarold Kieffer, *Aging* Magazine, February/March 1984, pp. 11-16, 47. Reprinted by permission of *Aging* Magazine.

137

5. RETIREMENT

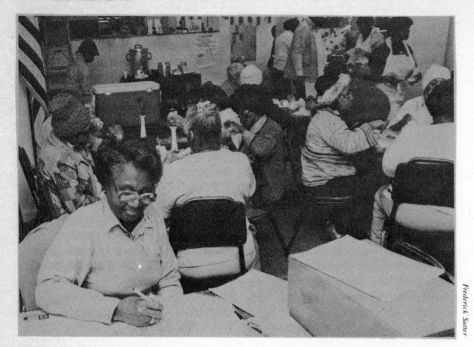

Frederick Sutter

Dorothy Holsey, 64, is an aide at the Barney Senior Center in Washington, D.C.

age 60, grew from 15.9 to 17.8 years. For women, the gain was from 19.6 to 22.7 more years. By the year 2000, when the Social Security retirement age starts to move up, average life expectancy for men at age 60 is projected to climb to 19.2 more years, while that for women of the same age will be 24.7 more years.

In acting to delay the Social Security retirement age and to steepen the disincentives for early retirement, policymakers were reflecting their concern that the demands upon the Social Security Old Age and Survivors Insurance Trust Fund could become unmanageable if present pro-early retirement policies were continued. These policies have been converting more and more taxpayers into retirement benefit receivers prematurely at the same time that greater life expectancy has extended the years that retirees and their survivors can be expected to receive benefits. Moreover, policymakers could see that the already rapidly growing numbers of people over age 55 would increase from 47.4 million (1980 Census) to 58.8 million by the year 2000 and then leap to 74.1 million 10 years later when the "baby boom" generation begins to reach the 55–60 year category.

No one can be sure whether the new Social Security provisions will induce people to work longer. Some analysts believe that they will not and that people will continue to retire as soon as they can. Others believe that the incentives to encourage people to delay retirement are inadequate.

However, several factors that could have a powerful influence on work versus retirement decisions really have not been addressed as yet by policymakers. One factor involves the whole attitude of older workers about staying productive. Another involves society's perception of older people as productive workers. Additional neglected factors are the availability of jobs and the atmosphere older people find in the workplace. If, indeed, national policy requires that older people work longer, then these factors will have to be given a great deal of attention.

No Incentives To Work Longer

From the end of World War II, employers, labor unions, and the federal government all seemed to agree that conditions should be established that would encourage older workers to retire as early as possible in order to open up or keep open jobs for younger workers. In part, this think-ing stemmed from fears that the post-war period would see a return of high levels of unemployment, and also it reflected the growing concensus that older people should not have to work until they died and that, as much as possible, they should have a right to retire with reasonable economic security.

Over the next several decades, a wide array of pro-retirement policies and conditions were put in place, and they were very effective. Between 1950 and 1983, the percentage of men over 65 still in the work force dropped from 45.8 percent to 17.8 percent. For men in the ages 55–64, the percentage dropped from 87 to 70. Middle-aged and older women joined the work force in large numbers during World War II and did so again on a longer term basis in the 1960s. However, less than 8 percent of those over age 65 were still counted in the work force in 1983. Among women in the age 55–64 category, work force participation peaked at 43 percent in 1970 but has dropped a little since that year.

Obviously, some of these people retired because they wanted to stop working. Many were in poor health and believed themselves, or were classed, as disabled. Even as late as 1950, a worker born before 1900 was part of an age group that had an average life expectancy at birth of less than 50 years. The then fledgling Social Security System offered workers who had survived to age 65 the possibility of retiring with a modest guaranteed income. Most older workers of that time had jobs in manual labor on farms or in factories. They had little motivation to keep working and welcomed the chance to have a few work-free years. Relatively low inflation rates and rising productivity during these years helped the pro-retirement thinking of workers and their employers and encouraged both private and public sector policymakers to believe that the economy could support an expanded practice of early retirement.

The nation's pro-retirement policies and practices were accompanied by a rapidly developed and accepted view that older workers were less productive, hard to teach, and hard to work with. In the workplace, workers in their 50's found that they were not considered worthy of being given further training and development. In a circular way, such personnel policies then assured that the skill status of such employees would decline, particularly in lines of work undergoing rapid technological and process changes. This situation, which still persists, then has influenced the determination of employers to ease older workers out of the picture as quickly as possible. Workers not only have been encouraged to quit early, but those who choose to stay after age 65 (and even younger ages) find that their pensions no longer gain in value with more years of service. Also, some find that their group life insurance stops or declines in value after age 65.

In these circumstances, even older workers who want or need to work longer have found that they are often considered a liability by their bosses and an outmoded relic by younger co-workers. These workplace attitudes have changed a little in the past few years but not much. In past and more recent times of economic downturn, older workers often have been advised that if they stayed on the job then younger workers with children to support would lose their jobs. Not surprisingly, even though the age of mandatory retirement was 65 until the late 1970s (and age 70 after then), employers have found ways of encouraging many workers to quit before age 65.

Studies of older worker attitudes about work versus retirement usually conclude that retirees sought retirement or thought they quit at about the right age. Yet, these views in many cases may have reflected the weak motivation of older workers to stay at work under such unpromising circumstances. Or, they may have accepted the judgment of their bosses and co-workers that they were less productive and stood in the way of younger workers.

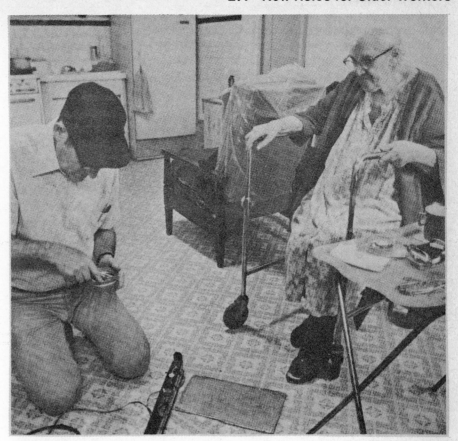

David Rosenberg, from Geri-Pare, Inc. in Brooklyn, N.Y., assists an elderly woman with home repairs.

Myths About Their Productivity

The exodus of older people from the work force has been reinforced by beliefs that older workers cost more to keep, get sick and are absent more, and are more prone to accidents. These notions, in addition to those about poorer productivity and teachability, have never been supported by important evidence comparing them with younger workers. Yet, in a remarkable way, such notions became the basis of personnel policies in the workplace and at the hiring door, and, for all practical purposes, still are.

Worse yet, the same notions about older workers became stereotyped along with those about older people generally and have been commonly used as the basis for caricatures in the motion picture industry, in the media, and in literature. Younger and many older people have become convinced that older workers are not interested in new ideas, really do not fit into the oncoming electronic world,

have poor memories, are ailing and often need physical help, and are marking time on the job until they can retire.

Such views persist even though ordinary observations should be sufficient to indicate that people age and decline in skills at varying rates. Moreover, in many kinds of work, technological change actually is easing the physical and, in some cases, other skill demands upon workers and further reducing the basis for using age as a critical factor in judging the capacity of people to perform their work duties. Most significantly, the overall health and physical status of most people over age 55 is remarkably good. Only about 5 percent are institutionalized or otherwise unable to care for themselves. Another 10–15 percent have some degree of physical or health limitation, although many among these would be capable of doing productive work.

Undoubtedly, many of the people over 55, particularly some who are retired, have no wish to continue to work or return to the workplace. However, it must be emphasized that the successful strategy of encouraging the mass of older people to leave and stay out of the workplace, plus the myths and stereotypes that developed to reinforce the pro-retirement policies still in place, has been carried out in the face of the enormous contradiction that their good health and physical status represents. Even if the groups noted above were left out of the calculation, we still would have eight out of ten of the people over age 55 with no important physical or mental limitations that would prevent them from joining in many kinds of productive activity, if they wanted to stay in the work force or rejoin it.

Furthermore, as a consequence of improved diets, more exercise, and changed life styles, people 55 and over seem to be in better condition than their counterparts were 10–20 years ago. People in this age group today also have higher levels and fresher types of educational and training experiences.

This means that in the same years that our society succeeded in encouraging the departure of most older people from the work force, we have been producing an older population unprecedented for its health status and educational and skill levels, factors that bear directly on the qualifications potential of people to remain in productive roles in the economy. Beyond the irony of this contradiction, we have yet to develop a strategy for gaining productive advantages from having an older population of this quality. This lack of a strategy is particularly striking in view of the fact that we have become well aware of the burgeoning costs projected in the retirement income and health care areas as a result of the great growth and increased life expectancy of the older population. We have become so used to writing off the productive capabilities of the older population that we are not thinking creatively about ways in which many able older people could help to reduce the retirement and health care problems rather

than adding to them by retiring prematurely and remaining non-productive for longer and longer periods.

We have yet to take hold of the idea that many of these people, if properly encouraged and helped, may well wish to extend their worklives, and that, in so doing, they would continue to pay both income and Social Security taxes and reduce the time they are retirement income beneficiaries. Some would be interested in longer worklives because they need the extra income; others believe that they will be healthier and have a better mental outlook if they keep busy. Still others would like to function in ways that help others.

The Need for Workplace Changes

A strategy to encourage able older people to extend their worklives would require changes in workplace policies and practices. A first step would be for employers to declare to their workers and job applicants that age will not be a barrier to the hiring, retention, promotion, and training of workers. While federal and, in some cases, state legislation bars age discrimination in these areas, a positive statement by employers would help clear up doubts in the minds of many older people. Also, older people only rarely can prove overt age discrimination. They tend to be left with their suspicions, but do not have the will, the time, or the resources to go the formal anti-discrimination charge route.

Then too, the visable lack of very many older workers still on the job or being hired, and the dearth of further training and promotion opportunities for older workers tends to shape the thinking of middle-aged and younger workers as to the probable duration of their own careers. Therefore, a turn-around in employer signals on older worker employment could help open up whole new perspectives among people of all ages as to the duration of worklives and the possibilities for further productive activity by workers as they gain in age.

Employers also can review their pension and fringe benefit plans to

remove or ease features that discourage older people from working longer. Workers at age 65 should be put on equal footing with younger workers in gaining added pension growth for additional years of service. Changes could be made in fringe benefits to recognize that older workers may have different needs than those of younger workers. For example, many older workers no longer have spouses, and their children are grown. Life insurance to protect survivors may not be a major need anymore. Some may want longer or shorter vacation periods. Some may wish to save unused vacation or sick leave and use it to finance a new educational or training experience, or a tax deferred annuity to which the employer and the worker jointly contribute so that the worker can have more retirement income after retirement. Then too, some older workers might wish to sacrifice other fringe benefits in favor of better protection for health care contingencies not well covered by the employers regular group health plan or Medicare. Flexibility, rather then rigidity in this area could help project a further indication that employers wish to encourage rather than discourage longer worklives.

More Job Options

A key factor in changing the workplace atmosphere is the bread and butter problem of the lack of job options. The U.S. employment picture is full of seeming contradictions. The number of people working is at a record high. However, simultaneously, unemployment is still at very high levels, though moving down from a record high in December, 1982. Some employers are rebuilding their work forces; others are under heavy competitive pressure to cut staff as one means of reducing their costs. Broad job reduction objectives have been adopted by many private and public employers. Elimination of programs, hiring freezes, and broader uses of labor-saving technologies are being used more extensively by employers to help achieve these objectives.

In these mixed circumstance, employers and labor unions are likely to respond unevenly to the idea of making major policy changes to encourage older workers to work longer. At the same time, we can expect that more older workers will challenge existing workplace policies and practices and allege that they are being subjected to age discrimination. Probably, more of these cases will be won by the older workers, and such an outcome will likely induce more employers to move increasingly toward age-neutrality in their hiring, retention, and training policies.

In the meantime, employers could consider several relatively simple steps that could broaden job options for older workers who may not prefer to retire or may wish to work again in some capacity.

• *Additional Training*. Employers, working with educational and training institutions, could assure that their workers, including those over age 50, keep up or acquire skills that enable them to be considered valued employees in the future operations of their employers. If older workers choose to stay on but are not kept up in their skills, they become a drag on productivity and morale, theirs and that of fellow workers, and increase employer costs.

• *Flexible Scheduling*. Where possible, older workers who wish to continue working, but on a reduced basis, could be helped by more flexible work and attendence arrangements. For example, they could be given longer vacation periods in return for proportionately reduced compensation and benefits. For workers eligible for pensions, partial benefits could be phased in gradually as worktime and wages are gradually reduced. Also, some workers could be put into work-sharing arrangements, where several employees, each on a part-time basis, carry out the functions of one job. Workers could be given broader leave-without-pay opportunities to pursue educational and training objectives leading to new or further careers, while kept in good standing in the employer's pension and benefit plans.

• *Productive Assignments*. Many workers, older and younger, feel dead-ended or used up in their current jobs. They commonly lack motivation and job interest. Some exhibit boredom, falling or uneven productivity, and growing error rates. They stay in place because they lack other job options, and cannot afford to sacrifice their pensions and group insurances. Usually, they retire early and become a long-term obligation of the employer. More job options could help ease this problem.

Most employers have a growing involvement in community responsibilities. Many encourage their employees to participate in community endeav-

---

A turn-around in employer signals on older worker employment could open up whole new perspectives.

---

ors. The practice of actually loaning employees to community problem-solving efforts could be expanded. The employers could cover some or all of the wages and benefits of the loaned workers and keep them in good standing in their company benefit programs. The employers would gain community goodwill as well as other values that develop from reducing costly community problems. The workers would gain the value of fresh challenge and possibly new or different career perspectives. In many cases, such loans of workers would cost the employer less over time than carrying them non-productively on the job for additional years and later in early and prolonged retirement.

New Problem-Solving Jobs

Both in the near- and long-term future, more jobs will be developed to help cope with stress areas in our communities. When the population was much smaller and scattered, social sensitivities and community well-being were less affected and troubled by the unmet needs and/or adverse behavior or difficulties of individuals. Their problems tended to

be dealt with by families, church groups, or voluntary organizations, or they were neglected. Today (and probably even more so in the future), the scale and complexity of these difficulties are much greater on account of population expansion, crowding, and mobility.

Large numbers of people suffer from dislocation, lack of family or group support, and alienation from community values. Large pockets of only partially assimilated immigrants are developing in many of our communities, and tensions flare because of crowding, cultural differences, and economic difficulties. Both unemployment and underemployment are becoming intergenerational, with growing numbers of families having no solid employment experience within them. As such, they exist in environments of lifelong public assistance and dependency, broken families, and shadowy activities outside the regular economy. While more people have been schooled than ever before in our history, we appear to have growing numbers of people without satisfactory employment skills and work habits. Rapid technological change and demands are threatening the employability of many current workers and job seekers and building higher barriers for the unskilled unemployed. The number of older people left alone is also steadily growing, and living and other support arrangements for them will have to be developed.

Increasing numbers of employers and many community leaders appreciate that these and other individual or family problems have become community problems. As such, they are producing both human and dollar costs that translate into rising private and public sector budgets, higher taxes, lower property values and tax bases, and diminished investment and business opportunities in many communities. Therefore, private and public sector policymakers are being challenged to evolve new concepts of cost-effectiveness to judge the utility of proposed remedial measures. Remedial measures that require greater

Frederick Sutter

Also, in the next ten years, our society, for cost, social, and political reasons, will have to face the challenge of dealing more effectively with the massive training and retraining needs of millions of people of varying ages who will want to be kept or made employable. Training and retraining demands are not new. What is new are the numbers of people who face skill obsolescence, the pressure on American producers to remain competitive, the huge numbers of unskilled and unemployable people for whom a productivity solution must be found, and the steadily larger pool of able older people that the economy has written off prematurely but will have increasing difficulty supporting in prolonged retirement. Major decision-making will be needed in the years ahead if we are to meet these challenges. However, once the decisions are made, a great demand will develop for teachers, trainers, job and career counselors, and placement specialists.

Other labor intensive sources for more jobs will arise from the need to provide a wide variety of health maintenance and care services outside of hospitals, from the need for more effective crime prevention and law enforcement efforts, from the demand for more effective transportation services, and from broadened programs to protect and enhance the environment. Many older and middle-aged people will find new or further career possibilities in these expanded job areas, and in other expanding fields, such as biomedical research, biomedical industry, communications, and hazardous waste management. The availability of more job options could influence many older people to extend their worklives, many middle-aged workers will see that they can have a lengthy period ahead in which to pursue a different career, and many able people who are already retired would realize that they have fresh opportunities to expand their income or find interesting new work to challenge them.

Many of these new or expanded fields of employment will produce jobs that will be considered self-

use of personnel may have to be judged on the basis of a broader test of cost-effectiveness.

For example, population figures show that in the 20 years between 1980 and 2000, the numbers of people over age 80 will nearly double—from 5.2 million to 10.1 million. In our communities, many of these people will require health care, feeding, living arrangements and services that will require the employment of large numbers of people. Finding adequate means to pay for these activities will be very difficult, but the needs must be met, and the jobs will be required.

supporting in a market economy sense. In other cases, as noted earlier, cost-effectiveness will have to be judged on the basis of new equations that compare the long-term costs to our economy of employing more people in order to alleviate serious individual and community problems with the growing human and dollar costs to the economy of failing to mitigate these problems.

These new cost-effectiveness equations also will be able to include the cost savings that will result when older workers lengthen their work-lives. This will reduce the number of years they will be beneficiaries of public and private retirement income systems and add to the years that they will be paying income and Social Security taxes on their work income. Further cost savings may accrue, because marginal earners who have a chance to work longer, or people who retired with only small benefits and can go back to work, can gain enough additional income to lessen their need for public assistance.

Some of the "problem-mitigating" jobs will likely require support from combinations of private and public resources. Foundations can help identify these situations by supporting pilot programs that seek to demonstrate how the training and use of additional workers (including older workers) could directly mitigate costly individual and community problems. The pilot programs could help determine the skills needed by the workers, training and service strategies, numbers of workers needed, practical employment arrangements, and the means of sustaining the jobs over the long term. Private and voluntary organizations, community service clubs, business associations, churches, and other organizations could help raise funds annually to support more problem-solving jobs.

In some communities, businesses are organizing and gaining approval for special taxing districts to raise revenue to support extra law enforcement, transportation, and neighborhood enhancement efforts in their areas. This concept probably will be expanded and could be used to fund problem-mitigating jobs. Also, some employers now are making direct contributions to strengthen community services of importance to them. Increasingly, businesses have recognized how more effective community services aid the morale of their work forces. Many also are recognizing that the reduction of serious community problems can help business prospects in many ways.

The additional jobs developed and maintained through these various efforts would not be restricted to older workers. Moreover, their existence would loosen up the job picture and give all workers more options for new or further careers. Workers of any age who leave their current jobs to take one of the new option jobs often will leave a place open for other workers, older or younger. When older workers realize that they could either stay productive in their current jobs or that they could do so in different jobs of interest to them, they will be able to weigh the work versus retirement decision in a wholly different context than has been possible up to now. Many will choose to extend their worklives, and the nation will gain from their choice.

As Early Retirement Grows in Popularity, Some Have Misgivings

Ronald Alsop
Staff Reporter of The Wall Street Journal

Harry Myers of Salem, N.J., always prided himself on keeping trim and healthy. He liked his job of estimating project costs at a Du Pont Co. chemical plant well enough and planned to work past 65, perhaps even until he turned 70.

But about a year and a half ago when he was 58, Du Pont made him a one-time retirement offer he couldn't refuse—a week's pay for each of his 40 years of service, plus all his other accrued benefits. "It was like finding money in the street," Mr. Myers says.

Within just two months, though, he realized he had made a grave mistake. He quickly tired of yard work and contracted a bad case of cabin fever. His hobby of making miniature wood furniture for doll houses seemed more like a job than a pastime. "I had seen only the dollar signs," Mr. Myers says. "I was too young, and my health was too good for me to retire. My wife wasn't ready for a rocking chair, either."

NEEDED AGAIN

At Du Pont, his skills were missed when business picked up late last year, prompting the company to offer him temporary part-time work. That makes Mr. Myers happy, for now at least. "Du Pont needs me again, and I need Du Pont," he declares.

As Mr. Myers's experience suggests, early-retirement incentive programs sometimes yield mixed results. The programs can be costly to finance and costly in terms of talent lost. They also can produce anger and depression among employees. Some feel pressured to quit. Others later regret retiring too soon. And if the plans aren't carefully designed, companies may leave themselves open to charges of age discrimination, as the law generally forbids forced retirements before age 70.

"I've tried to warn clients that early retirement programs can be a dangerous and costly strategy, but it's been like trying to stop a locomotive," says Lawrence Olson, senior economist with Coopers & Lybrand's management-consulting service.

During the recession, retirement incentives were promoted widely by such companies as Bethlehem Steel Corp., Deere & Co. and Firestone Tire & Rubber Co., as a way to slim bloated staffs. Some concerns, including American Telephone & Telegraph Co., BankAmerica Corp., Eastman Kodak Co. and Sun Co., are using them to adapt to turbulent change in their industries.

EFFECT OF RECESSION

Of 305 companies responding to a survey by Hewitt Associates, 28% said they had offered early-retirement incentive programs between 1980 and 1982. More state governments and colleges also are dangling incentives before their senior employees. In Ohio, for example, some 70 state colleges and public-school districts are crediting early retirees with as many as five additional years of service to fatten their pensions. Although new early-retirement programs have diminished in number as the economic recovery has gathered steam, a number of big companies are still offering them this year.

Known as "open windows" and "golden handshakes," voluntary early-retirement incentive plans usually are aimed at people over 50 with at least 10 years of service. But sometimes when companies must ax several thousand employees from the payroll, retirement sweeteners are offered to employees regardless of age or length of employment. Typically, the carrot is some combination of a pension bonus, medical-insurance benefits and a severance payment based on salary and tenure at the company.

Incentive programs are part of a long-term trend in the U.S. toward earlier retirement. Pension programs have been gradually liberalized over the years so that at many companies, workers can collect their regular benefits after 30 years of service or at age 55. "Early retirement was a huge ball gathering moss even before these incentive plans became so popular," says Malcolm H. Morrison, a visiting research associate at the University of Pennsylvania's Wharton School.

RETIREMENT TREND

Last year, 17.4% of men over 65 were in the civilian labor force, compared with 22.8% in 1973 and 46.8% in 1948. The ratio of men between 55 and 64 who were still working also continued to drop, to 69.4% in 1983 from 78.3% in 1973 and 89.5% in 1948.

Economists are disturbed that more companies these days consider early retirement incentives whenever an economic downturn or technological change requires cutbacks in the work force. The programs help reinforce the expectation for earlier and earlier retirement, critics say, at a time when the country should be starting to encourage people to work longer.

"Demographics are turning around," says James Schulz, an economist at Brandeis University's Policy Center on Aging. "In a few years people will have to work until they are 65 or 70." As the baby-boom generation ages, shortages of skilled workers are likely. Furthermore, later retirement will be necessary to keep the Social Security system solvent, economists maintain.

Retirement incentives clearly have some merits for both companies and employees. At the very least, they provide financially beleaguered companies with a bit of good public relations. Employers look more humane, offering early retirement as a way to keep layoffs of younger workers to a minimum. The plans also improve cash flow by reducing payroll expenses, and they clear a path for younger employees to move into management positions.

Many workers are delighted with their early-retirement decisions. The windfalls sometimes provide middle-aged employees with the means to start second careers or just to take life easy. For C. William Roos, the former director of technology administration at Monsanto Co., an incentive payment meant a chance to fulfill an ambition to teach. He now is an associate professor of chemical engineering at Auburn University. Executive secretary Patricia Keelan took advantage of a travel-discount inducement offered to early retirees at Pan American World Airways and spent much of 1983 touring Australia, France and Germany.

But these programs are far from panaceas. For one thing, they aren't cheap. Sears, Roebuck & Co. succeeded in thinning the executive ranks in 1980, but the retirement offer cost the company $66.7 million to put into effect. A plan offered by Kodak last year resulted in an after-tax $87.4 million charge against first-quarter earnings. New York state estimates the bill for its special early-retirement program at $145 million spread over five years and cautions that if many of the 8,000 jobs vacated last year are refilled, the state stands to lose money on the program.

"I'm not sure companies are looking closely at all the costs," says Thomas Wood, senior partner at Hewitt Associates. He mentions the soaring cost of the medical-insurance coverage that often is provided until Medicare kicks in, continued death-benefit expenses and supplemental payments that are sometimes offered until workers become eligible for Social Security.

Probably the most serious complaint lodged against early-retirement plans is that they aren't as voluntary as they are advertised to be. Richard Kobus, a former telephone-system designer for AT&T Information Systems, believes early-retirement was merely a sanitized way to fire him. "My boss said my job was going to be eliminated Dec. 31, 1983, and here is this voluntary retirement plan," the 37-year-old Phoenix man says. "The company shoved it down my throat."

A spokesman for the AT&T marketing unit responds: "It definitely was a voluntary program. But it's difficult to implement a national program like this and know how every manager handles it with his employees."

FEELING THE PRESSURE

Even Betty McCaul, a clerk at Parker Pen Co. who retired on friendly terms, felt pressured. "It was shaky back then at the company," she recalls. "You had to decide whether to stay and accept the risk of being laid off, or take what you could get and run."

Some workers also feel coercion from colleagues and union officials eager to save younger employees' jobs. What's more, companies usually give workers only two to four months to decide whether to retire, raising questions about whether that is long enough for such a critical choice.

A New Jersey woman says she was too hasty in accepting a fat early-retirement offer in 1982. She thought the money could help her grandson study at a seminary. "But I've never been so sad," she says. "I feel like I've lost my home."

Although pleased with his decision, Harold Scheule, a former assistant marketing manager in petroleum chemicals at Du Pont, says the early-retirement incentive program spoiled his vacation to Europe in 1982. "I lay awake nights wondering, 'Should I or shouldn't I retire?'" he says. "It was grueling. I knew I couldn't very well go back after retiring and say I had changed my mind."

United Nations Photo/Michael Tzovaras

Early retirement can be a bittersweet experience. While elderly people are free to do what they want, they can be bored at being alone.

FACING INFLATION

It is too soon to tell whether this recent crop of early retirees across the country will have financial difficulties after their severance bonuses expire. But Prof. Schulz of Brandeis says: "People leaving in their 50s had better have pretty decent pensions because they will be eroded by many years of inflation." He and other economists note that it becomes much harder to find jobs, even low-paying part-time positions, after the age of 50.

Some companies have chosen not to offer early-retirement incentives because they find them too disruptive to morale and productivity. Champion International Corp. rejected them during its "cash conservation" period in 1982, believing they would make workers feel insecure about their future with the company.

Morale can suffer in other ways, too. "Sometimes, these plans are perceived as rewarding poor performers," says Bill N. Rutherford, Sun Co.'s senior vice president for human resources and admnistration. Some people are ineligible for a retirement incentive because their departments are thriving and cutbacks aren't needed.

At Du Pont, for example, some workers were bitter because they wanted to retire but happened to work at plants that didn't offer any special inducements. "A lot of guys walked out of this plant grumbling," says Joseph Nidzgorski, an accounting clerk at a Du Pont titanium dioxide plant in Wilmington, Del. "It's a damned shame. Our retirees gave the same sweat and blood as other people, but left without getting anything extra."

PURPOSE OF PROGRAM

Du Pont executives dismiss such complaints as "short-sighted and selfish." Mark Suwyn, the vice president of employee relations, says, "Some people are looking to get a handout, but that wasn't the purpose of our voluntary termination incentive program. It was intended to protect younger workers' jobs where we needed to make permanent layoffs." So far, about 3,800 Du Pont workers have retired early.

A big risk to companies is the sacrifice of valuable employees. Companies the past few years have touted the fact that they were "slimming down" and becoming "lean and mean." But they may have lost some of their weight in the wrong spots. Because of the random nature of some retirement offers, companies sometimes try to compensate by hiring back needed former employees as consultants.

"History will prove the early-retirement incentives so prevalent in the 1980s to be a disastrous waste of human resources," says Rep. Edward R. Roybal of California, the chairman of the House's Select Committee on Aging. "The programs indiscriminately jettison the most experienced, loyal and talented members of the work force." Indeed, management consultants report that absenteeism rates often rise after a wave of early retirement because the departed older workers had a stronger work ethic and were more dependable.

UNIVERSITY'S PROBLEM

Miami University in Oxford, Ohio, may not reap the payroll savings it had expected from early retirements because of the mix of people being lost. The school hopes to replace tenured professors with younger faculty members earning no more than $25,000. But some professors in competitive fields such as accounting and economics are leaving, and the university may have to pay dearly to attract replacements.

Often, companies lose their best and brightest because such employees know they can take the incentive payment and easily land another job, perhaps an even better one. "I was arrogant enough to know I wouldn't have any trouble finding an attractive offer," says Richard Young, who took early retirement as executive vice president of marketing

at Polaroid Corp. and soon was hired as president of Houghton Mifflin Co., the book publisher.

Polaroid's early-retirement program also hurt two innovative programs it has been testing—"retirement rehearsal" and a "tapering off" program for older workers. Under the rehearsal option, employees can leave the company for three months and then decide whether they want to return to their jobs or make their retirement permanent. Workers also can retire gradually, by tapering off the number of hours worked each week.

"But when the incentives were offered people in our tapering-off program said, "My gosh, I'd better grab that money and leave now,' " says Joseph Perkins, the corporate retirement manager. "We're back at ground zero."

Companies sometimes try to coax valuable employees to pass up buy-out plans. But the wooing may come too late. "Xerox Corp. offered me a promotion right before I left, but I said, 'Where were you two years ago?' " recalls Douglas Vacanti, who retired at 40 and used his $31,500 incentive payment and $22,000 of profit-sharing to help establish Topaz Machine Inc. in Rochester, N.Y.

To protect their ranks, some companies exclude high-demand workers such as engineers and geologists, from retirement plans, and require that high-salaried executives get management approval. They also try to deter retirees from joining the competition. BankAmerica will cut off incentive payments to retired executives who defect to other banks. "It will be difficult for us to police, especially since it's hard to tell who your competition is in banking these days," says Robert N. Beck, the executive vice president for corporate personnel. "But we have a good network of friends."

The Experience of Dying

Modern science has allowed us some control over the conception of our children and has provided us with an ability to prolong life. But life and death still defy scientific explanation or reason. We can divide the world into two categories: sacred and secular. We use the sacred (that which is usually embodied in the religion of a culture) to explain all the forces of nature and our environment that we can neither understand nor control. On the other hand, we use the secular (defined as "of or relating to the world") to explain all the other aspects of our world that we *can* understand or control. Through scientific invention, we have been able to control more and more of the natural world. It still seems highly doubtful, however, that science will ever be able to give us an acceptable explanation of the meaning of death. In this domain, religion may always prevail.

Death is universally feared. Sometimes it is more bearable for those who believe in a life after death. Here, religion offers a solution to this dilemma. In the words of anthropologist Bronislaw Malinowski (1884-1942):

Religion steps in, selecting the positive creed, the comforting view, the culturally valuable belief in immortality, in the spirit of the body, and in the continuance of life after death. (Bronislaw

Malinowski, *Magic, Science and Religion and Other Essays,* Glencoe, Illinois: Free Press, 1948.)

Our fear of death leads us to develop defense mechanisms in order to psychologically insulate ourselves from its reality. We know that some day we will die, but we always think of death as occurring in the distant future. In this way, we are able to control our anxiety about death.

Losing a close friend or relative brings us dangerously close to the reality of death. We come face to face with the fact that there is always an end to life. Our latent fears become conscious. During times of mourning, we grieve not only for the dead but for ourselves and for the finiteness of our lives.

The readings in this section range from discussions of attitudes toward death to different methods of coping with death.

Looking Ahead: Challenge Questions

Is the fear of dying really universal? Do all people share it equally?

What are the techniques by which people alleviate their anxieties about dying?

Should patients be told the truth about their impending death, or should this information be withheld?

Are the elderly more afraid of death than the young?

Coping with the Reality of Terminal Illness in the Family

Elisabeth Kubler-Ross

Elisabeth Kubler-Ross is a Swiss physician now practicing in Chicago where she began a seminar on death and dying that was initially greeted with considerable resistance by physicians but was welcomed by terminal patients. In this selection taken from her book On Death and Dying, *Dr. Kubler-Ross introduces the family as a participant in the dying drama.*

Family members undergo different stages of adjustment similar to [those of the] patients. At first many of them cannot believe that it is true. They may deny the fact that there is such an illness in the family or "shop around" from doctor to doctor in the vain hope of hearing that this was the wrong diagnosis. They may seek help and reassurance (that it is all not true) from fortune-tellers and faith healers. They may arrange for expensive trips to famous clinics and physicians and only gradually face up to the reality which may change their life so drastically. Greatly dependent on the patient's attitude, awareness, and ability to communicate, the family then undergoes certain changes. If they are able to share their common concerns, they can take care of important matters early and under less pressure of time and emotions. If each one tries to keep a secret from the other, they will keep an artificial barrier between them which will make it difficult for any preparatory grief for the patient or his family. The end result will be much more dramatic than for those who can talk and cry together at times.

Just as the patient goes through a stage of anger, the immediate family will experience the same emotional reaction. They will be angry alternately with the doctor who examined the patient first and did not come forth with the diagnosis and the doctor who confronted them with the sad reality. They may project their rage to the hospital personnel who never care enough, no matter how efficient the care is in reality. There is a great deal of envy in this reaction, as family members often feel cheated at not being able or allowed to be with the patient and to care for him. There is also much guilt and a wish to make up for missed past opportunities. The more we can help the relative to express these emotions before the death of a loved one, the more comfortable the family member will be.

When anger, resentment, and guilt can be worked through, the family will then go through a phase of preparatory grief, just as the dying person does. The more this grief can be expressed before death, the less unbearable it becomes afterward. We often hear relatives say proudly of themselves that they always tried to keep a smiling face when confronted with the patient, until one day they just could not keep that facade any longer. Little do they realize that genuine emotions on the part of a member of the family are much easier to take than a make-believe mask which the patient can see through anyway and which means to him a disguise rather than a sharing of a sad situation.

If members of a family can share these emotions together, they will gradually face the reality of impending separation and come to an acceptance of it together. The most heart-breaking time, perhaps, for the family is the final phase, when the patient is slowly detaching himself from his world including his family. They do not understand that a dying man who has found peace and acceptance in his death will have to separate himself, step by step, from his environment, including his most loved ones. How could he ever be ready to die if he continued to hold onto the meaningful relationships of which a man has so many? When the patient asks to be visited only by a few more friends, then by his children, and finally only by his wife, it should be understood that that is the way of separating himself gradually. It is often misinterpreted by the immediate family as a rejection, and we have met several husbands and wives who have reacted dramatically to this normal and healthy detachment. I think we can be of greatest service to them if we help them understand that only patients who have worked through their dying are able to detach themselves slowly and peacefully in this manner. It should be a source of comfort and solace to them and not one of grief and resentment. It is during this time that the family needs the most support, the patient perhaps the least. I do not mean to imply by this that the patient should then be left alone. We should always be available, but a patient who has reached this stage of acceptance and decathexis usually requires little in terms of interpersonal relationship. If the meaning of this detachment is not explained to the family, problems can arise. . . .

The most tragic death is perhaps—aside from the very young—the death of the very old when we look at it from [the] point of view of the family. Whether the generations have lived together or separately, each generation has a need and a right to live their own lives, to have their own privacy, their own needs fulfilled appropriate to their generation. The old folks have outlived their usefulness in terms of our economic system and have earned, on the other hand, a right to live out their lives in dignity and peace. As long as they are healthy in body and mind and self-supporting, this may all be quite possible. We have seen many old men and women, however, who have become disabled physically or emotionally and who require a tremendous sum of money for a dignified maintenance at a level their family desires for them. The family is then often confronted with a difficult decision, namely, to mobilize all available money, including loans and savings for their own retirement, in order to afford such final care. The tragedy of these old people is perhaps that the amount of money and often financial sacrifice does not involve any improvement of the condition but is a mere maintenance at a minimal level of existence. If medical complications occur, the expenses are manifold, and the family often wishes for a quick and painless death, but rarely expresses that wish openly. That such wishes bring about feelings of guilt is obvious.

I am reminded of an old woman who had been hospitalized for several weeks and required extensive and expensive nursing care in a private hospital. Everybody expected her to die soon, but day after day she remained in an unchanged condition. Her daughter was torn between sending her to a nursing home or keeping her in the hospital, where she apparently wanted to stay. Her son-in-law was angry at her for having used up their life savings and had innumerable arguments with his wife, who felt too guilty to take her out of the hospital. When I visited the old woman she looked frightened and weary. I asked her simply what she was so afraid of. She looked at me and finally expressed what she had been unable to communicate before because she herself realized how unrealistic her fears were. She was afraid of "being eaten up alive by the worms." While I was catching my breath and tried to understand the real meaning of this statement, her daughter blurted out,"If that's what's keeping you from dying, we can burn you, by which she naturally meant that a cremation would prevent her from having any contact with earthworms. All her suppressed anger was in the statement. I sat with the old woman alone for a while. We talked calmly about her lifelong phobias and her fear of death which was presented in this fear of worms, as if she would be aware of them after her death. She felt greatly relieved for having expressed it and had nothing but understanding for her daughter's anger. I

encouraged her to share some of the feelings with her daughter, so that the latter might not have to feel so bad about her outburst.

When I met the daughter outside the room I told her of her mother's understanding, and they finally got together to talk about their concerns, ending up by making arrangements for the funeral, a cremation. Instead of sitting silently in anger, they communicated and consoled each other. The mother died the next day. If I had not seen the peaceful look on her face during her last day, I might have worried that this outburst of anger might have killed her.

Another aspect that is often not taken into account is what kind of a fatal illness the patient has. There are certain expectations of cancer, just as there are certain pictures associated with heart disease. The former is often viewed as a lingering, pain-producing illness, while the latter can strike suddenly, painless but final. I think there is a great deal of difference if a loved one dies slowly with much time available for preparatory grief on both sides, compared to the feared phone call, "It happened, it's all over." It is easier to talk with a cancer patient about death and dying than it is with a cardiac patient, who arouses concerns in us that we might frighten him and thus provoke a coronary, i.e., his death. The relatives of a cancer patient are therefore more amenable to discussing the expected end than the family of someone with heart disease, when the end can come any moment and a discussion may provoke it, at least in the opinion of many members of families whom we have spoken with.

I remember a mother of a young man in Colorado who did not allow her son to take any exercise, not even the most minimal kind, in spite of the contrary advice on part of his doctors. In conversations this mother would often make statements like "if he does too much he will drop dead on me," as if she expected a hostile act on the part of her son to be committed against her. She was totally unaware of her own hostility even after sharing with us some of her resentment for having "such a weak son," whom she very often associated with her ineffective and unsuccessful husband. It took months of careful, patient listening to this mother before she was able to express some of her own destructive wishes toward her child. She rationalized these by the fact that he was the cause of her limited social and professional life, thus rendering her as ineffective as she regarded her husband to be. These are complicated family situations, in which a sick member of the family is rendered more incapable of functioning because of the relative's conflicts. If we can learn to respond to such family members with compassion and understanding rather than judgment and criticism, we also help the patient bear his handicap with more ease and dignity.

The following example of Mr. P. demonstrates the difficulties that can occur for the patient when he is ready to separate himself, but the family is unable to

6. THE EXPERIENCE OF DYING

accept the reality, thus contributing to the patient's conflicts. Our goal should always be to help the patient and his family face the crisis together in order to achieve acceptance of this final reality simultaneously.

Mr. P. was a man in his mid-fifties who looked about fifteen years older than his age. The doctors felt that he had only a poor chance to respond to treatment, partially because of his advanced cancer and marasmus, but mainly because of his lack of "fighting spirit." Mr. P. had his stomach removed because of cancer five years prior to this hospitalization. At first he accepted his illness quite well and was full of hope. As he grew weaker and thinner, he became increasingly depressed until the time of his readmission, when a chest X-ray revealed metastatic tumors in his lungs. The patient had not been informed of the biopsy result when I saw him. The question was raised as to the advisability of possible radiation or surgery for a man in his weak condition. Our interview proceeded in two sessions. The first visit served the purpose of introducing myself and of telling him that I was available should he wish to talk about the seriousness of his illness and the problems that this might cause. A telephone interrupted us and I left the room, asking him to think about it. I also informed him about the time of my next visit.

When I saw him the next day, Mr. P. put his arm out in welcome and signaled to the chair as an invitation to sit down. In spite of many interruptions by a change of infusion bottles, distribution of medication, and routine pulse and blood pressure measurements, we sat for over an hour. Mr. P. had sensed that he would be allowed to "open his shades" as he called it. There was no defensiveness, no evasiveness in his accounts. He was a man whose hours seemed to count, who had no precious time to lose, and who seemed to be eager to share his concerns and regrets with someone who could listen.

The day before, he made the statement, "I want to sleep, sleep, sleep and not wake up." Today he repeated the same thing, but added the word "but." I looked at him questioningly and he proceeded to tell me with a weak soft voice that his wife had come to visit him. She was convinced that he would make it. She expected him home to take care of the garden and flowers. She also reminded him of his promise to retire soon, to move to Arizona perhaps, to have a few more good years. . . .

He talked with much warmth and affection about his daughter, twenty-one years old, who came to visit him on a leave from college, and who was shocked to see him in this condition. He mentioned all these things, as if he was to be blamed for disappointing his family, for not living up to their expectations.

I mentioned that to him and he nodded. He talked about all the regrets he had. He spent the first years of his marriage accumulating material goods for his family, trying to "make them a good home," and by doing so spent most of his time away from home and family. After the occurrence of cancer he spared every moment to be with them, but by then, it seemed to be too late. His daughter was away at school and had her own friends. When she was small and needed and wanted him, he was too busy making money.

Talking about his present condition he said, "Sleep is the only relief. Every moment of awakening is anguish, pure anguish. There is no relief. I am thinking in envy of two men I saw executed. I sat right in front of the first man. I felt nothing. Now, I think he was a lucky guy. He deserved to die. He had no anguish, it was fast and painless. Here I lie in bed, every hour, every day is agony."

Mr. P. was not so much concerned about pain and physical discomfort as he was tortured by regrets for not being able to fulfill his family's expectations, for being "a failure." He was tortured by his tremendous need to "let go and sleep, sleep, sleep" and the continuous flow of expectations from his environment. "The nurses come in and say I have to eat or I get too weak; the doctors come in and tell me about the new treatment they started, and expect me to be happy about it; my wife comes and tells me about the work I am supposed to do when I get out of here; and my daughter just looks at me and says, 'You have to get well'—how can a man die in peace this way?"

For a brief moment he smiled and said, "I will take this treatment and go home once more. I will return to work the next day and make a bit more money. My insurance will pay for my daughter's education anyway, but she still needs a father for a while. But you know and I know, I just cannot do it. Maybe they have to learn to face it. It would make dying so much easier!"

Mr. P. showed . . . how difficult it is for patients to face impending and anticipated death when the family is not ready to "let go" and implicitly or explicitly prevents them from separating themselves from the involvements here on earth. [One patient's] husband just stood at her bedside, reminding her of their happy marriage which should not end and pleading with all the doctors to do everything humanly possible to prevent her from dying. Mr. P.'s wife reminded him of unfulfilled promises and undone tasks, thus communicating the same needs to him, namely, to have him around for many more years to come. I cannot say that both these partners used denial.* Both of them knew the reality of the condition of their spouses. Yet both, because of their own needs, looked away from this reality. They faced it when talking with other people but denied it in front of the patients. And it was the patients who needed to hear that they too were aware of the seriousness of their condition and were able to accept this reality. Without this knowledge "every moment of awakening is pure anguish," in Mr. P.'s words. Our interview ended with the expression of hope that the important people in his environment would learn to face the reality of his dying rather than expressing hope for prolonging of his life.

This man was ready to separate himself from this world. He was ready to enter the final stage when the end is more promising or there is not enough strength left to live. One might argue whether an all-out medical effort is appropriate in such circumstances. With enough infusions and transfusions, vitamins, energizers, and antidepressant medication, with psychotherapy and symptomatic treatment, many such patients may be given an additional "lease on life." I have heard more curses than words of appreciation for the gained time, and I repeat my conviction that a patient has a right to die in peace and dignity. He should not be used to fulfill our own needs when his own wishes are in opposition to ours. I am referring to patients who have a physical illness but who are sane and capable enough to make decisions for themselves. Their wishes and opinions should be respected, they should be listened to and consulted. If the patient's wishes are contrary to our beliefs or convictions, we should express this conflict openly and leave the decisions up to the patient in respect to further interventions or treatments. In the many terminally ill patients I have so far interviewed, I have not seen any irrational behavior or unacceptable requests, and this includes . . . two psychotic women . . . who followed through with their treatment, one of them in spite of her otherwise almost complete denial of her illness.

THE FAMILY AFTER DEATH HAS OCCURRED

Once the patient dies, I find it cruel and inappropriate to speak of the love of God. When we lose someone, especially when we have had little if any time to prepare ourselves, we are enraged, angry, in despair; we should be allowed to express these feelings. The family members are often left alone as soon as they give their consent for autopsy. Bitter, angry, or just numb, they walk through the corridors of the hospital, unable often to face the brutal reality. The first few days may be filled with busy-work, with arrangements and visiting relatives. The void and emptiness is felt after the departure of the relatives. It is at this time that family members feel most grateful to have someone to talk to, especially if it is someone who had recent contact with the deceased and who can share anecdotes of some good moments towards the end of the deceased's life. This helps the relative over the shock and the initial grief and prepares him for a gradual acceptance.

Many relatives are preoccupied by memories and ruminate in fantasies, often even talk to the deceased as if he were still alive. They not only isolate themselves from the living but make it harder for themselves to face the reality of the person's death. For some, however, this is the only way they can cope with the loss, and it would be cruel indeed to ridicule them or to confront them daily with the unacceptable reality. It would be more helpful to understand this need and to help them separate themselves by taking them out of their isolation gradually. I have seen this behavior mainly in young widows who had lost their husbands at an early age and were rather unprepared. It may be more frequently encountered in the days of war where death of a young person occurs elsewhere, though I believe a war always makes relatives more aware of the possibility of no return. They are therefore more prepared for that death than, for example, for the unexpected death of a young man through a rapidly progressing illness.

A last word should be mentioned about the children. They are often the forgotten ones. Not so much that nobody cares; the opposite is often true. But few people feel comfortable talking to a child about death. Young children have different concepts of death, and they have to be taken into consideration in order to talk to them and to understand their communications. Up to the age of three a child is concerned only about separation, later followed by the fear of mutilation. It is at this age that the small child begins to mobilize, to take his first trips out "into the world," the sidewalk trips by tricycle. It is in this environment that he may see the first beloved pet run over by a car or a beautiful bird torn apart by a cat. This is what mutilation means to him, since it is the age when he is concerned about the integrity of his body and is threatened by anything that can destroy it.

Also, death . . . is not a permanent fact for the three-to-five-year-old. It is as temporary as burying a flower bulb into the soil in the fall to have it come up again the following spring.

After the age of five death is often regarded as a man, a bogey-man who comes to take people away; it is still attributed to an outward intervention.

Around the ages of nine to ten the realistic conception begins to show, namely, death as a permanent biological process.

Children will react differently to the death of a parent, from a silent withdrawal and isolation to a wild loud mourning which attracts attention and thus a replacement of a loved and needed object. Since children cannot yet differentiate between the wish and the deed . . . , they may feel a great deal of remorse and

*For a discussion of the mechanisms of denial, see Weisman's selection on this topic. -ED.

guilt. They will feel responsible for having killed the parents and thus fear a gruesome punishment in retribution. They may, on the other hand, take the separation relatively calmly and utter such statements as "She will come back for the spring vacation" or secretly put an apple out for her—in order to assure that she has enough to eat for the temporary trip. If adults, who are upset already during this period, do not understand such children and reprimand or correct them, the children may hold inside their own way of grieving—which is often a root for later emotional disturbance.

With an adolescent, however, things are not much different than with an adult. Naturally adolescence is in itself a difficult time, and added loss of a parent is often too much for such a youngster to endure. They should be listened to and allowed to ventilate their feelings, whether they be guilt, anger, or plain sadness.

RESOLUTION OF GRIEF AND ANGER

What I am saying again here is, let the relative talk, cry, or scream if necessary. Let them share and ventilate, but be available. The relative has a long time of mourning ahead of him, when the problems for the dead are solved. He needs help and assistance from the confirmation of a so-called bad diagnosis until months after the death of a member of the family.

By help I naturally do not assume that this has to be professional counseling of any form; most people neither need nor can afford this. But they need a human being, a friend, doctor, nurse, or chaplain—it matters little. The social worker may be the most meaningful one, if she has helped with arrangements for a nursing home and if the family wishes to talk more about their mother in that particular set-up, which may have been a source of guilt feelings for not having kept her at home. Such families have at times visited other old folks in the same nursing home and continued their task of caring for someone, perhaps as a partial denial, perhaps just to do good for all the missed opportunities with Grandma. No matter what the underlying reason, we should try to understand their needs and to help relatives direct these needs constructively to diminish guilt, shame, or fear of retribution. The most meaningful help that we can give any relative, child or adult, is to share his feelings before the event of death and to allow him to work through his feelings, whether they are rational or irrational.

If we tolerate their anger, whether it is directed at us, at the deceased, or at God, we are helping them take a great step towards acceptance without guilt. If we blame them for daring to ventilate such socially poorly tolerated thoughts, we are blameworthy for prolonging their grief, shame, and guilt which often results in physical and emotional ill health.

Choosing the Good Death

WAYNE SAGE

In the end, more and more Americans find themselves in the hands of medical authorities dedicated to keeping the patient alive at almost any cost. Too often, the last chapter is full of suffering, indignity and alienation. When to die? How? Who decides? The answers are still as opaque as death itself.

Wayne Sage is a freelance writer and contributing editor to HUMAN BEHAVIOR.

*With my own eyes I saw the Sibyl
suspended in a glass bottle at Cumae
and when the boys said to her,
"Sibyl, what is the matter?"
She would always respond:
"I yearn to die."*
— Satiricon, *by Petronius*

Patients in hospitals no longer die. They go to intensive-care wards. There, beneath the tubes and tents, they are made dead. The ordeal is long, and shrouded in deceptions and self-deceptions that fool no one.

"If you're going to write this, make it sound like hell," said one man currently dying at a large metropolitan hospital. He eyed with disgust the screen that had been erected between himself and his cronies on the cancer ward. "How we doin' over there, Tom?" he shouted through. There was no answer. His friend Tom had died the night before because those around him could no longer bear his living. Tom's family had been financially ruined and emotionally depleted as surgeons continued to cut and sew to no avail. His doctors had finally given up and turned off the respirator that was keeping him alive.

"He may be sleeping," I said.

The old man looked up in shock. "Why are you pretending Tom's still alive?" he asked.

In the intensive-care ward at another hospital in the same city an old soldier lay calmly discussing the benefits of euthanasia.

"You ready?" he said.

"What?"

"Get this," he said, and ripped the plasma needle from his arm. A small font of blood burst from the vein. He screamed and the staff was on him in an instant.

"That wasn't your fault," one of his doctors said consolingly as he walked me out the corridor. "He's done this kind of thing before. It's his way of getting attention."

In one of the rooms, a woman with brain cancer was screaming so loudly the windows seemed to shake. She believed giant cockroaches were eating her alive. "It's all in her mind," her nurses said. "She's in no pain."

In the hallway, another woman had been wheeled out of the way to a corner. Her skin was powdery and white, stretched almost to transparency over the sharp bones of her face. There was no sign of breathing, but there was a plasma needle in her arm so that one might presume her to be alive. She opened her yellow, watery eyes. "Come back tomorrow, Honey," she said. "I'll try and hang on till then for you." She died that afternoon. A telegram was sent to her only living relative, a cousin in St. Louis who cabled back her thanks and her relief at hearing the news.

"What we're advocating is a voluntary, passive euthanasia," says Elizabeth Halsey, executive director of the Euthanasia Educational Fund, the tax-exempt arm of the Euthanasia Society. Voluntary means it's done with the patient's consent. Passive means the physician simply stops treating the patient and allows him to die. As the society likes to define the term itself, *euthanasia* means "a good death"

(from the Greek words *eu*—good, and *thanatos*—death).

To the society, a good death is one without pain, lingering or medical heroics; one with dignity, honesty and compassion. Beyond such descriptions, the good death is as difficult to define as is the good life; yet Americans are beginning to pursue the former with all the fervor with which they once sought the latter. In the last four years, the Euthanasia Society has grown from 400 to 50,000 members. Thousands of people of sound health have signed the society's "living will," a personal plea to be allowed to die without medical interference when the time comes. Twenty-five percent of such requests come from the young. Social commentators are predicting that the right to euthanasia will be the next burning social issue to follow school integration and abortion. This time there will be no bystanders. Not everyone has school-age children or needs an abortion, but everyone dies; and the good death soon may be stalking those who do not yearn for it as well as those who do.

When medical science cannot make us well, it can often keep the catastrophic diseases from killing us, in the traditional sense. The machines await. When your lungs give out, a shiny new Bennett MA-1 respirator will be wheeled in to pump air into your lungs and suck it back out again. If you cannot eat or even digest food, an ingenious process known as "total parenteral nutrition" will catheterize your veins and inject nutrients directly into your bloodstream, drop by drop, around the clock. If your heart refuses to beat, electronic pacemakers will circulate your blood while sensors all over your body monitor the flow and warn of nascent gangrene.

Wealthy members of one midwestern family kept their grandmother "alive" for seven years under such paraphernalia because they considered it the humane thing to do. Finally, physicians convinced them to stop. The machines were turned off. Her brain had been dead for three years.

Such twilight spans are not the sole province of either the wealthy or the elderly. Following an automobile accident, the body of one 24-year-old New York woman was kept functioning for nine years, with no hope that she would ever recover. Her middle-income parents were left with nearly $300,000 in medical bills.

Gone are the days when we fell peacefully into never-ending sleep in our own beds at home with those we had loved nearby. Eighty percent of all deaths now take place in hospitals, where life-extending heroics are second nature to medical staffs.

In most geriatric hospitals and on every terminal ward, rumors spread of the "black bottle," a mythical potion hospital officials supposedly dole out to patients who "ought to die" and ask for it. Some beg for it, day after day, and spit obscenities at doctors and nurses who insist that it does not exist. When someone on the ward dies, others conclude he may have gotten his hands on it at last.

"The patients get the treatment all right," says renowned Houston heart surgeon Dr. Denton A. Cooley in his biography, *The Career of a Great Heart Surgeon* by Harry Minchee. "They get even more acutely ill; they puke; they bleed; they collect new pains that we gave them; they lose their resistance to infection. . . .

"As a dutiful medical warrior," he continues, "I am expected to inject poisons into dying peoples' veins in the name of 'chemotherapy,' of 'sound medical practice.' (I'm careful to avoid spilling any on my hands because it burns.) I send people downstairs to be bombarded—listen to the language —by isotopes. (That's 'radiotherapy'; again, I stand safely out of the way.) . . . They are denied their right to die in peace, in dignity, at home. With treatment they often live less comfortably, even miserably, certainly at more expense. But maybe they live a little longer. Maybe not. In some cases, documentably not."

During the course of such medical assaults, the time of death becomes largely an administrative matter. Traditionally, death has been legally defined by the absence of "vital signs" such as heartbeat and respiration. Since irreparable damage to the brain occurs within minutes when the flow of oxygen is cut off, such standards sufficed. But now that stopped hearts can be restarted and the "vital signs"

kept going without the brain's help, the time of death occurs more or less whenever the physician decides to pull the plug to the machines on which the bodies of their patients hang. The relentless drive of the medical profession to sustain life at all costs gives that science its impetus for advancement and perhaps can never be stopped. As one San Diego physician puts it, "The only way to a quick and easy death these days is to shoot yourself in the head—and that's illegal."

Laws are beginning to catch up with this reality. Many physicians want legislation to establish the cessation of brain functions as the legal criterion for death. Proponents of euthanasia also back brain-death bills since, under such standards, once a patient's EEG goes flat, all life-support equipment could be turned off without fear of lawsuits. (No patient with a flat EEG for a period of 24 hours has ever regained consciousness.)

The physicians, however, have something a little different in mind. If the brain (and therefore "the person") is dead, legally, but the heart and lungs are kept going, the body becomes a veritable storage bin for the organ-snatching transplant specialists who presently must time a patient's death precisely to coincide with their operations on the living.

For society at large, the stage seems set for the good death's hour upon it. One polling of the members of the American Association of Professors of Medicine found 87 percent in favor of passive euthanasia. Eighty percent had practiced it themselves. The usual procedure is the physician consults the family, and if they agree, the machines and other life support systems are wheeled away. All treatment ends except that which will keep the patient out of pain, if he gets those medications. One young psychologist sat night after night watching the light board at a large metropolitan hospital. Each time a patient signaled for help, the researcher recorded the room number and the time interval before the staff's response. When these data were matched with the charts on each patient, he found the more serious the patient's condition, the longer it took nurses to answer. Some, very near death, were ignored almost completely.

Active euthanasia, which means the physician deliberately kills the patient, occurs more often in those increasingly rare instances in our overcrowded hospitals when the doctor has become emotionally involved

with a patient he cannot cure and cannot bear to see suffer. The most common method is to begin increasing the dosage of pain-killing drugs. With all such injections, there is a point at which the medication itself becomes lethal, although the level varies from one patient to another and often can never be pinpointed precisely. When the toxic level is reached and the patient dies, the last dosage is recorded and there is no way for others to know positively that the intention was to kill rather than to relieve pain, if the doctor indeed knows that himself. In other cases, the physician will inject an air bubble into the patient's vein. Death from a "stroke" follows in minutes. One survey of specialists in problems of the terminally ill uncovered 15 percent who admitted anonymously that they had performed such acts.

Euthanasia can be either voluntary —the patient consents to or asks for it; or involuntary—his relatives or physician decide his fate for him. Usually his level of consciousness and mental competence, as judged by those around him, determine whether his wishes one way or the other will be respected. One 77-year-old Milwaukee woman, suffering from hardening of the arteries and gangrene, had already lost an arm and a leg. She refused to sign another surgical consent form and asked to be allowed to die. The hospital attempted to have her ruled incompetent so its surgeons could continue amputating her limbs. A county judge blocked the petition.

Then there are the individualized varieties of euthanasia that defy classification. They are sometimes worked out as tacit agreements by a physician and patient when neither can face the matter openly. For example, one San Francisco specialist relies on what he calls "the three-pill proposal." He leaves three tablets at the patient's bedside with the following instructions: "Take one every four hours through the night. If you took them all at once, it would kill you."

As far as the legality of euthanasia is concerned, its proponents would seem to have everything they want de facto if not de jure. No physician has ever been brought to trial in the United States for practicing passive euthanasia. No doctor tried for active euthanasia has ever been convicted, even though it is murder as defined by present legal statutes.

Gallup polls indicate the general public is becoming more accepting of the idea of euthanasia. In one survey of a national sample of college students, sociologist Glenn M. Vernon of the University of Utah found 54 percent of the students approved of euthanasia, at least in some cases, provided the lethal agent was self-administered or requested.

About the only group strongly opposed is the patients themselves. In one survey of the elderly in nursing homes, half rejected euthanasia altogether, opting instead for "life at any cost," leading researchers Caroline E. Preston and Dr. Robert H. Williams of the University of Washington to conclude that their elderly subjects, like the dying in earlier studies, are not "adamant about avoiding pain and senility." Only 25 percent wanted to be allowed to die if their situation became hopeless. There was no correlation between the current quality of the patient's life and his leaning toward euthanasia.

What terminal patients do seem to want from their doctors is honesty, which is what they seem least likely to get. In another such poll, 70 to 90 percent of the doctors interviewed said they would not advise the ordinary patient that he had a terminal illness, while 77 to 89 percent of the patients said they wanted to be so informed. In almost all such interviews, one finds terminal patients willing, even eager, to talk about the subject and seldom indecisive about their feelings.

In the words of one 78-year-old woman now dying in a Los Angeles hospital, "I just wish I could get up and drag that motherfucker in here and make him tell me to my face what's going on."

"If she knew, it would kill her," said her physician smugly.

She continually shouted contempt for the other terminal patients, vowing to outlive them all, but refused to accept their verdict for herself.

"You're dying, too, aren't you?" one young orderly told her in exasperation.

"Aren't you?" she said.

Cook County Hospital in Chicago is catacombed with underground tunnels connecting the various wings. "I've never seen a body going through the tubes," says Chaplain Cliff Eden, "but somehow they get them through to the morgue. There are no written rules, but it's the most efficient operation I've ever seen." The sight of a dead body is apparently something physicians don't want families to have to look at. "Doctors want the bodies down to the morgue as soon as possible while they keep the family away," Eden explains. "Then they can say the body's already gone to the morgue so they (the family) can't see it until the funeral."

Perhaps whom the members of the medical profession are really protecting is themselves. Studies consistently show that men and women who become doctors and nurses have an abnormally high fear of death. This is probably part of the reason they enter a profession whose goal is to preserve life. It is also probably among their motives for suppressing discussion of the subject. When Dr. Charles H. Goodrich and nurse Barbara Taylor of the Mount Sinai School of Medicine in New York recently asked the deans of 22 medical schools what they would do with any medical student who showed signs of difficulty in his encounters with terminal illness and death, almost everyone said, "We would send him to the psychiatrist."

In general, it seems, the arguments for and against euthanasia go on over the heads of the dying. One man in his early 30s lay totally paralyzed after major surgery from which doctors had decided he would never regain consciousness. His physician, the nurses and his relatives openly discussed "pulling the plug" and allowing him to die—in his presence, assuming he could not hear them. He recovered. He had heard every word but was unable to move or speak. Today he is the father of a newborn son.

From midnight until sunrise, Vivian Richmond, a student nurse at a large university hospital, monitors the infamous machines that enmesh with their tubes and wires the bodies they pump, squeeze and shock night after night, day after day, on the intensive-care ward.

Does she ever feel like pulling a plug?

"Never," she says.

But aren't they all dying, or dead?

"Yes," she says. "But then you never know. Sometimes, if you turn your back, they get up."

They do indeed. In medicine, as in life, there is just no such thing as true hopelessness. "We have all been embarrassed to have individuals who look as though they had only a few days to live . . . literally pack up their bags and go home and live useful lives for a year or two, or sometimes much longer," says Dr. Alfred Jaretzki, III, of the Columbia University College of Physicians and Surgeons. Radiologist Justine Stein of UCLA, for example, was expected to die of cancer 29 years ago. Today he is president of the American Cancer Society.

"This is not just an occasional situation," says Jaretzki. And the predictions are becoming increasingly difficult to make as medical science advances. With the very "heroic measures" that strip a patient of all dignity, as proponents of euthanasia describe them, surgeons may literally tear a patient's body apart and put it back together again when all reason would say stop. In the end, "we have extended someone's life unnecessarily and certainly in discomfort and without dignity," says Jaretzki. "(But) doctors . . . cannot help but be influenced by maybe even those two or three that we see in our offices as the years go on, happy, grateful, effective, useful in their families or in their retirement, whichever end of the spectrum they are on."

Every terminal ward has known its cases of inexplicable recovery. Studies show that chronically ill patients are generally much better at predicting the time of their own deaths than are their doctors, even when their doctors do not tell them the true medical prognosis.

Also, even the most adamant disciples of death with dignity, and their families, change their minds as the moment draws near; and many who wanted to be saved at all costs beg to be killed as their situation darkens.

Nevertheless, the good death is on its way for Americans of all ages, it seems, not just the ill and the elderly. Yale pediatrician Dr. Raymond S. Duff and Dr. A. G. M. Campbell of the University of Aberdeen, Scotland, recently made national headlines by disclosing that 43 infants were deliberately allowed to die during a 30-month period at Yale–New Haven Hospital. All were either deformed, hopelessly ill or both.

Many doctors who deliver a defective infant simply allow the baby to die and report to parents that they could not save it, intending to spare both parents and the child the agony of its life. In the instances at Yale, parents were consulted in each case and took part in the decision to give up. Some such children, Duff and Campbell explain, "have almost no capacity to be loved."

One who apparently did have that capacity was Saundre Diamond, who was born so severely brain damaged that doctors said she would never see, hear, speak or walk and that she would be mentally retarded. Permitted to live, she would spend her life

6. THE EXPERIENCE OF DYING

as a vegetable in one of the "dying bins" where such children are institutionalized. Her parents said no to both euthanasia and institutionalization and took her home. Today, Saundre Diamond is a counseling psychologist in private practice in Philadelphia.

Understandably, Diamond feels in no case should euthanasia be used on the deformed, "because then I wouldn't be here," she says.

The problem goes much deeper than just the frightening "potential for error," in Duff's and Campbell's terms, to which such decisions are subject. Admittedly, not all the deformed would grow up to be counseling psychologists if allowed to live. "But many such people I know achieve whatever they want to achieve," says Diamond, "or at least whatever society allows them to achieve. Being disabled is not intrinsically a burden," she says. "You feel like a 'person,' whatever that means. What makes it a burden is that society refuses to see you as one."

There have been studies that consistently show that the disabled are generally just as happy, well adjusted and satisfied with their lives as are "normal" individuals, for what the statistics are worth. But if a deformed child does escape euthanasia at birth, he must be on guard against it for the rest of his life.

"When you become ill for any reason, it is a major problem to stay alive," says Diamond. Not because of the disability, but because of the prevailing attitudes in society and especially within the medical profession. "The assumption is made that you don't have to give the disabled ordinary medical care because they're going to lead a horrible life anyway," she says. One disabled woman of 24 went into a hospital for a very minor, and common, menstrual problem that usually requires only an overnight stay. Two days later she was dead of pneumonia.

"Pneumonia is something we often die of," says Diamond. Pneumonia is common when one is bedridden after surgery and resistance to infection is low. It provides an easily explained death if antibiotics are withheld. "When I'm hospitalized, I always say 'Get me out of bed,' but often they won't. So my family comes and gets me out. Her family couldn't get there in time," Diamond says of her late friend.

Diamond herself was hospitalized after being caught in a fire. "Doctors freely said, 'You're going to die, prepare yourself,'" she recalls. "People speak freely in front of you as if you were a moron as they talk about how you would be better off dead. That's the assumption: disabled, therefore stupid. If you don't have a family, you're a goner. I know people who have died in hospitals who have gone in for very mild problems."

Not only must they fight to save themselves, the disabled often must be on guard to save their children. One mother and father, both victims of childhood cerebral palsy, were soon to become parents. Cerebral palsy is not hereditary. The child was expected to be normal. Yet the mother wound up surrounded by physicians who wanted to abort the baby at eight months because they did not think two disabled people would be fit parents. The father sneaked into the hospital at night and stole his wife from her room before they could carry out the abortion the following morning. Today, they are the parents of a happy, healthy girl.

In the case of both the deformed and the terminally ill, we seem to turn our deadly compassion on those we just don't want to look at, to accept as fellow human beings. Sociologist David Sudnow has discerned a strong relationship between the age, social background and perceived moral character of patients and the amount of effort that is expended to save them when the clinical "death signs" appear. Few efforts are made to revive suicide victims, dope addicts, prostitutes, criminals and vagrants, he notes. A Chicago ordinance requires the deformed to stay off the streets. Saundre Diamond is in private practice because the employers who offer the $25,000-a-year jobs for which she is qualified told her bluntly that they did not want their patients to have to look at her.

Although Diamond finds her private practice "wonderfully fulfilling," she considers herself an "underachiever" and does not like being cut off from her colleagues because they will not accept her. "I'm a damned good counseling psychologist," says she. "People are sometimes uneasy with me at first but, as we talk, they soon stop noticing the fact that I'm in a wheel chair, the jerks, the facial grimaces. We begin to relate to one another as two human beings trying to help one another.

"Even if a baby is born with two heads, it isn't fair to allow him to die," she says, "because you just don't know what's going on in those two heads. I'm different mainly because I can talk, so you know."

This includes the elderly and even the "vegetables" euthanasia proponents feel most desperately need their attention, she believes. "We don't know what that person is experiencing," she says. "You don't know if he is enjoying the feeling of cold sheets against his body, the temperature changes in the room. If he is, can we take this away from him? Can we shorten his time for experiencing life whatever his level of experiencing it?"

Those who ask to be killed or allowed to die, Diamond thinks, often are listening to society's mandate that they die. They sense from those around them that they are a burden, emotionally and financially. "That burden is based on what society's needs are," says Diamond. "As they hear the doctor saying, 'This (euthanasia) is the best thing for you,' I think his or her choice is based on what society dictates. I think they need careful, supportive counseling at these times so they can really see the options open to them of living, at whatever level, to enjoy the final stages of their lives."

Such therapy can be so effective as to cause reservations about ever indiscriminately granting a patient's plea for euthanasia. One such story is that of "the poet laureate of Governor Bacon," a man whom few would have been able to deny the good death. He had been one of the most successful stage managers in the theater. Following the death of his wife, severe arthritis reduced him from an active man of 5'10" and 175 lbs. to a gnome-like figure weighing less than 70 pounds. The death of his son, then his daughter, followed. Day after day, he sat alone in a wheel chair, an embittered little dwarf. If a nurse or anyone else attempted kindness toward him, he would pick up his urinal and throw its contents in their faces, as well as he was able with his gnarled fingers. At age 79, he was sent to Governor Bacon Health Center in Delaware, "virtually to die, as a prelude to the morgue," said Dr. Maurice E. Linden before a recent seminar of the Group for the Advancement of Psychiatry in New York.

Today, Governor Bacon's poet laureate is usually cheerful, reports Linden. "He writes at least one poem a week, with good form and good content. He entertains the other patients in his building and keeps up their spirits." With the little nubbins that are now his fingers, he paints and sculpts. He swims in the summertime, likes to go out, especially on automobile trips, and has a lady friend. He is 86 years old. The change followed intensive psychotherapy, occupational therapy and milieu therapy.

Perhaps part of the reason group therapy works so well among the elderly and the terminally ill is that it combats the loneliness and isolation society forces on them. "One of the reasons elderly people do not want to be revived and brought back after having 'died once' is that they sense a social mandate," says Dr. Lawrence F. Greenleigh of the University of Southern California Medical School. "They realize that those around them really feel it is their time to die, and to stay dead," he says. "It has been traditional for hundreds of years to place heavy tombstones upon the graves of the dead so that they may not get up out of their graves and return to life," he notes.

The burden of the dying on those around them and on society is real and immense. One woman in Montreal was kept alive for 12 years with no hope that she would ever recover. As a result, 312 patients were denied a hospital bed, her physicians estimate. The middle-income parents of one of Duff's and Campbell's ill-fated infants had spent over $15,000 on his hospital care before the decision to take him off oxygen. Other children in the fam-

ily had become mentally disturbed, and the marriage itself was falling apart. Arguments for euthanasia made on such grounds come closer to arguments for eugenics than most people can stand when a relative falls ill. But the knowledge that one must be such a burden to those around him is a prime source of the chronically ill's desire to die.

With or without euthanasia, the resulting mandate is lethal. According to Dr. Eric J. Cassell of the Cornell University Medical School, the physician does not have to withdraw treatment to bring about euthanasia. It can be done by suggestion. "They (such patients) don't really know it's within their power to die," said Cassell last year at the Euthanasia Society's fifth national conference. He describes the procedure as follows: "One has a discussion with her and it's made perfectly clear to her that everybody around her says it's all right, that she has permission to go. Within a relatively short time she will get pneumonia or something like that, have a heart attack and die. It's really simple—a family can do it, a clergyman can do it."

Most such conversations are shrouded in euphemisms, according to Cassell. There's an interplay going in which the patient tells you what to tell him," he says.

That death is often an act of will

seems manifest. Widows and widowers are well-known for their proclivity, and ability, to die soon after the deaths of their mates. One 78-year-old woman had been suffering for eight months at Long Island Hospital from cancer of the esophagus. After radiation treatments failed, complications increased her pain tremendously. Plans for drug therapy and surgery were put aside because neither promised to give her more than a few more months of intense suffering.

"I really can't do very much about it," Cassell told her. "I'm awfully sorry about that, but I really have nothing further to offer for your tumor. However, I have a great deal to offer you. You will be free from pain, you will be absolutely comfortable...."

The woman thought over Cassell's words, and the following day responded, "If I understand you correctly, you said I have to live with this. Is that what you mean? I have to accept it?"

"Yes," said Cassell. "That's what I mean. You have to accept it because I can't do anything else about it." She died a few days later.

"People have much more control over their own lives than they think they have," he says.

Perhaps it is just such powers we have gotten out of touch with. A sociological study of California found

The Hospice Haven

There is one way of dealing with the terminally ill that perhaps both proponents and opponents of euthanasia can accept. St. Christopher's Hospice in London was originally founded as a center for the control of chronic pain, but this hospice is much more. It is a haven for those whom medical science could not cure—the young as well as the old, but most often the middle aged, who are the most frequent victims of terminal cancer.

When physicians elsewhere finally give up on treating the disease, St. Christopher's takes over and treats the patient. Noticeably absent are the mechanical respirators, cardiovascular shock equipment, oxygen tents and intravenous feeding apparatus to which such patients are often made an appendage in hospitals. Present is a staff deftly alleviating pain. Here, many of the horrors that make euthanasia seem merciful evaporate in an atmosphere of comfort and safety.

The idea that the dosage of pain-killing drugs must be ever increased to prevent suffering has proven a fallacy at St. Christopher's. "Pain control is not simply tied to the drug," says the Reverend Edward Dobihal, chaplain at the Yale–New Haven Hospital. Dobihal has visited, studied and worked at St. Christopher's and is involved in efforts to start a similar facility in Connecticut. "There are all kinds of pain," he says. "There is physical pain, emotional pain, the pain of anxiety of being uncertain that someone is going to be able to help you. Those things are just not taken care of chemically.

"Hospitals don't handle pain—chronic continuing pain—very well," Dobihal explains. Doctors give drugs when patients complain. When the pain returns, the patient asks for further injections and they are given. The patient has felt pain and because he feels that it is coming back he may ask for it more and more frequently. At St. Christopher's, the patient is assured that the staff will control his

pain. A dosage is set with a routine that anticipates pain. The medication is then regulated through constant checks. Mood elevators, such as heroin, and medications to control the nausea that often accompanies such drugs are given in addition to the pain-killers, and alcoholic drinks are also supplied. The resulting combination is carefully geared to keep the patient painfree yet alert, neither euphoric nor depressed, so he can function normally in spite of illness.

Most such medications are given in liquid form. Pills are hard to swallow and needles cause distress in themselves. Since patients are alert and the staff has time to feed them normally, there are no intravenous injections of any sort. Pharmacologists who have carefully studied the chemical constituents in such procedures believe they will be able to duplicate such treatments here even without the use of heroin. The climate of confidence and safety that is built up with the patient is as important as the drugs themselves, they have found. Within

(continued on the following page)

24 to 48 hours of arrival, the patient's pain that could not be lessened in hospitals is under control at St. Christopher's. Not only does the dosage not have to be continually increased, it sometimes can be significantly lessened with time.

Part of the secret of such success is that physicians and nurses at St. Christopher's take a personal interest in the comfort of each patient and carefully sort out his complaints. They are ever aware that patients can have pain from other than their primary diseases. One 49-year-old woman was admitted with records marked "incontinent and confused." The hospice staff discovered that she was constipated—a problem quite unrelated to the malignant tumor her doctors elsewhere had assumed to be the source of all her problems. Once the constipation was corrected, she was seldom confused and began a long process of evaluating her life and sorting out her difficult relationship with her daughter. Another patient arrived suffering excruciating facial pain. Her doctors had assumed the cancer had gotten to her face and were fighting it with appropriate medical assaults. She had an abscessed tooth; the St. Christopher's team discovered and removed it.

"Doctors at acute hospitals begin to think very clearly about a disease," explains Dobihal. "I've heard doctors talk about 'that gall-bladder patient.' That mental attitude carries over to the point that the patient becomes only a disease. If you can't cure that, they decide there is nothing more you can do for him. There may be nothing more you can do for the disease, but you ignore all you can do for the patient."

"People shouldn't be so afraid and apt to run away and say there is nothing else that can be done," echoes Dr. Cicely Saunders, the founder and medical director of St. Christopher's. "There is always something you can do. We need to get back into general medicine the concept of the patient as a person and help with symptoms even when nothing can be done for the disease," says Saunders.

What's best for the treatment of the disease may not be what's best for the patient, it seems. About 10 percent of the patients referred to St. Christopher's are eventually discharged and sometimes go on to live comfortably for years afterwards. "I think acute treatment for a disease may be life shortening," says Dobihal.

One man Dobihal met at St. Christopher's had been expected to die two and a half years earlier. His doctors had referred him to the hospice with the verdict that he would be dead within five weeks. When he arrived, he was racked with uncontrolled pain and severe nausea. He was apathetic and withdrawn. Once his pain and nausea were under control, the staff found that he responded to particular foods. As the hospice dietician went to work providing food he was fond of, he began to take more nourishment and become stronger. He began to look around him and talk with the other three men on his section of the ward. He started to take care of the flowers brought in for him as well as those of the other patients and eventually took over the horticulture of the whole ward, getting up in the morning eagerly to begin his watering and seeding. At the end of the five weeks, rather than dying, he asked if he might go home—and did. He lived for another four years before returning to the hospice to spend his final days.

This situation is frequent at St. Christopher's. The patients often simply don't die as outside doctors expected.

Often, the psychological aspects of a patient's dilemma must be sorted out as well. One elderly lady would get out of bed at night and wander around confusedly. If returned to her bed, she would only get up again. Lack of sleep began to wear her down. When the hospice psychiatrist sat with her for a few nights, he discovered that she was afraid of the dark—or, more precisely, she was afraid she would die alone in the dark. The staff lowered her bed and put in a night-light and objects that could be seen in its glow. The next night she again got up—to go to the bathroom. On her way back to her room, she stopped at the nurses' station to say good evening and then returned to her bed and slept for the rest of the night.

Many of the issues set burning by the euthanasia movement simply do not apply in the hospice situation. The criteria for establishing death do not matter so much when a patient is allowed to die at a pace set by his own body. "If someone is dying who is not tied up to respirators and things, it is not important or difficult to say when the person is dead," says Saunders. "Lawyers and physiologists can talk around the matter of the time of death." Without such heroics, the vital signs tend to fade in unison and can take their time to dwindle to a stop. Without the tents and tubes to cut them off from their families, the staff and other patients, the patient's loneliness subsides. Some of the families of patients come to live at the hospice with their striken relatives in order to be near them until the end.

In America, medical insurance plans provide terminal patients with private or semiprivate rooms that actually increase their isolation and separation and perhaps help bring on their early demise, those who want to see hospices started in this country believe. "If one wanted to achieve alienation, one would have to fight very hard to do it better than in our modern hospitals with private and semiprivate rooms," says one American chaplain hoping to start a hospice in New York. At St. Christopher's, beds are set up in four-bed bays where patients and families can get to know one another. When a death occurs on a bay, the grief is shared by all. Some families "adopt" other patients and continue to visit them long after their own relative has passed away.

Finally, the honesty that is so lacking in present care of the terminally ill can be fostered in a hospice. "We're not saying, 'Look, you must know that you are going to die,'" says Dobihal. "I don't believe in that. We're saying, 'Look, you have these difficulties and we're going to help you with them.' When someone is feeling sick, that's what they want."

"Doctors should let patients tell *them* that they are dying," says Saunders. "People have more courage and common sense than we give them credit for." One woman came to St. Christopher's dying of cancer. As she came out of the pain and confusion of the acute treatment she had known at the hospital, she and her daughter began to work out, at last, the problems they had experienced in their relationship during life. Eventually, she valued even the illness that would end her life at age 49. "It's made me rethink life," she said five days before her death. "Made me think of what I am doing here and what I am in relation to people and my family and what I am in relation to God. It's made an enormous difference. . . . I feel I can trust in the future now."

"When you wake up in the morning, what do you think?" asked Saunders.

"I don't think I'm lucky to be alive as I used to," the woman said. "Now I expect to wake up. I expect death to be slow and that I can realize it when it does come. . . . I want to go out feeling as though I'm still alive." With those words, she summed up the essence of what the hospice movement offers.

the majority of the population preferred a description of death as a disease to be overcome by medical science to one that saw it as a natural part of the cycle of birth and life.

In an academy on the shore of the Baltic, a Swedish physician rigs up the bodies of dying men and women with an elaborate, sensitive system of weights and balances. Precisely at the instant of death, he finds, the scales tip, indicating a slight loss in weight. The departure of the human soul? If so, it weighs 24 grams. The weight of a sigh?

As we age, we detach ourselves physically from the decaying body around us, says psychiatrist Maurice E. Linden of the Jefferson Medical College in Philadelphia. Our physical shells are dying, we realize, but that we ourselves shall die we cannot really accept. Says Linden, "I have

found that whether a patient is atheistic, agnostic or absolutely religious, never knew he was religious before or never thought about it before, this experience of an aging soma and a nonaging psyche gives rise to a feeling of what might be called soul."

The soul, whatever its nature, seems to insist on triumph over the soma.

It is precisely the erosion of the control of the individual over his own body (and therefore his death) that has given the new death movement its impetus. Arguments for the right to voluntary euthanasia are essentially arguments for the right to suicide or, more precisely, the right to have others help one commit suicide if one is unable to carry it out oneself. Our ridiculous laws against suicide are based on the conviction that life is always better than death, and that anyone who decides differently for himself is certainly wrong and prob-

ably insane—a highly questionable presumption, at best. What the machines, the antideath warriors of modern medicine, grief-stricken relatives and the demands of society at large have stolen away, some are refusing to relinquish.

One Canadian couple, in their 80s, is an example. The woman was dying of cancer. Her husband did not want to live without her. They borrowed a car from their neighbor, parked it behind their house and ran a hose from the exhaust pipe into one of the windows. With rags, they sealed themselves inside airtight and started the engine. In the note they left behind, they promised not to leave the motor running. They didn't. As soon as the car was filled with carbon monoxide, they turned off the engine.

"It was beautiful," said their neighbor when he discovered them.

Death, Dying, and Bereavement in Old Age:

New Developments and Their Possible Implications For Psychosocial Care

Robert Kastenbaum, PhD

Dr. Kastenbaum, Ph.D, University of Southern California, is a psychologist who has been active in clinical, research, and educational roles with the aged and the dying-suicidal-bereaved of all ages. He is currently director of Cushing Hospital, Framingham, Massachusetts 01701, while on leave from his professorship at University of Massachusetts-Boston. Dr. Kastenbaum is past president of the American Association of Suicidology, and the Division of Adult Development and Aging, American Psychological Association, he is also editor of the International Journal of Aging & Human Development. Dr. Kastenbaum has been attempting to balance philosophical and research interests with practical and direct services to the vulnerable aged and life-threatened.

Are the aged still neglected? Is death still a "taboo" topic? The answer to both questions may still be in the affirmative, but now at least we must hesitate a little. The situations of both the aged and the dying person have come much more into public and professional-scientific awareness over the past quarter century. The development of the Gerontological Society, two White House conferences on aging, the establishment of the National Institute on Aging, and a proliferating network of peer and professional agencies concerned with the well-being of the elderly are among the evidences of greater visibility in this area. Death education courses from elementary school through advanced university seminars, establishment of journals devoted to "thanatology," seasonal crops of legislation and a lively stream of judicial rulings on "right to die" and related matters, along with the gradual emergence of the hospice concept—these are among the indices that our society has overcome some of its reluctance to acknowledge mortality.

It is probably no coincidence that interest in both topics has heightened over the same span of time. Aging and death have been intertwined from the most ancient days (Kastenbaum & Ross, 1975). Together they have posed for many a classic ambivalence: one does not want to die, yet one does not want to grow old. Ponce de Leon's famous quest for a a fountain of youth represents but one of innumerable efforts to break out of the die young / grow old dilemma. These stretch back to early myths and the foundations of alchemy and modern science (Gruman, 1963/1977), and extend into our own day (e.g., Rosenfeld, 1976). The link between aging and death must be examined with care, however. There are both factual and attitudinal considerations that require our attention if we hope to provide relevant and appropriate care for those in need. We begin, then, with a brief review and updating of the factual relationship between aging and mortality. This is followed by a similarly brief exploration of attitudinal

factors, and then by an examination of selected problems that confront the would-be helping person.

MORTALITY IN OLD AGE

Recent Trends in Mortality Rates

Brotman (1977) has presented us with a remarkable statistic: 75% of the American population now survives to age 65. This figure simultaneously emphasizes a major difference between ourselves and past societies and documents the intensified relationship between old age and death. More people are living to an advanced age than ever before; therefore, more are dying old. Historically, death at an early age has been the principal scourge. Infants, young children, and women in the childbearing phase of life have been at special risk. A large wave of people moving well into "old age" is a novel phenomenon in history; it could not have come into existence without markedly improved opportunities for survival in the early years of life. If we owe nature a death, as the saying goes, then this debt is now allowed to ride much longer before it is collected.

The facts about old age and mortality continue to change even as we attempt to fix them in our minds. Notice, for example what has been happening to the mortality rate for older Americans at three selected points in our history (Table 1).

One of the considerations raised by the data in Table 1 is the seemingly paradoxical rise and fall of mortality in old age at the same time. There are more 65-year-olds in our population now than in 1900, for example. This reinforces the association between old age and death, because there are more people in this age range who obviously did not die when they were younger. On the other hand, the mortality rate itself has decreased almost a fourth for white males and nearly two-thirds for white females: more deaths, then, but reduced mortality risk for any individual.

These data also suggest that the mortality rate is *continuing* to decline among the aged. This impression is supported by recent analyses such as those of Myers (Note 1). He has examined the brief span between 1970 and 1975 for the U.S. and ten other nations. Data for the U.S. are shown in Table 2.

Myers (Note 1) states that these declines are "rather large for such a time period, especially in the 65-69 age and 85-and-

TABLE 1
Mortality Rates at Ages 65 and 75*

Year	White Males		Nonwhite Males		White Females		Nonwhite Females	
	65	75	65	75	65	75	65	75
1900	41.7	88.4	54.2	99.5	36.4	80.4	54.1	86.9
1950	34.5	75.0	45.8	71.1	20.6	56.5	37.0	57.7
1975	30.3	68.1	35.5	74.5**	13.9	38.3	19.8	54.1

*per 1,000 in the population. **mortality of nonwhite males has been an exception to the general trend over the past decade. (Source of basic data: National Center for Health Statistics).

TABLE 2

Percentage Changes* in Age-Specific Deaths, 1970-1975

Men					Women				
65-69	70-74	75-79	80-84	85+	65-69	70-74	75-79	80-84	85+
11.3	5.4	4.4	5.7	9.6	14.9	8.8	8.7	11.1	12.7

*All changes are in direction of decreased percentages of death.

over categories for both males and females. . . . The annual declines in the five-year period for these age categories for males were 2.4 per cent and 2.0 per cent compared with the 1950-1975 period annual declines of .5 and .7 per cent respectively. The annual rates of declines for females were twice as large in this period as they were over the 25-year period" (p. 6).

Statistics such as these do not count for much when we are trying to be of service to a particular individual or family. They alert us, however, to the double-pronged message on the larger scene:

1. Elderly people continue to gain in the years remaining to them, thereby cautioning us against equating "old" with "ready for death"; yet

2. The terminal care situation will occur with increasing frequency in the extreme reaches of the life span, thereby reinforcing the old age/death association.

Where Do Old People Live and Die?

We need two answers for the above question. Unless we recognize clearly that the statistics indicate divergent answers, we are apt to make and act upon inappropriate assumptions. Population data routinely indicate that about 95% of those 65 and older reside in a noninstitutional setting. This implies a reasonable degree of social visibility for most older people and access to all the natural human support networks in the community: family, friends, neighbors, and all manner of clubs, groups, associations, and health maintenance agencies. It may also imply that the dying process will take place within a familiar interpersonal context. But this is rapidly becoming the exception. While most elders live in the community, most die in some type of

institution. And it is not just the last few days of a "death watch" that runs its course in an institution. Weeks, months, or years are spent in a final environment that has little relationship to the individual's time-arching lifestyle. The first study of this type indicated that approximately 25% of deaths in the 65+ age range occurred in institutional "homes" (Kastenbaum & Candy, 1973). In other words, about five times as many people *died* in such places as are usually assumed to be *living* there. Other researchers have confirmed this general finding and extended it (Palmore, 1976; Wershaw, 1976). When *all* types of institutions are included, the likelihood that an old person will end his or her life in the community shrinks to less than one in five.

The discrepancy between where-people-live and where-people-die statistics has come as a surprise to some geriatricians because they have failed to distinguish between cross-sectional sampling procedures and the longitudinal nature of life itself. At any one point in time there is only about one elderly person in 20 residing in an institution. But when we follow the *same* person over time (and through further aging and illness), the probability relentlessly increases that some form of institutional care will be forthcoming.

There are many implications for psychosocial care during the terminal phase of life. Almost everything that makes an institution "institutional" erodes the expression of individuality and the availability of intimate human relationships. The general literature on institutional impersonality is extensive and too well known to require detailing here, nor can geriatric institutions as a class claim exemption. Perhaps it is enough to remind ourselves that there are multiple processes which converge to imperil the self-esteem and dignity of the old person who faces death in an institution. These include but are not limited to:

1. The "stigma" of institutionalization itself (Goffman, 1960);

2. The loss of individual identity and its replacement by becoming in the world's eyes simply one old person among many others—forced identification with an all-too-visible, seven-day-a-week cohort of people who are dysvalued as a group;

3. The attenuation of self-esteem supports through reduction in environmental features that maintain life continuity and reduction in social contact with the larger community;

4. An intensification of all the above—stigma, identity loss, and stimulus/person deprivation once the individual is perceived as a *dying* person.

Old . . . institutionalized . . . dying. This constellation is becoming ever more typical. It is no longer possible to shrug off the problem as one that affects just a few people. Most people today do grow old, all do face death, and, increasingly, the final scene is played out in an institutional setting which offers no more adequate support for dying than it does for living (to the extent that these two sides of the coin can be meaningfully distinguished).

TRANSITION: FROM FACTS TO ATTITUDES

Some of the elementary facts about mortality in old age have been touched on. Unfortunately, these are not sufficiently well known to professionals, including those who have taken the responsibility to teach others. We are still told, for example, that the major "developmental task" of the older person is to prepare for death. This conclusion is hard to reconcile with the increasing *life* expectancy of old people—with their rich variation of resources and motivations. Alternatively, we are asked to attend chiefly to the well-functioning elder in the community. Presumably this person will not join the supposedly small minority who face death in the institution. Even where facts are relatively clear, our attitudes and assumptions often go their own way. And, of course, the facts frequently are far from clear. Lay person and professional alike have few restraints upon the exercise of their own biases when faced with the emotional challenges of terminal illness among the elderly. We must, then, with caution move into the attitudinal thicket.

ATTITUDES OF SOCIETY TOWARD DYING AND DEATH IN OLD AGE

There are several rather common attitudes toward dying and death in old age. Find any one of these attitudes and the others usually are hovering about as well:

1. The old person is thought to be "ready" if not actually "longing" to see the final curtain descend;

2. On a more philosophical level, death is "natural" and "timely" for the old person. Biologists make this point with emphasis on the preservation of the vigor of our species through the "necessary elimination" of weakened and impaired specimens;

3. On the pragmatic level, it is inappropriate to attempt to extend the life of a person who is conspicuously old and ailing; such an action is decried as "indignity" or "not cost-effective," depending on the speaker's preferred vocabulary;

4. The "social loss" (Glaser, 1966) when an old person dies is minimal and is not a factor that must be taken seriously;

5. Memorialization and rituals associated with the death also are not of particular importance; they may even extend the "morbid" aura of death over the surviving elders—in any event, the death has been expected so long that there is little need to prolong the scene with rituals of mourning and memorialization;

6. Little could be done to extend the life of a sick and imperiled elder; and

7. Limited social and medical resources should be applied to care of the young who still have so much life ahead of them.

Not only do these assumptions tend to cluster together, but they have at least two other commonalities:

1. None of them is well supported by empirical evidence;

2. All serve key needs of the people who espouse them.

Some of the attitudes and assumptions *could* be tested against empirical criteria. Others are statements of personal bias which only appear to be rooted in demonstrable fact. The fact/value mix in each proposition is difficult to ascertain. Take the biological argument, for example. Would this be settled by studying the "vigor" of societies that have varying populations of elders? Or is it rather a pseudoscientific way of declaring "I'd prefer to get old people out of the way"? I have often heard and read presentations of the biological species-preservation argument; never has it been accompanied by plea or plan to explore the question by objective research.

None of the assumptions cited above is well supported by the available data. Attention to a broad span of observations casts doubt on their validity. Case histories such as those presented by Miller (1976), for example, well illustrate the way in which the attitudinal climate can all but bury an old person who remains both viable and desiring of life if given a reasonable opportunity to survive. Munnichs's (1966) pioneering review of studies on death orientation in old age as well as his own research indicates diversity rather than homogeneous death-fear or death-ripeness. Similar results were found with different methodology (Weisman & Kastenbaum, 1968), and the power of the sociophysical environment to influence the timing and manner of death in old age has been shown repeatedly (e.g., Ekblom, 1964; Gubrium, 1975; Tobin & Lieberman, 1976). The latter, for example, find that the first few weeks of institutionalization tend to foster a preoccupation with death-related themes, presumably because there is a heightened generalized sense of loss and vulnerability.

Resources are more easily distributed elsewhere and the status quo more firmly protected if we assume that sick or institutionalized old people are ready to die and should not be deterred from their objective. The idea that there might be premature death even in old age and that environmental factors could contribute to early demise (e.g., Kastenbaum & Mishara, 1970) appears irritating and odd in this context. More would be expected of the care givers and of society in general if we had to believe that some old people do cherish their lives—and that how we respond can actually make a difference in their survival. Nursing personnel are probably expressing a view typical of the society at large when they report that the "best deaths" in their experience involved old people, while the "worst" involved young people (Kastenbaum, Ananis, & Ross, Note 2). So long as we can believe that old people are ready for death and that it is high time for them to leave the scene, we can also hold our emotional responses and professional services within acceptable limits. It should be noted that the tendency to see old people as appropriate candidates for death has a self-perpetuating character. If we just *know* that death is appropriate for old people, then there is little need to explore precisely what this old man or woman is thinking and feeling. And the social expectation that "it's about time for you to go" is not lost upon many elders. The person who is experiencing his own personal ambivalence about life and death may be impelled to accept the implicit life-forsaking judgment of others.

HELPING THE TERMINALLY ILL OLD PERSON

Let us consider now some of the ways in which social workers and members of allied professions can be of value to the terminally ill old person, along with some of the problems that interfere with good care.

Is This Person Terminally Ill?

The attitudinal climate and accompanying behaviors change appreciably when a person becomes regarded as "dying" (Kalish, 1970). There are so many different frames of reference and latent criteria that the same individual may be variously seen as dying and not dying at the same time (Kastenbaum, 1977a). It is helpful when at least one person in the situation recognizes the ambiguities involved and attempts to develop a clear communication network. We have already emphasized the tendency to assume that a person is terminally ill simply because of advanced age, illness, and/or institutionalization. It is also possible, however, to err in the other direction. Old people have been admitted to mental hospitals when, in fact, they were terminally ill, not emotionally disturbed (Markson & Hand, 1970). You can well imagine the implications of such a misguided action. In such a situation an alert and forceful social worker could prevent a tragedy of errors. The term "forceful" seems relevant, because the administrative and political climate in a particular situation can make it difficult for sound judgment to be reflected in practice.

The onset of the terminal phase of life may be difficult to identify, whether the elderly person is at home or in a congregate care facility. An old woman becomes unusually "bossy" and demanding; an old man becomes uncharacteristically confused or suddenly tries to take his life back into his own hands after a long period of depending on others. These are *sometimes* signs of a pending biological catastrophe. Disorganized, out-of-character behavior often is interpreted by others on a symptomatic level. If the old woman gets too bossy, she is to be put in her place. If the old man becomes agitated, then tone him down with whatever drug happens to be in fashion. The desperation underlying the old person's altered behavior may touch off increased anxiety on the part of others in the environment without its essence's being understood. The old person may be attempting to express or compensate for the premonition of catastrophe without being able to put this response into so

many words. Unfortunately, the environmental response may be punishment, chemical restraint (that often has the paradoxical effect of increasing agitation), or even further social isolation. A person who can see beyond the symptom to its possible source in a sense of internal disorganization can be of inestimable value in facilitating a more humane and appropriate climate of social response.

What Does This Particular Person Need?

Knowledge of aging and dying has increased considerably in recent years, but there is a limit to the value of generalities when the guiding principles themselves are off the mark. The stage theory of dying is a prime example. When Kubler-Ross (1969) organized her account of interviews with dying people into five so-called stages, she had no way of knowing how eagerly this would be seized on by the public, as well as by many professionals. It offered a ready-made framework for encompassing the challenging and often anxiety-arousing observations one makes when interacting with the terminally ill. Unfortunately, this formulation received immediate acceptance in many quarters rather than the thoughtful evaluation and testing it deserved. People who previously had no framework available for approaching and conceptualizing the dying process now could, with some comfort, view the terminally ill through the denial-anger-bargaining-depression-acceptance "stages." This has led at times to distorted and narrow vision. The stage theory suffers from methodological, conceptual, and empirical flaws that are too serious to disregard (e.g., Kastenbaum, 1975; Kastenbaum & Costa, 1977; Schulz & Aderman, 1974). It gives little attention, for example, to the individual's particular illness, mode of treatment, environmental press, ethnicity, and lifestyle, nor does it have acceptable definitions and a data base. From the practical standpoint, one of the unfortunate outcomes of the hasty acceptance of the stage theory has been the confusion between what is and what should be. The dying person may be pressured to "graduate" from one stage to the next. "Acceptance" (often conceptualized quite vaguely) may be implicitly demanded. It also becomes tempting to discount the dying person's very individual configuration of needs and resources and what specific aspects of the environment might be contributing to his despair. "She's just in the anger stage" is a convenient way of turning aside the obligation to discover precisely what it is in the total situation that might be arousing justifiable anger (e.g., being lied to, having decisions taken out of one's own hands, not receiving medications dependably). Kubler-Ross did not intend such misuse of her material, but it is more difficult to recall a defective theory for repairs than a misbegotten offspring from the assembly lines in Detroit.

Some of the most effective professionals in the terminal care situation have the knack of "forgetting" that they are dealing with a dying person. By this I mean that they are as thorough and careful in assessing the person's needs and resources as they would be with any other client. They do not go in with a preset, narrowed framework. Perhaps this particular individual has organized her life around the well-being of children and grandchildren. Perhaps, instead, finances are the prime concern, or the preservation of a particular object or piece of property. Perhaps there is a tremendous fear of becoming totally dependent on others. Perhaps, at the other extreme, there are such high expectations of receiving unstinting love and attention that these surpass fulfillment. The social worker's knowledge of ethnic patterns may guide her to the critical needs and deepest resources of a particular individual. But in another instance it may be the particular nature of the disease and disabling process that exercises the most influence. Still again, the terminally ill old person may have definite ideas about the kind of death or funeral arrangements that would be most acceptable, and this is the area that most requires attention. Looking, listening, making one's self available, not moving in with fixed expectations for *the* dying old person—these are the ways many effective professionals function.

Once a social worker believes he or she has grasped the central concerns and assets of a particular terminally ill old person, it may be necessary to move into an advocacy role. The advocacy itself may take on forms that appear trivial. Here, for example, is an old woman who does not have much time left. Why should time and effort be spent—along with the money—to provide her with a new pair of glasses? Yet the social worker may recognize that the difference between despair and self-integration in the weeks ahead could depend upon this woman's ability to complete something she is knitting, reading, or writing. Similarly, advocacy for a trip, a hairdresser's appointment, the opportunity to place long-distance calls, the addition of some favorite foods to the menu—any of these relatively "little" things can help make the difference in the maintenance of morale. Additionally, the social worker could have a strong influence in the medical and nursing regime if she is able to convey some dimensions of the patient's mind and character that have not become apparent to others. Too often, the terminally ill old person is treated in a rather condescending way, as though no longer a mature adult whose thoughts and desires command respect. This "put down" is familiar enough for hospitalized individuals in general, but intensified when the person is both aged and terminally ill. The social worker who is not afraid to joust with the establishment on behalf of the client will have many opportunities to do so in such instances.

What Kind of Help Do Family and Care Givers Need?

It is not only the terminally ill person who faces loss. Family and care givers often are in need of understanding and support as well. The death of young children is known to devastate many parents and health professionals (Burton, 1974). Such distress is not usually expressed so conspicuously by those who are close to the terminally ill old person. The dying process of an old person often follows what Glaser and Strauss (1968) have termed a "lingering trajectory." The situation has been chronic rather than acute. Expectations of recovery have been minimal. Little attempt has been made to respond with "heroic" measures when the end appears near. The death itself, as we have seen, typically occurs in a setting where nothing is more routine than an old person's fading away. This pattern reduces the probability of a crisis atmosphere or the perception of a sudden loss.

Yet sorrow, anxiety, guilt, and other painful affects exist beneath the surface more often than an outsider might expect. There may be a tense relationship between family and staff. For example, I have seen the following type of situation occur repeatedly:

The family of an institutionalized old person gradually has become more distant. They are learning how to adjust without the old man or woman at home. It is not convenient and perhaps not at all pleasant to visit. The old person's death is not discussed at home, but there is the feeling that it is only a matter of time. Meanwhile, quite the opposite process has been at work between the old person and the staff of a facility that has any "heart" at all. The staff are no longer strangers to this old person. They have emotionally adopted the old man or woman. Mental and behavioral quirks as well as physical problems have been accepted by the staff ("She's been a regular bear today, but I just kidded her along and she came out of it"). In effect, staff have become this person's *final family*. There is a continuity and immediacy to the relationship that no longer holds with the "official" family outside. Old person and staff are "in this thing together." This kind of arrangement sometimes makes the interior of a geriatric facility warmer and more nourishing than it might otherwise appear.

The success of a final family arrangement, however, sometimes invites grief (literally). Staff may feel themselves to be more attached to the old person than his or her own family. As death approaches, the staff undergo what some have termed "anticipatory grief." There is genuine sadness. After the old person dies, the staff may have to contend with a sense of loss that they do not feel quite entitled to express: it was not really "their" person who died. They have no license to grieve and mourn. We see then the paradox of an official family that does not have conspicuous grief to show, while the unofficial family does mourn but lacks license to express itself. Staff may then express anger toward the "unfeeling" family, which further intensifies everybody's discomfort. The family, for its part, may have dissipated some of its grief during the long period of preterminal decline. A delayed "thump of reality" may strike them only sometime after the death has finally occurred. This is just one of the ways in which staff and family may increase each other's difficulties after the old person's death as well as during the preterminal phase.

Whether the terminally ill old person is at home or in an institution, often there is one particular person who has made him or herself available for care and comfort. It may be spouse, child, friend, neighbor, attendant, volunteer—somebody who has stepped forward more than others to care for the dying person. In the long run this individual is likely to come out of the situation with a well-earned sense of accomplishment and completion. But this person is also more vulnerable. During the dying process and in the period soon after death, the core care giver may be experiencing a complex and demanding special relationship that is not quite like any other (although it could be compared imperfectly with the process of bearing a child and then separating from it at birth, as well as with other types of leavetakings). *Depletion* is perhaps as apt a term as any to describe the experience. Staff who reach out to relate to the terminally ill over and again (as distinguished from remaining professionally aloof) often describe themselves as "drained," "washed out," or "burned out." The same condition may be experienced by the relative caring for a loved one through the last days of life.

The social worker can be of real help in both types of situation sketched above. As a good listener and facilitator of communication, the social worker can assist family and/or staff to put their experiences into perspective, release pent-up feelings, and avoid creating new problems through misunderstandings. The "burn out" phenomenon, for example, can be alleviated to some extent by formation of peer support groups in the institutional setting, and by "vacations" in the family situation where another person is encouraged to step forward at times and not keep all the burden on the one individual who has been most willing to provide sustained care. Sensitive follow-up contacts with the core helping person after an especially "difficult" death can also be valuable.

There is now a reasonable literature to consult for suggestions on avoiding or minimizing problems such as these. Useful general material can be found in two NIMH publications, *A Social Work Guide for Long-Term Care Facilities* (Brody, 1974), and *Maintenance of Family Ties of Long-Term Care Patients* (Dobrof & Litwak, 1977). Previously cited works by Gubrium (1975) and Miller (1976) are among those which provide helpful glimpses of the social context of death in old age, with a more academic perspective offered by Kalish (1976). Both the groundbreaking Feifel essay collection (1959) and its recent follow-up (1976) offer insights useful to any professional who works with the terminally ill and their families. The SHANTI project of support for terminally ill people is but one of many constructive approaches reported in Garfield's new (1978) collection.

Every person who works with the terminally ill and their loved ones brings individual needs and resources into the situation. It is not surprising that "death educators" often urge that those who would help the dying not neglect their personal thoughts and feelings about death. Books are not the only or necessarily the most effective answer, of course, but among the many publications now available one is likely to find some that encourage useful self-confrontations. Koenig's wry "programmed" approach (Koenig, 1975) will speak to some people; Worden and Practor's (1976) *Personal Death Awareness* will be more useful to others. The self-help literature ranges from the academically oriented to the Sunday-supplement type. At any particular moment one might find stimulation or consolation in any of these sources. Workshops and courses on terminal care are available in many parts of the nation. These do vary much in quality as well as focus and level. Audio-visual materials of many types have been prepared. Some of these show up in readily available catalogs; others still must be obtained through

more roundabout means. The individual who is starting to explore the realm of aging and dying materials to support his/her clinical activities might find it useful to contact the Death Education Forum and look into the journals *Omega* (for a broad range of dying-death related articles) and *Death Education Quarterly* (for contributions specifically in this field). Books of a scholarly cast include those by Kastenbaum and Aisenberg (1972/1976), Kastenbaum (1977a), Schulz (1978); Cartwright, Hockey, and Anderson (1973, and Mack (1973). Clinically oriented works, in addition to those already mentioned here, include an especially rewarding book by Weisman (1972). Legal and ethical issues are explored in a variety of books, such as the useful contribution by Veatch (1976). The fact that a recent bibliography (Fulton, 1977) lists 3,800 references and is already in need of updating makes it plain that there is no longer cause to complain about the paucity of literature on this topic (although the quality is just as variable as one might expect).

TWO RECENT DEVELOPMENTS

Two quite contrasting recent developments by now will have come to the attention of most people who are interested in care of the terminally ill: "life after life" and the hospice movement. What are we to make of these two very different developments that have become so popular in the same span of time?

"Life After Life"

Raymond Moody's (1975) book of this title sparked widespread curiosity and discussion. Essentially, Moody listened to people who had experienced a very close brush with death. Conservatively, they might be said to have had near-death experiences; some have preferred to characterize them as actually being returned from the dead. Moody found some striking similarities among their reports. Chief among these was a sense of ease rather than of pain and suffering. The nearly deceased person often had the pivotal encounter of meeting a "being of light" who would send him back to life. The "life after life" state was so pleasant that the person hovering between life and death tended to resist the return trip. Once back among the living, the individual often felt that the idea of death had lost most if not all of its anxiety. Many others have reported similar experiences. The work of Osis and Haraldsson (1977) is perhaps the most useful contribution from a research standpoint and also includes references to many other examples.

In my judgment, there is no reason to question the integrity of these reports. They are often given by people of the most solid character who have not heard of such experiences before and who have nothing in particular to gain by inventing or adorning such tales. I heard "life after life" stories in my own childhood and early clinical experiences, and many others can say the same. Yet the most significant questions remain to be answered. What do these experiences "mean"? What implications do they have for our theoretical and practical approach to the dying person? Is the experience the same for the dying older as for the younger person? And have we, in fact, learned anything about death as such from these experiential reports?

The critical literature attempts to offer parsimonious explanations of what might be involved in the "life after life" state. In other words, what more familiar phenomena might account for these experiences, as contrasted with interpreting them as actual returns from the dead or transformations through spiritualistic experiences? Examples of this critical approach can be found in the work of Noyes and Kletti (1976) and Noyes (in press). It has also been pointed out that some people return from near-death experiences *without* such vivid memories (e.g., Kastenbaum, 1977b).

There is also concern that the pleasant or euphoric qualities attributed to death can detract from dedicated terminal care, as well as encourage serious suicide attempts (Kastenbaum, 1977b). It is feared that the supposed pleasures of the passage from life will be used by some as a rationale for withholding high-quality care to the terminally ill, especially those with low status value such as the aged ("Let him die; he'll enjoy it!"). This attitude fits too snugly with the already prevailing assumption that old people are or should be ready for death and might therefore translate the assumption into further action (or inaction). People in a suicidal crisis sometimes call a halt to their impulses because they are hesitant either to experience the dying process or enter the realm of the dead. If the passage and the destination both are portrayed as more pleasurable than life, the individual might then cross over the threshold into decisive action and carry out the self-destructive act.

There is a related phenomenon worth keeping in mind. Old people sometimes have the sense of being in contact with a particular deceased person even when they are not themselves in the borderland between life and death. In my own experience, these "visitations" generally bring a sense of comfort and assurance. They are not restricted to people who believe firmly in some form of afterlife, nor do they necessarily signify a regressive, senile, or psychotic state. The old person may be in good contact with the "real-life" surroundings. There is much that remains to be understood about such experiences. One impression: often the visitations or hallucinations occur in a context in which the old person has very little to hold on to. There is nothing in his room, in his environment that relates centrally to the kind of life he has lived, nobody on the scene who really means anything to him. The sense of contact with a particular deceased person seems to fill a void in the here-and-now social-support matrix. Perhaps it is best, in our limited state of understanding, simply to respect this type of experience and to avoid perceiving it as a demonstration of the old person's incompetence or need for more powerful medication.

The Hospice Movement

The "death awareness" movement at first generated discussion. There were times when it seemed as if "everybody's talking about death but nobody's doing anything about it." An increasing number and variety of people have, in fact, turned to practical actions intended to comfort the terminally ill person and his family. Much of this activity has centered around the establishment of "hospices." The term itself first appeared centuries ago in connection with shelters for pilgrims undertaking their long and arduous religious journeys. Later, the hospice spirit was extended to the care of impoverished, abandoned people who would otherwise have died by the side of the road. Today, *hospice* refers to a system of care that encompasses home and family as well as a physical facility designed expressly for the terminally ill. This means that some hospice systems may operate with only the home-care component until it is possible to add the backup physical facility. It is not always necessary for the terminally ill person to enter the hospice building per se. In some situations, family members can provide excellent care at home with assistance from nurses, social workers, and others. The identification of hospices with a physical facility, then, is not quite accurate.

The hospice system, as contrasted with traditional health services to the terminally ill, is more likely to concentrate upon relief of pain and other symptoms of distress. Accordingly, there often is greater expertise in the prescription *and* administration of pain-relieving substances. The tempo and attitudinal climate are in greater harmony with the natural flow of life. There is much less rushing around and fewer evidences of a medical-technological presence. The environment seems more successful in maintaining the individuality and dignity of the patient. Patient, family, and staff all seem to have firmer ideas about what is happening and how they can be helpful to each other. Much of the inspiration for the current hospice movement has come from the work of Dr. Cicely Saunders and her colleagues at St. Christopher's in London (Saunders, 1960; St. Christophers, Note 3). A useful overview of *The Hospice Movement* has recently been provided by Stoddard (1978).

It would be helpful for social workers to recognize clearly the differences between the theory and technique of the true hospice and some of the arrangements that have been proposed under this same term. Unfortunately, there have been proprietors of rather unsatisfactory nursing homes who have attempted to pass them off as "hospices" by making a few superficial adjustments. The fact that many people die in a particular place does not make it a hospice. The hospice is, on the one hand, an *attitude* of total caring and, on the other, a *constellation of services and techniques* developed for this purpose. The potential value of the hospice movement could be undercut by crude and hasty caricatures of the real thing.

Even "the real thing" has its difficulties, however. These include living within bureacratic guidelines and financial restrictions as well as the more direct challenges of preserving the patient's personhood and supporting the family as the family supports the patient. It is much too soon to evaluate the success of the hospice movement in the United States (even the criteria for evaluation are not entirely clear). It is also too soon to determine the relationship between the hospice concept and the sophisticated, multiservice extended-care facility. But it is reasonable to expect that people responsible for both types of facility could learn from each other.

CONCLUDING NOTE

By every indication, more of us each year will enter the ranks of the aged and dying. What lessons we can learn and apply today might well be of personal comfort in the future. Many of us are not temperamentally suited to work with the dying ourselves, at least at a particular phase in our own careers and lives. But we can respect the courage and sensitivity of those who are able to respond to this challenge, as well as the aged themselves who know life and death on such intimate terms.

REFERENCE NOTES

1.   Meyers, G. C. *Cross-national trends in mortality rates among the elderly.* Unpublished manuscript, Duke University Center for Demographic Studies, March 1978.

2.   Kastenbaum, R., Ananis, R., & Ross, G. *"Best" and "worst" deaths as seen by nursing personnel.* Unpublished report, 1978. (Available from the Bedford, Massachusetts, Veterans Administration Hospital.)

3.   St. Christopher's Hospice. *Annual reports, 1973-1977.* Unpublished reports, annual. (Available from St. Christopher's Hospice, Sydenham, England.)

REFERENCES

Brotman, H. B. Life expectancy: Comparison of national levels in 1900 and 1974 and variations in state levels, 1969-1971. *The Gerontologist, 1977, 17,* 12-22.

Brody, E. M. (Ed.). *A social work guide for long-term care facilities.* Rockville, Md.: NIMH, 1975.

Burton, L. (Ed.). *Care of the child facing death.* London & Boston: Routledge & Kegan Paul, 1974.

Cartwright, A., Hockey, L., & Anderson, J. C. (Ed.). *Life before death.* London: Routledge & Kegan Paul, 1973.

Dobrof, R., & Litwak, E. *Maintenance of family ties of long-term care patients: Theory and guide to practice.* Rockville, Md.: NIMH, 1977.

Ekblom, B. The significance of social psychological factors for the death risk, especially in aged persons. *Nordisk Psychiatrisk Tiddskrift, 1964, 18,* 272-281.

Feifel, H. (Ed.). *The meaning of death.* New York: McGraw-Hill, 1959.

Feifel, H. (Ed.). *New meanings of death.* New York: McGraw-Hill, 1976.

Fulton, R. *Death, grief and bereavement. A bibliography: 1845-1975.* New York: Arno Press, 1977.

Garfield, C. A. (Ed.), *Psychological care of the dying patient.* New York: McGraw-Hill, 1978.

Glasser, B. G. The social loss of aged dying patients. *The Gerontologist, 1966, 6,* 77-80.

Glasser, B. G., & Strauss, A. L. *Time for dying.* Chicago: Aldine, 1968.

Goffman, E. Characteristics of total institutions. In M. R. Stein, J. Vidich, & M. White (Eds.), *Identity and anxiety: Survival of the person in mass society.* Glenco, Ill.: The Free Press, 1960.

Gruman, G. J. *A history of ideas about the prolongation of life.* New York: Arno, 1977. (Originally published, 1963, American Philosophical Society, Philadelphia.)

Gubrium, J. F. *Living and dying at Murray Manor.* New York: St. Martin's Press, 1975.

Kalish, R. A. The onset of the dying process. *Omega: Journal of Death & Dying, 1970, 1,* 57-69.

Kalish, R. A. Death and dying in a social context. In R. H. Binstock & E. Shanas (Eds.), *Handbook of aging & the social sciences.* New York: Van Nostrand Reinhold, 1976.

Kastenbaum, R. Is death a life crisis? On the confrontation with death in theory and practice. In N. Datan & L. Ginsberg (Eds.), *Life-span developmental psychology: Normative life crisis.* New York: Academic Press, 1975.

Kastenbaum, R. *Death, society and human experience.* St. Louis: C. V. Mosby Co., 1977. (a)

Kastenbaum, R. Temptations from the ever after. *Human Behavior, 1977, 6,* 28-37. (b)

Kastenbaum, R., & Aisenberg, R. B. *The psychology of death.* New York: Springer, 1972/1976 (Concise edition).

Kastenbaum, R., & Candy, S. E. The 4% fallacy: A methodological and empirical critique of use of population statistics in gerontology.

International Journal of Aging & Human Development, 1973, 4, 15-22.

Kastenbaum, R., & Costa, P. T. Psychological perspectives on death. In M. R. Rosenzweig & L. W. Porter (Eds.), *Annual review of psychology* (Vol. 28). Palo Alto, Calif.: Annual Reviews, Inc., 1977.

Kastenbaum, R., & Mishara, B. L. Premature death and self-injurious behavior in old age. *Geriatrics, 1970, 26,* 70-81.

Kastenbaum, R., & Ross, B. Historical perspectives on the care of the elderly. In J. G. Howells (Ed.), *Modern perspectives in the psychiatry of old age.* New York: Brunner/Mazel, 1975.

Koenig, R. Counseling in catastrophic illness: A self instructional unit. *Omega: Journal of Death & Dying, 1975, 6,* 227-242.

Kubler-Ross, E. *On death and dying.* New York: Macmillan, 1969.

Mack, A. (Ed.). *Death in American experience.* New York: Schocken, 1973.

Markson, E. W., & Hand, J. Referral for death: Low status of the aged and referral for psychiatric hospitalization. *International Journal of Aging & Human Development, 1970, 1,* 261-272.

Miller, M. B. *The interdisciplinary role of the nursing home medical director.* Wakefield, Mass: Contemporary Publishing, 1976.

Moody, R. A. *Life after life.* Atlanta: Mockingbird Books, 1975.

Munnichs, J. M. A. *Old age and finitude.* New York: S. Karger, 1966.

Noyes, R. Near-death experiences: Their interpretation and significance. In R. Kastenbaum (Ed.), *Between the living and the dead: Psychological, personal, and humanistic studies.* New York: Springer, in press.

Noyes, R., & Kletti, R. Depersonalization in the face of life-threatening danger: A description. *Psychiatry, 1976, 39,* 19-27.

Osis, K., & Haraldsson, E. *At the hour of death.* New York: Avon, 1977.

Palmore, E. Total chance of institutionalization among the aged. *The Gerontologist, 1976, 16,* 504-507.

Rosenfeld, A. *Prolongevity.* New York: Avon Books, 1976.

Saunders, C. *Care of the dying.* London: Macmillan, 1960.

Schulz, R. *The psychology of death, dying, and bereavement.* Redding, Mass.: Addison-Wesley, 1978.

Schulz, R., & Aderman, D. Clinical research and the stages of dying. *Omega: Journal of Death & Dying, 1974, 5,* 137-143.

Stoddard, S. *The hospice movement.* New York: Stein & Day, 1978.

Tobin, S. S., & Lieberman, M. A. *Last home for the aged.* San Francisco: Jossey-Bass, 1976.

Veatch, R. M. *Death, dying and the biological revolution.* New Haven: Yale University Press, 1976.

Weisman, A. D. *On dying and denying: A psychiatric study of terminality.* Behavioral Publications, 1972.

Weisman, A. D., & Kastenbaum, R. *The psychological autopsy: A study of the terminal phase of life.* New York: Behavioral Publications, 1968.

Wershaw, H. The four percent fallacy. *The Gerontologist, 1976, 16,* 52-55.

Worden, J. S., & Practor, W. *Personal death awareness.* Englewood Cliffs, N.J.: Prentice-Hall, 1976.

A New Understanding About Death

Living wills, thanatology courses, self-help groups, the hospice movement—all are part of a widespread yearning to make sense out of life's ultimate mystery.

Death and dying, topics that Americans traditionally have spoken of only in private or have tried to ignore altogether, are intruding upon the nation's consciousness as never before.

Dramatic, life-prolonging medical advances, the desire of more people to "control" the act of dying, a growing population of elderly and concerns over funeral costs have spawned a panoply of nagging moral and ethical dilemmas. Just this year alone—

■ A pregnant California woman, declared legally dead from a severe brain seizure in January, was put on life-support systems to allow the fetus to mature. After a healthy baby was delivered on March 24, the woman was taken off the machines and immediately stopped breathing.

■ A Los Angeles judge dismissed charges that two physicians had violated their legal responsibilities by ordering that a comatose patient be taken off a respirator and intravenous feedings.

■ Writer Arthur Koestler, suffering from leukemia and Parkinson's disease, committed suicide along with his wife, adding fuel to the debate over euthanasia.

■ Barney Clark, a Seattle-area dentist who was on the verge of death last December 2, lived on for 112 more days with the help of an artificial heart.

■ A federal judge struck down the Reagan administration's "Baby Doe" rule that urged hospital employes to tell federal officials if defective infants were being denied food or medical treatment.

With such issues grabbing headlines, college professors report that courses on death and dying are among the most popular on campus, where young people, many of whom have never been to a funeral or visited a terminal patient, are trying to understand life's deepest mystery.

In what observers call the "gloom boom," more books on the subject—ranging from controversial manuals on how to commit suicide to studies of "near death" experiences—have been written in the last decade or so than in the entire last century.

Millions of people have taken out living wills, directing the sort of medical treatment they should receive in their last days. Others are shopping in advance for funeral arrangements to save their families the trouble of making costly decisions during a time of grief.

It all adds up to a more honest confrontation with an issue that most individuals would rather sweep from their minds. "It isn't an easy thing to do, but more people are at least trying to come to grips with death, grief and loss," says sociologist Vanderlyn Pine of the State University of New York at New Paltz.

The Right to Live—and to Die

One reason death is now less threatening to many Americans is that it has become, as sociologist Robert Fulton of the University of Minnesota puts it, "the monopoly of the elderly." Last year, more than 70 percent of the 2 million people who died in the U.S. were age 65 or older, and just 5 percent were under the age of 15.

Many of these elderly spend their last years in nursing homes—in effect, waiting to die. Other senior citizens have moved off to retirement communities or have been left behind themselves by children who have moved on to other cities. Whatever the reason for the separation, notes Fulton, many Americans have made an emotional break with their elderly relatives well before death occurs. Says Fulton: "There is a tendency to observe that these people have lived long, full lives and that it is only normal and natural that they be allowed to die in peace."

The idea of a peaceful and natural death, however, often comes in direct conflict with medical science, with its defibrillators to restore regular heartbeat, respirators to aid breathing, dialysis machines for failing kidneys and wonder drugs to ease pain, sustain blood pressure and enhance other key bodily functions. With 80 percent of deaths now occurring in hospitals and other institutions, physicians are confronted almost daily with whether to use these tools to prolong the lives of gravely ill patients. As often as not, it is a complicated, delicate decision made against a background of murky law.

In California, for example, physicians cannot legally take a patient off a respirator unless tests show a complete absence of brain function. Yet, with the permission of patients or their families, medical teams time and again are privately "pulling the plug" on severely brain-damaged patients who, they believe, have no chance of recovery. "It is a courageous and risky thing to do, but many doctors are doing it anyway," says the Rev. Ernie Young, a chaplain at Stanford University Hospital.

Such situations are made more difficult, however, when the patient or family disagrees with the advice of the doctor or when the patient is mentally incompetent, leaving no indication of how he or she would want to be treated.

Reprinted from *U.S. News & World Report* issue of July 11, 1983, pp. 62-65. Copyright, 1983, U.S. News & World Report, Inc.

For fear of prosecution by law-enforcement officials or out of a genuine belief that a patient might improve, some doctors or hospital officials still refuse to take patients off life-support systems. Last October, Peter Cinque, a painfully ill diabetic in New York, had to appeal to the State Supreme Court to get a Long Island hospital to stop dialysis and let him die as he asked. He died shortly after the court ordered an end to the treatment. In New Jersey, Karen Ann Quinlan—one of about 5,000 "permanently unconscious patients" in the U.S.—remains in a coma more than seven years after her parents won a State Supreme Court ruling to remove her respirator.

Yet observers say most physicians now are less tempted to press for the indiscriminate use of extraordinary or "heroic" means of keeping patients alive. "The vitalist approach—that a person must be kept alive no matter what—is now the minority view," says Alice Mehling, executive director of the Society for the Right to Die, a New York group concerned with the welfare of terminal patients. "There's a more realistic understanding that all technological mechanisms don't have to be used."

Needed: Advice, Guidelines

To give guidance to families and doctors, 14 states and the District of Columbia have passed "right to die" bills—and 22 more are considering such measures—that recognize the right of individuals to sign living wills. These documents specify whether or not patients want to be connected to life-sustaining machinery if they should become unable to speak for themselves.

Although more than 5 million of these wills have been distributed throughout the U.S. since 1967, they are by no means perfect. In some states, doctors in theory are bound to follow the directions specified in the wills; in other cases, the wills are merely advisory. A major problem is that the language is often vague. Many wills use phrases such as "my dying shall not be artificially prolonged" without mentioning the specific procedures that are to be avoided. Thus, a doctor has plenty of loopholes.

Experts note that the wills at least give physicians some idea of a patient's intent and make the medical team less fearful of legal prosecution if extraordinary treatment is withheld. However, a report released in March by a special presidential commission on ethical problems in medicine recommends another alternative: Giving power of attorney to a trusted friend or family member in the event one is too sick to make decisions. Some 42 states recognize this technique, which Dr. Joanne Lynn, director of the commission's report on "Deciding to Forgo Life-Sustaining Treatment," calls a more effective and flexible means of "controlling the course of dying."

That report, which emphasizes the right of a mentally competent patient to halt treatment when there is no hope of recovery, recommends that hospitals set up a regular system of internal review to help physicians make decisions about difficult cases involving dying patients.

What these patient's-rights issues show, experts say, is the need for medical staffs to become much more sensitive to the requirements of dying individuals—a class of patient

that doctors traditionally have viewed as "medical failures." More medical schools are beginning to add courses on gerontology, and more hospitals are hiring philosophers and chaplains trained in ethics.

At Montefiore Hospital in the Bronx, staff philosopher John Arras works with nurses, social-services personnel and physicians in dealing with dying patients and their families. Among the cases he has addressed:

■ Should an elderly man, with failing mental powers, have the right to refuse an operation to detect cancer, or should the hospital overrule him for his own good?

■ Should the hospital respect the wishes of a woman in her early 40s dying of cancer to keep her condition secret from her family?

Says Arras: "There is a great deal of legal confusion, and doctors still are supercautious. In unclear cases, they will usually choose to maintain life."

ILLUSTRATION BY HAROLD SMELCER

Books on "near death" experiences describe people being bathed in a bright but comforting light.

Suicide and Mercy Killing

Also spurring debate is the question of whether it is ever proper for a suffering, terminally ill patient to take his or her own life—or for others to help that process along. While many—if not most—doctors, clergy and legal authorities publicly disapprove of euthanasia, there are signs of growing sympathy in U.S. society for the practice.

There were few public outcries, for example, when Arthur Koestler, the ailing 77-year-old author of *Darkness at Noon* and other works, committed suicide in London in early March along with his wife by taking an overdose of barbiturates. Koestler was a member of a voluntary-euthanasia group called EXIT.

Since Koestler's death, membership has grown in the Hemlock Society, the U.S. version of EXIT, according to the group's founder, Derek Humphry. He helped his wife—then dying of cancer—to commit suicide in England in 1975. Started in California in 1980, Hemlock now claims 7,500 members, only 10 percent of whom are described as terminally ill.

"We encourage people to hang on to life," says Humphry, "but when the end does come, we are saying that individuals ought to be able to control how they die and not have to suffer terrible pain or lose control of mental faculties and bodily functions." Humphry, who last year published *Let Me Die Before I Wake,* a manual on suicide that gives specific lethal doses of drugs, says some 40 people have committed suicide with the help of the guide.

Many experts on death and dying condemn such an approach outright. "We as Christians believe that pain is part of salvation and that it can be a healing thing and a force to bring people together," says the Rev. Miles Riley, a Roman Catholic priest in San Francisco who has written a book on preparing for death.

Nevertheless, says sociologist Fulton, who heads the Center for Death Education and Research at the University of Minnesota, "I suspect that sympathy for euthanasia is on the rise. If I took a poll of students in my classes and asked if gravely ill older people should be allowed to take their own lives, more than half would say 'Yes.'"

Others note that it is extremely rare for someone to go to

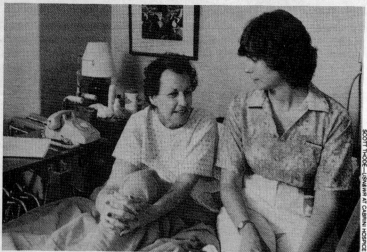

Hospices try to create a more homelike setting for dying patients.

jail for mercy killing. In February, a distressed father was released without bail after he walked into the Army's Walter Reed Hospital in Washington, D.C., and fatally wounded a son who had suffered severe burns in a suicide attempt. He has yet to be indicted. Similarly, in early April, a grand jury in Florida refused to indict a 79-year-old man who had shot and killed his wife, whose mind had been devastated by Alzheimer's disease.

In dealing with dying patients, there is often a fine line between treating a person for pain and mercy killing. Massive doses of morphine regularly given to patients dying of cancer, for example, have the potential of leading to a respiratory shutdown. In an issue of *Nursing Life* magazine earlier this year, 8 percent of nurses surveyed in a study on ethical dilemmas admitted to intentionally giving overdoses of narcotics to dying patients.

Despite such developments and the increased interest in studying euthanasia, many authorities worry that legal approval of mercy killing could bring with it many abuses and would be a harmful step toward social engineering.

Understanding Death—the New Obsession

Whether the issue is euthanasia or how to cope with grief, Americans can't seem to get enough of the subject of death. Since 1959, when Herman Feifel wrote his pioneering work, *The Meaning of Death,* nearly 1,000 books have been written on death and dying.

One of the top-selling books last year was *When Bad Things Happen to Good People,* written by Harold S. Kushner, a Massachusetts rabbi trying to come to grips with the death of his 14-year-old son from progeria, a disease that causes the aging process to escalate dramatically. Kushner has been inundated with letters from other grieving parents throughout the country, and funeral directors and health associations have ordered thousands of copies to help families deal with the loss of loved ones.

Also popular: Books describing the near-death experiences of individuals resuscitated after cardiac arrest or other medical crises. In his *Recollections of Death,* published last year, Atlanta cardiologist Michael Sabom related the experiences of 116 such patients, many of whom described how they seemed to rise out of their bodies and observed the medical team trying to revive them. Many also told of enjoying a tremendous feeling of peace, of being bathed in a bright light, of undergoing a life review or encountering deceased relatives.

While critics have labeled these experiences mere dreams, fabrications or hallucinations brought on by painkilling drugs or release of chemicals in the brain, at least a half-dozen books have been written attempting to give scientific evidence of the phenomenon. The International Association for Near Death Studies also has been set up at the University of Connecticut to foster research in the area. "Whatever the explanation, we know from extensive studies that something extraordinarily interesting happens to many people at the moment of death," says Connecticut psychologist Kenneth Ring, who stresses that near-death experiences do not prove the existence of afterlife but merely show that the act of dying may not be the agonizing event many people fear.

Beyond these studies and the swelling literature in the field, courses in death and dying are attracting thousands of students nationwide. Courses at the University of Maryland involve everything from discussions of ethical and legal issues to work with dying patients. Students go so far as to fill out their death certificates and predict the dates and causes of death. "The purpose is not to dwell on death for its own sake but to improve the quality of living," says Prof. Daniel Leviton of Maryland. "If we all realize that we could die tomorrow, then we will do a better job of setting our priorities in life and make every day count."

When Someone Dies—How to Cope

Not only is thanatology—the study of death, from the Greek word *thanatos*—becoming widespread, but, when death does strike, families are getting help from many directions. In more cities, counseling centers are being set up to advise doctors, nurses and other medical personnel in the more sensitive treatment of dying patients and to assist families in coping with grief. Typical is the St. Francis Center in Washington, D.C., which also puts on workshops for high-school students and other groups and even sells simple, low-cost pine coffins.

In Buffalo, the Life and Death Transitions Center conducts many of the same activities, but also has a special program for cancer patients. Based on theories advanced by such physicians as Carl Simonton, who has worked successfully with cancer victims in Houston, the program follows the view that stress and depression help to bring on and worsen cancer. Thus, individuals are instructed in methods of exercise and relaxation and advised to exert more control over their lives.

"Taking control" is an idea heard often in reference to the process of dying and the events after someone dies. As leading thanatologists see it, Americans have abdicated their role in death and dying to professionals—doctors, funeral directors and clergy. This is in contrast to the practice in this country before World War I and in many foreign countries now, where people die at home surrounded by family, where relatives build a coffin for the deceased, wear black armbands and dig the grave.

One step in regaining that control is the growing hospice movement, which attempts to put dying patients in a more humane, relaxed environment. Whether the care takes place in a special hospital wing or in a patient's home, the concept is the same: A team of health practitioners, clergy and volunteers deals with the patient's physical, psychological and spiritual needs—and counsels the family as well. Pain-reducing drugs keep the dying person as comfortable as possible, but expensive life-sustaining machinery is avoided, which saves the enormous medical bills of traditional hospitals. From only one program in 1974, the hospice movement in the U.S. has grown to some 1,100, with many more in the planning stages.

More families also try to exert greater control once a relative dies. Many ask more questions of funeral directors, choose lower-cost alternatives to expensive arrangements and make church and memorial services more personal by featuring readings by family and close friends.

The Rev. William Phipps, a Presbyterian minister and professor of religion at Davis and Elkins College in West Virginia, says more families now hold a private graveside ceremony for close relatives and a memorial service at a later date for friends that focuses on the life of the deceased. Catholic funeral services have traded black vestments for white and replaced the somber Gregorian chant with joyous hymns that emphasize the passing of a soul into eternal life—though some critics feel the switch gives too little attention to the reality of family loss.

Rabbi Earl Grollman of Belmont, Mass., notes an increased interest in ritual on the part of Jewish families in Reform congregations. Rather than "sanitize" the process, he notes, more families watch while the casket is being lowered into the grave. More survivors of the deceased also show up at daily services where the kaddish, or prayer of mourning, is said. "Until recently, the emphasis was on being strong and getting back to a normal routine in a hurry," says Rabbi Grollman.

The therapeutic value of sharing grief with others is

DARRYL HEIKES—USN&WR

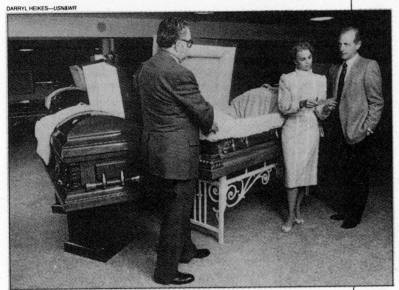

More families are making funeral arrangements in advance.

behind the surge in self-help groups. Rather than face the loneliness that often exists when friends and family depart after a funeral, people can meet regularly with others who have gone through similar experiences. Among the many groups: Widow-to-Widow; Parents of Murdered Children; Candlelighters, for parents of leukemia victims; SHARE, serving parents who have suffered miscarriages or had children die at birth, and Compassionate Friends, for families of young people who have died from accidents, by suicide or other causes. Sociologists note that, in a society where most deaths involve older people, the sudden death of a child or youth can be particularly devastating to a family.

Letting people have time for grief, experts say, is an important part of an honest approach to death. "It used to be that if a person didn't snap out of it in three months, we'd say, 'Get with it, what's wrong with you?'" observes the Rev. William Wendt, director of the St. Francis Center. "But we now know that it takes much longer than that. In fact, you never really get over the death of someone you love; you just learn to live with it."

By LAWRENCE MALONEY

Funeral Costs Still Draw Ire Of Regulators, Consumers

Two decades after Jessica Mitford published *The American Way of Death,* an attack on lavish and costly burials, the funeral industry remains on the hot seat for promoting what critics view as unnecessary products and services.

Much is at stake. Americans spend 6.5 billion dollars a year on funeral expenses, with average burial costs exceeding $2,500. Many services run $3,000 or more.

To make sure the public gets a fair shake, the Federal Trade Commission plans to initiate regulations requiring funeral directors to provide customers itemized price lists of goods and services and to disclose prices by telephone on request. The rules, which could take effect as early as next January unless blocked in the courts by the industry, would also bar funeral directors from falsely saying that state laws require embalming or purchase of a casket for cremation.

Some consumer groups say the FTC action doesn't go far enough. It does not, for instance, prohibit such practices as displaying cheaper caskets in unattractive colors or fabrics. But William Rutherford, president of the National Funeral Directors Association, claims the evidence does not support a need for regulation. To back his argument, Rutherford, owner of four funeral homes in the Columbus, Ohio, area, cites the experience of ThanaCAP, the industry's new program for answering consumer complaints. Since it began in April, 1982, just 30 complaints have been forwarded to the organization's national offices—and only five of those will be submitted to binding arbitration.

Money loss. Even so, the industry continues to lose revenue to lower-cost burial alternatives. In the last decade, the total of Americans cremated each year—a process that often costs $500 or less—has doubled. More than 900,000 people have joined memorial societies, which arrange cremations or negotiate lower-cost traditional funerals in advance with undertakers.

As a result, mortuaries have declined in number from 24,000 in the 1960s to between 20,000 and 22,000 today. More firms are being taken over by giant companies, such as Service Corporation International, which owns 279 funeral homes, 51 cemeteries and 40 flower shops and had sales of 208.5 million dollars for the year ended April 30, 1983. Reflecting growing public desire to hold down costs and make choices prior to death's emotional turmoil, the company has collected more than 83 million dollars in prepaid funerals.

While many sociologists applaud the trend away from showy funerals, many fear that the swift disposal of bodies from place of death to crematories without a memorial service—a practice that occurs in 20 percent of all deaths in some parts of the West—denies the reality of death and ignores the fact that a life has been led. There have been recent reports in Los Angeles, too, of large crematories mixing the ashes of several deceased persons without notifying families.

"To abandon funeral and grieving rites is to walk away from an important event that gives continuity to both family and community life," notes sociologist Robert Fulton of the University of Minnesota.

Living Environments
in Later Life

Old age is often a period of shrinking life space. This concept is crucial to our understanding of the living environments of older Americans. Upon retirement, older people find that they travel less frequently and lesser distances, both because they no longer work and because most neighborhoods have stores, gas stations, and churches in close proximity. As the retirement years roll by, older people may begin to experience hearing and vision problems as well as other health losses and, therefore, feel less in control of their environments. As the aging process ensues, the elderly are likely to restrict their mobility to the areas where they feel most secure. For many, this means that they spend an ever-increasing amount of time inside their houses or apartments. It has been estimated that individuals sixty-five and over spend eighty to ninety percent of their lives in their home environments. Of all the other age groups, only small children are so house- and neighborhood-bound as are older people.

The house, neighborhood, and community environments are, therefore, more crucial to the elderly than to any other age group in the adult population. The interaction with others that the elderly experience within their homes and neighborhoods can be very stimulating or foreboding, pleasant or threatening. Across the country, older Americans find themselves living in a variety of circumstances, ranging from desirable to undesirable.

Approximately seventy percent of the elderly live in a family setting, usually a husband-wife household, and twenty percent live alone or with non-relatives. The remaining five percent live in institutions such as nursing homes. Although only about five percent of the elderly will be living in nursing homes at any one time, a total of twenty-five percent of the persons sixty-five and over will spend some time in a nursing home setting. The longer one lives, the more likely he or she is to end up in a total care institution. Since most older Americans would prefer to live independently in their own homes for as long as possible, their relocation—to other houses, apartments, or nursing homes—is often accompanied by a considerable amount of trauma and unrest.

The fact that the aged tend to be less mobile and more neighborhood-bound than any other age group in the adult population makes their living environments most crucial to their sense of well-being. Some of the issues of residential location, housing, relocation, and institutionalization are examined in this section.

Looking Ahead: Challenge Questions

As medical technology increases the life expectancy of the average American, will it be more or less likely that individuals will spend some of their later years living in a nursing home setting? Discuss both the positive and negative aspects of nursing home life.

As both the number and percentage of older Americans in the total population increases, will the extent to which neighborhoods are age-segregated become more common?

What new kinds of living arrangements will become more common for older Americans in the future?

The Risk of Institutionalization Before Death

Leticia Vicente, PhD,
James A. Wiley, PhD,
and R. Allen Carrington, MA

The authors are, respectively, Research Sociologist, Research Specialist, and Research Analyst at Human Population Laboratory, California State Dept. of Health Services, 2151 Berkeley Way, Berkeley, CA 94704.

The provision of care in institutional settings for disabled elderly people has attracted much attention in recent years. Concern has been expressed regarding the quality of institutional care which, often, has been found to be substandard or even dangerous (see for example, Moss & Halamandaris, 1977). Institutional care is also expensive. For all but the most severe levels of impairment the cost of providing care is higher in institutions than at home, even when voluntary services are assigned a dollar value and included in the total cost of care (U.S. General Accounting Office, 1977). Another reason for concern is based on evidence that many institutionalized old people are receiving more care than they actually need (Davis & Gibbin, 1971; Dunlop, 1976). Such cases of inappropriate placement can be attributed in part to a bias towards institutionalization in federal reimbursement policy. In addition, other factors besides medical condition and physical disability are believed to influence the risk of institutionalization in old age. Among these are socioeconomic status and family structure (Riley & Foner, 1968; Townsend, 1965).

In spite of these concerns, not much information is available on the risks of being placed in an institution or on the factors related to these risks. Two recent studies indicate that the cumulative chance of being placed in an institution before death is much higher than the 4 to 5% prevalence rate which can be observed at any point

This research was supported by Grant No. HS 02627 from the National Ctr. for Health Services Research. Computer programming for the analysis was done by Terry C. Carnacho. The authors would like to thank Drs. R.S. Burt, Ira Cisin, Joseph Hochstim, Erdman Palmore, and Ethel Shanas for helpful comments.

in time. Kastenbaum and Candy (1973) estimate that in 1971 23% of deaths among persons over age 65 in Detroit occurred in long-term care institutions. Palmore (1976) found that 26% of his sample had been institutionalized before death. The longitudinal design of Palmore's study also permits identification of the factors that increase total risk of institutionalization: living alone, being separated or never married, having few or no children, being female, adequate finances, seven or more years of education, and being white.

This paper reports further evidence on the risks of institutionalization before death and discusses the factors associated with increased risk. As in Palmore's study, these factors are measured at a fixed point in time (1965) before institutionalization.

The Sample

In 1965 the Human Population Laboratory (HPL) of the California State Department of Health conducted a survey on health status and patterns of living among a probability sample of 6,928 Alameda County residents. Annual checks of California's vital statistics records showed that 521 (29.9%) of the survey participants who were age 55 and over in 1965 had died as of January 1975. It is this group of decedents that constitutes the sample for the study we are now reporting.

Data Collection

The first step in collecting data consisted of abstracting personal information on each of the 521 decedents from the questionnaire they had filled out in 1965. This material was transferred onto a special case record along with selected information from each individual's death certificate. We also recorded telephone numbers and addresses for decedents and for the friend or relative they had named in the 1965 questionnaire as a "contact." Addresses and phone numbers for all cases were brought up to date by checking telephone directories and the address records of the California State Department of Motor Vehicles.

Our data collection procedure consisted essentially of telephone interviews with relatives, friends, doctors

From THE GERONTOLOGIST, Vol. 19, No. 4, 1979. Copyright 1979 by the Gerontological Society. Reprinted by permission.

and other informants who could help us reconstruct an "institutional history" for each of the 521 decedents in the sample. Because we did not contact these informants prior to the telephone interview, a somewhat structured but open-minded protocol was used to enable interviewers to quickly introduce themselves, describe the study, and establish rapport. Special protocols and/or referral procedures were devised to deal with informants who were initially hostile or suspicious, who had complaints about neglect or ill treatment in specified institutions or wanted help in locating a "good place," or who simply wanted to share their experiences—sometimes amusing, but more often heartbreaking—with long-term care institutions. Efforts in tracing informants were often difficult and tedious. Because most members of the sample had died at advanced ages, we frequently found that their age peers among family and friends (who were most likely to be informed about the decedent's institutional history) were also dead. When immediate family members of the decedents could not be found, much ingenuity was often needed to locate their more distant relatives. A variety of sources were useful (e.g., former neighbors, employers, attorneys who handled the disposition of decedents' estates, and records of funeral directors). These last provided the names of persons who had arranged or attended a decedent's funeral.

The follow-up record for a case was considered "complete" whenever: (a) an informant—usually a relative—stated definitely that the decedent did not stay in a long-term care facility between 1965 and his/her death; or, (b) we were able to reconstruct an institutional history for an individual which included information on the name, location and type of each institution in which the individual stayed, dates of admission and discharge for each stay, and a specification of the place (acute care hospital, home, etc.) the patient was admitted from and discharged to. For cases in category (b) data supplied by informants were almost always verified by checking patient records at each institution identified by name. We encountered some difficulties here because long-term care facilities in California are required to keep records for only seven years after a patient is discharged. Fortunately it was often possible to reconstruct the needed information from transfer records kept by acute-care hospitals. When the institutional history was completed for a case, the information was summarized and entered in chronological order on a form we called the institutional record.

At the end of the period we had set aside for collecting data, we had complete records for 79.1% (412) of the sample, and partially complete records for 8.3% (43), producing an overall completion rate of 87.3%. We could not obtain any information on 12.7% (66) of the sample.[1] These "lost" cases are excluded from our

---

[1]The characteristics of the 66 cases with unknown institutional

analysis, reducing the number of cases from 521 to 455.

Table 1 presents findings concerning the relationship between risk of institutionalization and selected independent variables. The rate of institutionalization is measured in two ways: (1) percentage of sample members who had been admitted at least once to a long-term care facility; (2) percentage of sample members who had stayed at least six months in a long-term care facility. The period of risk under consideration is between 1965 (the year of HPL's first survey which provides us with measurements of the independent variables) and each individual's year of death. The reader should also note that in this analysis institutionalization refers only to admission to facilities—most often called nursing homes or convalescent hospitals—which provide long-term medical or skilled nursing care. Excluded from the analysis are acute-care hospitals, homes for the aged and other institutions that provide room, board, and other non-medical services, rehabilitation hospitals, and facilities for the mentally disturbed or retarded.

Total Chances

We found that 177 of the 455 (38.9%) persons in our sample had stayed in a convalescent hospital or nursing home at least once before death. Among persons with one or more stays, about 40% were institutionalized for long periods of six months or more. Overall, numbers of patient days exceeding six months were observed for 65 of 441 (14.7%) sample members (we did not have data on duration of stay for 14 persons). The rate of institutionalization we found is much higher than the rates reported in the studies we cited. Part of the discrepancy between our 38.9% figure and Kastenbaum and Candy's 23% (1973) may be attributed to differences in study design. By using death certificates as the source of data, Kastenbaum and Candy's findings on the use of long-term care facilities are restricted to stays that terminated in death: "any person who resided in a nursing home but did not die there would not be counted among those deceased in institutions. Our data indicated that Kastenbaum and Candy are correct in pointing out that reliance on death certificate information creates a downward bias in estimating institu-

histories were compared with those of the 455 cases whose records were complete or partially completed. There were significant differences (i.e. $p < .10$) on only one of the characteristics listed in Table 1. The "no information" cases were less likely to be married at the beginning of the follow-up period compared to the rest of the sample (43% married vs 53% married). There were no significant differences between the two groups with respect to distributions of age in 1965, sex, race, year of death, family income in 1965, years of schooling, household size in 1965, and an index of physical health status. Since unmarried persons have higher rates of placement in long-term institutions than married persons (see Palmore, 1976 and Table 1 of this paper), the "no information" cases may have a somewhat higher risk of institutionalization than the other group whose rates are presented in Table 1. Thus, the overall rate in Table 1 may be biased downward.

Table 1. Percentage With at Least One Stay in a Nursing Home and Percentage Who Stayed Six Months or More by Selected Characteristics.

Variable	At least one stay				Stayed 6 months or more			
	%	Base N	x^2	p[a]	%	Base N	x^2	p[a]
All persons	38.9	455			14.7	441		
Marital Status, 1965								
Married	29.1	244			7.5	241		
Single	35.5	31			14.3	28		
Separated/Divorced	42.9	35			18.2	33		
Widowed	55.2	145	26.4	<.001	26.6	139	26.1	<.001
Household size, 1965								
One person	54.5	123			24.3	115		
Two persons	37.0	230			13.3	225		
Three persons	25.0	56			7.1	56		
Four or more persons	23.9	46	21.8	<.001	6.7	45	13.7	<.008
Sex								
Male	32.9	228			10.8	222		
Female	44.9	227	6.4	<.011	18.7	219	4.9	<.027
Physical Health Status, 1965[b]								
Some disability	41.0	222			17.2	209		
Chronic conditions	37.9	145			16.0	144		
Symptoms	40.0	35			8.6	35		
No complaints	32.1	53	1.5	NS	5.7	53	5.7	NS
Race								
White	40.5	393			16.2	382		
Other[c]	29.0	62	2.5	NS	5.1	59	4.2	<.040
Family income, 1965[d]								
Inadequate	49.6	133			23.0	126		
Marginal	40.5	74			13.7	73		
Adequate	33.8	136			6.8	132		
Very adequate	23.8	63	14.1	<.003	9.7	62	15.3	<.002
Years of schooling								
0-8	37.3	220			14.2	212		
9-12	39.9	138			16.3	135		
13 or more	40.9	88	0.4	NS	14.1	85	0.3	NS
Age in 1965								
55-64	17.7	113			3.6	110		
65-74	34.8	164			11.9	159		
75-84	53.7	147			23.2	142		
85 and over	67.7	31	47.0	<.001	30.0	30	25.5	<.001
Year of death								
1965-1968	24.4	164			8.2	159		
1969-1971	41.8	153			16.6	145		
1972-1974	52.9	138	26.5	<.001	20.4	137	9.4	<.009

[a]Probability of a chi-square value equal to or larger than the observed value under the null hypothesis of no difference between the two groups.

[b]The health status categories are based on a seven category index developed by Belloc et al. (1971).

[c]The "other" category includes Blacks (N = 46), Spanish-American (N = 9), and Asians (N = 7).

[d]The family income categories measure total household income in 1965 adjusted for household size. For a family of three of four, an annual income of $10,000 or more in 1965 is considered "very adequate," between $5,000 and $9,999 is "adequate," $3,000-4,999 is "marginal," and below $3,000 is considered "inadequate."

tionalization rates. About one-fourth (44 out of 177) of all persons in our sample with at least one stay in a nursing home or convalescent hospital died elsewhere, usually in acute-care hospitals. Such stays were usually not noted in death certificates even when individuals who died in acute-care hospitals had been admitted there directly from nursing homes.

Explaining the size and direction of the difference between our institutionalization rate of 38.9% and Palmore's 26% (1976) is more difficult. It would have been reasonable to expect a higher rate for Palmore, given his wider definition of institutionalization (which includes stays in homes for the aged) and a longer follow-up period (20 years, compared to our nine). Without more knowledge of Palmore's data we can only offer conjectures to account for the discrepancy in rates.

(1) Certain characteristics—such as health status—of Palmore's volunteer sample from Piedmont, NC, may be different from the characteristics of our sample of Alameda County decedents.

(2) The geographical settings of the two studies may differ in terms of availability of long-term care institutions.

(3) The long duration (1955-1976) of Palmore's follow-up suggests that in comparison to our sample, many more deaths would have occurred prior to 1965—the year Medicaid and Medicare were enacted. By increasing the ability of older persons to purchase care at long-term care institutions, these programs provided financial incentives to increase the supply of such services and facilities. Thus, a higher rate of institutionalization may characterize the Alameda County sample since many more of its members would have spent their last years in an environment of increased access to, and availability of, institutional long-term care.

Factors Related to Institutionalization

The data on characteristics of our sample members come from the original survey HPL fielded in 1965. As presented in Table 1, these can be grouped into several categories: socio-economic (family income, education); demographic (age, sex, race); potential availability of social supports (household size and marital status); and physical health status. For each of these classes of

[2]Using death certificate information alone, we computed an institutionalization rate (persons with at least one stay before death) of 29.3% for our sample.

[3]There were 4.4 long-term care beds per 1,000 population (i.e., beds in nursing homes, rehabilitation hospitals, and mental institutions) in Alameda County in 1966. By 1973 there were 6.0 beds per 1,000. This increase in supply is one possible reason for the finding—reported in Table 1—that persons who died late in the follow-up period had higher rates of institutionalization than those who died earlier. (Bed supply figures are based on unpublished data from the California State Dept. of Health Services.)

independent variables our findings are as follows:

(1) Income as a measure of socioeconomic status is significantly associated with institutionalization while education is not. Our analysis shows that poorer people were more at risk of being institutionalized, perhaps because they are more likely to qualify for insurance programs (e.g., Medi-Cal, California's version of Medicaid) which pay for long-term institutional care. People with higher incomes would not pass the required "means" test; in addition, they are more able to postpone or avoid institutionalization by buying services that enable them—despite mental or physical infirmities—to live at home. Our findings on income run counter to Palmore's and are more in keeping with prevalence data reported by Riley and Foner (1968).

(2) Being female and being white are associated with higher risks of institutionalization. On these demographic characteristics, our findings replicate Palmore's. However, our results on age are very different from Palmore who reported no relation between age at the beginning of follow-up and consequent risk of institutionalization. This finding is surprising because prevalence rates of nursing home residence increase with age (cf. Brody, 1977). Moreover, certain risk factors such as poor health and widowhood are more typical of older age groups. Palmore explains the absence of an association between age and institutionalization as follows: increased risk with age due to changes in level of need for or access to long-term institutional care is counterbalanced by a shorter duration of risk before death among older persons in the sample. "Thus, the younger persons in our study had lower annual risks of institutionalization but more years ahead to be at risk, while the older persons had higher annual risks but fewer years ahead" (Palmore, 1976).

In contrast to Palmore we find a striking difference between rates of institutionalization among different age groups in our sample. The proportion with at least one stay rises from a low of 17.7% in the youngest age group to a high of 67.7% among persons who were 85 or older in 1965. Similarly, rates of long stays are 3.6% in the 55 to 64 age group and climb to a high of 30% among the oldest members of this sample. Since the rates used in this paper measure *cumulative* risk, it is not surprising that they are also associated with the duration of exposure to risk as indicated by year of death. For those who died in 1965-1968, the rate of at least one stay in a nursing home is 24.4%; rates are 41.8% and 52.9%, respectively, for those who died in 1969-1971 and 1972-1974. That age and duration of risk do not cancel out each other's effects may be due to their relatively low correlation ($r = -.09$) in our nine-year follow-up data. This correlation is undoubtedly higher in Palmore's 20-year data, though its size is not reported in his article.

(3) The indicators for availability of social supports are significantly correlated with risk of institutionalization. Persons who did not have spouses, or who lived

alone, or in households with only one person had higher rates of institutionalization, probably because such persons are less able to get care or help when they fail mentally or physically. However, we do not have data on number of living children. This is a serious omission because presence of children has been found to be associated with decreased risk of institutionalization (Palmore, 1976).

(4) For our sample, health status is measured by a set of categories defined by presence or absence of functional disabilities, chronic conditions, and symptoms. The measure was developed by Belloc et al. (1971) in a study of the impact of life style on generalized susceptibility to illness. Unexpectedly, we found that rates of at least one stay in a nursing home do not vary significantly over health status categories; persons who reported disability in 1965 (activity imitations lasting more than six months) were not much more likely to be placed in a nursing home than those with more minor complaints. However, there is a significant association between health status categories and long stays in nursing homes of at least six months.

The data presented in Table 1 suggest that several factors influence the risk of being institutionalized before death. Since the correlations between some of these factors are substantial, assessing their relative contributions to risk of institutionalization requires multivariate analysis. The method we used is multiple discriminant analysis, which weighs and linearly combines the different factors so that groups of cases are forced to be as statistically distinct as possible. The analysis allows us to construct a profile (consisting of variables selected from the list in Table 1) of individuals who run the highest risk of institutionalization.

Two separate discriminant analyses were performed and their results are as follows:

(1) The first analysis attempts to discriminate between persons with no stays in nursing homes and persons who had at least one stay. Persons at high risk of being institutionalized are profiled as follows: they were unmarried, lived alone, were over age 75 in 1965, and died late in the follow-up period. This multivariate analysis excluded race, income, initial health status and sex from the profile of persons in the high-risk group. The reader will recall that most of these variables were significantly associated with risk of institutionalization in Table 1.

(2) The second analysis attempts to identify factors which discriminate between those who stayed in nursing homes less than six months (included in this category are persons with no stays); and persons who stayed for six months or more. The multivariate profile of an individual at high risk of a lengthy stay includes most of the elements identified in the first analysis: being unmarried, over age 75 in 1965, and dying late in the follow-up period. However, other elements are added to this profile which did not show up in the earlier one: being white, having "inadequate" or "marginal"

Table 2. Multiple Discriminant Analysis of Variables Related to Institutionalization.

Variable[a]	Standardized Discriminant Function Coefficients	
	At least one stay (+) vs no stays (−)	Stayed 6 months or more (+) vs stayed less than 6 months (−)
Married (= 1)	−.21*	−.45**
Lives alone (= 1)	.28*	−.04
Lives with one other person (= 1)	.22*	.13
Male (= 1)	−.11	−.08
No chronic conditions or disabilities (= 1)	.03	−.23*
White (= 1)	.04	.22*
Inadequate income (= 1)	.09	.36*
Marginal income (= 1)	.11	.17*
55-64 years old (= 1)	−.76**	−.52**
65-74 years old (= 1)	−.51**	−.45**
Year of death minus 1965	.64**	.45**
Wilks' lambda[b]	.790 (p < .001)	.849 (p < .001)
% of cases classified correctly[c]	.69.2%	74.0%
Number of cases for this analysis[d]	406	393

*indicates p < .10   **indicates p < .05

[a]All predictors except duration of risk (i.e., year of death minus 1965) are coded as 1/0 dichotomous variables. Persons who have the characteristics listed in the table are coded as 1 while persons who do not have the characteristics are coded as 0.

[b]Wilks' lambda tests the overall discriminating power of the set of predictor variables. The null hypothesis is that lambda equals 1 (i.e., no discrimination between the two groups) in the population from which the sampled cases were drawn.

[c]Probabilities of category membership (e.g., at least one stay vs no stays) are derived for each case from the results of the discriminant function analysis. A case is assigned to the category for which it has the greatest probability of membership.

[d]The sample sizes differ from those given in Table 1 due to missing information about predictor variables for some cases.

income, and reporting health problems in 1965.

These results indicate that there are important differences between risk of entry into an institution and the risk of staying there for a long time. In the multivariate analysis, factors such as marital status, income, race and initial health status bear a stronger relation to duration of stay than to cumulative risk of at least one stay. Perhaps further study of the correlates of various utilization patterns in nursing homes will suggest explanations for the differences we observed. In any case, these findings justify the practice of using several different measures of institutionalization in studies of this kind.

The results of both discriminant analyses show that age is an important discriminating variable. It makes a large contribution to risk of institutionalization, *even when controlling for variations in factors such as marital status, income, and health at the beginning of the follow-*

up period. This finding suggests that age represents, or is associated with, other factors that increase the risk of institutionalization before death. Among these one might include access to insurance plans—such as Medicare—which pay for institutional care of the elderly; undocumented changes in the personal characteristics of sample members which occurred after our 1965 survey; and preferences among professionals (such as physicians) for institutional rather than home care for the very old. Unfortunately, the additional data needed to evaluate these interpretations of the age effect are not available for our sample.

In each analysis duration of risk (year of death minus 1965) is included as a control variable. We mentioned earlier that we expected duration of risk to be positively correlated with entry and length of stay because institutionalization is measured cumulatively over the period at risk in the study. It appears, however, that there may be other reasons for this association besides cumulation of risk. For persons in the same age cohort in 1965, number of years lived beyond 1965 is perfectly correlated with age of death. In turn, age at death may be related to other factors that predict institutionalization, such as the length of an individual's period of decline and consequent dependency before death. In addition, the number of years lived beyond 1965 brackets the period during which a person was exposed to risk of institutionalization. If time-specific prevalence rates were increasing over the follow-up period, death late in the period would be associated with a higher risk of institutionalization for all age groups.

Summary and Conclusion

Of the findings presented in this report, perhaps the most important is the high risk of institutionalization we observed for our sample. Among its members, 38.9% were admitted to a nursing home at least once before death. We also found a substantial incidence of long stays in nursing homes: approximately 40% in the group which had at least one stay (or 15% of the entire sample) were institutionalized for six months or more.

If our findings are generalizable to other populations, estimates in current use of the risk of institutionalization would have to be drastically revised upwards. This would mean that much larger numbers of people than has previously been supposed are exposed to the shortcomings and deficiencies of institutional long-term care.

Our multivariate analysis shows that the chances of being institutionalized vary, depending on an individual's characteristics. Being unmarried, old, and living alone are associated with high risks of entry into a nursing home. The profile of persons most at risk of long stays is somewhat different. To the list of characteristics we just mentioned should be added being white, poor, and having chronic conditions and physical disabilities. Among all these factors, the best predictor of institutionalization is age: in general, increased longevity is associated with higher risks of entry and longer stays in nursing homes.

The association between factors such as old age and poverty, on the one hand, and increased risk of institutionalization on the other, indicate that medical need may not be the sole or even major determinant of entry or length of stay in nursing homes. This raises questions regarding the influence upon the process of institutionalization of factors external to elderly persons, such as reimbursement policies under Medicaid or Medicare, and professional biases towards institutional care among physicians. Obviously, further study is necessary to determine more precisely what factors are responsible for the higher rates of institutionalization in various population subgroups.

This study of institutionalization was based on a follow-up of persons who were originally interviewed for different purposes. Our experience suggests that already existing survey or longitudinal samples can be utilized for research on the use of long-term facilities. The follow-up methods we used worked very well, enabling us to reconstruct complete institutional histories for nearly 80% of our sample. We hope that other studies based on similar samples and data collection methods will be conducted, to determine if our findings can be generalized to other populations.

References

Belloc, N.B., Breslow, L., & Hochstim, J.R. Measurement of physical health in a general population survey. *American Journal of Epidemiology,* 1971, *93,* 328-336.

Brody, E. *Long-term care of older people.* Human Sciences Press, New York, NY, 1977.

Davis, J.W., & Gibbin, M.J. An area-wide examination of nursing home use, mis-use, and non-use. *American Journal of Public Health,* 1971, *61,* 1146-1153.

Dunlop, B.D. Need for, and utilization of, long-term care among elderly Americans. *Journal of Chronic Disease,* 1976, *29,* 75-87.

Kastenbaum, R. & Candy, S. The four percent fallacy. *Aging and Human Development,* 1973, *4,* 15-21.

Moss, F.E., & Halamandaris, V.J. *Too old, too sick, too bad.* Aspen Systems Corp., Germantown, MD, 1977.

Palmore, E. Total chance of institutionalization among the aged. *Gerontologist,* 1976, *16,* 504-507.

Riley, M.W., & Foner, A. *Aging and society, vol. 1: An inventory of research findings.* Russell Sage Fdn., New York, NY, 1968.

Townsend, P. The effects of family structure on the likelihood of an admission to an institution in old age. In E. Shanas & G.F. Streib (Eds.), *Social structure and the family.* Prentice Hall, Englewood Cliffs, NJ, 1965.

U.S. General Accounting Office. *Home health: The need for a national policy to better provide for the elderly.* HRD-78-19, USGPO, Washington, DC, Dec., 1977.

Positive Consequences of Institutionalization: Solidarity Between Elderly Parents and Their Middle-Aged Children

Kristen Falde Smith, MS
Director of Social Services
Southland Lutheran Home & Geriatric Center,
Norwalk, CA 90650

Vern L. Bengtson, PhD
Director, Laboratory for Social Organization & Behavior,
Ethel Percy Andrus Gerontology Center,
University of Southern California, Los Angeles, CA 90007

Long term institutional care for the elderly is associated with many negative images. Of these, perhaps none is more pervasive than institutionalization symbolizing the failure of family support to an aged member.

It is generally agreed that institutionalization represents a last resort in providing for an aged family member. This reflects a widespread belief that the majority of American institutions (primarily nursing homes, but also board and care facilities) provide substandard care. This popular opinion is supported by an abundance of professional literature which indicts institutions with poor care and treatment (Anderson & Stone, 1969; Butler, 1975; Gottesman & Bourestom, 1974; Kahana, 1973; Mendelson, 1974; Moss & Halamandaris, 1977; U.S. Senate, 1974). Nursing homes are viewed as "houses of death" (Butler, 1975), or "the human junkyard . . . halfway between society and the cemetery" (Moss & Halamandaris, 1977).

Accompanying the negative image of long term care institutions is the negative image of the elderly persons who are residents or patients in these institutions. Studies indicate that the institutionalized elderly are highly depersonalized (Coe, 1965; Kahana & Coe, 1969), withdrawn and isolated (Jacobs, 1969), and have

Presented at the 31st Annual Meeting of The Gerontological Society, Dallas, TX, Nov. 16-20, 1978.

very weak links to the social system (Coe, 1965). Lieberman (1969) summarizes characteristics of the institutionalized elderly suggested by repeated studies: They tend to be depressed, unhappy, intellectually ineffective, possessing a negative self-image, docile, submissive, and having low interest in surroundings.

The elderly and their families often hold similarly negative views, so that institutionalization becomes the least desirable alternative when an older person begins to require support and assistance (Kahana, 1971; Shanas, 1960). It has become difficult to extract any positive aspects of long term institutional care, especially when considering the family in relation to institutionalization of an older family member. It is frequently assumed that those in institutions have been abandoned by their families, or that the family failed in its role of service provider. That the elderly who reside in long term care institutions have strained family ties thus becomes a widespread notion that fits into the general arena of negative attitudes about institutions and those they attempt to serve.

Recent literature of the family, however, does not seem to uphold the notion of family breakdown (Bengtson, 1978). Researchers are now identifying the events which precede institutionalization: Death of spouse and/or children, multiple physical disabilities, mental confusion, assaults of aging on the children, changing neighborhoods, exacerbation of old family conflicts (Brody, 1966; Brody & Spark, 1966; Miller & Harris, 1965). Treas (1977) cites demographic trends indicating that it is unreasonable to assume that families can effectively deal with all of the age-related problems of parents. She and others (Brody & Spark, 1966; Dobrof & Litwak, 1977; Simos, 1970; York & Calsyn,

1977) discredit the belief that children have abandoned their parents in the institution.

The main purpose of this study was to discover how institutionalization of an elderly parent affected the relationship between the parent and the child who was instrumental in placing the parent in the institution, as seen by both generations. In identifying what happens to key relationships throughout the institutionalization process, we can more fully understand several issues of institutional care. The issues of importance here involve changes, whether positive or negative, in family interaction following institutionalization. Data collection focused on whether or not the prevalent family pattern among the institutionalized elderly is one of isolation from family as is so commonly believed, or whether close family relations are also present among the institutionalized elderly and their children. In addition, we wished to explore what factors specific to an institutional setting accounted for the negative or positive consequences.

How the Study Was Done

Open-ended interviews were held over a period of two years with resident-patients of an institutional setting and with the child who was most involved with the parent at the time of entrance to the facility (N = 100). Interviews were conducted with *both* parents and children, since the perceptions of each are likely to reflect differences between them in "generational stake" (Bengtson & Black, 1973). The interviews lasted from one to three hours. All interviews were conducted by the first author. Coding categories were constructed by both authors directly from verbatim case protocols.

The interview focused on pre- and post-admission issues. With regard to pre-admission, information was obtained on the amount of contact between parent and child, what types of activity this contact involved, and feelings of family closeness and affection. Subjects were then asked to look at these three factors as they existed following institutionalization of the parent and describe any changes—whether positive or negative—which had occurred. The events which led to the decision for the parent to enter the institution also were explored.

The institutional setting used in this study is a 195-bed, multi-level care facility, consisting of residential care, intermediate nursing care, and skilled nursing care. Resident-patients of this facility range from 51 to 101. The age range of the resident-patients whose interviews pertained to this study was 70 to 92. The age range of their children was 50 to 71.

The facility and its clientele may not be typical of other institutional settings, since the resident-patients are predominantly Scandinavian, middle-class, and with families. The facility has a good reputation, and therefore, is popular. Full occupancy is a constant and a long waiting list for all levels of care continuously exists. Since Jan. of 1977 when 120 beds of nursing care were added to the facility, the total number of admissions has been 300.

34. Positive Consequences of Institutionalization

Consequences of Institutionalization for Relationships

Our research suggests six "ideal types" reflecting consequences for family relations following the institutionalization of an elderly parent. Five were directly manifest in interviews from the institutional population; the sixth was added on the basis of clinical observation and experience in other settings. These types are not meant to be exhaustive of all possible patterns, but they represent frequently recurring themes among the families interviewed. The six types reflect improvement, continuation, or deterioration of family relationships following institutionalization, and were distributed among families in the present study as follows: Renewed closeness and strengthening of family ties (30%); Discovery of new love and affection (15%); Continuation of closeness (25%), Continuation of separateness (20%); Quantity without quality interaction (10%); and Abdication: Institutions as a dumping ground. These percentages are deliberately presented as approximate, since in several cases judgement had to be made on the basis of data from only one generation (the parent was confused, or not as explicit as the child) and since the single-site sample makes generalization tenuous.

Improvement of Family Relationships

Renewed closeness: Strengthening of family ties.— Families who have experienced institutionalization of an aging parent often suggested a history of affection, respect, frequent contact, and feelings of closeness between parent and child. The long-term closeness, however, frequently has been strained by the traumas leading to institutionalization. Pre-admission events such as multiple physical disabilities or confusion of the parent may have created numerous and unnatural demands on the child and threatened to sever previously close ties.

In most of our cases, institutionalization was sought out by the child for the parent. After placement, the child became more free to provide the psychosocial, emotional aspects of care. A renewed closeness was developed, with some families expressing a closer relationship than ever before. About 30% of the families interviewed could be classified in this category.

Mr. P., 82, had retired from business and lived alone on a large Idaho ranch for several years. Then his health began to decline due to lung problems. He had always been closest to his 50-year-old daughter Grace, having lived with her previously following a separation from his wife. Thus, he moved out to California to live with her again.

Mr. P. and Grace both note that they "had always had great affection for each other." However, as his breathing difficulties worsened, Mr. P. became more and more fearful, and began to constantly call Grace at

7. LIVING ENVIRONMENTS

work. Mr. P., "demanded access to someone 24 hours a day." Grace began to respond in ways to her father in which she had never responded before, and which she did not like in herself. She became very nervous and felt irritable toward her father and toward her siblings whom she accused of not taking their share of the responsibility for the father.

Mr. P. and Grace openly discussed the growing problems and both agreed that he should enter some type of an institutional setting. Mr. P. entered skilled nursing care in Feb. of 1977.

Mr. P. improved remarkably in his physical health and strength following institutionalization. With regular IPPB treatments for his breathing and 24 hour supportive care, he was able to advance to intermediate care. Mr. P. says that "we are closer now than we ever have been. The entire family is closer and we all see each other more often." Grace says that her father has changed. He is "sweeter than he used to be, valuing people and friendships more than business and material wealth, and verbally expressing love and appreciation for his family for the first time."

Mr. P. and Grace are representative of many other families who expressed a renewed and strengthened relationship following institutionalization.

"The last two years, I was closer to my dad than ever before . . . the important point is to stay in touch and let the relationship grow." (Son, age 60)

"My son has become everything to me. He is always with me." (Father, age 82)

"We are closer now because the 24 hour pressure of taking care of my mother is lifted. She is doing more for herself here than she did at home." (Daughter, age 56)

"I feel more comfortable in our relationship now because my daughter doesn't have to constantly worry about me." (Mother, age 82)

In some instances, although the child experienced a renewed closeness with the parent, the parent was not fully aware of the pre-admission strain and therefore viewed the relationship more in terms of an uninterrupted closeness. This may be a result of the child not having expressed negative feelings which were arising or the parent's inability to accept and be aware of increasing needs and demands.

"I don't think she consciously realized that she had been taking her resentments toward the physical effects of her stroke out on me." (Daughter, age 56)

The overall picture, however, still illustrates a strengthening of family ties, as one member of the relationship was nearing a point of dependency which would have broken a previously close bond. Instead, through the supportive services of the institution, the child was able to draw close to the parent and grow in the relationship.

Another variation of renewed closeness appeared when the parent was suffering from a marked level of confusion. Pre-admission events were traumatic to the child. Following placement in the institution, the child was more fully able to understand and accept the confusion and find a new type of closeness to the parent. (In these cases the parent was not able to be interviewed, so an interpretation of the relationship was made from the child's point of view.)

Mrs. E., now an 89-year-old resident of skilled nursing, comes from a family whose concept was to keep her at home. For the past eight years, according to her 54-year-old daughter Alice, Mrs. E. had been getting progressively more confused to the point where she did not know her own family. Alice quit her job and took her mother into her home.

Alice did not want to be a martyr, so took a very practical approach. She charged her mother for staying with her to cover the expenses and to hire people to stay with her mother when she wanted to get away.

Mother and daughter lived together for a few years. Alice says of this time, "I did not recognize my mother's problems; I didn't want to accept them." Then Mrs. E. began to sneak out for walks, and as Alice's home was on a hillside, she suffered numerous falls. However, the last thing Alice wanted was to place her mother in an institution. Finally, it was obvious, however, that the only way to insure the physical safety of Mrs. E. was to move out of the hillside home which had been Alice's home for 29 years. At this point, Alice began to look for a nursing home for her mother.

Mrs. E. entered skilled nursing in March of 1977. She resides on a floor which specializes in rehabilitation for disoriented persons. She is happy and can often be seen pushing others in wheelchairs. Her daughter visits about once a week, and to her surprise, Mrs. E. always recognizes her. At home, Mrs. E. had often referred to Alice as the maid or the cook.

Discovery of new love and affection.—A second category, represented by about 15% of our respondents, consisted of families who, after institutionalization of the parent, experienced a close relationship for the first time. The history of these families revealed duty and obligation to be the criteria for interaction between parent and child. Interaction was often based on some type of specific task. As the tasks took on aspects associated with problems of aging, the child became instrumental in placing the parent in an institutional setting.

Mrs. W., an 80-year-old widow, lived in an apartment close to her only child, Pauline (age 58). Mrs. W. had been diagnosed as having cerebral arteriosclerosis and was beginning to display serious symptoms of the disease.

Mrs. W. and Pauline had weekly contact, but the affection had been strained throughout their past. Mrs. W. as described by Pauline, "was always a very depressed and depressing person." "She never was outgoing nor did she ever seem to laugh and enjoy herself.

She was possessive of me and expected me to be constantly attentive to her. She had always tried to live her life through me."

Pauline, realizing that a change was drawing near, returned to school in order to achieve a higher degree and bolster her income so that she would be in a better position to help her mother financially with care and services. Pauline began to feel the strain of constant concern for her mother, yet she knew that she could not bring her into her own home as her husband and mother had never really gotten along due to Mrs. W's chronic depression and possessiveness.

Mrs. W. entered residential care in January of 1977 under the persistence and persuasion of Pauline. During the first six months, Mrs. W. was resentful of her situation and frequently expressed anger at her daughter and at the staff of the facility. Pauline, however, refused to accept this anger and to consequently feel guilty, as she still was convinced that this was the best solution.

After six months, the picture changed for both Mrs. W. and Pauline. Through the supportive services offered in residential care, Mrs. W. has been able to face and accept her limitations. Without having to struggle with meals and daily maintenance, she has found a freedom to do what she has the energy for. She no longer feels angry at her daughter or at the facility, and is becoming involved in running the home's gift shop, which gives her a feeling of competence, and is actively participating in group activities.

Pauline now feels relief and pleasure when talking about her mother. She indicated that, "this Christmas was the first time I have ever seen my mother actually enjoy herself." She feels that, "my mother—who had never accepted life's limitations—has accepted them now and is finally free to be herself and not try so hard to be something or someone else." Mrs. W. and Pauline now have a more satisfying relationship than ever before. For Pauline, it is the first time she has emotionally felt close to her mother.

The job of the institution is to take over the technical tasks of care giving (Black & Bengtson, 1977; Dobrof & Litwak, 1977). After institutionalization, it was no longer necessary for the child to perform these tasks, thus allowing for interaction to be based on the child wanting to see, to talk to, to do for the parent. In these cases, a relationship of love and affection was created and explored for the first time.

> "My mother demanded rather than earned respect and love. We had a poor past relationship—a love/hate relationship. Now I can do for her because I want to. I can finally love her because I want to." (Daughter, age 57)

The older member of the relationship in which this pattern emerged did not always reveal as explicitly the history which had caused the child to feel uncomfortable in parent/child interactions. Yet, the parent did affirm a close relationship with the child following placement in the institution, and also claimed to be satisfied with the services of the institution—services which had previously been performed by the child.

> "I like the camaraderie here. And I feel very secure. I feel sorry for people who have only sons—I'm so grateful to have my one daughter." (Mother, age 76)

Continuation of Family Relationships

Continuation of closeness.—Many times when parent and child express feelings of closeness after the parent has been institutionalized, it is the expression of an uninterrupted closeness which appears throughout the family history. Institutionalization was sought as a realistic solution to the parent's growing needs and disabilities and the child's lack of training to effectively provide for them.

> "The relationship to my mother hasn't changed. We are still close. It's just as though she has moved and I am relieved of the responsibility." (Daughter, age 56)
>
> "I don't see how anyone could have a better relationship than I have with my daughter. What would I ever do without her?" (Mother, age 82)
>
> "We have remained close. We are realistic about her limitations and about ours to take care of her." (Daughter, age 57)
>
> "I don't feel at all neglected or far away in a corner." (Mother, age 87)
>
> "We have tailored our lives in order to stay close to my parents." (Son, age 71)

An underlying value of this pattern of continued closeness seemed to be that of the importance of independence between parent and child. Institutionalization was seen as a way for independence to be maintained.

> Mrs. T. and her daughter Janet, ages 82 and 56 respectively, had always considered themselves to be good friends as well as mother and daughter. After Mrs. T's husband died, she moved into an apartment just a few blocks from her daughter. Mrs. T. didn't drive and needed assistance with shopping, going to the doctor, and other errands.
>
> This arrangement continued for 13 years. Mrs. T. and Janet enjoyed their relationship. They saw each other about four times a week. In exchange for Janet providing her with transportation, Mrs. T. helped Janet with her housework. As Janet's husband traveled extensively, her mother was a welcomed companion. They shopped, went out for lunch, and talked about family and world events. Yet, they also maintained a definite independence from each other. Mrs. T. always did as much for herself as was possible. Janet often traveled with her husband.
>
> Suddenly one day, as Mrs. T. described it, she had "a type of breakdown." She felt nervous and weak, possibly as a result of a facial neuralgia which had been bothering her. Because of her weakness, she was not able to prepare meals or do any housework. She also lost

confidence in walking, which was an activity she had always enjoyed.

Mrs. T. began to spend weeks at a time with Janet as she no longer wanted to be alone. Janet accepted this willingly and allowed her mother to stay with her until she felt ready to return to her own apartment. Mrs. T. states, "I had never wanted to live with my children. I have seen too many cases that resulted in resentment and bitterness among family members."

She wanted to remain independent from her daughter. Consequently, Mrs. T. decided that she would move into an institutional setting. She did not ask her daughter what she thought about it, but told her that this was what she was going to do.

Both Janet and Mrs. T. seemed pleased that Mrs. T. is receiving 24 hour care. Janet states, "I was beginning to worry about whether or not I could provide permanent care for my mother and am happy that mother made the decision herself to enter an institution." Mother and daughter still see each other every week and talk on the phone several times a week. There are no feelings of separateness between them, but both are happy with the independence that they have. Mrs. T. and Janet continue to describe themselves as "good friends."

Many families—parents and children—expressed this same desire to maintain an independence within a close relationship.

"I want my daughter to travel now that her husband has retired. That's what my husband and I did. That's what she should do." (Mother, age 77)

"Mother took care of her own mother and loved it. Yet, she never wanted to live with her own children though they would have gladly taken her in. She's too independent—a doer and a goer." (Daughter, age 60)

"I never wanted to live with my children—it wouldn't be good for them or for me. But we have always been very close." (Mother, age 83).

"No one put me here as some other people say. I came here because I wanted to be independent and free my daughter from having to worry about me." (Mother, age 82)

About one out of four of the families in this population could be categorized as reflecting continuation of closeness following institutionalization.

Continuation of separateness.—In another category of respondents, institutionalization reflected a clear history of distance and lack of meaningful involvement between parent and child. Since family support was not available, the parent had no recourse except to seek out professional care giving services. About 20% of the families interviewed portrayed this pattern.

An 83-year-old widow, Mrs. B., had been living in her own apartment and doing quite well except for some arthritis in her knees. She lived about seven miles from her 49-year-old daughter Eileen but the two saw each

other only about once a month. Mrs. B and Eileen never were intimately close as their ideas about life differed markedly.

One day with no forewarning, Mrs. B. suffered a stroke. When Mrs. B. was ready to leave the hospital, her doctor encouraged placement in a nursing home as she was in need of full care. Mrs. B. was not able to make decisions at that time and Eileen never questioned but that her mother needed institutional care.

Over a period of months, Mrs. B's physical status improved. The question then was whether she would return to her apartment, move into Eileen's home, or go into an intermediate care facility. Eileen felt it would be "too difficult to have mother in my home. I work full-time and don't want this kind of responsibility." In addition, she stated she had never been comfortable around her mother. She had never been free to be herself when they were together. Mrs. B. thought she could go back to her own apartment but the doctor didn't advise this. Eileen strongly encouraged Mrs. B. to enter an intermediate care facility and make it her permanent home. Mrs. B. felt "I really had no choice."

Mrs. B. now has made her permanent home within an institutional setting. She and Eileen see each other regularly, but the visits are not enjoyable for either. Mrs. B. feels that Eileen should come more often and tells her this when she does come. Eileen says, "there is nothing much to talk about when I come, so I try to leave after about one-half hour. Yet, I want my mother well taken care of, even if I'm not willing to do it myself."

Deterioration of Family Relationships

Quantity without quality interaction.—Some families (about 10%) depicted a history of frequent contact and involvement, but indicated the motivations for such had been ambivalent. Negative feelings between parent and child appeared to be beneath the surface, but not allowed to be openly admitted.

Following institutionalization, contact between parent and child increased, following the earlier pattern of frequent contact, but again, with ambivalent motivations. Often, the child expressed guilt about the parent being in an institution; the parent, anger at his or her circumstances. Neither party appeared to enjoy the time spent together, with negative feelings becoming more acute, although both insisted on maintaining the increasing frequency of contact.

Susan, a 53-year-old housewife, always feared the day that her parents, ages 85 and 75, would require extensive assistance from her. Mr. L., a very strong-headed individual, had always made demands on the family members; demands which they met, but with growing resentment.

When Mrs. L. began to display signs of confusion and withdrawal, Mr. L. decided to enter a residential care facility. Susan felt guilty if she did not visit almost everyday, although when they were in their own home, she visited only about once a month. Yet, she was worried about her mother and knew that the rest of the family would not be very supportive.

Susan did not enjoy her visits. Mrs. L's confusion had become so great that she did not at all respond to her daughter. Mr. L. demanded that she run numerous errands for them and became angry if she declined to do so. The guilt which Susan felt, however, forced her to increase her visits to her parents and take on all of the responsibilities which the family might have shared. Susan stated, "After my parents came here, I felt like I had to be here all the time. I felt guilty when I wasn't here. My dad kept calling for me to do this, to do that. My brothers and sisters hardly ever come—the family has never really enjoyed being around them, because my dad was always so rude."

Some children were able to resolve the inner conflict which drove them to visit at an increasing rate despite the lack of enjoyment, and bring the relationship at least back to the pre-admission level of interaction and closeness.

A different coping mechanism sometimes used by children who were involved in a quantity without quality relationship, however, was to become demanding and critical of staff. As the parent expressed displeasure (which likely was a symptom of the parent's anger toward the child), the child would blame staff for the parent's unhappiness and show his or her concern for the parent by making unrealistic demands concerning the care. Negative interactions thus became three-fold among parent, child, and staff members.

"His family has become so unreasonable—they're dissatisfied with everything we do. Yet, when they're (the family) not here, he is perfectly content with his care." (Female, age 50)

Abdication: Institutions as a dumping ground.—None of the families interviewed from the facility used in the present research fit the stereotype of a middle-aged child abandoning an elderly parent. However, clinical observation and experience can testify to this occurrence. Seemingly, the parent had more at stake in the relationship, with the child feeling only moderately tied to the parent. Institutionalization was seen as all responsibility being lifted from the child. Visits from the child dwindled to seldom. The parent felt lonely and rejected though would tend to use the excuse of how "busy" the child always was, not wanting to put the child or the relationship in a totally unfavorable light.

As the interviews did not uncover any instances where the child had, in fact, abandoned the parent, it seems probable that in those relationships in which this had occurred, the child or parent was not honest about the relationship during the interview, or the child was not available to be interviewed.

Why Strengthening Seems to Occur

The findings of this study do not perpetuate the

stereotype that elderly persons in institutions are abandoned by and isolated from their families. Although two of the six consequences represent a negative change in family relationships, these negative changes occurred in only about 10% of the families interviewed. The most predominant patterns were that of renewed and strengthened closeness and a continuation of family closeness. These two patterns, as expressed by both generations, represented over one-half of families interviewed.

The pattern of renewed closeness is especially interesting as it not only fails to perpetuate the notion that families have abandoned the institutionalized elderly, but also suggests the opposite—that institutionalization of an elderly member has served to strengthen family relations. Many respondents explicitly noted such positive outcomes of institutionalization, giving various explanations.

The most frequently cited reason was the alleviation of pre-admission strains on the family, caused by the multiple and acute needs of the parent. One whose mother's increasing disorientation had created many difficulties for several years, said:

"Now since she has been here, I can see her for what she really is—accept her confusion—and feel closer to her as a person." (Daughter, age 54)

It should be noted that portions of the interview in this study focused on events at the time of admission when the relationship may be at its worst: the parent feeling abandoned and the child feeling guilty. Improvement in this case is more likely to occur than if the interview had been before the decision to seek institutional care (Tobin & Leiberman, 1976). In any case, the alleviation of acute strains on the family by institutionalization represents an important reason for improved parent-child relations.

A second factor in renewed closeness was the physical and/or mental improvement displayed by the parent following institutionalization. This was attributed to the professional 24 hour care and skills of the institution's staff. Many families felt that they were not adequately trained to deal with the parent's problems and had felt guilty, knowing that nothing was being done to help the parent. This physical and/or mental improvement of the parent led to a greater acceptance of limitations and a more realistic approach for living within them.

Being able to spend time with the parent that was focused on socio-emotional interaction, knowing that other basic needs were being provided for, led to more enjoyment of the time spent together. Time could be spent in conversation, reminiscing, and going out for social events; as Litwak phrases it, in providing non-technical aspects of care (Dobrof & Litwak, 1977).

Another reason mentioned by respondents for the strengthening of family relationships was the parent's involvement with other residents in the facility. Some parents found themselves being able to help others and to grow close to others. The parent then had something to look forward to besides family visits. Growth of new relationships also led to growth of family relationships.

> "My father is so much sweeter now. He always valued business. Now he has learned to value other people. He cherishes his relationships with some of the other men. He feels needed. He wants to be competent." (Daughter, age 56)

During these interviews, a fairly positive attitude about aging was expressed, even though these were the families of older people and older people themselves who had suffered various degrees of infirmity.

> "Having to deal with an elderly parent helps me to cope with my own aging, to deal with attitudes and stereotypes. I see the elderly as coping very well, accepting less than optimum conditions and making changes they didn't ask for." (Daughter, age 50)

Most families felt that the trauma of institutionalization had, in retrospect, provided opportunity for learning and for growth. Few children appeared devastated by having a parent in an institution, although most had suffered some degree of guilt prior to and just following placement. The majority of parents had, after a period of time, adjusted quite well to the facility.

Many parents and children interviewed expressed the need for more extensive community services. There seemed to be a particular dearth of such services for the mentally confused. One child said she was "going to write a book on the frustration of trying to get knowledgeable and trained persons in the home to help with some of the problems associated with physical limitations and mental confusion." If in-home services had been more available, some children and parents would have opted for them. But, in looking at what was available and in realizing the need for 24 hour services, most felt that the right thing had been done.

> "The only thing I fear is that some day you will call and say that mother can't stay here because her confusion and behavior is so bad. Then, what could I possibly do?" (Son, age 51)

The interviews held with the elderly parents were often not as detailed as those held with the children. Parents tended to not share the details of pre-admission events and were more inclined to generalize the situation with words such as:

> "We felt it was time for me to come here." (Mother, age 76)

Also, parents saw the relationship more in terms of a continued closeness rather than a renewed closeness. Renewed closeness would have indicated the existence of a strain, however temporary, on the relationship. The interviews with the parents did, however, reveal positive attitudes about family and expressions of pride in what their children were doing. On the negative side, some parents did express a frustration that life had become so busy that their children didn't have much time for them. Usually, however, blame was not placed on the child, but on societal circumstances in general.

A final point to be recognized for this discussion was the satisfaction of both parent and child with the quality of care in the institution from which subjects were drawn. The idea of "shared functions" and "balanced coordination" between primary groups and formal organizations (Black & Bengtson, 1977; Dobrof & Litwak, 1977) was successfully utilized in the facility. Families felt that technical tasks, such as restorative nursing care and rehabilitation, provision of nutritious meals, and personal care and hygiene, were of high quality. The facility also encouraged the involvement of families in the nontechnical aspects of care. Family members felt welcome and comfortable when they came to be with their parents. Had quality of care been different, and had not the institution's policies encouraged parent-child interaction, the effect of institutionalization on family relationships may have been less positive.

Implications for Policy and Practice

The positive family consequences of institutionalization present a challenge for policy makers and practitioners. The identification of specific consequences of institutionalization for families and the patterns which underlie them may lead to more effective counseling for families who are seeking assistance for an elderly parent. Counseling of families following institutionalization may be more effective. Perhaps much of the guilt that so many children feel because they cannot take care of their parents could be lifted if consequences are realistically explored.

The findings here indicate that family members are involved with their institutionalized parent. The program of the institution, then, must involve not only the resident-patients, but also their children and grandchildren. Families must be encouraged to be involved and not treated as intruders within the institutional setting. Dobrof and Litwak (1977) give several suggestions for incorporating family members into the services offered to resident-patients. Some of their ideas include special Sunday entertainment for families, arts and crafts exhibits, family programs on special holidays, and days set up just to honor families such as Grandparent's Day.

The facility used for this research has an extensive program for families. Families are invited to activities throughout the year and are instructed in ways which they can give care to their parent. Orientation sessions and educational programs are also available to families so that they come to have a better understanding of long term care and of the aging process. Too few facilities do more than cater to the guilt of adult children by merely assuring that their parents will be well cared for. More institutions should actively plan orientation, information, and programmatic involvement of middle-aged children. At the policy level there should be reimbursable cost formulas worked out to include orientation and educational programs and informational letters to adult children.

In short, the focus of the institution can become a *service to families, not to isolated individuals.* Such an orientation to the family concept will not be developed in most institutions, however, until gerontologists, other concerned professionals, and the American public begin to involve themselves with the policies that regulate the definition of quality care in our long term care institutions.

Summary and Conclusion

This research questions the frequent observation that elderly persons in long term care institutions are isolated from their families, and that institutionalization is the final step in the breakdown of family relations. Data consisted of open-ended interviews with institutionalized elderly parents and with the child most involved with the parent at the time of placement (N = 100). The interview explored pre-admission events, amount and type of contact between parent and child before and after placement, and quality of the relationship prior to and following admission.

The data suggests six general patterns reflecting consequences for family relationships as a result of institutionalization: (1) Renewed closeness and strengthening of family ties (30%) (2) Discovery of new love and affection (15%); (3) Continuation of closeness (25%); (4) Continuation of separateness (20%) (5) Quantity without quality interactions (10%); and (6) Abdication: Institutions as a dumping ground. Thus, consequences of institutionalization reflect improvement; continuation; or deterioration of family relationships.

The findings presented here indicate that many elderly persons in long term institutional care are close to and involved with their families. For some families, an uninterrupted closeness before and after admission was evident. Institutionalization, in these cases, was mutually sought as a realistic solution to the parent's problems. For a large number of families, institutionalization of the elderly parent resulted in a strengthening of family ties or a renewed closeness between parent and child. A major reason for this improvement of family relationships was the alleviation of strain and pressure caused by the multiple physical and/or mental problems of the parent. For these families the effect of institutionalization was actually to enhance the relationship between parent and child.

There was little support for the stereotype of institutions as a "dumping ground" for unwanted elderly kin. Only about 10% of parent and child combinations experienced a negative effect on their relationship following institutionalization. Some parents who were not involved with their children apparently never had been in the past, so no change in the relationship was perceived. Guilt was a predominant factor among those children who did experience a deterioration of the relationship. In general, however, the families interviewed for this study were involved with each other, enjoyed their time spent together, and expressed strong feelings of family closeness and affection.

The professional 24 hour care provided by the institution can be and has been an intervention which supports the family structure. Institutions provide for the technical needs of elderly parents, and free the family to perform the nontechnical functions of its natural role as a primary group. Unfortunately, the lack of interest among constituents and advocates, including gerontologists, in long term institutional care allows many facilities to provide substandard care, thereby lending support to the negative stereotypes which surround the institution. Only when the positive consequences of institutionalization, such as those presented here, become more widely recognized and encouraged, and the factors which lead to positive consequences more fully developed, will long term institutional care reach its service potential and be accepted as part of the continuum of care offered to older people.

References

Anderson, N. N., & Stone, L. B. Nursing homes: Research and public policy. *Gerontologist,* 1969, *9,* 214-218.

Bengtson, V. L. You and your aging parent: Research perspectives on intergenerational interaction. In P. K. Ragan (Ed.), *You and your aging parent.* Univ. Southern California Press, Los Angeles, 1978.

Bengtson, V. L., & Black, K. D. Intergenerational relations and continuities in socialization. In P. Baltes & K. W. Schaie (Eds.), *Life-span development psychology: Personality and socialization,* Academic Press, New York, 1973.

Black, K. D., & Bengston, V. L. Implications of telecommunications technology for old people, families, and bureaucracies. In E. Shanas & M. B. Sussman (Eds.), *Family, bureaucracy, and the elderly.* Duke Univ. Press, Durham, NC, 1977.

Brody, E. The aging family. *Gerontologist,* 1966, *6,* 201-206.

Brody, E., & Spark, G. Institutionalization of the aged: A family crisis. *Family Process,* 1966, *5,* 76-90.

Butler, R. N. *Why survive? Being old in America.* Harper & Row, New York, 1975.

Coe, R. M. Self-conceptions & institutionalization. In A. M. Rose & W. A. Peterson (Eds.), *Older people & their social worlds.* Davis, Philadelphia, 1965.

Dobrof, R. D., & Litwak, E. *Maintenance of family ties of long-term care patients.* NIMH, MD, 1977.

Gottesman, L. E., & Bourestom, N. C. Why nursing homes do what they do. *Gerontologist,* 1974, *14,* 501-505.

Jacobs, R. H. One Way street: An intimate view of adjustment to a home for the aged, *Gerontologist,* 1969, *9,* 268-275.

Kahana, E. Emerging issues in institutional services for the aging, *Gerontologist,* 1971, *11,* 51-58.

Kahana, E. The humane treatment of old people in institutions,

Gerontologist, 1973, *13*, 282-289.

Kahana, E., & Coe, R. M. Self & staff conceptions of institutionalized aged. *Gerontologist*, 1969, *9*, 264-267.

Lieberman, M. A. Institutionalization of the aged: Effects on behavior. *Journal of Gerontology*, 1969, *24*, 330-339.

Mendelson, M. A. *Tender loving greed.* Alfred A. Knopf, New York, 1974.

Miller, M. B., & Harris, A. Social factors & family conflicts in a nursing home population. *Journal of the American Geriatrics Society*, 1965, *13*, 845-851.

Moss, F. E., & Halamandaris, J. D. *Too old, too sick, too bad.* Aspen Systems Corp., MD, 1977.

Shanas, E. Family responsibility and the health of the older parent.

Journal of Gerontology, 1960, *15*, 408-411.

Simos, B. G. Relations of adults with aging parents. *Gerontologist*, 1970, *10*, 135-139.

Tobin, S., & Leiberman, M. A. *Last home for the aged.* Jossey-Bass, San Francisco, 1976.

Treas, J. Family support systems for the aged: Some social & demographic considerations. *Gerontologist*, 1977, *17*, 486-491.

U. S. Senate, Special Committee on Aging, Subcommittee of LTC. *Nursing home care in the U.S.: Failure in public policy,* Introductory report, reports 1-7, Washington, DC, 1974.

York, J. L., & Calsyn, R. J. Family involvement in nursing homes. *Gerontologist*, 1977, *17*, 492-499.

Innovative Living Arrangements: A Source of Long-Term Care

Patrick H. Hare and Margaret Haske

Patrick H. Hare is a Washington, D.C. housing consultant who is nationally known for his work on more efficient use of the housing stock. Margaret Haske is a research associate at Georgetown University Department of Community and Family Medicine. Their article is excerpted from a paper they prepared for the American Association of Retired Persons but does not necessarily reflect AARP policy.

Data on the demand for and financing of long-term care facilities point to a need for alternatives. The rapid growth of the elderly population, coupled with efforts to reduce government spending, suggests that the demand for long-term care will outstrip the supply.

David Banks, president of a major chain of nursing homes, Beverly Enterprises, estimates that over the next decade the U.S. will require 300,000 additional nursing home beds at an estimated cost of between $5 and $6 billion. Banks states that this cost is beyond the scope of private industry (Meyer, a, 1981). Dwindling government resources suggest that this cost is also beyond the means of the public sector. Finally, with nursing home care costing about $17,000 per year, it is already beyond the means of most families (Meyer, a, 1981).

There are also statistics showing that there may be a significant number of people in long-term care facilities who do not need to be there. Inappropriate placement is widely recognized as an expensive mistake. The Congressional Budget Office has reported that between 10 and 20 percent of skilled nursing home patients and 20 to 40 percent of intermediate care patients were placed at a level of care higher than necessary. (CBO, a, 1977, p. 18). It should be noted that this picture may have improved recently due to more sophisticated methods of assessing patients' needs for purposes of Medicaid reimbursement and to a greater demand for facilities (Billings, 1982).

Even if those elderly persons inappropriately placed in nursing homes were to be deinstitutionalized, a 1977 Congressional Budget Office report indicates that the need for sheltered living arrangements and home health care would greatly exceed the supply.

Care In Community Preferable

Common sense alone dictates that, in most cases, living in a nursing home is less desirable than remaining in the community. Noninstitutional settings are less likely to sever meaningful ties and relationships. Professor William May of Georgetown University's Kennedy Institute of Ethics states: "Many nursing homes mock the word 'home' . . . These facilities are often little more than geriatric barracks." (Meyer, be, 1982)

Although some residents of nursing homes maintain ties and relationships in the community or develop new ones in nursing homes, institutionalization is often traumatic. The Congressional Budget Office summarizes several studies in a 1977 report: "To many, institutionalization represents rejection by family and friends, loss of independence, isolation, and separation from society." (CBO, a, 1977, p. 26).

Many long-term care patients already receive support and/or home care in noninstitutional settings. The Congressional Budget Office estimates in a report released in February of 1977, that 3 to 6.7 million people may be receiving basic long-term care services in the home from their families. (CBO, a, 1977, p. 17). This is far more than the 1.3 million people now in nursing homes. (Meyer, a, 1982).

Constraints on Home Care

There are, however, major constraints on the availability of care in the home. These include increased participation by women in the workforce, the desire for privacy, the need to travel to provide care to elderly relatives living alone, and the expense of formal providers of in-home services.

The initial source of informal in-home support is usually a spouse or sibling of the person in need. In other words, the "caretaker" is likely to be

"Innovative Living Arrangements: A Source of Long-Term Care," Patrick H. Hare and Margaret Haske, *Aging* Magazine, December 1983/January 1984, pp. 3-8. Reprinted by permission of *Aging* Magazine.

191

Innovative living arrangements may also increase, because older homeowners have the surplus space the baby boom generation needs.

of the same age and to have an equal likelihood of being frail. In the event of his or her death or incapacitation, the role of caretaker is usually taken over by a daughter or daughter-in-law. (Johnson, 1982). Serious impediments to providing care exist for these women, including care of other dependents, other marital and family priorities, and most important, employment. As more women enter the workforce, fewer are able to provide the services required to maintain elderly individuals in their homes.

The need for privacy is also a major factor inhibiting home care of the elderly. Research in Long Island and Connecticut shows that 81 percent of a sample population of homeowners over 55 with large homes would prefer installing separate apartments in their homes to sharing their homes with another person. Privacy, like independence, is highly prized in U.S. society.

Travel time is another problem for many family members. For example, 28 percent of the elderly live over 31 minutes away from their nearest child, necessitating an hour long trip to visit a parent. At these distances, the travel time required to provide more than the most minimal care becomes impractical for most people.

Similarly, overhead and travel are major parts of the cost of service provision for formal in-home care providers. The economy of scale of nursing home care is lost when services are disbursed throughout the community. The Visiting Nurses Association of Washington, D.C., for example, estimates that providers spend 13 percent of their time in travel and that travel and overhead costs amount to 25 percent of the total agency budget.

Problems of Living Alone

Due to the practical stumbling blocks to in-home care of the elderly, many aged people continue to live alone. This, however, is often not a satisfactory solution. Living alone limits the ability of others to provide security. The physical separation from the elderly of family and friends prevents them from providing security from the fear as well as the reality of crime and accidents.

Living alone is also a restraint on the ability of others to detect health problems before they become critical. In the home services literature, the "discovery effect" is well documented. (Stassen, 1981, p. 204.) It refers to the fact that the medical needs of isolated people often go undiscovered and therefore untreated until the problem is critical.

The numerous problems cited above make it clear that there is a need for innovative living arrangements that can both preserve privacy and reduce the financial and personal costs of providing in-home long-term care to the elderly.

Accessory and ECHO Housing

Accessory apartments are complete, independent living units installed in the surplus space of a single-family home. They result in two independent households living under one roof.

ECHO housing (also known as granny flats) refers to small, temporary, living units placed in the yard of single-family homes so that adult children can care for aging parents. Older people can also install them in their own yards and rent their houses in return for income and services. The ECHO unit is removed when no longer needed.

Both housing types create living arrangements in which two independent households are close enough to permit extensive caregiving by one household while retaining a great deal of the independence of both households.

In spite of the growing literature on accessory apartments and ECHO housing, the degree of their acceptance is not generally appreciated. There is a growing commitment to the concepts by organizations like the American Association of Retired Persons. California has passed legislation that effectively required every community which did not already permit one or the other type of second unit to amend their zoning to permit them by July 1, 1983, or submit a report explaining the reasons for not doing so. In addition, state departments of housing and/or aging have expressed serious interest in the concepts in Connecticut, Maine, Minnesota, Wisconsin, New York and New Jersey, and the list is growing rapidly. Finally, the Administration, specifically the Department of Housing and Urban Development and the Administration on Aging, are increasingly interested in the concepts.

Accessory apartments and ECHO housing provide privacy with proximity. They eliminate or reduce travel costs for caregivers. Finally, these living arrangements provide security to the elderly and make detection of health problems easier.

Shared Housing

Shared housing is another type of innovative living arrangement. Two or more unrelated individuals live in the same home, each having a private room, but, in contrast to accessory apartments and ECHO housing, they share other common areas. Shared housing may involve one or more boarders, as was common in this country prior to the 1930's. It also may involve the provision of care and services by a tenant to a homeowner in return for a reduction in rent. This arrangement for long-term care may be set up by a community agency, as it is, for example, in Madison, Wisconsin by an organization called Independent Living.

Shared housing, like accessory apartments and ECHO housing, can be an alternative to institutionalization.

Shared housing also refers to a situation in which an agency provides help in structuring communal living in a home, with all occupants sharing responsibilities. The agency, rather than the individuals, assumes ultimate responsibility for the arrangement.

In contrast to a home in which a service exchange has been arranged to meet some of the long-term care needs of the elderly homeowner, an agency-sponsored shared home often requires signed prior commitments on the part of residents that they will move out if their health deteriorates beyond some defined standard. The standard itself varies from home to home.

It is clearly possible, however, that agency-sponsored shared housing, with proper organization and age integration, can provide a source of substantive long-term care. Independent Living of Madison, Wisconsin structures service exchanges with tenants that are designed to keep older homeowners living independently. These exchanges include such services as meal preparation, cleaning, and physical therapy.

In other words, shared housing, like accessory apartments and ECHO housing, can be an alternative to institutionalization for some people. In addition, all three housing types offer the opportunity to use tenants or housemates as formal service providers. Doing so eliminates some of the major costs incurred in using formal providers of long-term care.

The Tenant-Homeowner Match

Careful matching of tenants and homeowners is a prerequisite, to insure that they are compatible.

Exchange of services in accessory apartments, ECHO housing, and shared housing requires, at a minimum, a good working relationship between the individuals involved. In culturally homogenous Denmark state-built homes with accessory apartments, called "Kangaroo housing" are used to link unrelated households to exchange services. In our society, with substantial variations in lifestyles and ethnic values, finding compatible individuals is more difficult.

If the individuals are incompatible, there is the potential for unpleasantness and for both physical and psychological abuse or neglect. Marjorie Levenson, founder of Operation Match in the Washington, D.C. area, points out that there is also a need to eliminate incorrect assumptions about service exchange during the matching process. (Levenson, 1982.)

Training and Back-Up Support

Greater availability of training for caregivers, whether family or recruited tenants, is necessary.

An extremely high proportion of skilled nursing services can be taught to a lay person, even though "intrusive" procedures and higher level skills must be left to professional providers. It appears that one of the most appropriate times for such training is upon discharge from a hospital when trainers are available and a discharge plan is made. Roughly 32 percent of entrants to nursing homes come directly from hospital discharge. However, discharge planning is generally underfunded and understaffed. The discharge planners and/or relatives are often forced to make an ill-informed immediate placement which results in nursing home care, because that is the conventional placement for the elderly. (GAO, b, 1979, p. 66.)

Some provision may also have to be made for the care receiver while training is being given to the caregiver and living arrangements readjusted. One family had an accessory apartment installed within 10 days to accommodate an aging parent, but not everyone can work that fast. In general, education about living op-

tions needs to be better integrated with discharge planning if the provision of long-term care in innovative living arrangements is going to increase rapidly.

There is another type of training that may also be useful. The formal service system for community care is often referred to as a "non-system" because of the confusing array of programs available. (GAO, b, p. 70.) With training in the types of services available, the caregiver should be able to act as a broker of services for the elderly person. The National Conference on Social Welfare states: "In many instances, family and friends should be able to assist clients in obtaining a relatively few reliable services of good quality and in monitoring their continued performance.

Support groups for caregivers are also a good idea so they can develop the assertiveness to protect themselves from excessive demands made upon their lives.

It is generally accepted that most people have a hard time adjusting to role change stemming from the dependency of a person upon whom the caregiver was previously dependent. In addition, caregivers, in general, and relatives, in particular, often have a difficult time deciding where responsibility to the care receiver ends and responsibility to themselves begins. Counseling and support groups appear to make these problems more manageable for many people. (Gray & Felt, 1982.)

The GAO reports that lack of respite care is another serious problem for families providing care to elderly relatives. Independent Living in Wisconsin will no longer set up service exchange matches unless a specific provision is made for respite care. In order for the caregiver to continue to provide services, that person's need for relief must be addressed.

Emergency back-up services are

Services to improve the ability of families and tenants to provide long-term care in innovative living arrangements are being developed.

also necessary supports for the caregiver. It has been demonstrated in England that the presence of emergency back-up services increases the amount of care that family and friends are willing to provide. The program in England assures that a doctor will come to the home within 3 hours of a request. (Heumann, 1980.) "Lifelining" is a similar service demonstrated in the U.S. in which the elderly person has direct access to emergency help. Here, as in England, the availability of such services affects people's willingness to care for those needing long-term care in an innovative living arrangement. (Sherwood, 1982.)

A Tenant's Legal Responsibility

Clarity about legal liabilities is necessary if tenants are to be caregivers in any significant number. If an elderly person is especially frail, brokering a match for someone to provide services in return for housing is similar to placement in the care of foster parents. The tenant will have agreed to provide services. It is no longer a matter of a friend following through with a favor, but a responsibility for an apparently simple task that may, in fact, fill a critical need. Until the question of tenant responsibility and liability is addressed, these arrangements cannot be confidently promoted.

One agency and a tenant it matched already have a lawsuit on their hands (Kay, 1982.) None of the agencies contacted in the course of preparing this paper were clear about the legal liabilities involved for the tenant. Most have a disclaimer which normally protects the agency from liability but not the tenant. It appears, at a minimum, that the potential liability of tenants will restrict service provision primarily to "hands-off" care.

The second half of this question is the matter of the tenant's rights. At what point is the tenant being overloaded with responsibility? Presumably, the tenant will provide more services as the homeowner becomes more frail. In one case recently reported, a tenant shared a home with a person who was independent initially but became very ill. Much more was demanded of the tenant than he had originally agreed to. The tenant will, in most cases, instinctively agree to assist with an emergency situation. It is not clear, however, at what point an emergency situation or acute illness surpasses the commitment made by the tenant to the landlord.

The lack of clear definitions of legal liabilities and responsibilities will limit the use of innovative living arrangements in general and service exchanges in particular.

New Services Spur Changes

Many of the services necessary to improve the ability of families and tenants to provide long-term care in innovative living arrangements are being developed as part of other efforts to increase the effectiveness of the informal support system. The Medicaid waiver program is a major inducement to explore and encourage alternative methods of providing long-term care. There are some in-home services covered by Medicaid, but as yet these services make up a relatively small percent of the Medicaid budget for long-term care. (CBO, b, 1977, p. 9.)

Similarly, long-term care channeling demonstrations, funded by the Department of Health and Human Services, are examining the most efficient method of providing services to long-term care patients. (Simpson, 1981, p. 11.) Many of these demonstrations involve training, respite care, and other programs needed to develop the potential of innovative living arrangements.

It is also important to note that extensive training courses are provided by the American Red Cross to families who care for individuals needing nursing services, and that there are many registered nurses who can and do give such training as a matter of course. (Seidl, 1982.)

Aged Can Provide Child Care

The potential of innovative living arrangements as a source of long-term care may also be developed to some extent by current trends, including the need of working mothers for grandparent assistance in childrearing.

Nearly 50 percent of women with children under 6 were in the labor force as of March, 1982. This figure implies a greater role for grandparenting. That role may be given a further boost by the fact that the percent of women 30 or over having a first child doubled between 1970 and 1979. (U.S. News and World Report, 1982.) The parents of this group of women will be approaching old age at the same time that caregivers' children are young, creating a double dependency situation for many working mothers.

For some families the answer to this problem will be to provide care for the elderly in exchange for their assistance in childrearing. The need for childrearing assistance is also indicated by the fact that there are now twice as many children in need of day-care as there are slots available nationwide. (Shreve, 1982.)

The High Cost of Housing

Innovative living arrangements may also increase because older homeowners have the surplus space the baby boom generation needs for small apartments. House prices are too high for many young families to afford. In contrast, about 70 percent of the elderly do own their homes, and those homes are often too large for the elderly household. (Hare, 1981.) Their housing reflects earlier income and family size and results in payments for heat, taxes, and maintenance of extra space that adds little to their lives.

One solution to this disequilibrium is the installation of accessory apartments. Another is shared housing. Both uses are likely to grow regardless of the homeowners initial need for long-term care. However, the relationships structured by the living arrangements before care is needed will increase the likelihood of care being given once it is needed. (Spohn, 1981.)

Per Capita and Public Costs

Although accessory apartments, ECHO housing and shared housing may reduce per capita costs for long-term care, these arrangements will not reduce public costs.

Private payments for non-medical services will be reduced because those services will be provided primarily by family or tenants. Housekeeping services are the ones most often used by elderly persons living alone. These services are expensive if provided by an agency. In the Washington, D.C. area, agencies charge roughly $5 an hour for housekeeping, usually for a minimum number of hours per visit (most often a 4-hour requirement).

A homemaker health aide is a worker who provides housekeeping and personal care services (bathing, dressing) and is even more expensive. The average charge for a homemaker in the District of Columbia is roughly $8 an hour for a minimum of 4 hours per visit. This cost is often charged to Medicaid. If formal services could be used for only medical needs with other assistance being provided by a family member or tenant, the total cost to the elderly person would be substantially reduced.

Private payments for medical services will increase because of the inefficiency of providing them to dispersed patients. There is an economy of scale when providing services to individuals in close proximity. Physical therapy, for example, is much less expensive to provide in a nursing home than in private homes because the therapist's

United Nations Photo/John Isaal

Many aged people live alone. Clearly, because of the problems of crime, accidents, loneliness, and the general physical separation from family and friends, there is a need for innovative living arrangements for the aged.

time and equipment are used more efficiently. In general, when medical services are provided in the home the cost of those services will be greater than if they are provided in an institution. Individuals who live in innovative living arrangements and have

medical services brought into their homes will pay more for those medical services than if they were institutionalized.

At levels of service below skilled nursing care, savings for non-medical services will probably exceed added costs for providing medical services to dispersed patients.

The "breakeven" or "savings" point will vary for each individual as a function of the individual's service needs. A person requiring frequent skilled nursing services probably would not lower his or her costs through an innovative living arrangement even if all housekeeping services were free. In contrast, a person requiring infrequent skilled nursing services, along with housekeeping or home upkeep services, could save money by living in an innovative living arrangement.

However, it is important to add to this equation the quality of life of the care receiver. Those able to afford to stay out of an institution may want to do so, regardless of an economist's abstract view of their choice. Given a choice, many people want to pay a little more for medical services in return for a much higher quality of life.

The Medicaid waiver program cannot pay significant amounts for long-term care patients kept in innovative living arrangements or it will end up paying for many people whose care now costs little or nothing. A number of attempts have been made to determine whether or not in-home services can save public funds now subsidizing institutional care. The results are not conclusive. Two complicating factors are relevant to innovative living arrangements. If in-home services and/or subsidies were provided only to individuals who would otherwise be institutionalized, a savings might be apparent.

In fairness, however, they would also have to be provided to the many individuals who already need them but are receiving necessary support from their families or by other informal means. As indicated earlier, such people far outnumber those in institutions.

The second complicating factor is the "discovery effect." This is the phenomenon mentioned earlier of more services being provided to individuals whose needs are noticed. (Stassen & Holahan, 1981, p. 204.) An isolated individual does not receive as many services as an individual in contact with other people because there is no one to respond to an isolated person's needs.

Studies show that families and friends are often instrumental in helping a person obtain services. (Simpson, 1981, p. 11.) The potential of innovative living arrangements in providing long-term care builds upon this principle. The tenant or family member sharing an innovative living arrangement may, in addition to providing services directly, help the older person obtain other services as well. In fact, it is suggested that this is a role caregivers should play. Innovative living arrangements may reach individuals who otherwise would remain underserved, thereby increasing total public costs.

In conclusion, innovative living arrangements should be encouraged as a way of reducing the institutional provision of long-term care and increasing the quality of life, but not, under existing legislation, as a way of reducing the demand for public subsidies for long-term care.

For a complete copy of this paper and references please write to: Housing Coordinator, American Association of Retired Persons, 1909 K Street, N.W., Washington, D.C. 20049.

A list of materials relating to the housing alternatives discussed in this article can be obtained by sending a self-addressed stamped envelope to: Patrick H. Hare Planning and Design, 2027 Que Street, N.W., Washington, D.C. 20009.

Alternatives to Institutional Care of the Elderly: Beyond the Dichotomy

Robert L. Kane, MD

Senior Researcher, The Rand Corporation, 1700 Main St., Santa Monica, CA 90406, and Associate Professor, Department of Medicine, UCLA, Los Angeles, CA.

Rosalie A. Kane, DSW

Social Scientist, The Rand Corporation and Lecturer, School of Social Welfare, UCLA, Los Angeles, CA.

The majority of those over age 65 in the U.S. reside in the community, enjoy at least moderate financial well-being and, although they consume disproportionate amounts of the health care dollar, perceive themselves to be in reasonably good health. Public attention, however, has increasingly focused on a different segment of the elderly—namely, the 5% who live in nursing homes or other institutions. In contrast to the first group, the institutional residents are likely to be very old, lack social supports, suffer from multiple physical disabilities as well as some degree of disorienting mental disability, and to perceive themselves in a much less optimistic light. Once an individual achieves age 65, he has one out of four chances of someday entering a nursing home (Kastenbaum & Candy, 1973). Institutional care for the aged is an increasingly expensive item in the federal budget, accounting for the fact that about 40% of the Medicaid bill now goes to services to the elderly (Hudson, 1978).

The nursing home is viewed by professional, patient, and citizen alike as an undesirable solution to the problem of dependency in old age. The call for alternatives to nursing home care has thus become a theme and a slogan spurred by public attention to fraud and abuse in the nursing home industry. The sense of outrage occasioned by the mounting bill is exacerbated by recognition that the taxpayer is not getting his money's worth.

Strong pressures, therefore, combine to encourage the search for alternatives to institutionalization for the elderly. The term "alternative" is an imprecise rallying cry; those who gather under its banner imbue the term with differeent shades of meaning depending on their own goals and reasons for dissatisfaction with the status quo. Some proponents are seeking a source of care to substitute for the institution so that a patient destined to become one of the 5% of institutional residents might be diverted elsewhere. Others have focused on the current population of nursing home residents, deriving estimates of how many might be cared for under alternative auspices. A third group champions a preventive approach, arguing that an investment in various forms of care for the elderly could prevent institutionalization in the future; here there is a lack of clarity between the goal of prevention and that of postponement of admission to an institution. Depending on one's definition of the concept "alternative," one may view the nursing home as an organization which should be phased out as soon as possible or as one which should be strengthened as a rehabilitation center facilitating return to the community.

Discussions of long-term care alternatives tend to resemble cacophony more than symphony. In addition to confusion over different meanings of "alternative," other social themes are discordantly interspersed. There is no consensus on the reasons for the pursuit of alternatives; they may include desires to check costs, prevent fraud or abuse, or provide a better way of life for the elderly in their later years. Alternatives are pursued in the hopes that they will be both better and cheaper, yet such an ideal synthesis may be difficult to achieve. There has been almost no public discussion of what should be done if alternatives prove to be simultaneously better and more costly. While such value-laden discussions have been avoided, it has been at the cost of careful discussion of the goals which alternative programs seek. It would be indeed ironic if alternative mechanisms for care of the elderly such as a home services network were developed only to prove more expensive than nursing home care without eliminating fraud and abuse or even improving the well-being of the elderly.

The problem, then, which we address in this paper is one of identifying appropriate populations at risk, the strategies which might improve their conditions (or at least minimize the rate of deterioration) and the costs of such approaches. Crucial to this process is measurement of the health and social status of the various elderly populations at risk; without this ability it is impossible to specify the advantages or disadvantages of various alternatives in terms of their anticipated

This paper is based on work prepared for the American Association for the Advancement of Science, AAAS Intergovernmental R & D Project Workshop on Health and Human Resources: The Elderly, Dec., 1978.

effects on the service recipients. In our discussion of anticipated benefits, we will also need to differentiate between long-run and short-run benefits—some alternatives may need to be put into place years before their expected benefit in terms of preventing institutional placement (e.g., preretirement counseling). It is always methodologically difficult to demonstrate the effectiveness of the preventive dollar or to make confident decisions about preventive expenditures given future uncertainties.

In assessing the costs of various alternative strategies, we require a common language which will distinguish between unit costs, program costs, and target group costs. We must apply epidemiological techniques to insure that we are comparing equivalent groups and assessing the relative benefits of alternative approaches. If, for example, alternatives to nursing home care are most useful for those who have a home in the community and it was found that nursing homes most often serve those who do *not* have a home in the community at the time of admission, discussion of the comparative effectiveness of the two modalities would be severely compromised. Similarly, researchers proposing to utilize cost effectiveness analysis must be prepared to look at the full range of costs, including the costs of services provided by family and friends as well as the basic cost of living (Doherty & Hicks, 1975). Failure to do so will lead to inappropriate comparisons between institutional care and its alternatives (U.S. Comptroller General, 1977).

The Nursing Home as a Hybrid

The nursing home evolved as a hybrid between the hospital and a family surrogate. First deemed as an alternative to family care for a growing group of elderly without family resources, the nursing home gradually took on the configuration of a more medical model, in many ways the pale imitation of the hospital.

Families have traditionally provided both instrumental caretaking and affective, companionate services to elderly members. In some situations these roles may be effectively played by other types of informal social networks. The absence of the concrete caretaking services and the inability to perform them oneself propels the individual into a nursing home; it is important to differentiate between the instrumental and affective aspects of family ties since the latter may be present or absent independent of residence in a nursing home. If the need for instrumental services is responsible for many admissions, then alternative planning requires provision of direct personal services at a low level of technology and skill. The ability to sustain someone in the community may require assistance with chores such as cooking, cleaning, shopping, personal care, managing incontinence and doing the laundry. However, the provision of open-ended services of domestic laborers may be viewed by some as a frivolous

use of tax dollars to provide luxuries at a time of growing economic austerity.

The decision to institutionalize is often made at a time of crisis, usually due to illness. The physician thus becomes a pivotal force; unfortunately, he is both inadequately trained to make such a decision and under tremendous pressure from external forces to act quickly and decisively. The path of least resistance may lead to the door of another institution like the nursing home.

Admission to a nursing home appears to be rather a final step. While it is true that almost three-fourths of the patients in nursing homes are discharged alive, the large majority of those patients are, in fact, discharged to other health facilities only to cycle back into the nursing home system. Only about one-quarter of all discharges see patients return to their places of residence (NCHS, 1978). This observation can be traced to both physical and social causes. An individual entering a nursing home may cut off his access back to the community; most importantly, housing is relinquished and cannot be replaced at anywhere near the same cost. The nursing home milieu is often counter-therapeutic. Patients are likely to deteriorate within the institution and thus become increasingly less able to leave the institution the longer they remain within it (Kane, et al., 1976). Our nursing home institutions have been characterized as custodial rather than rehabilitative; few provide the necessary rehabilitative services to encourage independent living (Austin & Kosberg, 1976), nor are they reimbursed under a system which would encourage them to do so.

The Problem of Shifting Targets

Current market conditions place a premium on the medical rather than the social model. Funds are more abundant for individuals labeled as patients rather than as clients. Reimbursement mechanisms currently favor institutional care rather than alternatives. However, it would be erroneous to simply condemn the present funding posture as one born of ignorance or oversight. The problem is a far more subtle one which may be viewed epidemiologically.

Fig. 1 is an attempt to illustrate the dilemma. The simple bar graph labeled "A" approximates the current situation in which about two-thirds of the elderly population function without any support, another 30% function with only minimal support and about 5% require substantial support. Suppose we were to develop a set of alternatives designed to reduce the proportion of individuals requiring institutionalization. These alternatives would be targeted toward the group in greatest need, but would also have great appeal for those currently functioning with minimal or no support. Providers would be especially attracted to this latter group because they are likely to make fewer demands and to show better results. The resulting distribution may resemble that shown in "B." The provision of increased services may thus lead directly to increased dependency. The likelihood of such an event will depend heavily on our ability to establish appropriate entrance requirements for such programs. These entrance-monitoring techniques will, in turn, depend heavily on the philosophic orientation of the program, that is, whether they are viewed as preventive alternatives, substitutive alternatives or institutionalization alternatives. The degree of utilization of these new programs will depend upon the social and economic incentives that are developed for them and within them.

There is no certainty that provision of additional services will actually have impact on the total amount of nursing home services rendered unless such programs are carefully tailored to meet the needs of specific target groups; moreover, each alternative program will necessarily embrace those who might profit by the service despite the fact that they are unlikely to require nursing home care. Thus, altering the centrality of the nursing home in our national care delivery system, which came about because of the interplay of economic and social forces and public policy, will not be easy.

Status of Present Policy

Our present policy for care of the aged has a strong institutional bias and our present policy rhetoric favors shifting the balance of community-based programs.

Articulation of future policy will depend upon our ability to distinguish between several types of alternatives. A basic question, as yet not directly addressed, is the extent to which funding for alternatives is expected to be offset by savings resulting from a decrease in institutionalization. If the policy to pursue alternatives is used as a legitimizing vehicle to reduce the current support for institutions, some savings may occur although the savings may have no relationship to the improvement of care.

The recent painful experience of implementing "deinstitutionalization" in state mental hospitals is illustrative of the potential problem. The policy of deinstitutionalization, accompanied by a program of community mental health center development, did not lead to a higher level of care for former mental patients (Ruchlin, 1978); in fact, the newly established community mental health centers ultimately served a different population than the ex-mental hospital patient. Ex-hospital patients placed in nursing homes and newly-created boarding homes and hotels did not find the "community" a hospitable or receptive environment (Schmidt et al., 1977). Donahue (1978) has outlined the predictable and disastrous effects of the deinstitutionalization program in mental health. It might be emphasized that while the follow-up information available (since many state mental hospitals kept no records, this information is sketchy) shows former patients almost completely bereft of services, the new policy thrust did *not* result in less money being spent on mental health services.

The experience of deinstitutionalization of the mental hospitals makes one cautious of plunging into similar initiatives for current nursing home patients (some of whom are these same former state hospital patients). Several studies have suggested that patients currently placed in nursing homes could be cared for under other auspices (U.S. Congressional Budget Office, 1977; Williams, et al., 1973); however, this is not equivalent to saying that, once in the nursing home, patients may be returned to the community. The ability to leave an institution and return to the community depends on the quality of the institution and its ability to prevent "institutionalization," as well as the availability of appropriate support systems. We have already indicated that avenues of return to the community are often cut off at the time of nursing home admission.

Policy development has been hampered by an arti-

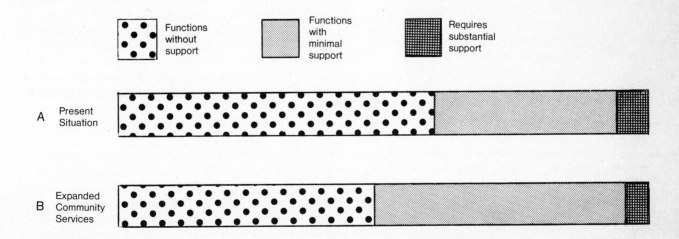

Fig. 1. Hypothetical distributions of the elderly population under two service provision programs.

ficial distinction between institutions and their alternatives. In fact, the utility of alternatives often depends on the presence of a high quality, institutionally-based service capable of diagnostic and rehabilitative functions, temporary admissions for social reasons (e.g., vacations of caretakers) and high quality of service for that subset whose social and health needs might be better met in institutions. In the British system, for example, a geriatric hospital service is used to assess new admissions in a triaging function. Those patients deemed rehabilitatable for community living are routed into appropriate treatment units. A similar program is followed in Scandinavia; these countries have discovered that successful community programming depends on ready access to health care, including flexible and reliable readmission procedures.

Unfortunately, despite the enthusiasm with which this pattern of patient triage has been adopted, there have been few hard studies to demonstrate its cost-effectiveness. Few explicit criteria for rehabilitation are available which have been tested in terms of their ability to avoid both false positives and false negatives. Long-term followup studies to document the results of a rehabilitative investment are infrequent.

Ironically two of the main thrusts for deinstitutionalization—concerns about fraud and abuse and concerns about costs—may be even more difficult to control under community placement alternatives. The greater degree of decentralization of service provision, the more difficult it will be to regulate practices. Similarly, the more numerous the units of service, the more costly the service may become. Original assumptions that community services would be cheaper were sometimes based on apples-to-oranges comparisons of a day of nursing home care with its complete housing function to the nursing and housekeeping aspects of home care *without* including the costs of shelter.

A policy that favors increasing activity in the area of alternatives may encourage providers of those services to reach out to those in less need in order to show a greater effect. To the extent that outcomes are compared to costs, the tendency to serve the most accessible and least needy will predominate. Thus recreational activities and congregate senior centers tend to serve the most socially active rather than reach out to the socially isolated. This creaming phenomenon is similar to events in the health insurance field which led to the passage of Medicare.

An antidote to such a contingency is the active pursuit of case finding and monitoring. For example, in Sweden municipalities are obliged to insure that all persons living within their boundaries receive what care and assistance they need. In Stockholm this has been translated into a detailed survey of needs and a monitoring of services received. Several programs in this country (e.g., ACCESS in Monroe County, New York and TRIAGE in Connecticut) have sought to build upon the model of the health maintenance organization and

appoint some organization—perhaps day care centers—to take direct responsibility for entire populations of the elderly within their jurisdiction. Without careful and costly monitoring, however, such a system may prove as ineffectual as Community Mental Health Center responsibility for ex-mental patients in their regions.

Status of Research

Unfortunately, research in the area of alternatives to nursing home care suffers from inadequate conceptualization of the issues, inappropriate comparisons, and fragmentation of efforts. Rarely do common premises underlie research efforts regarding definitions of good outcomes. The distinction between social and medical models emerges acutely. It is not clear what functions are to be maximized in programs at the cost of what other functions. Are there certain basic levels of outcomes that should be achieved by all in the targeted groups? For example, is it really possible to discuss the relative benefits of recreational activities vs primary medical care? If one is to choose between such alternatives, one must have a basis for determining their relative effectiveness that is not presently available. In fact, since programs are developed and evaluated in relative isolation, one is often left unsure of the comparability of different populations or even the extent of services received in addition to those of the program being evaluated.

Focusing the research effort.—One sign of the medical-social schism is the dichotomy between the major types of instruments proposed to identify the needs and outcomes of patients. The Department of HEW has championed a Patient Appraisal, Care Planning and Evaluation (PACE) Program which was developed by a consortium of universities. This instrument places heavy emphasis on the medical and nursing needs of long-term care patients—the PACE instrument and its derivatives may be said to represent the medical model. In contrast, the Duke Center for the Study of Aging and Human Development, under funding from the Administration on Aging, developed a multidimensional functional assessment tool known as the OARS (Older Americans Resource and Services Programs) method. The OARS instrument uses data self-reported by the client to assess five general areas of impairment (social resources, economic resources, mental health, physical health, and activities of daily living) and may be said to represent the social model.

This instrument has been the keystone in a study conducted by the U.S. Government Accounting Office with the collaboration of Duke Univ. Utilizing the OARS instrument to measure various categories of impairment, 118 service agencies in Cleveland have been testing a procedure for disaggregating the actual components of service provided to individuals. When this system is in place it should be possible to measure changes of impairment level over time and to link the rates of those changes with the provision of comparable units of service; it will also be possible to examine natural rates of changes in impairment which occur in the absence of any particular service (Maddox & Dellinger, 1978). The disaggregation of services currently breaks out 25 functions in three general categories; these are basic living components (such as living quarters, transportation, unprepared foodstuffs), supportive care elements (such as periodic checking, continuous supervision, meal preparation), and remedial care components (physical therapy, nursing, counseling, retraining).

Another dimension to the issue is the question of identifying appropriate target groups. Data from several research projects suggest that different groups of patients may do better under different auspices.

In a quasi-experimental study, Mitchell (1978) compared cohorts of VA patients receiving nursing home care and home care. She found that the patients with the best prognoses tended to do best on home care while those with the worst prognoses did best with nursing home care. In general, those patients who received home care had fewer limitations in terms of their functional status index; and the functional status index at the outset of the experiment was the best predictor of future functional status.

Weissert (1978) has similarly expressed a note of caution about comparisons between adult day care and nursing homes. He notes that day care is not intended to be a wholesale substitute for nursing home care, but is appropriate for that subset of nursing home patients who should not have been placed there in the first place or who no longer required such services. He also provides an important distinction between the day care center (also termed the multipurpose day care center) and the day hospital. The former tends to put far more emphasis on social, recreational and nutritional services while the latter is more firmly based in the medical model.

The importance of the effort to establish units of service cannot be exaggerated. The fact that this seminal effort is taking place does, however, highlight issues about the instrument used to measure the impairment. The OARS instrument has the advantage that it is self-administered, non-instrusive and relatively inexpensive. Its use in this context points up a number of issues. For example, the current level of analysis uses highly aggregated measures of impairment in order to make the calculations manageable. A number of assumptions are made in that process: Impairments in different categories are equivalent; various degrees of impairment for a given item can be usefully reduced to a dichotomy; various patterns within a category are equivalent. Much the same questions can be raised about the admittedly simplified classification of services. The effort at finding a common taxonomy for services suggests that a service has an intrinsic effect. It may well be that the effectiveness

(and certainly the efficiency) of a given service will depend upon the context in which it is delivered.

Nonetheless, this effort represents an important beginning at addressing the issue at the heart of any discussion of alternatives to nursing home care. Clearly, further work will be needed to determine what level of aggregation of data is most useful in targeting impairment, what specific items are most associated with overall impairment, and how useful the instrument is in predicting future needs.

The whole question of the validity of self-report must also be given hard scrutiny. There is some evidence that the aged often present an optimistic picture in questionnaire responses, partly because they make comparisons to situations which "could be worse." It is also possible that once problems occur affecting housing, relationships or any particular area, a halo effect will influence all responses in a negative direction. In descriptions of populations, the under- and over-reporting might balance out; however, when further correlations are made to service requirements, the under- and over-reporting may introduce distortions that call all conclusions into question. Finally, there is the caveat that once an instrument is used as the basis for policy decisions (e.g., for allocation of services or resources) it is inevitably subject to contamination (Campbell, 1975).

Demonstration projects—Often service delivery approaches are first developed in the demonstration project context. In the U.S., the widespread concern over the cost of nursing home care and its deficiencies led to the series of demonstration projects funded under the authority of Section 222 of Public Law 92-603. These projects were intended to produce comparative data about the relative cost effectiveness of covering day care and homemaker programs under Medicare in six sites.

Unfortunately, the wide variation in the program activities, program costs and program participants across the several sites rendered summative evaluation difficult. Some intriguing tendencies emerged from the reanalysis of the data by staff of the National Ctr. for Health Services Research that attempted to control for the multiple confounding variables. Mortality rates were generally lower among those receiving expanded benefits than those who did not use them. Those using day care benefits had fewer SNF days and were more likely to retain their level of functioning than were the controls; no similar effects were seen with users of homemaker services. For both groups, however, the total Medicare payments were greater for the experimental groups than for the controls (Weissert et al., 1979). It must be recognized that these findings cannot readily be generalized in view of the potential for self-selection in utilization of the expanded benefits.

This extensive investment in the Section 222 Projects, together with several other federally sponsored projects of a similar nature (e.g., the Connecticut Triage project which used a quasi-experimental design to compare outcomes of clients receiving intensive coordinated services with those receiving regular care) highlight the difficulties in this type of research. Perhaps the most critical problem is the lack of a clearly defined research protocol. All too often, either by policy or circumstance, the evaluation effort is grafted onto a demonstration project already underway. If we are to invest in expensive *prospective* experiments such as these, they should be undertaken with well-conceived protocols, clearly delineated analysis plans and tight research designs.

Developing a technology for alternatives.—So much attention has been given to development of services to substitute for the nursing home that comparability with nursing home care has seemed to be the usual focus of research. There has been very little organized investigation of various packages within an "alternative" program. For example, it would be of interest to know whether hospital-based home health differs in any way, including cost, from home-health programs based in health departments or community agencies. It would also be important to explore the implications of the proprietary movement in home health, day care, and homemaking services to determine whether the auspices of the service or other organizational factors are associated with different outcomes. It would be useful to develop a research agenda around the various mixes of personnel that could be utilized on service delivery teams.

A well-developed research agenda in each specific program area (i.e., home health, day care, etc.) would begin to address questions framed in terms of the actual goals these programs can hope to achieve. As stated earlier, the elderly individual may have both instrumental and affective needs which cannot be met by relatives. Is it possible for the same personnel to meet both the practical and emotional needs of the client? Are such needs often enough combined in the same individual to make such dual focus on the part of the homemaker or health aide useful? Can one make effective use of nonprofessional workers who share the client's background or of elderly individuals themselves as workers or volunteers? What kind of day care programming is most helpful for various target groups? Should primary health services be linked to day care programming? Is it possible to develop streamlined techniques that would reduce the costs of home health and homemaking services? A host of similar program-specific questions suggest themselves. Thus far we have only made rudimentary beginnings at development of a technology for any of the alternative programs and have devoted more attention to finding ways of making alternatives cheaper than institutional care than to developing the most cost-effective approach to each individual alternative.

In the area of housing, there has been some research attention given to the desires of elderly persons and the adjustment levels associated with different kinds of housing patterns. For example, there is some preliminary data associating age-segregated housing with higher survival rates compared to age-integrated housing (Harel & Harel, 1978). Brody (1978) and her colleagues are conducting a multifaceted project to examine the effects of various community housing arrangements; an intriguing early observation from this work is that individuals who decide not to move from their former housing have an increased mortality rate, compared to both those who follow through with moves to the sheltered housing and those who make other independent moves. Sherwood et al. (1978) used a quasi-experimental design to compare effects of admission to a medically-oriented sheltered housing project among physically impaired elderly with a carefully matched group of applicants who were not admitted. Results indicate that significantly fewer of the experimental group were admitted to long-term care facilities during the followup period. At the same time, the mortality rate for the experimental group was also lower. On the other hand, the experimental group experienced more hospitalizations and incurred more acute hospital days than did the control group. This decreased mortality rate among movers was also found in Carp's eight-year followup of a San Antonio housing project, but she also noted better health indices among the experimental group (Carp, 1977).

The decision to enter an institution, to leave an institution, or to seek alternative community services deserves some attention because of the growing body of research regarding the importance of personal control in the life of the individual (Seligman, 1975). It has been found among elderly groups in particular that the adverse effects of institutionalization may be an effect of lack of choice in entering the facility and that mortality rates on relocations may be due again to lack of choice rather than transfer trauma; Schulz and Brenner (1977) have reconciled opposing research findings through this explanation. We are just beginning to develop research thrusts that address the problem of reversing some of the deleterious effects of institutionalization, including the phenomenon of "learned helplessness" (Mercer & Kane, 1978). A hypothesis worthy of study is that alternative programs such as home health or day care may not be able to prove effectiveness unless they are chosen willingly by recipients.

Impact of Research

It is difficult to point to any direct relationships between the research going on in the area of alternatives to LTC and the changes in policy for those alternatives. These decisions appear to depend more on political pressures than on empirical information. As is often the case in this type of social research, the findings are not sufficiently clear that they can be unequivocally presented. Advocates for alternative points of view are more likely to cite selectively those points which support their preconceived position. Adding to this problem is the state of the art. The vast bulk of information, both from this country and abroad, is anecdotal rather than analytic. The few exceptions to this rule present findings from small numbers of cases from which generalizability is difficult. The lack of clear-cut, unambiguous results substantially reduces the impact of any research. Unfortunately, statistically significant differences on derived scales are not easily translated into meaningful results for the decisionmaker.

The problem of utilizing knowledge to assess the costs and benefits of alternatives to nursing home care may be illustrated by a simplified decision tree such as that shown in Fig. 2. We begin with a distribution of patients (or clients) which can be stratified according to a set of definable characteristics; these might include demographic characteristics, functional status, income, assets, family and friends, and individual preferences. For each subset of patients, a placement decision is made. For the purposes of the model here we have shown the decision as a dichotomous one between the nursing home and an unspecified alternative. The alternative could refer to a specific single alternative or some combination of services.

Once assigned to either nursing home or the alternative, a proportion of patients will have been suitable and a proportion unsuitable for the assigned service. The placement for each group will lead to one of several outcomes. At a point in time it is then possible to examine the results from each contingency. These results may be expressed as a function of the costs accrued to date and the state of the patient. (The latter can be expressed in a variety of ways from the amount of support required to some comprehensive measure of health status or some measure of self-actualization.) The question of how to weigh different combinations of outcomes (e.g., improved physical functioning, decreased mental status, improved life satisfaction) introduces a further wrinkle: whose value system should be used to determine the utility weights for the various probabilities? Should the patient's values always be used to determine utility weightings or, for publicly supported programs, must we tap the value system of the public?

The model is presented to illustrate several points:

(1) We lack the techniques at present to measure many of the results.
(2) We lack the data to estimate the probabilities.
(3) The number of different combinations of services and patient characteristics is vast.

Nonetheless, the model does serve as a framework to guide our work by identifying the kinds of research questions that need to be addressed. Where empirical data become too cumbersome or costly to collect, we will have to rely on expert judgment gathered in an organized fashion. Even this level of subjective data may be useful in distinguishing those alternative

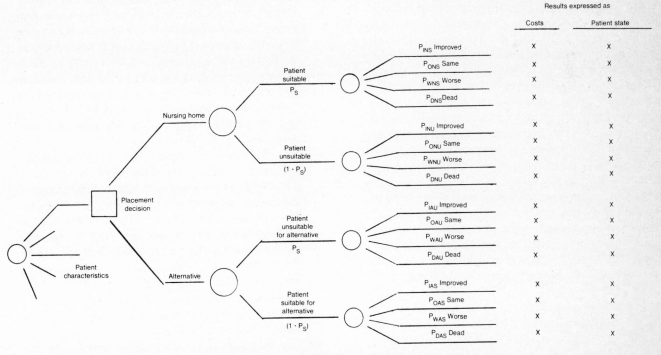

P_S - Probability of pt being more suitable for NH than for alternative

P_{IXY} - Probability of patient improving given a placement X and suitability Y (of placement)

P_{OXY} - Probability of patient staying the same given a placement X and suitability Y (of placement)

P_{WXY} - Probability of patient getting worse given a placement X and suitability Y (of placement)

P_{DXY} - Probability of patient dying given a placement X and suitability Y (of placement)

Fig. 2. Decision tree for placement of LTC patients.

packages that appear to have the most potential for serving defined subgroups of the elderly.

Technology Transfer

The discussion up to now might suggest that we have little definitive knowledge to transfer into practice. On the other hand, within the last decade there has been considerable summarizing activity of our knowledge to date in the area of LTC and its alternatives.

Similarly, there has been attention in the professional and lay press on the subject of long-term care and a growing number of national meetings have turned their attention to aging, including the economics of aging. The Health Care Financing Administration of DHEW has announced its intention to formulate a clear long-term care policy. This policy may separate long-term care from the rest of health care financing in anticipation of a program of national health insurance.

The need for better education of health professionals and others engaged in the delivery of services to the elderly has begun to be recognized (Inst. of Medicine, 1978). While that debate may continue for some time as to whether the providers of geriatric care should be geriatric specialists or generalists with additional training in geriatrics, there is general recognition that the training of physicians, nurses, social workers and others must be substantially augmented to offer information on aging and the aged. This training should include biologic and social aspects of aging, techniques for caring for the aged, services needed by the aged and the problem faced by the aged in obtaining these services.

A related problem in technology transfer concerns the fragmented delivery system for alternative programs. Presently the numerous small programs created under the Older Americans Act as well as an assortment of small and large voluntary and proprietary agencies are responsible for delivering the alternative programs (Binstock, 1978). In some instances, the funding base is too small to afford innovation; in other instances the competition between organizations and the pressure to show the best organizational results militates against careful coordinated application of research knowledge about targets most at risk and how to reach them.

Finally, one must address the problem of incentives for action. In the nursing home area, application of technology has certainly lagged behind its development, largely because there have been no incentives in the industry for improved performance. Technology directed toward achievement of particular outcomes is unlikely to be applied in alternative programs either unless appropriate incentives are developed to encourage the organizations to try to achieve the outcome. Reimbursement mechanisms seem the most likely kind of incentive which will foster transfer of technology.

In summary, there is currently great enthusiasm for the development of alternative models for institutionalization of the elderly. There is less evidence, however, that any type of technology is being transferred to buttress this enthusiasm on a foundation of meaningful information. Until the issues noted above are more widely discussed and some level of reconciliation achieved, it is unlikely that a great deal of progress will be made.

Recommendations

Before we can define our goals we must know more about where we want to go. We offer the following recommendations as next steps toward clarifying these goals. These recommendations are addressed broadly to both those who would undertake the tasks and those who would commission them.

(1) A clear delineation of the alternative mechanisms to provide long-term care must be developed with a common vocabulary and a consensus as to measures of the outcomes, target populations, and costs that will be considered.

(2) Preliminary decision analysis strategies should be utilized to evaluate the most feasible routes toward dealing with subsets of the population. Decision analysis will necessitate a clarification and specification of what types of outcomes we wish to maximize and how these different outcomes should be weighted relative to each other. The repertoire to outcomes should be broad enough to encompass socially desirable ends such as happiness and quality of life as well as the more usually considered elements such as functional status and costs.

(3) Methodological issues in measuring health status of the elderly must be clarified; these include testing the validity and reliability of self-report and the predictive as well as face validity of the measures.

(4) Specific research should be directed toward developing the concept of common units of service so that costs can be compared across differing programs (e.g., a refinement of the work described by Maddox and Dellinger (1978). This research should place particular emphasis on assessing the context in which such service units are delivered.

(5) The emphasis on developing alternatives to nursing homes should not obscure the need for careful study of the cost-effectiveness of various strategies *within* given alternatives (e.g., day care, home health, sheltered housing).

(6) The enthusiasm for alternatives should not detract from the need to improve institutional care. A finite proportion of the elderly will continue to need care in such institutions, either as a prelude to reentering the community or as a strategy of choice. The need for careful targeting of institu-

tional programs to subgroups of clients is crucial. In this regard, attention should be given to determining the best solution-based technology for serving extremely disoriented individuals.

(7) More attention should be given to the potential role of sheltered housing as an efficient and highly satisfying mode of delivering service. If priorities are given to the study of different kinds of alternatives, the sheltered housing concept seems to merit the highest consideration.

(8) To aid in the development of appropriate alternatives, further research must be conducted around the abilities of different family groups to provide care for the elderly. Here we must distinguish between physical care in the home of the relative, physical care in the home of the aged person, and emotional support.

(9) On the other side of the coin, the process of deinstitutionalization, especially in early phases, merits careful descriptive study. If it becomes a matter of policy to remove individuals from institutions to alternative arrangements, records should be kept of the kind of alternatives implemented and their outcomes at various time intervals. Follow-up of representative samples of those discharged is important to provide a minimum data base about the effects of deinstitutionalization policies in terms of the outcome measurements—health status, happiness, etc.—that have been developed. Here we would wish not to replicate the problem of mental health organizations which implemented deinstitutionalization programs but did not determine what happened to the individuals discharged.

(10) New methods of financing and developing incentives for providers to use technology must be considered. Emphasis here should be placed on reimbursing providers on the basis of the outcomes achieved (Kane & Kane, 1976). Such a comparison would require the development of adequate predictors of function for either individual clients or well-defined subgroups of clients.

(11) Professional education of physicians, nurses, social workers and other service providers should be augmented to include sufficient information on aging and the needs of the aged to allow these professionals to function effectively as both providers of care and brokers at those critical times when decisions about institutional placement are made.

References

Austin, M., & Kosberg J. Nursing home decision-makers and the social service needs of residents. *Social Work in Health Care*, 1976, *1*, 447-456.

Binstock, R.H. Federal policy toward the aging. *National Journal*, 1978, *10*, 1838-1845.

Brody, E.M. Community housing for the elderly: The program, the people, the decision-making process, and the research. *Gerontologist*, 1978, *18*, 121-129.

Campbell, D. T. Assessing the impact of planned social change. In G.M. Lyons (Ed.), *Social Research and Public Policies*, (1975), Hanover, NH, The Public Affairs Ctr.

Carp, F.M. Impact of improved living environment on health and life expectancy. *Gerontologist*, 1977, *17*, 242-249.

Doherty, N.J.G., & Hicks, B.C. The use of cost-effectiveness analysis in geriatric care. *Gerontologist*, 1975, *15*, 412-417.

Donahue, W.T. What about our responsibility toward the abandoned elderly? *Gerontologist*, 1978, *18*, 102-111.

Harel, Z., & Harel, B.B. On-site coordinated services in age-segregated and age-integrated public housing. *Gerontologist*, 1978, *18*, 153-158.

Hudson, R.B. Political and budgetary consequences of an aging population. *National Journal*, 1978, *10*, 1699-1705.

Inst. of Medicine. *Aging and medical education*. Washington, DC, National Academy of Sciences, 1978.

Kane, R.L., & Kane, R.A. *Long-term care in sex countries: Implications for United States*. DHEW Publ. #NIH 76-1207, USGPO, Washington, DC, 1976.

Kane, R.L., Olsen, D.M., Thetford, C., & Byrnes N. The use of utilization review records as a source of data on nursing home care. *The American Journal of Public Health*, 1976, *66*, 778-782.

Kastenbaum, R., & Candy, S.E. The 4% Fallacy: A methodological and empirical critique of extended care facility population statistics. *Aging and Human Development*, 1973, *4*, 15-21.

Maddox, G.L., & Dellinger, D.C. Assessment of functional status in a program evaluation and resource allocation model. *Annals of the American Academy of Political and Social Science*, 1978, *438*, 59-70.

Mercer, S.O., & Kane, R.A. Helplessness and hopelessness in the institutionalized aged: A field experiment. *Health and Social Work*. (in press)

Mitchell, J.B. Patient outcomes in alternative long-term care setting. *Medical Care*, 1978, *16*, 439-452, 1978.

National Center for Health Statistics. A comparison of nursing home residents and discharges from the 1977 National Nursing Home survey: United States. *Advancedata* No. 29, GPO, Washington, DC, May 1978.

Ruchlin, S. When schizophrenia comes marching home. *Psychiatric Quarterly*, 1978, *50*, 202-210.

Schmidt, L.J., Reinhardt, A.M., Kane, R.L., & Olsen, D.M. The mentally ill in nursing homes: New back wards in the community. *Archives of General Psychiatry*, 1977, *34*, 687-691.

Schulz, R., & Brenner, G. Relocation of the aged. *Journal of Gerontology*, 1977, *32*, 563-573.

Seligman, M. *Helplessness*. Freeman, San Francisco, 1975.

Sherwood, S., Greer, D.S., & Morris, J.N. A study of the highland heights apartments for the physically impaired and elderly in Fall River. In T. Byerts (Ed.), *Gerontological Monographs*, Garland, NY. (in press)

United States. Comptroller General. *Home health—the need for a national policy to better provide for the elderly*. HRD 78-19, GPO, Washington, DC, 1977.

United States. Congressional Budget Office. *Long-term care for the elderly and disabled*. GPO, Washington, DC, 1977.

Weissert, W.G. Cost of adult day care: A comparison to nursing homes. *Inquiry*, 1978, *15*, 10-19.

Weissert, W.G., Wan, T.T.H., & Livieratos, B.B. *Effects and costs of day care and homemaker services for the chronically ill: A randomized experiment*. DHEW/NCHSR, Hyattsville, MD, 1979.

Williams, T.F., Hill, J.G., Fairbank, M.E., & Knox, T.G. *Appropriate placement of the chronically ill and aged: A successful approach by evaluation*. Journal of the American Medical Association, 1973, *226*, 1332-1335.

Social Policies, Programs, and Services for Older Americans

It is a political reality that older Americans will be able to obtain needed assistance from government programs only to the degree that they are perceived as politically powerful. Political involvement can range from holding and expressing political opinions, voting in elections, participating in voluntary associations to help elect someone or some party, and holding political office.

Research has indicated that older people are just as likely as any other age group to hold political opinions, are more likely than younger people to vote in an election, are about equally divided between being Democrats or Republicans, and are more likely than young people to hold political office.

Older people, however, have shown little inclination to vote as a bloc on issues affecting their welfare. Current activists, such as Maggie Kuhn and the leaders of the "Gray Panthers," have encouraged senior citizens to vote as a bloc, but so far they have not been successful in convincing them to do so.

Gerontologists have observed that the major factors contributing to the increased push for government services for the elderly have been the publicity on their plight generated by such groups as the National Council of Senior Citizens and the National Retired Teachers Association, and adult children's desire to shift the financial burden of aged parents from themselves to the government. The resulting widespread support for such programs has almost guaranteed their passage in Congress. While service programs for older Americans have required an increasingly larger share of the national resource, to date there has been no organized resistance or opposition to these programs. Moreover, these programs are being administered by a sizable group of young professionals, whose careers are dependent upon the programs' expansion.

Looking Ahead: Challenge Questions

What new programs should the federal government institute in the next five years to assist older Americans?

What service programs for senior citizens could be more efficiently handled by state and local governments than by Washington? Give some examples.

Are some of the current service programs for senior citizens not working well? Should they be changed or eliminated? Give examples.

As senior citizens' consciousness is aroused by the ever-increasing publicity about their problems, will they be more likely to vote as a bloc?

Do you agree with Mary Burnett that the elderly are often abused in the name of protection? Explain why or why not.

Model Project Reduces Alienation of Aged From Community

Patricia Rowe

Patricia Rowe was formerly Editorial Assistant for Aging Magazine.

By the year 2000, there will be an estimated 30 million older persons in the United States, 95 percent of whom will continue to live independently in their communities. This lifestyle will necessitate innovative approaches to community-based delivery systems if their independence is to be meaningful.

To help meet the needs of those elderly living in the community, the Administration on Aging funded the *Mutual Help for Community Elderly: A Mutual Help Model.*[1] Conducted from July 1, 1976 to December 31, 1979, this model project sought to gauge the effectiveness of a community based, neighborhood service delivery system built on the concept of involving the elderly in "mutual help" opportunities. The agency developed

[1] Free copies of the two-volume report are available from Phyllis Ehrlich, Rehabilitation Institute, Southern Illinois University, Carbondale, Illinois 62901.

to test the mutual help model of service delivery was the Benton Neighborhood Program for the Elderly in Benton, Illinois. The grant for the three-year period, including the research component, amounted to some $300,000.

The basic structure of the mutual help model consists of a decentralized program of small groups built on natural neighborhood boundaries. Each group utilizes the ability of its elderly members to organize, assess their own needs, and then plan to meet these needs primarily through their own efforts and resources. Thus, each group, with its emphasis on neighborliness, as well as neighborhoods, provides an organizational opportunity for the elderly to be both providers and recipients of services.

Several sociological studies related to the model have indicated that the critical distance for adequate use of services and facilities for the aged is three blocks with a neighborhood defined as no more than ten blocks. Social ecology research suggests that social and personal interventions for the elderly can be most effective when they are available to them within this distance.

Much research has documented the lack of formal service utilization by the aged. A study completed by sociologists E. Kahana and B. Felton in 1977 in Detroit indicates the tendency of two distinct ethnic populations to bring problems to significant others who live in the neighborhood rather than to formal agencies.

There appears, then, to be agreement in gerontological literature that, as social scientist, M. Cantor, asserts,

mately 2,000, or 28.9 percent, of its 7,000 residents were elderly and because the community lacked formal service programs for the elderly. A further reason for this choice was that the elderly residents appeared to place strong reliance on personal autonomy—a factor highly interrelated with program philosophy.

Predominantly a coal mining town, Benton's other occupational opportunities include business, the education system, and the county government, which have spawned a small professional class of lawyers, judges, and others. Members of the younger generation are leaving the town and those that remain tend to maintain the occupations and living patterns of previous generations.

The 1973 area agency on aging plan documented that other than a few services and the usual, but limited, assistance of public aid and Social Security offices, there were no formal services in Benton—to say nothing of a network of services—to meet the elderly's needs. It listed a number of professional and intermediate nursing homes, but their services had an institutional focus with no community orientation.

Shirley McCann, Benton's City Commissioner and Board Chairman, explains how her "romance" with the mutual help concept began in 1976 when Phyllis Ehrlich contacted the mayor to discuss the idea she had to help the elderly.

"At this time," she recalls, "I was a freshman City Commissioner and very interested in social programs for Benton. Mayor Mundell, representatives of the Oakwood Senior Citizens Club—the only organized group of elderly in Benton, consisting mainly of the residents of a small Housing Unit—and I met with Phyllis. She was considering submitting a proposal to demonstrate the mutual help idea in Benton. After hearing the concept of this terrific program and what she wanted to do for us, I must admit my first thought was, 'We should be so lucky; we'll never see her again.' Well, thank God—we did!"

"Social support tasks most essential to mental health can be carried out on a day-to-day basis by neighbors and friends . . . ."

Traditional service delivery systems have been designed to meet specific needs of the elderly through categorical programs provided in a continuum from agency to client. Although this system frequently attempts to involve the elderly in some phases of service planning and delivery, such involvement is usually token and, at best, minimal.

A Neighborhood Where Everyone Has Moved

In 1969, Phyllis Ehrlich, Project Director of the *Mutual Help Model Project* and Assistant Professor of the Rehabilitation Institute at the Southern Illinois University at Carbondale, opened a community action agency for the elderly in a neighborhood of University City, Missouri, that was already characterized as a neighborhood in which "everybody has moved." Since it was suspected that this was not true for the elderly, a store front office was rented, the area was bombarded with brochures in English and Yiddish, and a population identification and needs

assessment study was organized. Trained volunteer interviewers climbed the steps of every three-story apartment house in the area and located 1,000 elderly in a neighborhood where "everyone had moved." At the end of a year and a half, in spite of the application of recognized community organization techniques, there were only about 100 elderly residents highly involved in the successful social action program. At the city sponsored senior center, one saw that the same people who attended the Jewish Center in the area were now taking advantage of the new program as well. The other 900 in this geographically close neighborhood, which had been bombarded with information and visible services, were still behind closed doors.

This experience convinced Ms. Ehrlich of the need to design a new service in which the elderly themselves were the service providers for each other. The neighborhood focus was based on her belief that if "Mohammed can't come to the mountain, the mountain should go to Mohammed."

Small Town America

Mrs. Ehrlich chose Benton, Illinois, as the site for her neighborhood mutual help project because approximately

8. SOCIAL POLICIES, PROGRAMS, AND SERVICES

Community Workers

The primary criterion for hiring staff for the mutual help model project was that they be Benton residents because they would bring knowledge of their community to the program, and increase the potential for the program's continuation after the Federal funding period. Twelve half-time community workers were hired. The criteria for selecting workers, in addition to residence in Benton, was a history of community involvement, such as church or civic activities.

The community worker conducts outreach to all homes in the neighborhood to locate the elderly, organizes the operation of neighborhood groups, and assists both mobile and homebound elderly to work together. The community worker also works with other agencies and community organizations, encouraging linkages between elderly residents and the community, and performs such administrative functions as record keeping or statistical work determined through staff planning.

Betty Cunningham relates how she became a community worker:

"I heard about the job with the Benton Neighborhood Program for the Elderly from my daughter, Carolyn. She had heard the announcement on the radio and knew I was looking for a part-time job. The job was supposed to be two and a half days a week but our enthusiasm soon turned it into three days and more.

"I was interviewed by Phyllis Ehrlich and told there were no education or age requirements. She wanted people who were concerned about people and who had been active in school and church work. I think I was hired because of my excitement about people getting together and helping each other, or helping someone in need."

All workers were given a two-week intensive orientation/training program before the initial outreach period. The orientation program, developed with the cooperation of Southern Illinois University faculty and the Illinois Department on Aging staff, included lectures in social gerontology, physiology of the aging process, group leadership and community skills, and interviewing techniques.

Outreach as Phyllis Ehrlich describes it is "a never ending process." It is important, she stresses, to make initial contacts with as many elderly as possible so that "they know a program opportunity is being brought to them."

Betty Cunningham recalls outreach efforts on the part of workers to identify and find the hard-to-locate and the first meeting of one of the neighborhood groups:

Armed with coffee and goodies, each of us fanned out to greet the long-dreamed-of neighborhood group.

"Phyllis had already been in Benton a month getting an office, a secretary, and lists of elderly from various sources, like the United Mine Workers and different clubs. The Precinct Captains of both Democratic and Republican parties supplied lists and told us who was 60 and over. To get other lists, we went to churches and clubs, etc. We got lists every place we could. We began to sort out names using the telephone book, the city directory, and local contacts.

"On Saturday, before the first meeting of a neighborhood group, we mailed letters to each person who had been initially contacted, telling them of the upcoming meeting. Armed with coffee and goodies, each of us fanned out to greet the long-dreamed-of neighborhood group. Our secretary told us people would come to anything if we had food. Much to our surprise and delight, the neighbors came. I found, at the very first meeting, that these people didn't know who lived on their block. As time passed, they got acquainted with each other at the meeting and because most of them walk, they would stop on their way to and from the meeting to visit with neighbors in yards and small gardens. The group meetings are like a big happy family reunion now."

According to Carolyn Neafus, another Benton community worker, the community worker must become a familar face on the streets of the neighborhood. A worker who stays in the office can't do the job she says. Visiting the active participants, the non-participants, the homebound, the isolated, the storekeepers, and "gatekeepers" of the neighborhood are key responsibilities. Involvement of neighbors is the effective way to pyramid people-to-people contacts, she asserts, because one worker can't do it all.

She remarks: "It is impossible to fill all the needs of the elderly without the help of the neighbors and the neighborhood group. I begin every group meeting with that all-important question, 'Do we have anyone in the neighborhood who needs help or do you know of anyone who is sick?' We also discuss any casework that we have been involved in as a group. This is not gossip; the group members are really interested in the well-being of their neighbors."

Traditional case work or counseling implies a one-to-one helping relationship between a worker and client, but according to Ms. Neafus, historically the elderly have not requested such services in large numbers. Work with individuals in the mutual help model, she relates, is more broadly interpreted to include enabling the well elderly to meet daily needs, as well as providing counseling or direct service for the frail elderly, and it develops through the group process.

She reports on the case of an 86-year-old woman who was a complete recluse. Mrs. W's home was located in a busy neighborhood but appeared to have been abandoned some years ago. Before the neighborhood group began, many of the neighbors did not even know the house was occupied. Mrs. W. had some contact with other agencies in the community but everyone saw her as a difficult person and believed she belonged in a nursing

---

The first time I called on her at her home, she was very hostile towards Benton. She spoke about how her neighbors never spoke to her except for a passing nod, but after joining the Autumn Leaves, Mrs. X's outlook changed entirely.

---

home. But with the help of the group and an FHA grant, Mrs. W was able to get a new bathroom, heating system, and screening for her front porch. Neighbors have taken her food, house slippers, and other household items and have provided many needed services that would never have been possible before.

"Neighborhood" Becomes a Household Word

At the end of 12 months, the community of Benton had 10 well-established neighborhood groups. The director, community leaders, and participants observed that "neighborhood" had become a household word for the Benton elderly. One major value of participation in a neighborhood group was the elimination of loneliness and isolation through social experience with people living nearby.

Weekly or bi-monthly meetings became the place to enjoy oneself, share news about neighbors, develop plans to assist if needed on a one-to-one basis, and to speak out regarding community problems. The concept of membership was expanded to incorporate neighbors who were homebound as well as mobile.

During the 17-month period, 350 elderly participated through attendance at meetings; 131, though homebound, received help through worker or group contact; 139 received case management assistance from the worker or group; and 680 came to the office for such traditional services as assistance with completing forms or emergency needs. The challenge to the project, as it developed the neighborhood unit programs, was to re-educate and thus reverse the service policy that places the elderly solely in the recipient role by working with both the elderly and community service system.

Winter Emergencies

A report on neighborhood group activities during the January 1977 and 1978 winter crises provides an example of the impact of the mutual help model on the Benton elderly and the community.

During both winters extremely hazardous weather and inadequately cleaned streets made even the mobile elderly homebound, but the 1978 winter crisis affected the elderly in their pocket-

---

A 92-year-old woman, who had been totally opposed to the program at its inception, called to offer her home if someone was out of fuel.

---

books as well. A lengthy coal miner strike at the same time led to the cut-off of pensions for the large number of retired miners in the area and made it also impossible to get coal for home heating. In 1977, at the start of the program, community workers responded as best they could to such emergencies as frozen water pipes, lack of food, or refilling of prescriptions. In January 1978, workers' outreach phone calls to group participants indicated active neighborhood networks which included assistance, particularly with shopping, from neighbors' children as well. A 92-year-old woman, who had been totally opposed to the program at its inception, called to offer her home if someone was out of fuel. One group member called to offer money to pay for coal for an isolated neighbor who had never come to the meeting but about whom the group had become concerned.

In preparation for the winter season, the staff had developed a Youth Emergency Corps, again using the

neighborhood concept to recruit and assign volunteers. The youth program had problems in its operation but was important for snow shoveling. The higher involvement of the elderly participants and the activation of the youth emergency service thus freed the staff to provide new services, including contacts with the union and coal companies to obtain and deliver coal to the elderly and handicapped. This service became vital not only to the elderly but to other Benton residents in need as the staff and ministerial alliance worked together.

Satisfaction With The Program

A survey taken of both participants and non-participants in the Benton community shows a very favorable response to the project. A total of 78 percent of elderly participants were rated as "very satisfied," 94 percent of relatives of the elderly felt the program was "excellent," and 97 percent of community leaders rated the project as "very good." An analysis of the Mutual Help Model indicates increased development of friendships and helping relationships, greater involvement in community concerns, and a reinforcement of social roles with a community orientation (as distinguished from home or family) through increased participation in social organizations and church activities.

"The first time I called on her at her home, she was very hostile towards Benton. She spoke about how her neighbors never spoke to her except for a passing nod, but after joining the Autumn Leaves, Mrs. X's outlook changed entirely. She became acquainted with her neighbors and they became acquainted with her. When Mrs. X was ill a couple of winters ago, friends from the group checked on her on a regular basis and carried meals to her. Mrs. X also carried food to other group members when they were ill. Mrs. X moved out of the Autumn Leaves neighborhood a year ago into an isolated area on the other side of town. There is no neighborhood group organized in this area, and Mrs. X has reverted to her previous hostile attitude and her behavior and isolationism have become a real concern. She *needs* a neighborhood group with which to identify."

One 75-year-old Benton resident, who was a worker involved in the project, noted that, "The most wonderful thing that has happended in my group, called the South Benton Neighbors, is the fact that a lady of 82 who had lost the will to live, to have friends in her home, has been made to know that her neighbors care about her, love her, and

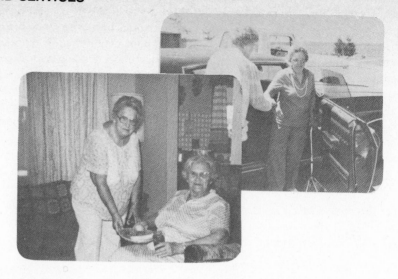

want her love and friendship. She had Parkinson's Disease so bad she could not drink liquid except with the aid of a tube without spilling it. She shakes so badly, crumbs fall from a cookie while she is trying to put a piece into her mouth. She now attends the meetings regularly and knows everyone will make her welcome and has helped by buying some cookies. She plays bingo with the group with the aid of others. She has been living in a shack, where she had a little coal and wood stove for heat. We were able to get her into the government housing project on October 31, 1977."

Many activities developed in Benton during the demonstration period suggest program ideas that can be adopted by other services. These included: neighbors helping neighbors with shopping and laundry, regular phone calls to shut-in neighbors, helping to hang a door in a neighbor's house, picking up groceries for a sick neighbor, inviting a lonely neighbor for Thanksgiving dinner, spending time with a neighbor after the death of the neighbor's spouse, transportation for a neighbor to visit a sick relative in a distant city, helping a neighbor with the physical work of moving, or visiting neighbors at home, in the hospital, or in the nursing home.

Social Activism

Carolyn Neafus also talks about the mutual help model's successful efforts to raise the social consciousness of the elderly in the communities where the neighborhood projects have been set up. She comments:

"Many times we organized the elderly of the community for social betterment. Participants and staff attended

After hearing the concept of this terrific program and what she wanted to do for us, I must admit my first thought was, we should be so lucky; we'll never see her again. Well, thank God—we did!

County Board, City Council, or Township Board meetings. It is difficult to organize the elderly for this purpose. In a small town they are not accustomed to speaking out for social or community betterment We did get them one by one. After a few meetings they were pros."

The Benton Neighborhood Program for the Elderly is now an established agency in the community, funded by the Illinois Department on Aging, with matching funds from the City, Township, and County governments, as well as from individual contributions and participant projects.

Its presence ensures that a portion of the town's elderly, at least, will have the social interaction and services support needed to maintain them as viable and integral parts of their community.

At the time of selection, it was suggested that the findings of a demonstration program developed in Benton could be applicable to the large part of the United States representing "small town" America. It was also felt that the similarity of problems for the urban and rural elderly are greater than their differences, indicating the potential application of this research to larger communities as well.

The program's emphasis lies not in a strong centralized structure but in the decentralized location of the service and the implementation of the mutual help concept. The neighborhood groups are not intended to replace formal agencies as service providers but to add to the community's resources by organizing the informal and formal systems into a supportive network.

The staffing pattern for the model is a traditional one, including the supervisor who serves in an administrative/supervisory position. The responsibilities of the local residents who serve as community workers are a blend of outreach worker, group worker, case manager, and community organizer. To provide program continuity, paid workers rather than volunteers are recommended. Each full-time worker could be assigned three groups, or neighborhoods, plus short term or special assignments.

In the mutual help model, the participants and staff *are* the program. Community workers, as local residents, represent the agency during working hours and afterwards—in the office, supermarket, or church. Considering that staff spend the majority of their time outside the office and that they may be part-time as well, it is essential that there be one day when no regular neighborhood meetings are held. This allows for staff meetings and supervisory conferences as well as the opportunity to build team work.

The model is based on the assumption that services for the elderly can be designed to reinforce social roles, increase opportunities for reciprocal relations, and prevent or delay the loss of roles and independence.

A major factor mitigating against the continuation of a satisfying life style in old age is the change caused by social role loss. Many, studies have documented declining social roles and their effect on the aged population, but the mutual help philosophy believes that social role loss need not be irreversible.

The neighbor role is reinforced in a flexible manner which takes into consideration the changing physical health needs and the abilities of the elderly. The process enables the elderly to participate in the neighbor role just as younger aged people can, rather than only adjust to progressive role loss in this area.

Participation in the neighborhood group program provides a social role opportunity as a group member. The roles of friend, group leader, or participant offer new leisure role opportunities while reducing the potential for social isolation and loneliness—factors related to social role loss. At this level, the roles of neighbor and group member are integrated, creating within the neighborhood an alternative to isolation and role loss, with its consequent perception of uselessness.

For some there is yet another community level of social role opportunity including leadership roles as social activist and community organizer. The opportunities for such activities move far beyond reversing negative social isolation and instead center on positive involvement in community betterment.

Gerald Caplan, in a 1974 study on *Support Systems and Community Mental Health*, explores a positive community environment and concludes that individual responses during crises are influenced not only by stress and the individual's ego strength, but by the quality of emotional support provided by social networks. He saw even superficial links with neighbors as significant and encouraged their support by the professional community, but cautioned that such networks should not be forced into a professional mold.

GERIATRIC DAY CARE

The Options Reconsidered

Eleanor Gurewitsch

Mrs. Gurewitsch, who recently completed her doctoral studies at the Union for Experimenting Colleges and Universities in Cincinnati, has written a number of articles in the field of gerontology.

In most instances it is extremely difficult, if not impossible, to make arrangements for third party reimbursement of day care facilities in the U.S. Physicians who are well aware that in many instances day care would be a desirable alternative to full-time institutionalization do not normally have this option available to them.

Supposedly in the interest of economy, most medical payment providers aren't yet willing to reimburse for day care service. It seems ironic that it is precisely those groups which have the greatest interest in cost containment with respect to health care for the elderly which have raised the most serious roadblocks to the establishment of geriatric day hospitals in our country.

I have talked with administrators of hospitals, skilled nursing homes, intermediate care facilities, extended care facilities, homes for the aged, even of senior centers, who have the space

for and the interest in establishing geriatric day care facilities. In each case the failure to do so can be directly traced to the nonexistence of third party reimbursement. How many patients can a day care center hope to attract, even at a modest daily rate, when payment must come from the patient's own pocket? For the medically indigent, full-time institutional care is virtually gratis (it is the taxpayers who pay) and therefore a "better buy," even if the per diem cost to the taxpayer exceeds the modest day hospital charges.

Even members of the middle class with their private health insurance policies tend to think along similar lines. Insurance will pay for expensive hospital care; it does not yet reimburse for geriatric day hospitals. For the individual, institutionalization becomes the more economic solution to nearly every problem.

I wrote my first article about a geriatric day hospital in 1974. At some length I described for readers of Switzerland's Neue Zurcher Zeitung the Felix Platter Day Hospital in Basel. Because this day hospital was designed after an English model, I subsequently travelled to England to visit the Cowley Road Hospital in Oxford which was the first English day hospital

(opened in 1958) and presided over by Dr. Lionel Cozins, who pioneered the entire concept. On this same occasion I visited the day hospital at Manchester which is administered by Prof. J. C. Brocklehurst, Professor of Geriatric Medicine at the University of Manchester, Prof. Brocklehurst has a particularly innovation-oriented setup. In the autumn of 1978 I had an opportunity to visit several day hospitals in the States, and to complete the circle so to speak, during 1979, I participated briefly but intensively on a regular basis in the work of a Swiss geriatric day hospital in a rural setting.

Visiting many different kinds of day hospitals in three different countries has clarified my thinking on this subject. It has permitted me to meet many individual patients for whom day care is unquestionably the more satisfactory, less expensive long-run solution. But I have also met a smaller number for whom the expense of geriatric day care seems to be warranted only on a very short-term basis, if at all. Yet for these persons as well, some kind of sheltered day care is obviously essential if institutionalization is to be avoided.

The reluctance of the reimbursers to take on the commitment to subsidize geriatric day hospital care is under-

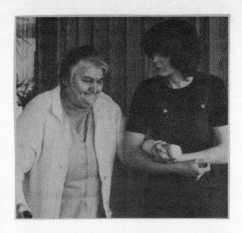

standable. Theoretically, care of a frail individual who returns home to his family each night should be less expensive than institutional care around the clock. The ideal geriatric day hospital patient does have someone to return home to. The key words lie in the phrase—*returns home to his family*. Relatives, friends, neighbors, a "significant other," or informal communal living may be able to provide an adequate support system. But this arrangement usually proves to be either unrealistic or extravagantly expensive in practice unless the frail elderly person actually lives under the same roof with one or more people committed to assisting with his or her care on a long-term basis.

The stubborn, rugged individualist who wishes to live alone, within his four walls, and expects not only reimbursement for access to a geriatric day hospital several days each week (including door-to-door transportation of course) but, in addition, requires cooks, nurses, cleaning help, and other support personnel, more or less on a round-the-clock basis makes third party health care providers understandably uneasy.

Under these conditions, the experts are in complete agreement. Geriatric day hospital care plus an expensive, third party paid personal support team at home is no bargain. With perfect justification private insurance companies and government-funded health plans do not to offer to pick up the tab for that kind of care for our most senior generation.

Several geriatric day hospitals are described below. Their experiences tend to confirm one point made above.

The ideal geriatric day hospital patient does have someone who provides physical and moral support at home during non-hospital periods.

There is another aspect to this entire matter. Even when a community provides geriatric day hospital care, inpatient care, and social centers for comparatively healthy, independent seniors, not all of the required alternatives are necessarily being offered. The English doctors Woodford-Williams and Alvarez have suggested that there must be additional gradations and have commended what are, in effect, four tiers of sheltered geriatric day care ranging from day clubs, workshops for the elderly and day wards through genuine day hospitals.

Day hospitals are of several general types. Some are rehabilitative in character, others calling themselves by the same name, are basically sheltered, somewhat medically oriented long-term "holding operations." (No one honestly expects a relatively healthy woman of 95 to recover her lost youth and a totally independent mode of operation.)

A Rehabilitation Day Hospital

The first patient entered the Rehabilitation Day Hospital of Jacobi Hospital (part of the Bronx Municipal Hospital Center) in May 1977. Experiences with this program to date have been most positive.

The program offers intensive rehabilitation services that have tentatively been provided on an outpatient basis. To be eligible for the Rehabilitation Day Hospital, patients must have appropriate diagnosis (diagnostic groups of particular interest are cerebrovascular dysfunction, amputations, and other muscoloskeletal problems). The patient must be at least 15 years of age (this is not a geriatric program, although a large number of patients fall in this age group) and have a family member or friend capable of caring for him or her at home.

Patients who are interested in receiving rehabilitation in the day hospital are screened. Their "helpers" and home conditions are screened as well.

Inpatients and outpatients get identical rehabilitation programs. The basic difference is that a family member (or friend) of the day hospital patient receives one or two days of special training geared to the needs of the patient for whom he will assume responsibility at home. The day patient has round-the-clock MD access coverage, and the patient's "helper" has been trained to recognize when to make use of this service.

A majority of the patients have had strokes or amputations. Results indicate that day hospital patients return to normal society and to their families sooner than inpatients. Their families are more involved in an understanding of the rehabilitation program. In addition, according to the administrator of the program, patients are reluctant to drop out when their intensive rehabilitation training is concluded. It seems likely that modified post-rehabilitation daycare may be a logical next step.

Setting up a Rehabilitation Day Hospital has vastly expanded the capacity of the hospital. At present there are 37 inpatient beds available on the Rehabilitation Medicine Ward. Now it is possible to treat 20 additional patients on a day hospital basis. Outpatients get transportation by ambulette. This has included patients who live in fifth floor walk-ups.

The positive human aspects of living at home coupled with hospital rehabilitation are immediately obvious for those patients fortunate enough to have someone to care for them at home. The financial aspects are equally appealing. The day care outpatient charge is $66 per day plus the ambulette charge. Inpatient charges are reimbursed by Medicaid at the rate of $373 per day. Thus the daily rates are $373 versus $99 daily. But the actual saving is even higher. Inpatients receive no therapy on weekends and holidays, but their per diem must be paid in any case. Day patients are charged only for actual rehabilitation therapy days. Additional expenses at home have not been calculated here. Family members or friends are assumed to be contributing their time on a voluntary basis.

The rehabilitation day hospital described above is obviously not a typical American institution. For other reasons the day hospital directed by Prof. J. C. Brocklehurst which is attached to the large geriatrics ward of the University Hospital of South Manchester (England) is not precisely typical either. In Manchester day hospital, patients (some of whom may have recently graduated from in-patient status) share elaborate rehabilitation facilities with inpatients. The average number of visits a patient makes to the day hospital is approximately 13. This day hospital provides medial treatment and rehabilitation programs tailored to the medical needs of the individual patient and helps train him for daily living at home. The day hospital has a more or less typical home style kitchen and bathroom where patients can practice skills they will need in their own homes. There are various kinds of stairs. Patients learn to negotiate the stairs most like those they have in their own residences.

As part of the day-hospital package in Manchester, social workers and nurses visit with the patient in his home and help rearrange furniture and equipment to permit the patient to achieve the maximum possible independent or semi-independent living after dismissal from the day hospital.

There is a Geigy Unit for Research in Aging based on the biological and sociological aspects of gerontology located in Manchester, and Prof. Brocklehurst serves as its director. Much attention is given here to developing new techniques, medications, and also new equipment and methodology to ease the various problems which arise with advancing age.

Adult Day Care in the Bronx

In 1973 HEW funded four model projects related to day care hospitals and health centers. One of them was a "Day Center for the Elderly in a Community Center Setting." It is located in the Mosholu Montefiore Community Center in the Bronx, New York which offers a variety of services to all age groups. Included are a nursery school for young children, after-school activities for junior and teenagers, physical education and cultural arts programs for people of all ages.

By a fortunate coincidence, the entrance to the Mosholu Montefiore Community Center building is located about 200 yards from the out-patient section of the Montefiore Hospital and Medical Center. This particular Day Center was able to continue in existence after initial three-year HEW funding expired in 1976. New York State agreed to fund this program on an exceptional basis. The official brochure describes the situation in the following words: "The Day Center for the elderly is funded by the State of New York through Montefiore Hospital and Medical Center. This program is designed to maintain frail and impaired elderly in the community and is considered as an alternative to institutionalization."

Coming into the day center, one becomes quickly aware that the room set aside for the frail and impaired elderly is small and overcrowded with a group of 35-40 people. There are some activities going on—crafts, conversations, discussions of future outings, but there is no semblance of hospital-type care or a hospital-like atmosphere.

People participating in this program have lunch in a large dining room shared with healthy older adults from the senior center program which is under the same roof. Those from the day center program who are able to do so may also share in club and other activity programs conducted on a regular basis for the "well elderly."

Everyone I spoke to who is involved with this program in any way is totally convinced of its importance. Most say, however, that it is "not necessarily

cost-effective, rather that it is benefit-effective." Costs run to $22 per person per day which, it must be pointed out in all fairness, includes not only sitting space in a crowded lounge-type room, but also includes visits, as required, with doctors and psychiatrists and trips to the therapy rooms in the hospital next door. There is also the help in the day center proper of two RN's, an LPN, an occupational therapist and occupational therapy clinic, and a social worker. Transportation charges, also paid for by Medicaid, are extra. The Center has a contract with the same cab company that serves the hospital. Dr. Myron Gilbert of the Montefiore staff who is Physician-Consultant to the program tells of patients "so arthritic it is hard for them to move within the center. They would otherwise be in a nursing home." He refers also to patients with "psychological problems, organic brain syndrome, senility, and loss of contact."

Dr. Gilbert says flatly that most of the 35 to 40 patients who come to the day center daily would "not be able to survive without this program. Many are people living alone—in total isolation." Dr. Gilbert goes on to compare their daily lives with what is considered the worst penal punishment worldwide—solitary confinement.

Geriatric Day Care in a Swiss Setting

The Bronx is not New York City and even less is it New York State or the United States. Attractively situated suburban day care is available in suburban sections of our country. I have visited a day hospital in the gar-

denlike setting of The Burke Rehabilitation Center in White Plains[4] and in an equally attractive though vastly different southern setting at the Palm Beach County Comprehensive Community Mental Health Center in Florida which serves patients under psychological stress (patients with all degrees of mental, emotional or social disturbance). Here patients have ample time, space and attention.

We cannot wave a magic wand and transform older overcrowded inner city buildings into spacious modern facilities, but it is surely useful to have realistic yet attractive models to study and hopefully to emulate. With that thought uppermost in my mind, I spent enough time in an innovative new Swiss day hospital in a rural setting to become well acquainted with staff and patients alike. Below is a brief description of how this one day hospital functions, how it is integrated into the other health facilities available in this community. The lessons it offers are self-evident.

Affoltern am Albis is a political unit called a *Bezirk*. Within its boundaries are 14 separate communities with a total population of 27,000. In other words, it is definitely a rural setting. In the capital of this Bezirk there is a hospital which has an older building for acute care patients and a new one nearby for long-term patients, most in the senior citizen class.

In this modern long-term care hospital which accommodates 70 inpatients, there are 13 patients who come on a daily basis. Most arrive in a small converted Volkswagen bus chauffeured by a young psychologist who works half-time for the hospital. He drives about 100 kilometers daily and picks up the patients at their doorsteps in two tours. He is far more than "just a chauffeur," he is a key member of the caring team.

Upon arrival, the first patients sit in a spacious lounge room which they share with ambulatory patients from the hospital. They chat, play games, drink tea, and if needed take medication, and have their blood pressure checked. By the time the second shift of patients arrives, it is close to ten

a.m. All move to the physical therapy room where there are simple gymnastics and games performed in a sitting position, some done to music. The class lasts about an hour. The group is presided over by an RN and an LPN who take turns leading the gymnastics exercises. By this time it is 11:15. The group goes back to the lounge for lunch, prepared in the hospital kitchen and keyed to the individual needs of the patients if this is required. Then it is time for a rather long nap. The women share a room with eight beds, the men have one with four. Since many of these people cannot walk independently and some need help in using the bathroom, the more robust patients often help some of the patients who are less independent.

About two p.m., when naptime is over, the patients and the nurses return to the lounge where they sit and chat over coffee and cookies or cake. During this period post-stroke patients often go for individual physiotherapy, others have an opportunity to visit the hairdresser or the dentist, or take advantage of other hospital services as required. The balance of the afternoon is spent in a large room on the ground floor set aside for arts and crafts. During this period the room is used exclusively by members of the day hospital group. The day hospital staff members devote much time and thought to individualized craft projects and set up work which results in attractive objects most of which are subsequently sold in the hospital store. In view of the very limited abilities of some of the patients, this is a very creative effort on the part of the staff. On nice days the patients can take walks. Some of the patients seem to spend a great deal of time lost in their own thoughts, but they are always a part of the group in any case.

This hospital is different from American day hospitals I have visited partially because patients do have an opportunity to sleep during the day. Another difference is the large degree of integration this program has with other facilities for seniors in the local communities (homes for the aged, hospitals, household service in homes,

and visiting nurses). Every month, representatives of the major health care and social agencies meet to discuss common problems and individual patients. For example, if a patient must move from a day hospital to a home for the aged, he may continue to visit the day hospital for a transition period. Staff members from both organizations discuss with each other the special needs of each individual. People who can live independently in the daytime but panic frequently at night, can use the sleeping room of the "day hospital" as a "night hospital." There is a team spirit among these delivering health and social services to seniors, and the patients are moved from one facility to another with a certain style and grace that is not evident when groups seem to be competing for clients or areas of jurisdiction.

Dr. Peider Mohr is in charge of the day hospital as part of his duties in the Affoltern hospital. He was responsible for establishing the day hospital and is one of its most ardent supporters. He is the first to admit that his hospital's cost accounting is such that it is not possible to demonstrate exactly what the day hospital per patient costs are. Nevertheless he has been able to obtain public and private health insurance reimbursement for day care. Insurance reimburses for 32 francs* of the 40 franc per day charges. The patient pays the remaining 8 francs plus a 12 franc transportation charge. The total charge is 52 francs daily, 20 of which is supplied by the patient. Patients come on the average of 2-3 times per week. The fact that they are able to come to the day hospital often makes the difference between continuing to live at home or being forced to accept placement in an institution on a permanent basis.

The photos shown here are of some of the Affoltern Day Hospital patients during a one-week vacation at a hotel on the shores of Lake Lucerne. They give the impression of people who are, to some extent robust and capable of independent living. The pictures are

---

* At present writing $1.00 = about 2 Swiss francs; or one Swiss franc = fifty U.S. cents.

misleading to a certain extent. Some of these people cannot walk unassisted, others have poor vision, and still others suffer from such poor memory that they cannot be left alone for any length of time. A few are post-stroke patients with a fairly positive prognosis.

A young housewife and mother is more likely to look after an aged relative if she has relief on a regular basis. For many of the day hospital patients, the medical care, reactivation, and socialization received are important, but the improved prospects for long-range home and family living, thanks to regular relief time for those family members in charge, are often more important. Even people with a tendency to self-sacrifice and martyrdom break down when faced with a long-range untenable work load. Caring for a household with young children and aged parents often constitutes such a long-range untenable responsibility.

Some of the women patients are married to men who still work full-time. Since their wives are looked after adequately during working hours, these devoted husbands are able to keep their wives at home.

The staff members of this day hospital team are dedicated young people who give their patients care which is warm and loving, not just merely competent. The atmosphere is truly remarkable, totally unlike the resignation which often afflicts both staff and patients of long-term, round-the-clock care facilities.

The English experience is corroborated by what I saw at Affoltern. The majority of elderly day hospital clientele do not require very sophisticated medical care most of the time (at Affoltern a staff doctor normally spends about 3 hours weekly with the patients—more of course if this is required). Sheltered day care centers,

less expensive than real day hospitals of the type described earlier in this article, could easily be incorporated into many senior centers and homes for the elderly. The robust elderly could be encouraged and trained to assist their frail contemporaries who are sharing a facility on a temporary basis.

In Zurich the city is building sheltered senior apartments, residential homes for seniors, and skilled nursing homes at a rapid pace in order to cope with the problems which arise when more than 20 percent of the population is in the 65 + category. The buildings now moving from the drawing board to the construction stage in Zurich are nearly all designed with supplementary day care facilities. In addition many have public rooms for use by neighborhood seniors as well as full-time residents, and coffee shops open to the general public.

Acquainting older people with residential facilities in a non-threatening way is important. The person who enters a building regularly as a day care patient will, in addition to the immediate benefits, have a long-term advantage. Because he already knows the buildings, some of the permanent residents, and some members of the staff, his entrance on a full-time basis will be less traumatic.

Subjecting older people to an unfamiliar and, simultaneously, permanent entrance into a long-term care facility, suitcases in their hands, is cruel, however essential the move to the facility may be. Attendance at a day care program in the same building or, if there is no alternative, merely to a program in a similar type of institution, will do much to ease a transition which is difficult under the best of circumstances.

The need for adequate day care for

the frail elderly far exceeds the supply at present. Public and private insurers are not going to take the first steps. Whether the impetus will come from the medical community or from the seniors themselves remains to be seen. Perhaps a coalition of both groups would be the most effective. Already, in scattered communities, groups are renovating unused schools and hospitals (both school and hospital buildings are in oversupply in many locations) and trying to establish adult day care facilities. Help is needed in this effort—both at the local and the national levels.

REFERENCES

"Geriatrische Tagesspitaler, Beispiel Felix Platter Klinik in Basel," Gurewitsch, Neue Zurcher Zeitung, May 17, 1974, page 24b.

"Four Years' Experience of a Day Hospital in Geriatric Practice." Wood E. Woodford-Williams and A. S. Alvarez. Georontologia Clinica, Vol. 7, 1965. pp. 96-106.

"The Geriatric Day Hospital." J. C. Brocklehurst. King Edward's Hospital Fund for London, 1973. p.13-14.

"Rehabilitation Day Hospital," Department of Rehabilitation Medicine, Bronx Municipal Hospital Center, and the Albert Einstein College of Medicine of Yeshiva University. Jacobi Hospital, Room 2N28. Bronx Municipal Hospital Center, Pelham Parkway South, Bronx, N.Y. 10461.

"Services of the Aged," Mosholu-Montefiore Community Center, 3450 DeKalb Ave., Bronx N.Y. 10467.

"The Day Hospital: An Alternative to Institutionalization." $3.00. The Burke Rehabilitation Center, 785 Mamaroneck Ave., White Plains, N.Y. 10605.

"Pal, The Miracle on 45th Street," Palm Beach County Comprehensive Community Mental Health Center, Inc., 1041 45th St., West Palm Beach, Fla. 33407.

"Das Alterspfiege-Modell Affoltern am Albis". Peter Rinderknecht, Zeitlupe, Das Senioren-Magazin. Postfach, 8027 Zurich pp. 6-14. Provides supplementary information about this hospital. October 1978 No. 5.

"The Geriatric Day Hospital," p 14.

"Directory of Adult Day Care Centers," U.S. Health Care Financing Administration. Washington D.C. U.S. Government Printing Office, 1978. 116 pp. $3.

The Elderly Person

Joan M. Krauskopf and Mary Elise Burnett

Joan M. Krauskopf is a professor of law at the University of Missouri-Columbia School of Law.

Mary Elise Burnett is a third year law student at the same school of law.

Thomas G. Kochel

When Protection Becomes Abuse

The number of elderly persons in the United States has rapidly increased since the beginning of this century at which time it totaled three million. As of 1981, the older population had increased to over 26 million persons representing 11.4 percent of the total population.[1] It is currently projected that by the year 2000, there will be 35 million individuals age 65 and older, representing 13 percent of the total population.[2]

As this segment of the population has grown, various groups, organizations and individuals have demanded recognition of the rights of elderly persons. One such right of the older individual is to retain as much autonomy as possible. This requires that the remaining segments of society recognize the fact that aging does not automatically render a person incapable of caring for personal needs or financial affairs.

The increase in demand for autonomy creates a conflict with the theory that the older population requires protection due to its vulnerability. As evidenced by reports of elder abuse and neglect, there is definite need for some of the protective aspects of current legislation. However, these laws also can be a source of abuse. The form may be as blatant as trying to gain control over substantial assets, or as subtle as limiting a person's autonomy merely because of differences in values concerning lifestyles.

Reprinted by permission from *TRIAL* magazine, December 1983, pp. 61-76, The Association of Trial Lawyers of America.

Caught in the middle of this conflict is the attorney who is asked to represent the elder person. What is his or her role to be? The attorney must decide if it is to be that of a strong advocate for the "legal rights" of the client, or that of a "guardian" offering representation within the attorney's perception of the client's "best interests."[3] The trial attorney who sees her or his selection to represent an elderly person as an opportunity to preserve or vindicate individual rights has a growing body of law and services with which to work.

"Protective" Devices

Three areas of recently enacted or revised legislation that have a protective purpose, and yet are potential sources of abuse, involve guardianship/conservatorship, involuntary civil commitment and elder abuse.

The current trend in the first area is to separate the concepts of guardianship of the person and conservatorship of the estate. Theoretically, the purpose of such a distinction is to allow the individual to maintain as much control as possible with the court ordering only the assistance necessary to ensure the person's well-being, whether it be physical or financial. This reasoning is also the basis for a legislative trend toward providing for a limited guardianship or a limited conservatorship. The court should impose only those specific limitations on a person's liberty necessary to ensure basic physical or financial well-being. The limitations should be the least restrictive possible to protect the elderly person only, rather than others who would benefit from controlling the person or preserving his or her property. The duties and powers given to the limited guardian or limited conservator should be specifically delineated and designed to encourage the individual's self-reliance.

The second area of the law which has incurred change is involuntary civil commitment. As expressed by the United States Supreme Court in *Addington v. Texas*,[4] the possibility of involuntary commitment poses a substantial threat to a person's liberty and thus requires procedural due process protection.[5] There has been a noticeable movement in court decisions toward holding that substantive due process requires five basic findings which must be supported by evidence in order to justify an involuntary commitment. These five are:

- that the individual is mentally ill;
- that the individual is dangerous to others or himself;
- that the individual is in need of care or treatment;
- that the proposed commitment is the least restrictive necessary for the protection of the public or of the individual;
- if the commitment is for the protection of the individual alone, that he or she lacks the ability to decide if taking that action is desirable.[6] Most recent state commitment statutes expressly or impliedly require these five findings as well.

The third legislative area experiencing recent activity concerns elder abuse. Due to different definitions of what is considered abuse of the elderly, the statistics vary concerning the extent of the problem. Typically, the definition includes physical, psychological, and financial abuse. Following are some of the more common forms of abuse. The forms are not mutually exclusive. *Physical abuse* includes: lack of personal care (38 percent), lack of supervision (38 percent), bruises and welts (31 percent), lack of food (19 percent), direct beatings (15 percent). *Psychological abuse* often includes: verbal assaults (58 percent), isolation (58 percent), fear (50 percent) and threats (46 percent). *Material or financial abuse* often includes: misuse of money or property (46 percent) and theft of money or property (12 percent). A fourth category of abuse includes *extremely unsatisfactory individual environment* such as dirt in the house (38 percent) and odor like urine in the house (19 percent).[7]

A number of states have legislation covering abuse. The statutes may be one of three types: adult abuse legislation with a mandatory reporting requirement; elder abuse legislation with a mandatory reporting requirement; and adult or elder abuse legislation with no mandatory reporting requirement. Generally, the minimum age for the elder abuse legislation is from 60–70 years old.

Inroads into the elder person's autonomy with such a statute can exist in the form of the "protection" or "solution" to the problem. Institutionalization or imposition of a guardianship frequently is used, both of which can be devastating to the person striving to maintain his or her autonomy.

Potential for Abuse

These current trends serve very important purposes in that people often do require help in management, health or protection. However, upon the institution of guardianship/conservatorship or involuntary commitment proceedings, the potential for loss is tremendous. Imposition of an unlimited guardianship or conservatorship can result in a complete deprivation of personal rights and civil liberties. The individual is reduced to the legal status of a child, generally losing the rights to contract, make gifts, write checks, to vote, to marry and to obtain a driver's license.[8] The psychological impact of being deprived of the right to care for one's personal needs and the right to control one's financial matters can destroy one's sense of self worth entirely. For the elderly individual struggling to maintain independence and self-esteem in the face of forced inactivity due to mandatory retirement, the loss of control over assets earned as a result of his or her efforts may be a severe blow to the individual's sense of integrity.[9] Involuntary commitment takes on the additional specter of the loss of physical freedom and forced submission to medical treatment.

With either of these proceedings, in addition to the loss of personal and economic freedoms and rights, the elderly person also could suffer from the stigma of having been adjudicated of unsound mind.[10] The guardianship proceeding has a particularly threatening nature under a typical statutory scheme that allows a person to be involuntarily committed by his or her guardian who asserts that it is in the ward's best interest.

The problem with the elder abuse statutes is of a more hidden character. While these statutes do not directly involve the loss of personal and economic rights or freedoms, there does exist the potential for diminishing one's autonomy. Theoretically, elder abuse statutes are identical to child abuse statutes promulgated on the theory that a child, because of age and circumstance, is in need of protection. This assumption is not as accurate for an elderly population as it is for inexperienced and uneducated babies and young children. To the contrary, most people over age 65 do not need protection. To proceed on the theory that they do creates possibilities for abuse. Mandatory reporting, required in a number of states and common to child abuse statutes, reinforces the ageism that with age one needs help, further infantilizing the older population as a whole.[11]

The elder abuse statutes have the potential to replace personally initiated commitment and guardianship as a means of controlling and eliminating the autonomy of the very individuals the statutes were enacted to protect. Typical of this type of "elder abuse" statute is that of Missouri which requires reporting and "protective" action when there is a "likelihood of serious physical harm." In this statute, three of the four types of physical harm which form the basis for interference with a person's life involve, not what others have done to the elderly person, but rather the person's own inadequacies.[12]

The statutory protections for these "abuse" problems are often state initiated institutionalization or appointment of a guardian. Because of the fear of such "protection" the older individual may be reluctant to seek help from governmental agencies. This is apparently well founded for according to a survey conducted in Connecticut, 60 percent of those individuals receiving short term care resulting from "elder abuse" reporting did not return home.[13]

Resisting Unwanted "Protection"

The attorney is likely to represent the client who resists "protection" best by being a source of information concerning alternative and acceptable help to the elderly person. Social service agencies in many areas of the country are striving to provide various types of services which can be put together as a package to serve as an alternative to institutionalization. An example is an area where payment has been authorized by the Medicaid program for personal care services, respite care and adult day care. With knowledge of what is available in a particular community, the attorney may be able to direct a client to appropriate and welcome resources which will avoid the unwanted imposition of more drastic "protections." At a minimum, the attorney should inquire of the local Area Agency on Aging.

The appointed attorney for the client facing guardianship or commitment proceedings has the obligation of resisting unnecessary confinement or guardianship. This is the only assurance for the elderly client of due process to prevent unwarranted loss of liberty.

The attorney's initial task is to make sure that the individual realizes he or she is entitled to counsel of his or her own choice. The individual likely will be satisfied with the attorney, but this step will have reinforced the attorney's independence and interest in the client.

As is true of any trial preparation, the attorney should begin by fully exploring the facts.[14] In addition to information gathered from the client personally, the attorney should obtain all records filed with the court, especially the medical record upon which the petition was based. The attorney also should obtain whatever documents are in existence at

> *A shift in attitude toward respect for elderly autonomy should result in relatively less deprivation of elder rights...and also should lead readily to tort recovery....*

hospitals, in doctors' offices, or social agencies. Interviews with those having contact with the client should be conducted including neighbors, relatives and professionals. These interviews should explore the possibility of alternatives to the unwanted "protection" being sought. These preliminary factual inquiries should be directed to the extent of the client's self-sufficiency, the ability to use available supporting services, the ability to function without harming oneself or others, and the ability to care for oneself and one's property.

The next task is to discuss the information gathered with the client and with those in a position to influence the

outcome of the proceeding. The goal is to arrive at a settlement, using feasible alternatives, which is acceptable to the client. Consultation with the client should be in an advisory role. Knowing the facts, the attorney should be able to assess the probability of the petition being granted. If the attorney believes the client is mentally competent to make a judgment concerning alternative treatment, the attorney should discuss the possibilities and ascertain the client's wishes, rather than make an independent decision.

If no settlement is reached, the task facing the attorney is the preparation to defend. Initially, the attorney should make sure that all procedural requirements have been met. Even the smallest defect may be treated as jurisdictional and, therefore, a basis for a motion to dismiss the petition and discontinue the hearing. Preparation is critically important for commitment proceedings.

The attorney, preferably with the client's cooperation, must determine whether to request a formal open court proceeding and whether to request a jury. Both will increase the probabilities for success and should be pursued unless the client possesses characteristics which would render it inadvisable. However, not all states provide for jury trial by statute and it has not yet been held that a jury trial is constitutionally mandated for commitment proceedings.[15]

The attorney should prepare the client to take part in the hearing by fully explaining its nature and what to expect when being questioned. The client should be instructed to tell the truth but to only answer the questions directly without volunteering information. The attorney should go over all records so the client recalls their content and can answer conformingly. If the client believes the records contain a discrepancy, this belief should be explored and investigated prior to the proceedings. The attorney also should watch for changes resulting from medication which can produce marked differences in appearance and the ability to communicate.[16]

Psychiatric Dimensions

Various writers have explained that failure to properly represent commitment and guardianship clients often results from to the attorney's fear of "taking on" a psychiatrist due to the attorney's lack of knowledge of psychiatry.[17]

The deprivation of a client's liberty should not go by default to the unquestioned opinion of a psychiatrist. The following points are intended to aid the trial attorney who wants the court to rigorously analyze all evidence in relation to the five requisites for commitment outlined above.

First, most statutes require a showing of mental disorder, mental illness or mental disease as a basis for a commitment order. Mental illness is the ultimate legal issue to be determined by the trier of fact, not by a psychiatrist.[18] Second, these terms have no definitions in the American Psychiatric Association Diagnostic and Statistical Manual of Mental Disorders.[19] Psychiatrists, properly questioned, should acknowledge that these words have no medical meaning and many merely connote behavior that should be of concern to psychiatrists.[20]

In addition, psychiatry is an imprecise discipline.[21] The American Psychiatry Association (APA) has attempted to organize the discipline's theories in the Diagnostic and Statistical Manual (DSM) which labels groups of behaviorial characteristics. However, there is disagreement among the profession as to the categories and labels. Because there is no scientifically verifiable basis for these categories, the DSM was adopted and is revised periodically by committee drafts and a final vote of the APA membership. The consequence is that some characteristics are so broad as to permit the diagnostician to "shoehorn into the mentally diseased class almost any person he wishes, for whatever reason..."[21]

The attorney for an elderly person for whom commitment is being sought should expect the psychiatrist's diagnosis to use one or more of these terms: cerebral arteriosclerosis or atherosclerosis, "primary degenerative dementia," "chronic brain syndrome," "dementia," "organic brain syndrome," Alzheimer's disease, or "senile dementia."[22] These terms refer to essentially the same condition which has the primary manifested characteristics of memory loss and mental deterioration. Contrary to earlier thought, within the past 15 to 20 years, it has been discovered that numerous physical disorders can cause dementia symptoms. Approximately 15 percent of dementia patients can be corrected and an additional 20 to 25 percent improved with treatment.[24]

An invalid diagnosis of untreatable "primary degenerative dementia" could needlessly consign an elderly person to an institution for the remainder of his or her life. It, therefore, is essential that the attorney question the psychiatrist both concerning tests done to exclude specific physical causes which could be treated and about the least restrictive method of treatment feasible. If the attorney's prior investigation reveals even minimum self-sufficiency, it is crucial that the psychiatrist be questioned about the client's ability to do everyday simple tasks in his or her home with whatever assistance various alternatives can provide. The probability is that the psychiatrist does not have first hand knowledge about the client's ability. A person exhibiting symptoms of dementia nevertheless may be self-sufficient with help. Thus, diagnosis of dementia alone would not be adequate to commit.

Furthermore, the attorney should check the statutes of the particular jurisdiction. Recently enacted or amended statutes may explicitly exclude, or be interpreted as excluding, from the mental illness category those persons diagnosed as chronic brain syndrome or dementia.[25] Such statutes may exclude from mental illness conditions caused by "advanced years" or "senility." Since these concepts often are linked with dementia, a psychiatrist's testimony may combine them sufficiently to block commitment. Since there is no agreed upon cause of dementia, the expert might indicate aging as the cause. Absent other evidence, a statement that dementia is most often observed in the elderly may be sufficient for a finding that it is caused by advanced years. If the link can be made between a diagnosis of dementia and "advanced years," "senility" or the like, the statute may preclude the diagnosis as a basis for commitment.

Recovering Damages for Misuse of "Protective" Devices

There are several actions available to the client who has been wrongfully committed or against whom various protective measures have been wrongfully instituted. A shift in attitude toward respect for elderly autonomy should result in relatively less deprivation of elder rights than previously, and also should lead readily to tort recovery when it has occurred. Earlier case law reveals a pattern indicating that courts historically have tended to find against the elder person in conflict with another family member as opposed to third parties.[26] With the greater concern for the rights of the elderly and increased use of various tort remedies, this earlier pattern should change to favoring the elderly both against third persons and family members. The two primary causes of action are malicious prosecution and false imprisonment or false arrest, often being joined.

Malicious Prosecution

Malicious prosecution is the use of process for its ostensible purposes, but without probable cause. Generally, the elements include: (1) institution or continuation of a legal proceeding; (2) by, at the instance of, or abetted by, the defendant; (3) termination of the prior proceeding in favor of the person asserting malicious prosecution;[27] (4) absence of probable cause for the institution of the prior proceedings; (5) malice, and (6) injury or damage to the plaintiff.

A recent example of the potential for success with this cause of action is illustrated by the 1.2 million dollar judgment in the Texas case of *Dahl v. Akin*.[28] A father, Mr. Dahl, brought an action for malicious prosecution against his daughter and son-in-law, the Akins, for instituting guardianship and mental illness proceedings. Prior to these proceedings, differences had arisen between the parties with the initial focus on the objection to the father's proposed remarriage and his criticism of the Akins' spending habits. Mrs. Akin applied for and was appointed temporary guardian of her father. In a letter dated April 24, 1978, Mrs. Akin filed an application alleging her father was mentally ill and required observation and/or treatment. Mr. Dahl was arrested the following day and confined in a hospital for about two weeks. At hearing, the judge dismissed the mental illness proceeding. Amending the guardianship application, Mrs. Akin sought appointment as a permanent guardian. Upon a jury verdict that Mr. Dahl was not of unsound mind, the application was denied.[29]

In the suit brought by Mr. Dahl, extensive evidence was introduced to establish the elements of malicious prosecution based on the previous guardianship and mental illness proceedings brought by the Akins. To establish the termination of the prior proceeding in Mr. Dahl's favor, evidence was introduced that the earlier mental illness proceeding was dismissed and that, upon trial, the temporary guardianship was terminated and application for permanent guardianship was denied based on the jury's verdict that the father was not of unsound mind. The evidence introduced by Mr. Dahl from which the jury found a lack of probable cause for the institution of the prior proceeding consisted of testimony that the family doctor who relied on the Akins' statements that competency proceedings were appropriate had not seen Mr. Dahl in over two years. Additionally, friends and associates who were in frequent contact with Mr. Dahl testified as to his intelligence and competency. While this appears to be evidence similar to that required to defend an initial guardianship proceeding, the court pointed out that Mr. Dahl did not have to prove he was of sound mind and had no mental illness in order to recover.[30] In establishing malice, the court initially reiterated the long established principle that malice may be inferred from the proof of lack of probable cause. However, in addition, evidence was introduced outlining particular circumstances bearing on malice. This consisted of the Akins' objection to Mr. Dahl's proposed remarriage and their annoyance at his objection to their spending habits; evidence concerning the falsity of representations made with regard to the initiation of the earlier proceedings; personal motivations for the earlier proceedings; and the extreme degree of interference with Mr. Dahl's personal liberty and property rights.

Finally, evidence concerning injury consisted of the Akins' taking charge of his property, removal of private papers and securities which were not returned, and having an audit of the father's business made, all of which resulted in personal suffering and irreparable harm to his professional reputation as a world renowned architect.[31] Evidence offered to support his claim for damages included: achievements made by Mr. Dahl prior to the institution of the proceedings; his local, national and world recognition as an outstanding architect; his success as a businessman; testimony concerning the mental effect of his hospitalization and ensuing doubts about employability; testimony by witnesses concerning damage to reputation as an architect and possible injury to Mr. Dahl's ability to obtain credit.[32]

The jury's findings, upheld on appeal, were that this evidence established a lack of probable cause, malice and conspiracy between the daughter and son-in-law. The jury awarded $2,140,000 in actual damages and $500,000 in exemplary damages for the mental illness proceedings. This was subsequently reduced to $1,190,000. The court of appeals held the amount not to be so excessive as to require further *remittitur*. In upholding the amount of exemplary damages, the court stated that the evidence and reasonable inferences drawn from it were based upon appropriate considerations including: the nature of the wrong, character of the conduct, degree of culpability, the situation and sensibilities of the parties and the way such conduct affects a public sense of justice

> *Ensuring the rights of the elderly, particularly the right to maintain control over one's affairs and person, requires a compassionate understanding of the laws and their implications.*

and propriety. Moreover, the court held that expenses, including attorney's fees and expenses, were a proper consideration for a jury as part of exemplary damages in a malicious prosecution action.[33]

Abuse of Process

Abuse of process is a secondary cause of action often confused with malicious prosecution. This differs from malicious prosecution in that it is the use of a regularly issued process but for a purpose and to obtain a result not lawfully warranted or properly attainable. The test for abuse of process is whether the process was used to accomplish some end which is outside the regular purview of the process.[34]

The elements are: (1) the defendant made an illegal, improper, perverted use of the process; (2) the defendant had an ulterior motive or purpose; and (3) damage resulted. In some situations this action may be better than malicious prosecution because the plaintiff need merely show use of the process for an improper purpose without having to show lack of probable cause or a favorable termination of the prior proceeding.

However, a line of cases hold that merely having bad motives or intentions will not be sufficient.[35] For example, a person who resorts to legal process to have an individual declared incompetent or committed to a mental hospital does not commit an abuse of process, regardless of motives, if the person makes use of the proceedings for the purpose of attaining its proper ends.[36]

False Imprisonment

The other major cause of action may be for false imprisonment or false arrest which is detention of the person without valid legal authority regardless of malice or lack of probable cause. Generally, legal authority for the plaintiff's detention will bar this action, but a person still may be liable for false imprisonment if bad faith, abuse of process, or malicious prosecution can be shown. For example, in *O'Rourke v. O'Rourke*,[37] a man obtained an order to have his sister committed on the grounds that she was insane. Aroused from her sleep, the sister was committed for several hours in a mental hospital and given a cursory exam. There was evidence the two had been hostile toward each other for many years, but the court found it was due to her fault only to a slight extent. The court held the defendant had acted with malice and without probable cause and, therefore, was liable for damages resulting from the commitment.

Miscellaneous Causes of Action

In addition to the remedies outlined above, the attorney may consider several others. The first is the intentional or reckless infliction of emotional distress. The limiting factor in the tort is that the defendant's conduct must have been so "extreme and outrageous" as to be beyond all possible bounds of decency, regarded as atrocious and utterly intolerable in a civilized community.[38] The attorney who can effectively sensitize the trier of fact to the client's desire for and ability to control his or her personal liberty and financial freedom may find outrageousness particularly applicable.

Another remedy worth considering is the *"prima facie tort"* which can be established by showing that the defendant, with the intention to injure the plaintiff, committed an otherwise lawful act that caused injury to a legally protectable interest of the plaintiff.[39] Upon sufficient showing of intent, conduct and injury, the plaintiff will be entitled to recover unless the defendant has pleaded and proved a privilege, i.e., a justification for the action.[40] Two views exist with regard to the mental element for this tort. The harsher is that of New York requiring the defendant to have been solely motivated by a desire to hurt the plaintiff.[41] Contrasted is that adopted by the Restatement which states that intent to injure, without purpose, desire or motivation to injure, could be sufficient.[42] "Intent" includes not only a purpose to affect the plaintiff, but also a knowledge of consequences substantially certain to affect the plaintiff.[43]

Consequently, taking steps known to be substantially certain to infringe on a person's liberty or property would constitute the tort. However, the attorney should also be aware that some attempts to use this cause of action (arising primarily in a business context) have failed as merely an attempt to recover for abuse of process or malicious prosecution under a different legal theory.[44] The attorney should avoid using *prima facie* tort as a "catch-all" alternative for causes of action that fail because he or she cannot establish the essential elements of a traditional tort.[45]

A final remedy the attorney might consider is "wrongful interference with prospective advantage." In modern times there has been an increase in actions for interference with advantageous relationships. The interest being protected is the chance to achieve a monetary gain without anyone interfering. If employment or business opportunities are diminished, this tort may be appropriate. While historically arising in the context of a contract situation, this cause of action would be proper where instituting incompetency proceedings has prevented some economic benefit to the subject of the proceedings.[46] Mr. Dahl's situation without mental distress would constitute this tort. The plaintiff in this cause of action has the burden of proving that the defendant's interference was unjustifiable.[47] The plaintiff is not required to prove specific intent or malicious motive.[48]

A potential problem with bringing an action arising from an improper use of statutes with mandatory reporting requirements is the effect of immunity from liability which may be available to the person reporting. However, most such statutes have as a condition for mandatory reporting that the person so reporting have a reasonable belief that the elderly individual is in need of protection.

Conclusion

Most of the trends to "protect" the elderly serve an important purpose and are based upon humanistic motivations. Yet, with the number of elderly increasing there exists a growing potential for damaging effects from either the improper use or the thoughtless use of the statutes. Ensuring the rights of the elderly, particularly the right to maintain control over one's affairs and person, requires a compassionate understanding of the laws and their implications. No one is better suited for that than the trial lawyer.

[1] Bureau of the Census, STATISTICAL ABSTRACTS OF THE UNITED STATES 1982–83, 26 (103d ed.).

[2] *Id.* at 8.

[3] Gelt, *Psychological Considerations in Representing the Aged Client*, 17 ARIZ. L.R. 293 (1975).

[4] 441 U.S. 418, 99 S. Ct. 1804, 60 L. Ed. 2d 323 (1979).

[5] Outside the scope of this article, and yet of great importance is the growing concern for an individual's rights once committed. *See Youngberg v. Romeo*, _____ U.S. _____, 102 S.Ct. 2452, 73 L. Ed. 2d 28 (1982), for the substantive due process post-commitment rights of involuntarily committed persons with respect to safe conditions, freedom from undue restraint and such training as may be required.

[6] *See Addington v. Texas*, note 4, *supra*; *O'Connor v. Donaldson*, 442 U.S. 563, 95 S.Ct. 2486, 45 L. Ed. 2d 396 (1975); *Lynch v. Baxley*, 386 F.Supp. 378 (M.D. Ala. 1974), *rev'd* 651 F.2d 387 (5th Cir. 1981); *Lessard v. Schmidt*, 349 F.Supp. 1078 (E.D. Wis. 1972), *vacated on other grounds*, 414 U.S. 473, *modified*, 379 F.Supp. 1376 (E.D. Wis. 1974), *vacated and remanded on other grounds*, 421 U.S. 957 (1975); *State ex rel Hawks v. Lazaro*, 157 W.Va. 417, 202 S.E.2d 109 (1974). Also, see Krauskopf, ADVOCACY FOR THE AGING, § 4.4 (West, 1983).

[7] Block and Sinnott, *The Battered Elder Syndrome: An Exploratory Study* (1979).

[8] Horstman, *Protective Services for the Elderly: The Limits of Parens Patriae*, 40 Mo. L.R. 215, 231 (1975).

[9] *Id.*

[10] *Id.* at 234.

[11] Faulkner, *Mandating the Reporting of Suspected Cases of Elder Abuse: An Inappropriate, Ineffective and Ageist Response to the Abuse of Older Adults*, 16 FAM. L. Q. 69, 87 (1983).

[12] Mo. Rev. Stat. § 660.250(6)(1980).

[13] Also evidencing the firm basis for such a fear is the fact that mortality is higher in institutional populations. Excluding those acutely ill who die in the first three months after admission to a psychiatric hospital about 25 percent are dead within the first year, over 40 percent by the end of the second year, over 50 percent by the end of the third year and the percent dead after four, five, six and seven years is 65 percent, 73 percent, 79 percent and 82 percent respectively. *Horstman* at 274 quoting Special Senate Comm. on Aging, Mental Health Care and the Elderly: Shortcomings in Public Policy, S. REP. NO. 38–596, 92d Cong., 1st Sess. 11 (1971).

[14] For more detail on pre-hearing preparation *see* Mutnick and Lazar, *A Practical Guide to Involuntary Commitment Proceedings*, 11 WILL. L. J. 315, 320 (1975); Cohen, *The Function of the Attorney and the Commitment of the Mentally Ill*, 44 TEX. L. REV. 424, 446 (1966); and Note, *Civil Commitment of the Mentally Ill*, 87 HARV. L.R. 1190 (1974). *Also see* Krauskopf, *Advocacy for the Aging*, Ch. 3 (West, 1983).

[15] R. Brown *et al.*, *The Rights of Older Persons*, A.C.L.U. HANDBOOK, 312 (Avon 1979).

[16] B. Ennis and L. Siegel, *Rights of Mental Patients*, A.C.L.U. HANDBOOK, 295 (1973).

[17] Ennis and Litwack, *Psychiatry and the Presumption of Expertise: Flipping Coins in the Courtroom*, 62 CALIF. L. REV. 693, 745 (1974); Cohen, *The Function of the Attorney and the Commitment of the Mentally Ill*, 44 TEX. L. REV. 424, 450 (1966).

[18] Hardisty, *Mental Illness: A Legal Fiction*, 48 WASH. L. REV. 735 (1973); J.B. Aker, A. Walsh, and J. Beam, *MENTAL CAPACITY, MEDICAL AND LEGAL ASPECTS OF AGING*, 38 (1977).

[19] THE DIAGNOSTIC AND STATISTICAL MANUAL OF MENTAL DISORDER, American Psychiatric Association, 5 (Third Edition 1980).

[20] R. Allen, E. Fester, H. Weihofen, MENTAL IMPAIRMENT AND LEGAL INCOMPETENCY 6, 42 (1968).

[21] Pollack, *Principles of Forensic Psychiatry for Psychiatric-Legal Opinion-Making*, LEGAL MEDICINE, Annual (1971); Ziskin, J., COPING WITH PSYCHIATRIC AND PSYCHOLOGICAL TESTIMONY, Vol. I, 42–43 (3d Ed. 1981). This latter publication provides the most comprehensive considerations connected with the use of psychiatric testimony in legal proceedings.

[22] Livermore, Malmquist, Meehl, *On the Justification for Civil Commitment*, 117 U. PA. L. REV. 75, 80 (1968).

[23] J.B. Aker, A. Walsh, and J. Beam, MENTAL CAPACITY, MEDICAL AND LEGAL ASPECTS OF AGING, Introduction (1977). This is a good source for *lawyers* interested in learning about theories of the aging process and its effect on mental capacity.

[24] C. Wells, DEMENTIA 250 (1977). See chapter 12 for an excellent exposition of the possible treatable conditions that should be explored and suggested diagnostic methodology.

[25] For example, the Illinois Statute excludes from "mental disorder" "a person whose mental processes have merely been weakened or impaired by reason of advanced years." Ill. S.H.A. ch. 91½ ¶ 1–1. In Missouri, commitment is inappropriate for such "disorders as senility..." Mo. Rev. Stat. § 630.005.1(20).

[26] *See* for example, *In re Stokey*, 170 Ohio St. 125, 10 Ohio Op.2d 16 (1959) (despite evidence by three physicians, son appointed guardian after failing to receive requested loan from aged parent); *In re Wilson*, 23 Ohio App. 390, 155 N.E. 654 (1926) (no hesitancy to appoint a son guardian of 70-year-old mother despite absence of evidence of dissipation). In contrast *see*, *Fisher v. Adams*, 151 Neb. 512, 38 N.W.2d 337 (1949) (guardian appointed in an attempt by children to annul the marriage of their 80-year-old father); *Kutzner v. Meyers*, 182 Ind. 669, 108 N.E. 115 (1915) (guardian appointed for an adult who gave $3800 estate for $1.00 to a woman who would care for him).

[27] Disagreement exists as to what constitutes a favorable determination. *See*, *Fetterly v. Gibson*, 210 Cal. 282, 291 P. 411 (1930) (restoration insufficient); *Coulter v. Coulter*, 73 Col. 144, 214 P. 400 (1923) (restoration sufficient); *Sutherland v. Palme*, 93 Cal. App. 2d 307, 208 P.2d 1035 (1949) (dismissal sufficient).

[28] 645 S.W.2d 506 (Tex. App. 1982).

[29] *Id.* at 512.

[30] *Id.* at 519.

[31] *Id.* at 512.

[32] *Id.* at 520.

[33] *Id.* at 521–22.

[34] *Coplea v. Bybee*, 290 Ill. App. 117, 8 N.E.2d 55 (1937).

[35] *Hauser v. Bartow*, 273 N.Y. 370, 7 N.E.2d 268 (1937), *reh'g denied*, 274 N.Y. 489, 8 N.E.2d 617 (1937) and *Holiday Magic, Inc. v. Scott*, 4 Ill. App. 3d 962, 282 N.E.2d 452 (1972); *Harvey v. Pincus*, 549 F. Supp. 342 (E.D. Pa. 1982).

[36] *Barnette v. Woody*, 242 N.C. 424, 88 S.E.2d 223 (1955).

[37] 69 So.2d 567 (La. Ct. App. 1954), *amended on other grounds*, 227 La. 262, 79 So.2d 87 (1955).

[38] Restatement (Second) of Torts § 46 (1979).

[39] *Id.* at § 870. *See also* Forkosch, *An Analysis of the "Prima Facie Tort" Cause of Action*, 42 CORNELL L. Q. 465 (1957).

[40] Restatement (Second) of Torts § 870, comment j (1979).

[41] *Reinforce, Inc. v. Birney*, 308 N.Y. 164, 124 N.E.2d 104 (1954).

[42] Restatement (Second) of Torts § 870, comment b (1979).

[43] *Id.* at § 8A.

[44] *Scully v. Genese Milk Producer's Cooperative, Inc.*, 78 App. Div. 2d 982, 434 N.Y.S.2d 48 (1980).

[45] *Belsky v. Lowenthal*, 62 App. Div. 2d 319, 405 N.Y.S.2d 62 (1978).

[46] *See*, for example, *Harmon v. Harmon*, 404 A.2d 1020 (Me. 1979), where the court held an expectant legatee could maintain an action in tort against a third party for the wrongful interference with an intended legacy. Plaintiff would have to prove that, but for the tortious interference of another, he would in all likelihood have received a specific profit from the transaction.

[47] *M.J.S. Resources, Inc. v. Circle G. Co.*, 506 F. Supp. 341 (E.D. Mo. 1980); Restatement (Second) of Torts §§ 766B, comment d, 767 (1979).

[48] *Yaindl v. Ingersoll-Rand, Co.*, 281 Pa. Super. 419, 422 A.2d 611 (1980) (citing Restatement (Second) of Torts § 766B, comment f (1979)).

Toward an Aging Policy

Elizabeth A. Kutza

ELIZABETH A. KUTZA is assistant professor in the School of Social Service Administration at the University of Chicago. This article is excerpted from The Benefits of Old Age: Social-Welfare Policy for the Elderly *by Elizabeth A. Kutza by arrangement with the University of Chicago Press.*

The 1980s are beginning with a slightly altered perception of the "aging problem" from the one that prevailed a mere decade ago. As a result of political activism on their behalf, the elderly poor have realized many gains. Old Age Insurance (OAI) benefits are higher than ever before and are now "inflation-proof." Older persons are insured against the financial risks of most acute health hazards, and their publicly financed coverage is at least as good as coverage the nonelderly are able to purchase on the open market.

While poverty still exists among the elderly, it is declining, and the elderly have better public support than most nonelderly poor. They are guaranteed a minimum annual income through a program that has universal standards of eligibility and benefits. They occupy a higher percentage of low-income housing than their actual numbers would call for, and they are beneficiaries of a social-services advocacy structure within the federal bureaucra-

cy that has realized unparalleled growth in the past ten years. In sum, the impact of federal policy initiatives for the elderly in the past 15 years has been in the direction of desired change.

These gains are applauded by most, but an underlying dissatisfaction remains. Even staunch supporters of age-based programs are becoming alarmed by their cost. They are also puzzled. How can so much be spent on the elderly and still leave substantial numbers of them with incomes that support only a dog-food diet, with chronic health problems that lead to neglect and abuse in nursing homes, and with dwelling places that lack even minimum standards of decency? As the 1980s begin, these two concerns—the high cost to society of programs for the elderly and the failure of these programs to address the worst cases—are the common themes of the policy debate.

INTERGENERATION REDISTRIBUTION

Until very recently, concern for the elderly was focused on those who had become intrinsically dependent, that is, enfeebled by the aging process. In the nineteenth and twentieth centuries, however, society has witnessed the creation of a group of extrinsically dependent old persons who are excluded from participating in the nor-

mal channels of resource exchange in society, that is, in the bilateral exchange of the marketplace. The result has been a widespread economic dependency among the elderly that necessitates a transfer, a redistribution, of resources.

The effect of Social Security payments to the elderly on the overall income distribution in society demonstrates its redistributional impact. Danziger analyzes the 1974 income level and income distribution, before and after Social Security cash transfer, of all families and then of families headed by nonaged persons (younger than 62 years) and those headed by aged persons (older than 61 years). The income level is measured by mean income; the income distribution, by the Gini coefficient.* As a result of Social Security transfers, mean total money income for a family headed by an aged person increased by about 33 percent; for those headed by a nonaged person the increase was less than 2 percent. For all families, Social Security transfers were mildly redistributive, reducing the Gini coefficient by about 9 percent, but for families with an aged head these transfers reduced inequality by about 33.3 percent. There is thus substantial redistribution

*The Gini coefficient is a summary measure of income inequality that ranges from zero, where all individuals have equal incomes, to one, perfect inequality. Thus, a decline in the Gini coefficient represents a decrease in inequality.

from the whole society to the aged through Social Security. However, as Danziger notes, the incomes of the elderly remain lower, and continue to be more unequally distributed, than those of the rest of the population.[1]

Yet, as Okun points out, "neither the government nor any private group makes a big deal out of that reshuffle. Today's young know their turn will come, and so they foot the bill without gripes. To the aged, Social Security benefits are a right, so they cash those checks without guilt."[2] Okun, writing that in 1975, had no way of knowing that within a few short years there *would* be some "griping" about the intergenerational burden of the OAI transfer. The substantial tax increases voted in 1977 and due to take effect throughout the 1980s produced an enormous, unexpected public outcry and led to remarks like the following, which appeared in a *Wall Street Journal* editorial written by a Stanford University professor of economics:

A combination of slower productivity growth, slightly longer retirement periods, and a lower private savings rate between now and the baby boom generation's retirement does not augur well for our ability to avert what will almost certainly be the sharpest polarization of a society perhaps in history: one based on age rather than more traditional factors.[3]

In less than five years the implicit intergenerational pact upon which the Old Age Insurance program was premised went from unquestioning acceptance to an issue that, according to some, is about to rend the republic in two. How serious a matter this redistributive issue will become in the future remains unclear. It is certain, however, that the *fact* of intergenerational redistribution in the system, heretofore obscured, will increasingly become a matter of political debate.

The elderly constitute a larger proportion of the total population than ever before. And because of policy decisions made before their numbers had become so large, they are drawing more than their relative share of public benefits. Now 11 percent of the population, they receive benefits amounting to over 24 percent of the federal budget. James Schulz, in a paper presented before the National Congress of the American Medical Association in 1974, noted that because of public attention to the problems of aging in the preceding decade, a revolution had occurred in the development of public and private programs. He alluded to a threatened backlash to these efforts by quoting from a *Washington Post* column, which concluded with these words:

The significant, semihidden story in the . . . federal budget is that America's public resources are increasingly being mortgaged for the use of a single group within our country: the elderly. The benefits being paid to them are rising faster than any other major category of federal spending, and the taxes being levied—mainly on their children—to finance those benefits are also going up faster than any other.[4]

But the young not only shift resources to the old through formal systems such as OAI, they do it informally too—through intrafamily transfers of about $6 billion per year—half flowing to the younger extended family from the aged nuclear family, but the other half flowing in the opposite direction.

AGE AS A PREDICTOR OF NEED

Many current complaints about policy for the aged in America explicitly object to age as an organizing principle in the development of policies and programs.

Chronological age is not a good indicator of an individual's circumstances. No problem occurs in old age that does not occur also in other age groups, whether it be poverty, mental or physical disability, isolation, or malnutrition. Fourteen percent of persons 65 and over were poor in 1977, but 15.5 percent of American children aged five through 17 also lived in poverty. While 3.8 million elderly are prevented from carrying on major activities—such as working, keeping house, or going to school—by chronic health problems, 3.3 million nonelderly are similarly afflicted. Finally, the highest incidence of limitation of major activity due to chronic disability is found among the poor, regardless of age. A high percentage—indeed, the majority—of elderly persons can function adequately, from both a societal and individual perspective, through at least their seventies and are in need of rather limited resources to facilitate independent living.

The weakness of using chronological age as a basis for distributing public benefits is straightforward: age is simply not a useful indicator of changes within a person. Since any changes occurring with an individual occur at a pace that is unique to him or her, a more useful way to understand the needs and attributes of individuals is to examine their development on other dimensions of time—social time, biological time, and historical time—the dimensions along which the events of their lives have been patterned. Chronological age has not been shown to relate systematically to individual development along those other dimensions of time. Thus, knowing an individual's chronological age cannot give us any sure information about the person other than the number of years that have elapsed since his or her birth.

Recent trends also suggest that the life cycle is becoming increasingly fluid. Great variability in modal patterns as regards the relationship between chronological age and social age is becoming evident. Persons in their fifties, sixties, and seventies are returning to school, pursuing second careers, and starting new families. Such facts have led Neugarten to conclude that chronological age may be losing its utility both as a means of social organization and as a clock for the timing of events over the course of a lifetime.[5] Moreover, there are enormous individual differences on the rate and timing of physiological changes as well. Two individuals of different chronological ages may be of the same biological "age," while two others, born in the same year, are likely to have very different biological capabilities. Adding to this individual variability are the past life experiences of older persons. The present population over the age of 65 is comprised of cohorts born as much as 40 years apart. The significance of past historical events is different for each cohort. The current cohort of 65-year-olds, for example, were just teen-agers during the decade of the Great Depression, while persons now 80 were then young adults, trying to support families with young children. Given the independence of chronological age and individual development, then, the use of age as a predictor of individual needs and attributes is seriously limited.

Nevertheless, it is often argued that chronological age is an orderly, systematic, and meaningful index of need across the whole population of elderly persons. However, even when aggregated, data describing the elderly population present no unified picture. If variability is still the norm when individual differences are aggregated, then the utility of age as a predictor of group need remains questionable.

The heterogeneity of the over-65 population prompted Neugarten to suggest that the elderly population can be broken down into at least two subgroups, the "young-old" and the "old-old." Differentiated not by age but by biological and social attributes, the young-old are recent retirees who are relatively affluent, relatively healthy, and interested in leisure pursuits; the old-old, on the other hand, tend to be sicker, weaker, and more socially restricted, although the majority can still function adequately with limited intervention.[6] In his book on the history of old age in America, Achenbaum remarks that

another universal of old age has been the marked variations within the aged population. Since people at extremely dissimilar ages have typically been designated as "old," it is not surprising that the elderly population has always been a heterogeneous group.[7]

In fact, the cohort of the old *are* probably less homogeneous than younger cohorts. The accumulation of distinct social, biological, and historical experiences among the old results in increasing levels of internal heterogeneity. Hence, the present group of eight-year-olds is more diverse than the present cohort of 50-year-olds, and they, in turn, are more heterogeneous than the cohort of persons now 20 years of age.

Yet, while within-group differences are widening, between-group differences may be lessening. Recently, the Administration on Aging funded a study of aging and its effects on the quality of life. The researchers were struck not by the differences between the young, middle-aged, and old but by the similarities: "When the picture is examined as a whole," they conclude, "the most striking aspect is how much alike were the values placed on

quality of life factors regardless of age and how relatively little people's needs seem to change over time."[8]

USING AGE TO ALLOCATE PROGRAM BENEFITS

The history of age-based policies is clear. The Old Age Insurance program was the first major effort directed at the needs of older persons. It was a program related to retirement, a condition inevitably associated with aging in a modern industrial society. Thus, need and age in this program were closely related. Planning on the basis of age in other areas, however—areas where age and need are less clearly correlated—gives rise to serious inefficiencies.

Those in favor of age-based programming argue that these inefficiencies are outweighed by specific advantages. Generally, programs that distribute benefits on the basis of age and are aimed at a group having attributed rather than demonstrated needs are administratively simple. There are fewer eligibility disputes, less concern with fraud, no necessary recertifications. Such programs are politically popular and usually gain public support. Bell, Lekachman, and Schorr argue persuasively for such universal, categorical programs. (A program is categorical if it is limited to certain groups in the population, such as the aged or children; it is universal if its benefits are available to everyone in the group, regardless of income.) "Politically," they assert, "programs decline or prosper depending on their mix of beneficiaries. When the mix includes an entire population, like Medicare, they thrive. When the mix is limited to poor people, like Medicaid, they become embattled."[9]

It is also argued that universal, categorical programs are less stigmatizing than income-tested programs. To declare oneself poor in order to receive benefits leads to loss of pride and an acknowledgment of personal failure. Associated with this stigma is the danger that poor beneficiaries may be treated like second-class citizens. Many advocates of age-based programs would rather accept inefficiencies in the distribution of benefits than move to need-based programming.

Two facts weaken these arguments, both of which look backward rather than forward. Proponents of age-based

universal programs look back and see that in the past these strategies succeeded, while the alternative—need-based strategies—failed. It is historically true that universal programs have provided substantial benefits for poor persons and that means-tested programs have turned out to be "mean programs." But history is not our best guide in this matter. The two new facts that must alter our vision are these: the size of the elderly population has greatly increased, and our national economic and productivity rates have declined.

The liberal belief in an economy that always has more for everyone is now being questioned. It has been observed that what the Great Depression was to the generation of the thirties, inflation will be to the generation of the eighties. Difficult choices will face policy makers of the future, choices directly related to the most efficient and equitable way to allocate scarce resources. Public monies will need to be more judiciously spent and effectively targeted. Inflation affects everyone, but the poor are affected most seriously. In the future the inherent inefficiencies of universal, categorical programs will not only become more costly to the society; the burden of these costs will be increasingly borne by those at the bottom. The past successes of old strategies are thus poor indicators of future outcomes because economic conditions are changing.

A second belief strongly held by proponents of age-based programs is also due for revision. Means-tested programs have often proved punitive, stigmatizing, and demeaning for clients, but it is inaccurate to assume that more effective programs must incorporate such features. New programs that are equitable, efficient, effective, and enlightened can be developed. For example, the model of the tax- and welfare-simplification plan developed by Danziger and Haveman at the University of Wisconsin promises to be such a system. Reporting in the *National Tax Journal* they present a reform of the current personal income-tax and welfare systems that would provide increases in average disposable income to low-income households in a way that would eliminate stigma and discrimination.[10] The proposed plan would also be more beneficial to aged heads of households in income classes ranging from under $2,000 to about $10,000 than the current combined tax and welfare systems are. Using the standard poverty line as a base, Danziger and Haveman show that, under their plan, the rate of poverty among aged couples would drop from 13.25 to 1.42.

Studies of stigma, drawn primarily from surveys of attitudes of the general public and of recipients of aid toward the Aid to Families with Dependent Children (AFDC) program, may also be misapplied by those dealing with programs for the aged. The Old Age Assistance program, forerunner of SSI, has enjoyed a high degree of public support since the 1930s, and surveys have found that support increasing over the years. An Institute for Survey Research study made in 1971 found nearly 70 percent of respondents, from all income classes, supportive of more government spending on the aged poor.[11] Cook's more recent work on public support for social-welfare groups, cited earlier, parallels these findings.[12] In 1974 Ozawa surveyed elderly SSI recipients in part to assess their subjective feelings of stigma, and her findings call into serious question our long-held assumptions about the stigmatizing nature of income-tested programs for the elderly. She found that 80.3 percent of the recipients had no feelings of stigma from receiving SSI benefits; 88.5 percent reported no embarrassment at all; and 86.8 percent did not feel that their community had less respect for them because they were receiving assistance. Ozawa concludes that the findings of her study raise questions about the universal applicability of the stigmatizing nature of all antipoverty programs and all types of recipients. The arguments seem least applicable to income-support measures that benefit older poor persons.[13]

Since policy decisions involve choices among whom to serve, it is likely that programs will remain categorical, that is, aimed at a category of persons. The critical issue, of course, is how the category is defined. What is being argued here is that the use of age to delineate a category of beneficiaries may result in inefficiencies because benefits become available both to those who need them and to those who do not. Additionally, some critical needs within the group—the needs of

the most vulnerable persons—may not be well served. If the category is defined by need—that is, by low income or disability—the monies spent should effectively address need.

Measuring need is, of course, difficult for program-planners. Economists, for example, regard need as a normative reflection of individual values and wishes. Because need is normative, it defies attempts at standardized measurement. An illustration from the area of long-term care will highlight the problem.

Civil libertarians and classical economists argue that the individual is the best judge of his or her own need (i.e., preference) for service. Except for persons who need highly specialized medical management and persons of limited mental capacity, the typical consumer seems capable of judging his or her own needs. In the long-term-care area, where service must address living arrangements, the tasks of daily living, and personal care, the argument seems supportable. Yet self-report surveys of needs are notoriously poor guides when it comes to developing new public services, for what a person "objectively" needs and will use may be modified by his or her personality (dependent versus independent), motivation, and ingenuity in simplifying life and making it manageable.[14] Thus, personal standards of need and wants are too variable to be of much use to program planners.

As an alternative to the self-report approach, or, more usually, as an adjunct to it, outside observers estimate need by assessing level of functioning on a case-by-case basis. The level of functional incapacity is then used to measure the need for long-term-care services.

Over the years, large numbers of tools for assessing levels of functioning have been developed. This kind of assessment has been described as "any systematic attempt to measure objectively the level at which the person is functioning in any of a variety of areas such as physical health, quality of self-maintenance, quality of role activity, intellectual status, social activity, attitude toward the world and toward self, and emotional status."[15] Indexes of limitations of function generally measure an individual's capacity for self-care in terms of daily activities like bathing, dressing, eating, walking, us-

ing the telephone, shopping, doing laundry, and so forth.

The major shortcomings of these assessment tools is that the level of functioning they measure is not readily translated into need for service. For example, a person may score poorly on mobility. A response to that problem can take various forms: a wheelchair, a walker, a cane, better shoes, podiatry services. Kleh notes that in the long-term-care field there is no appropriate scheme for classifying patients in terms of service needs. Because of this lack, the judgment of the need for service rests with professional service workers, each of whom may apply a different standard.[16] In studies comparing the institutionalized and the noninstitutionalized elderly, for example, different levels of functional ability have been found to be poor predictors of placement. In 1975 a study of long-term care in Illinois estimated that about 33 percent of the clients receiving care (not necessarily formal) within their homes had limitations that met or exceeded those of elderly in long-term-care institutions.[17]

Answers to questions such as who needs service (by age, sex, race, location), what types of service they need, and how much or how often they need it are basic to decisions about program eligibility, service-delivery mechanisms, and financing. Without such data, service development and projections are risky. To date, however, we know very little about the level of demonstrated need for many social-welfare services in American society, and we know even less about how that need may be distributed throughout the society.

AGE-BASED EXCLUSION

Reorganizing the current age-based service system, of course, entails serious bureaucratic and political problems. Existing administrative agencies would only reluctantly relinquish authority over programs and services now in their domain. Special-interest groups, unable to concentrate their activities on constituent agencies, would resent becoming weakened advocates. In sum, replacing an age-based policy system with one that is need-based involves trade-offs. Further public debate on the question is needed so that the benefits of economic efficiency can be carefully weighed against the political and bureaucratic costs.

Clearly, those advocates of the elderly who fight discrimination on the basis of age are somewhat inconsistent when they then lobby for special treatment on the basis of age. Since the same range of needs found in the elderly population can be found in the larger population, planning on the basis of age is exlusionary. A guaranteed minimum income (Supplemental Security Income) and a national health insurance (Medicare) are important for the well-being of the larger citizenry (and critical for certain subgroups). One cannot argue that only the elderly need these provisions.

Equity considerations under age-based programs have become a critical element for review under the provisions of the Age Discrimination Act as amended. Although enacted in 1975, the Act is not yet fully implemented. The final regulations were not published until June, 1979. They call for a reexamination of all federally assisted programs that use age distinctions for receipt of benefits. The intent is to determine under what circumstances age may be a "reasonable" factor to consider in programming. The impact of the Age Discrimination Act is unknown, but it is likely to bring the question of age-based policy-making into the forefront of debate.

NOTES

[1] Sheldon Danziger, "Income Redistribution and Social Security: Further Evidence," Social Service Review 51 (1977), pp. 179–184.

[2] Arthur M. Okun, Equality and Efficiency: The Big Tradeoff (Washington, D.C.: Brookings Institution, 1975), p. 107.

[3] Michael J. Baskin, "The Social Security Deficit," Wall Street Journal (Dec. 6, 1979), p. 24.

[4] James H. Schulz, Have We Done Enough for the Elderly? (A paper presented to the National Congress of the American Medical Assocation, Chicago, Ill., 1974.)

[5] Bernice L. Neugarten, "Policy for the 1980s: Age or Need Entitlement." (Paper prepared for the conference "Aging: Agenda for the Eighties" sponsored by the National Journal, held in Washington, D.C., November, 1979.)

[6] Bernice L. Neugarten, "The Future and the Young-Old," Gerontologist 15 (1975), pp. 4–9.

[7] W. Andrew Achenbaum, Old Age in the New Land: The American Experience since 1790 (Baltimore: Johns Hopkins University Press, 1978), p. 2.

[8] John C. Flanagan, Identifying Opportunities for Improving the Quality of Life of Older Age Groups (Palo Alto: American Institutes for Research, 1979), p. 5.

[9] Winifred Bell, R. Lekachman, and Alvin Schorr, Public Policy and Income Distribution (New York: Center for Studies in Income Maintenance Policy, 1974), p. 32.

[10] Sheldon Danziger and Robert Haveman, "Tax and Welfare Simplification: An Analysis of Distributional and Regional Impacts," National Tax Journal 30 (1977), pp. 269–283.

[11] Eva Mueller, "Public Attitudes toward Fiscal Programs," Quarterly Journal of Economics 77 (1963), pp. 210–235.

[12] Fay Lomax Cook, Who Should Be Helped? Public Support for Public Service (Beverly Hills: Sage Publications, 1979).

[13] Martha N. Ozawa, "Impact of SSI on the Aged and Disabled Poor," Social Work Research and Abstracts 14 (Fall, 1978), pp. 3–10.

[14] See Edward A. Powers and Gordon L. Bultena, "Correspondence between Anticipated and Actual Uses of Public Services by the Aged," Social Service Review 48 (1974), pp. 245–254, for a discussion of these problems.

[15] M. Powell Lawton, "The Functional Assessment of Elderly People," American Geriatriacs Society 19 (1971), pp. 465–481.

[16] John Kleh, "When to Institutionalize the Elderly," Hospital Practice 12 (1977), p. 121.

[17] State of Illinois, Department of Aging, "Summary of the Major Findings of the Long-Term Care Study," mimeographed (Chicago: Booz, Allen, & Hamilton, 1975), p. 15.

Planning for an Aging Work Force

Raymond J. Donovan
Secretary of Labor

Amerrican society—and America's work force—are growing older. Today, more than 20 percent of the U.S. population is aged 55 or older, compared with less than 10 percent at the beginning of this century.

This trend is expected to peak dramatically within the next several decades. By the year 2010, 25 percent of our population is projected to be at least 55 years old. A special U.S. Census Bureau report issued in September 1983 warns: "In less than 30 years, an aging society will be upon us, whether we have prepared for it or not."

We can and we must begin to prepare now. As a nation, we have long focused much of our attention and concern on the needs of our large and still relatively youthful World War II baby-boom generation. Now that this generation is maturing and the growth of our younger population has slowed, we face some changing needs in the future. These changes will affect and involve many different institutions and sectors of our society: government, business, labor, education, voluntary and nonprofit orga-

> **Older workers drop out of the labor force because they perceive lack of opportunities to continue working.**

nizations, as well as individuals of all ages. Our effectiveness in meeting the needs of older citizens will help determine the quality of life for all Americans.

Priorities In An Aging Society

For our nation to grow older gracefully and make a smooth social and economic transition to the future, three interrelated priorities must be met:

• We must assure that our growing ranks of older citizens have opportunities to remain as productive as possible in their later years of life. We cannot allow vast numbers of Americans—those who want or need to continue working in their later years—to fall on a retirement scrap heap; forced idleness coupled with the reduced incomes and the increased health care costs of aging can erode living standards and create financial hardships. On the other hand, we may also have to find ways to encourage more highly qualified older workers—who

increasingly are opting for early retirement—to remain in the labor force as the supply of younger workers diminishes.

• We must continue seeking to strengthen and improve mechanisms which help provide long-term financial security for older Americans, especially our private pension systems. This includes encouraging the expansion of employer pension programs, individual retirement savings plans, and other income security measures that will alleviate the strain on existing pension programs and public resources as the ratio of older beneficiaries to active workers increases.

• We must continue on a sound course of national economic policy that sets the stage for long-term economic growth. Economic stability and industrial expansion will be essential if we hope to create adequate job opportunities for Americans of all ages; to generate revenues necessary to sustain our public and private pension systems; and to keep a firm grip on inflation, the greatest enemy of older Americans on fixed or reduced incomes.

These priorities are basic to policies that President Reagan and his Administration have followed since he took office. Among the results of

8. SOCIAL POLICIES, PROGRAMS, AND SERVICES

these policies are the following:

• Under the President's economic program, inflation has dropped from a record-breaking siege of double-digit levels to its lowest rate in many years; unemployment has dropped as a result of the nation's strong, broad-based recovery from recession.

• President Reagan in 1983 signed into law amendments to the Social Security Act which greatly strengthen old-age and disability programs and ensure their long-range stability as a source of income for elderly citizens.

• Effective administration and enforcement of the Employee Retirement Income Security Act (ERISA) have been assigned top priority in the Labor Department, and improvements have been made which make this law a stronger tool for protecting the multi-billion-dollar assets of more than 50 million participants in 650,000 private pension and welfare benefit plans.

• In September 1983, President Reagan sent to the Congress the Pension Equity Act, which, if enacted, will amend ERISA to equalize the pension rights of women workers and enhance the pension protections this law affords widows and divorced spouses.

• In 1982, President Reagan proposed that mandatory retirement be eliminated in private industry, as it already had been eliminated in the federal government.

Deterrents to the Older Worker

The federal government has and will continue to have an important role in setting policies and administering laws and programs that influence the status and welfare of older Americans. But government alone cannot bring about all of the changes necessary to meet our demographic challenges of the future.

Awareness, concern and cooperation among many different groups and individuals will be required to adapt our social and economic structure to the needs of our aging population.

We can start by eliminating handicaps imposed on older people—and on the rest of our society—by pervasive, but unfair and erroneous, beliefs and assumptions about this age group. Some of the most harmful of these misconceived ideas concern the abilities, role and potential contributions of older people in our workforce. Included are the generalized beliefs that age is a deterrent to productivity, that jobs are not a significant issue for older Americans and older Americans are not a significant factor in employment. We need to put such notions to rest and take positive steps to increase older workers' employment opportunities.

For example, too many people still believe that older workers should retire or be retired at some arbitrary age because of declining work ability, or that advancing age correlates with diminishing value on the job.

The government's experience in enforcing the Age Discrimination in Employment Act has shown beyond a doubt that many older workers lose their jobs, get demoted or otherwise are treated unfairly solely because of their age, rather than their work performance. Data from the Labor Department's Bureau of Labor Statistics show that once older workers lose their jobs, they are likely to stay unemployed longer than younger workers; one reason for the duration of older workers' unemployment is the mistaken idea that this age group is less productive, less capable or less energetic than younger workers.

In fact, research continues to document that learning ability, intelligence and productivity do not necessarily decline with age. Employer surveys have shown that, in comparison with younger workers, older workers in general have less job turnover, higher job satisfaction and at least equal productivity rates.

America's highly educated, well-trained and maturing work force com-

Dick Swartz

Increasing older workers employment opportunities will be fiscally and economically desirable.

prises a growing resource of talent and seasoned experience for employers. The wisdom and perspective that people acquire only with age can enhance their contributions and value as employees. Instead of arbitrarily restricting employment opportunities for older workers, the future demands that we look for ways to take better advantage of what these men and women have to offer.

Up to now, however, there has been little motivation among employers to boost older workers' employment opportunities, largely because of another traditional, but increasingly outmoded, belief: Older workers should step aside and make room for younger workers at the top.

As Social Security and private pension benefits have become more widely available and Americans have placed increasing value on leisure time, we have seen a trend toward retirement at earlier ages. At the same time, many older workers who lose their jobs drop out of the labor force prematurely because they perceive or encounter lack of oppotunities to continue working. From society's standpoint, this has not yet been a major concern. After all, large numbers of younger workers have steadily streamed into our labor force, ready and able to replace departing older workers.

Over the next several decades, however, this stream of younger labor force entrants will slow considerably. The talents, skills and experience of older workers will become more valuable and will be important factors in our nation's industrial productivity. Today's emphasis on early retirement could become tomorrow's scramble to hire and retain older workers. Smart employers will reassess their employment and retirement policies accordingly.

A Desirable Economic Goal

As noted earlier, slower growth in the younger segment of our population will also mean that fewer active workers will be making payments into public and private pension programs, while more and more older workers

The skills and experience of older workers will become important factors in our nation's productivity.

will be eligible to draw pension benefits. For employers and society as a whole, increasing older workers' employment opportunities will be fiscally and economically desirable.

If the present is any guide to the future, we may not experience any serious shortage of older men and women who are willing and able to prolong their stay in our labor force if given the opportunities to do so. But much will have to be done to create jobs and design work environments suited to the needs and desires of older people; simultaneously, we must assure that older workers are prepared and qualified for the jobs that our labor market has to offer.

Already, a substantial number of men and women are staying in our labor force well beyond presumably "normal" ages of retirement, because they want to or must for financial reasons.

In 1981, more than 80 percent of men aged 55–59, almost 60 percent of men aged 60–64, and one out of eight

men aged 70 or older were still in the labor force. Older women have dramatically increased their presence in our work force over the past several decades: some 42 percent of women aged 55–64 were working in 1982, compared with only 27 percent in 1950.

A Labor Department study completed in 1981 showed that more than one of every five older Americans who retires returns to work at least part-time. Those who retire completely and at earlier ages are most likely to be workers who have the financial security afforded by private pension plan coverage; those who lack pension coverage are more likely to continue working full-time or part-time until later in life.

At present, only about half of the U.S. work force is covered by pension plans. Vast numbers of Americans lack access to this type of income security; among them are employees changing jobs frequently, having frequent breaks in their employment and working in smaller, unorganized industries where pension programs have not been established. We must remember, too, that pension programs vary widely in the level and quality of benefits they provide to retirees and their survivors.

Here is further evidence that jobs are important to older Americans: The Census Bureau recently reported earnings accounted for 25 percent of the total money income of elderly citizens aged 65 and older in 1981. Earnings were second in importance only to Social Security benefits, which accounted for 37 percent of total income among the elderly, and ranked far ahead of pensions, which accounted for only 13 percent.

Earnings are one of the few unfixed sources of income available to the elderly that can help offset rising living costs. Increasingly, these earnings are coming from part-time jobs. In 1981, almost half of the working men and more than half of the working women aged 65 and over were employed in part-time work, up substantially from the percentage working part-time in 1960. Most of these peo-

ple on part-time schedules in 1981 reported that they chose to work part-time, rather than being forced to for economic reasons.

As life expectancy continues to lengthen and jobs continue to be an economic mainstay for older Americans, we have every reason to expect that large numbers of these men and women will be available to work if given the opportunities to do so. We can prepare for this by assuring that recruitment, training and employment practices are geared to the interests and needs of this age group.

Several years ago, the President's Commission on Pension Policy issued results of studies indicating that part-time jobs, flexible work schedules, the redesign of jobs, and phased retirement programs—which enable workers to split their time between jobs and leisure—are already being used to some degree in industry for the mutual economic benefit of employers and older workers. Given today's emphasis among labor and management on such issues as industrial efficiency, cost effectiveness, job security and the financial stability and rising costs of pension programs,

much more can and should be done in this area.

A related issue that jointly concerns labor, management and educators is the availability of training and retraining for older workers. In our rapidly changing, technology-based economy, older workers cannot be excluded from opportunities to keep their skills and knowledge current with the changing demands of occupations and the labor market as a whole. Workers themselves must accept the probability that training acquired in their youth will not be valid for a lifetime, and they may have to change jobs or career paths more often than people have done in the past.

An ideal scenario for America's future would be to strike a perfect match between the needs and desires of older people to work and employers' demand for the skills and experience that older workers have to offer. Perfection is difficult to achieve. But with foresight, planning and cooperation among the many players in this scenario, we can meet the future well prepared.

Widower Self-Help Groups: A Preventive Approach

Audrey Gartner

Bereavement following the death of a spouse has been recognized as a period of extreme stress—a period in which the surviving spouse is vulnerable to emotional and physical illness, particularly in the months immediately following the loss. Research studies show heightened impairment in widowed persons' mental and physical health when compared to married persons of the same age. The widowed consult physicians more often, consume more drugs, and generally have higher symptom and illness rates.

The importance of these findings is underlined by the size of the population currently and potentially at risk. The 12 million widowed persons in the United States already number almost 5 percent of the total population. The projected increase in the size of the older population suggests that the proportion of widowed persons will continue to increase.

Although it is women who comprise the bulk of the widowed—as high as 75 percent—it is men who appear to suffer more from widowhood. One community survey of 2,500 people across marital status groups found widowed males were more depressed than widowed females.[1] At a Congressional hearing on health and long-term care by the House Select Committee on Aging in 1983, evidence was presented that widowers over 75 had the highest alcoholism rate in the country. In addition, mortality figures indicate that bereavement has a more direct effect on wid-

> **Widowed men had a 28 percent greater mortality rate than their married counterparts.**

owers than widows. For men, risk is especially evident for homicide, cirrhosis of the liver, and suicide.

Since the primary work of Durkheim in 1897, attention has been drawn to the fact that the rate of suicide is higher among the widowed: "The suicides occurring at the crisis of widowhood . . . are really due to domestic anomie resulting from the death of a husband or wife."[2] And there is evidence that suicide rates are higher for widowers than widows. Gove, for example, in an extensive analysis of United States National Statistics for the years 1959 to 1961, computed age-specific suicide rates for the widowed and married aged 25 to 64 and found that for each age group the rates were greater for men than for women.[3]

Further indication that the death of a spouse has a severe impact on widowers is dramatically pointed up in a 12-year survey of more than 4,000 widowed persons that was conducted at the Johns Hopkins School of Hygiene and Public Health. The survey found that widowed men had a 28 percent greater mortality rate than their married coun-

terparts; moreover, widowers between the ages of 55 and 65, who made up more than one-fourth of the people in this study, had a mortality rate 60 percent higher than that of married men of the same age. Conversely, the study showed that a husband's death had almost no effect on the mortality rate of women.[4]

There is evidence, mainly from studies of the elderly, that men typically experience greater social isolation and loneliness in widowhood than women. Yet widowers are less likely to find alternative sources of support than widows. For widowers at risk, early intervention may have a significant effect upon their well-being.

WIDOWERS AND SELF-HELP GROUPS

In the last 15 years, a growing number of self-help groups have been established to serve the needs of the widowed, including NAIM (a Catholic-sponsored organization), THEOS (They Help Each Other Spiritually), Widowed Persons Service, Widow-to-Widow, and Community Centers for the Widowed. While most of these organizations include widowers as members, their programs are not typically directed toward men, and those men who do join often drop out.

Self-help groups help the widowed adjust to their new life by bringing them together with others who are facing and solving similar problems. One two-

United Nations Photo/F.B. Grunzweig

Recent studies indicate that men typically experience greater social isolation and loneliness after the death of their spouses than do women.

year study of post-bereavement adaptation in two groups of a total of ,62 widows demonstrated that widows receiving self-help intervention in an experimental widow-to-widow program adjusted to their bereavement more rapidly than did participants in a control group.[5]

Similarly, positive results of self-help groups' effectiveness are reported in a large-scale follow-up survey of widows and widowers who were participants in the self-help group THEOS.[6] Based on two questionnaires mailed a year apart, seven indices of mental health—depression, anxiety, somatic symptoms, psychotropic drug use, self-esteem, coping mastery, and well-being—were examined in terms of the extent of the respondents' participation in the organization. Both current and former THEOS members who

helped each other through their social network consistently showed better results. Those who were less involved (attended fewer meetings and did not establish social networks) showed greater levels of depression, lower self-esteem, and used more psychotropic medication and alcohol than those who were more involved.

Self-help groups have developed, in part, to replace the natural support networks that have been lost or have become disconnected as society has changed with the disintegration of the traditional extended kinship system and the isolation of mobile nuclear families. While the stresses placed on the newly widowed were once addressed in the family setting, in contemporary America support groups have come to play an important role.

Self-help groups provide social sup-

port to their members through the creation of a caring community, and they increase members' coping skills through the provision of information and the sharing of problem solutions and experiences. They carry out a variety of activities, offering (1) opportunities to participate with a group of people sharing the same problem; (2) a protected setting and a safe opportunity to try new behaviors; (3) role models showing what can be done and how, as well as how to cope successfully; (4) insight that is grounded in direct experience; (5) contacts that may serve both to deisolate the individual as well as to provide access or entry to additional sources of help; and (6) an ideology of empowerment, of being helped through helping others. This mechanism has been described by Riessman as the "helper-therapy" principle.[7] In its simplest form, it states that those who help are helped most.

In an era when formal services have been characterized as too costly, too impersonal, too bureaucratic, and too distant from their consumers, self-help groups have grown at an unprecedented rate. Such groups are considered complementary to formal services, and fill gaps between needs and services that could not be met by professional agencies.[8] There are currently about 500,000 self-help groups involving 15 million people in the United States. The U.S. Department of Health and Human Services predicts that by 1990 the number of persons reached by mutual-support self-help groups should double in order to reduce the gaps in mental-health services.[9]

Most support programs for the bereaved, such as widow-to-widow programs and services like "widow hotlines," are directed primarily to the needs of women. Yet widowers have been shown to be in special need of support. Many might join a self-help group if one suitable to their needs existed—an all-widower group, for example.

In an era when formal services have been characterized as too costly, too impersonal, too bureaucratic, and too distant from their consumers, self-help groups have grown at an unprecedented rate.

Self-help groups can provide a low-cost, accessible, and relevant mode of preventive intervention for the widowed. This approach has already been developed and tested as an effective model of intervention for facilitating resolution of the grief of widows. However, the health of widowers in particular is at risk, and early intervention may lessen their need for medical and social services. Therefore, the development

of effective self-help models for widowers will contribute an important component to comprehensive prevention programs for the aging.

NOTES
[1] L. Radloff, "Sex Differences in Depression: The Effects of Occupation and Marital Status," *Sex Roles,* vol. 1 (1975), pp. 249–265.
[2] Emile Durkheim, *Suicide: A Study of Sociology* (Glencoe, Ill.: The Free Press, 1951). Originally published, 1897.
[3] W. R. Gove, "Sex, Marital Status, and Suicide," *Journal of Health and Social Behavior,* vol. 13 (1972), pp. 204–213.
[4] Knut J. Helsing and Moyses Szklo, "Mortality After Bereavement," *American Journal of Epidemiology,* vol. 114 (1981), pp. 41–52.
[5] Mary L. S. Vachon, et al., "A Controlled Study of Self-Help Intervention for Widows," *American Journal of Psychiatry,* vol. 137 (1980), pp. 1380–1384.
[6] Morton A. Lieberman and Leonard D. Borman, "The Impact of Self-Help Intervention for Widows' Mental Health," The National Research and Information Center's *National Reporter,* vol. 4 (1981), pp. 2–6.
[7] Frank Riessman, "The 'Helper-Therapy' Principle," *Social Work,* vol. 10 (1965), pp. 27–32.
[8] Audrey Gartner and Frank Riessman, "Self-Help and Mental Health," *Hospital and Community Psychiatry,* vol. 33 (1982), pp. 631–635.
[9] *Promoting Health, Preventing Disease: Objectives for the Nation* (Washington, D.C.: U.S. Department of Health and Human Services, 1980).

State Units Launch Employment Initiatives

Susan Coombs-Ficke and Ann Lordeman

Ms. Coombs-Ficke and Ms. Lordeman are on the staff of the National Association of State Units on Aging.

Despite recent improvements in the nation's economy, long-term unemployment for middle-aged and older workers remains a problem. According to a recent report of the House Select Committee on Aging, "unemployment among older Americans is now the highest since the Government began measuring joblessness after World War II.

"More than 770,000 Americans, 55 and over, are out of work—1.1 million if one adds to the 'officially' unemployed those so-called discouraged workers whom the Government no longer counts as unemployed because they've stopped looking for work."

Do older people want to work? The response is mixed. To be sure, there are many for whom retirement is a welcome event, offering an opportunity to pursue other types of involvement or a respite from undesirable working conditions. To a great extent, early retirement has been hailed a symbol of social progress made possible by advances in public and private pension and disability benefits.

Regrettably, however, there are still a significant number of older men and women for whom retirement and the subsequent loss of income present serious problems. "Inflation, increasing energy bills, rising taxes, and relatively fixed retirement incomes," says the Federal Council on the Aging, "combine to suggest that earnings through continued employment, either part-time or full-time, is an option that older Americans may be forced to consider."

Older workers, 65 and over, comprise about 1 percent of the total population seeking employment. Consistently, however, this figure is described as an underestimate of interest since older people don't always seek employment through the traditional agencies that are a source of unemployment statistics. More effective for the older people are special programs that provide outreach, offer placement assistance, flexible

Norman Tavan

Norman Tavan

"State Units Launch Employment Initiatives," Susan Coombs-Ficke and Ann Lordeman, *Aging* Magazine, February/March 1984, pp. 18-22. Reprinted by permission of *Aging* Magazine.

working hours, some supportive services, and gradual movement into the unsubsidized job market.

Older workers, according to a 1981 Harris survey, especially those age 65 and older, desire and actively seek jobs with reduced hours.

A call to increase alternatives to retirement was also a consistent theme of the State White House Conferences on Aging held throughout the country during 1981. At the 1981 White House Conference on Aging in Washington, D.C., 9 out of 14 committees passed recommendations on employment-related issues. Fourteen recommendations specifically addressed the need for part-time, flexitime, and job-sharing work strategies to help increase the availability of public and private sector employment options.

Through Title V of the Older Americans Act, the Senior Community Service Employment Program, and the more recent Job Training Partnership Act, State Units on Aging are playing an increasingly important role in stimulating the creation of new jobs and encouraging the expansion of alternative work options.

The State Units on Aging are also supporting federal and state legislation that would raise the mandatory retirement age above 70 and are promoting state laws against age discrimination in employment. Pre-retirement seminars and training on age biases and stereotypes have been highly successful actions taken by the states for calling attention to employment problems of older workers. The State Units employment agenda is also directed toward ensuring that state personnel policies and practices are responsive to the needs of older workers.

The Senior Employment Program

Until recently, the major response of most states to employment problems of the elderly has been through their involvement with the Title V Senior Community Service Employment Program (SCSEP), authorized under the Older Americans Act.

Title V has three primary objectives. They are (1) to provide part-time employment for low-income per-

sons, 55 and over, (2) to enhance the general welfare of a community by bolstering its human services capacity, and (3) to encourage the transition of older workers to the unsubsidized job market through training, job finding support, and counseling.

Title V is now a $319.45 million program, supporting some 62,500 jobs. Administratively, Title V is managed by the U.S. Department of Labor which, in turn, allocates funds to the states and to eight national contractors. They include: Green Thumb, Inc., an affiliate of the National Farmer's Union; the National Council on the Aging; the National Council of Senior Citizens; the American Association of Retired Persons; the U.S. Department of Agriculture's Forest Service; the National Center on Black Aged; the Associacion Nacional Pro Personas Mayores; and the National Urban League.

The states' share (currently, 22 percent of the total) is allocated to the respective Governors who, in turn, decide which agency in state government should have authority for program management and oversight. In 41 states, responsibility has been turned over to the State Unit on Aging.

In recent years, Title V has served as a springboard for many states to become more actively involved with the private sector in helping older Americans to continue working or to re-enter the labor force. A change brought about by the 1981 amendments to the Older Americans Act involves a new emphasis on private sector employment of older workers. Already underway, program innovations at the state level in partnership with business are expected to have a positive impact on the employment situation of older workers. Later sections of this article will highlight some of these innovative state programs.

The Job Training Partnership Act

As involved as the State Units on Aging have been in job training issues through their participation in the Title V Senior Community Service

Employment Program, their role in this area is, in many cases, greatly expanding because of the Job Training Partnership Act (JTPA).

Enacted in 1982, the Job Training Partnership Act, like the Comprehensive Employment Training Act (CETA), expresses a federal commitment to help people who face serious employment barriers to become productive, working members of society. But, this program differs from its predecessor in several ways. First, JTPA redirects program funds from salaries and wages for workers to job training. Second, it redirects the overall thrust from public service jobs toward job creation in the private sector. At the same time, it greatly increases the responsibilities of state and local governments to determine the appropriate mix of employment-related activities to be supported in a given state or area.

Title I, Section 124 provides the authority for special training programs for economically disadvantaged older workers, 55 and over. The program is designed for older people not currently in the work force and specifies that 3 percent of the funds available under JTPA for state and local programs must be spent on older worker training.

The law requires Governors to coordinate all JTPA activities statewide. The Governors are assisted at the state level by Job Training Coordinating Councils. In most states, the State Units on Aging are represented on the councils and play an important role in helping to assess the extent to which local implementation plans address the concerns of older people. In addition, some State Units administer the older worker programs funded under JTPA. Others develop state guidelines for the programs, review and comment on applications for older worker and dislocated worker programs, and provide technical assistance on the implementation of JTPA to Area Agencies on Aging and to Service Delivery Areas established by the new law.

Of note, 70 percent of the funds allocated to the Service Delivery Areas

Kevin Reals

must be spent on job training as opposed to paying salaries and wages. Also, whereas local public officials were involved as prime sponsors under CETA, the new emphasis under JTPA is on establishing an

equal partnership between local governments and private enterprise. At the local level, Private Industry Councils (PIC's), together with elected officials, decide what activities will be funded under Title II,

"Training for Disadvantaged Adults and Youth."

Changing State Policies

A number of State Units on Aging have identified personnel policies and practices that adversely affect older worker employment opportunities in state government. Some efforts of the State Units to increase the responsiveness of state personnel policies and practices include (1) encouraging State Civil Service Commissions to allow, wherever feasible, credit for experience to substitute for college degree requirements, (2) working with State Civil Service Commissions to establish affirmative action policies for older workers, and (3) promoting legislation to establish state task forces and commissions to examine state and private sector employment policies and practices.

In addition, eight states currently have laws eliminating mandatory retirement, and legislation is pending in three states that would eliminate an age ceiling. Individual laws vary in their applicability to the private and public sectors, the kinds of exceptions permitted, the types of protection provided, the upper age limit, if any, and the enforcement provisions.

Innovative State Programs

What kinds of new programs are the State Units on Aging developing to create job opportunities for older people? The programs described below were selected because they illustrate the wide variety of approaches being adopted nationwide to solve the senior employment problem.

Delaware. One of the approaches adopted by the State of Delaware has been to target specific industries as potential employers of older people in permanent full- or part-time positions. "We believe that there are many job opportunities for older workers," says Eleanor Cain, Direc-

tor of the Delaware Division on Aging. "Our task is to identify those opportunities and to assist older workers in receiving the necessary training."

For example, the Division believes that more older workers can be employed in the hotel and restaurant industry. In 1983, the Division initiated an experimental project combining classroom training with work experience to prepare older job seekers for occupations in hotels and restaurants. Academic coursework is provided by the Widener University School of Hotel and Restaurant Management; the work experience is supervised by

professional staff of the Sheraton-Brandywine Inn, located on the Delaware campus of Widener University.

Funded under Title V of the Older Americans Act, the project trained five persons the first year in positions such as accountant, public relations representative, housekeeping supervisor, front desk clerk, and cook. As a result of the training, four of the five are now employed full-time; the fifth enrollee moved to another state before completing the program. During the project's second year, 13 older workers will receive training.

Missouri. In 1983, the Missouri Division of Aging initiated a small business micro-computer demonstration project in cooperation with the Central and Mid-East Missouri Area Agencies on Aging. Funded under Title V of the Older Americans Act, the project was designed to create second-career training opportunities for persons 55 and over in the field of micro-computer applications. Course content included familiarization with micro-computer hardware, concentration in one specialty, and a detailed explanation of various employer/contractor relationships.

Approximately 100 persons participated in the 10-week computer training program, followed by a 3-week program of job search assistance. Fifty-six participants obtained employment following the training.

New Jersey. In New Jersey, the Title V program, which is administered by the Division on Aging in conjunction with the National Council on the Aging, supports about 470 low-income older workers in community service jobs. Each of the state's 21 counties has an Employment Resource Specialist who provides job placement assistance to older workers; the six most populous counties have also hired assistants to the resource specialists.

In addition to placing eligible Title V enrollees into subsidized community service jobs, during 1981–1982 the state's Employment Resource Specialists found unsubsidized employment for 2,000 individuals who fell slightly beyond the Senior Employment program's eligibility guidelines. Division officials say the estimated cost per placement in this public/private sector cooperative venture was less than $170 per job and generated at least $4 million annual income for older workers in the state.

Kansas. The Kansas Department on Aging funds three employment programs which place older workers in the private sector through job development and training activities that match the skills of older workers with available jobs. The Kansas Legislature, in establishing the programs in 1982, mandated that they be located

in a city, a rural area, and a medium-sized town. "The programs," says Sylvia Hougland, Secretary of the Kansas Department on Aging, "are designed to serve two kinds of older workers—those persons seeking full-time work and retirees who want part-time employment. Different kinds of job development and training were required for the two kinds of workers." This year, 1,400 persons have participated in the programs which have worked closely with private industry in placing older workers. Recently, the Department has developed Older Worker Councils to provide input on the needs of older workers to the Service Delivery Areas established under JTPA. The Councils also review and comment on the plans of the Service Delivery Areas for spending the 3 percent of JTPA funds earmarked for older worker training.

Idaho. The Idaho Office on Aging operates its Older Worker Program under the Job Training Partnership Act through contracts with the Area Agencies on Aging. Intake and eligibility determination for the program are conducted through senior citizen centers. Workshops are arranged to address the various needs of older individuals seeking employment. Training covers such topics as job search assistance, skills development, self-employment, motivation and confidence-building.

In addition, on-the-job training is developed in cooperation with the local job service and the Private Industry Councils. Participants in the training will be encouraged to market their skills by developing and seeking employment opportunities on their own, thereby minimizing a dependency on the program. However, the program will contact prospective employers for participants who need special assistance. The staff will also publicize the benefits of hiring older workers through the media and civic organizations.

Wisconsin. The Wisconsin Bureau of Aging recently completed a two-year pilot project providing counseling and job readiness training for displaced homemakers. Funds for the

project were authorized by the Wisconsin Legislature out of general revenues. Upon completion the project was taken over by the Wisconsin Board of Vocational, Technical and Adult Education. It has since been expanded from its initial pilot center located in Madison to 14 centers located throughout the state.

Pennsylvania. The Pennsylvania Department of Aging initiated a demonstration program, called "Project POWER," in 1981. Project POWER has two objectives (1) to deliver employment services more efficiently to older people, and (2) to promote a more accurate image of the older worker among employers, society at large, and older persons themselves. POWER—which stands for Provide Older Workers Equal Rights—has four components (1) coordination, (2) public relations, (3) establishing contacts with employers, and (4) maintaining a skills/job bank, a project that includes intake, screening and counseling for older people looking for employment; referral to training and/or job placement; and follow-up.

A successful project, POWER has demonstrated that through a brokerage system matching applicants with skills needed by employers, job placements can be found for older workers. Implemented in eight Area Agencies on Aging, 519 persons were placed in jobs in the private sector during the first 6 months of the 1982 fiscal year.

When the Job Training Partnership Act was passed, the Department realized POWER was ideally suited to form the basis of a statewide employment program for older job seekers. Using a portion of the 3 percent of JTPA funds specifically targeted for older workers, the project has now been expanded to all 49 Area Agencies on Aging, each employing a full-time Older Worker Employment Specialist.

For further information on state programs focused on older workers, please contact: The National Association of State Units on Aging, 600 Maryland Ave., S.W., Suite 208, Washington, D.C. 20024. Tel: (202) 484-7182.

Index

Credits/ Acknowledgments

Cover design by Charles Vitelli

1. The Phenomenon of Aging
Facing overview—UN Photo by Gaston Guarda.
2. Longevity and Aging
Facing overview—EPA Documerica.
3. Societal Attitudes Toward Old Age
Facing overview—UN Photo/Milton Grant.
4. Problems and Potentials of Aging
Facing overview—UN Photo by Michael Tzovaras.
5. Retirement
Facing overview—UN Photo by Sebastiao Barbosa.
6. The Experience of Dying
Facing overview—EPA Documerica.
7. Living Environments
Facing overview—United Nations.
8. Social Policies, Programs, and Services
Facing overview—United Nations photo by John Isaac.

ANNUAL EDITIONS: AGING, Fourth Edition

Article Rating Form

We Want Your Advice

Here is an opportunity for you to have direct input into the next revision of this volume. We would like you to rate each of the 43 articles listed below, using the following scale:

1. **Excellent: should definitely be retained**
2. **Above average: should probably be retained**
3. **Below average: should probably be deleted**
4. **Poor: should definitely be deleted**

Your ratings will play a vital part in the next revision. So please mail this prepaid form to us just as soon as you complete it.
Thanks for your help!

Annual Editions revisions depend on two major opinion sources: one is our Advisory Board, listed in the front of this volume, which works with us in scanning the thousands of articles published in the public press each year; the other is you—the person actually using the book. Please help us and the users of the next edition by completing the prepaid article rating form on this page and returning it to us. Thank you.

Rating	Article	Rating	Article
	1. Profile of Tomorrow		26. Reconsidering Retirement: Understanding Emerging Trends
	2. Acting One's Age: New Rules for Old		27. New Roles for Older Workers
	3. Successful Aging and the Role of Life Review		28. As Early Retirement Grows in Popularity, Some Have Misgivings
	4. America's Neglected Elderly		29. Coping with the Reality of Terminal Illness in the Family
	5. A Generation at Risk		30. Choosing the Good Death
	6. Growing Old Absurd		31. Death, Dying, and Bereavement in Old Age
	7. Creative Aging		32. A New Understanding About Death
	8. Entering Middle Age		33. The Risk of Institutionalization Before Death
	9. Living Longer		34. Positive Consequences of Institutionalization: Solidarity Between Elderly Parents and Their Middle-Aged Children
	10. The Aging Body		
	11. Surgery and the Elderly		
	12. Are Companion Animals Good for Your Health?		35. Innovative Living Arrangements: A Source of Long-Term Care
	13. Ageism		36. Alternatives to Institutional Care of the Elderly: Beyond the Dichotomy
	14. Continuity: A Gift from the Older Generation		37. Model Project Reduces Alienation of Aged from Community
	15. Will You Still Love Me?		
	16. The New Ageism and the Failure Models: A Polemic		38. Geriatric Day Care: The Options Reconsidered
	17. Sex in the Nursing Home? For Lord's Sake, Why Not?		39. The Elderly Person: When Protection Becomes Abuse
	18. Visual Booby Traps for Our Aging Population		40. Toward an Aging Policy
	19. Alcoholism and the Elderly		41. Planning for an Aging Work Force
	20. Hazards of Drug Use Among the Elderly		42. Widower Self-Help Groups: A Preventive Approach
	21. Growing Old in Rural America		43. State Units Launch Employment Initiatives
	22. The Black Elderly Today		
	23. Therapy After Sixty		
	24. Symbolic Interaction and Retirement Adjustment: An Empirical Assessment		
	25. A New Wrinkle in Retirement Policies		

(continued on

ABOUT YOU

Name _____ Date _____

Are you a teacher? ☐   Or student? ☐

Your School Name _____

Department _____

Address _____

City _____ State _____ Zip _____

School Telephone # _____

YOUR COMMENTS ARE IMPORTANT TO US!

Please fill in the following information:

For which course did you use this book? _____

Did you use a text with this Annual Edition?   ☐ yes ☐ no

The title of the text: _____

What are your general reactions to the Annual Editions concept?

Have you read any particular articles recently that you think should be included in the next edition?

Are there any articles you feel should be replaced in the next edition? Why?

Are there other areas that you feel would utilize an Annual Edition?

May we contact you for editorial input?

May we quote you from above?

AGING 85/86

BUSINESS REPLY MAIL

First Class   Permit No. 84   Guilford, CT

Postage will be paid by addressee

The Dushkin Publishing Group, Inc.
Sluice Dock
Guilford, Connecticut 06437

No Postage
Necessary
if Mailed
in the
United States